CHANTREY LAND

Harold Armitage

NORTON POST OFFICE

From a water colour drawing by Charles Ashmore.

CHANTREY LAND

BEING AN ACCOUNT OF THE NORTH DERBYSHIRE VILLAGE OF NORTON

BY

HAROLD ARMITAGE

WITH A FRONTISPIECE AND EIGHTY-THREE
DRAWINGS BY CHARLES ASHMORE
AND OTHER ILLUSTRATIONS

CONTAINING TWO SUPPLEMENTARY
CHAPTERS WHICH HAVE NEVER BEEN
PUBLISHED IN PREVIOUS EDITIONS

"A more agreeable subject for the topographer than the parish of Norton can
hardly be found." – JOSEPH HUNTER, F.S.A., Author of *A History of Hallamshire*.

applebaum

First published 1910
by Sampson Low Marston & Company

Reprinted 1981
by Sheffield City Libraries

This edition published in 1998
by Applebaum
Advantage Book Company Limited
208 West Street, Sheffield, S1 4EU

Editing: Many thanks to J. M. Olive and D. Hindmarch

Printed by Biddles Limited
Guildford, Surrey

ISBN: 0 906787 07 6

WITH KINDEST THANKS TO EDWARD JESSOP AND
JOHN CAPES, GEMS AMONGST MEN, WITHOUT WHO'S HELP
THIS EDITION WOULD NOT HAVE BEEN POSSIBLE.

IN MEMORY OF EDWARD JESSOP, PROBABLY THE MOST
FOREMOST COLLECTOR OF LOCAL HISTORY THIS CENTURY,
WHO SADLY DEPARTED THIS LIFE SHORTLY BEFORE
PUBLICATION OF THIS EDITION.

Since this book was originally written further historical
research has been carried out, which has rendered certain
facts contained in the text inaccurate. However, the
publisher felt that it would be wrong to alter the original
text in this latest edition, therefore it has been
reproduced true to the manuscript of Harold Armitage.

TO

JEANIE

A DAUGHTER OF THE CAMERONS

WHO CAME INTO DERBYSHIRE

NOT IN THE '45

NOR TO WREST A THRONE

AND YET

TO REIGN AS QUEEN

IN THE HEART AND HOME

OF

THE AUTHOR

PUBLISHER'S DEDICATION

TO

GORDON

AS A CELEBRATION FOR THIRTY YEARS

IN PARTNERSHIP

Provincialism is the nursing-mother of character, morality, intellect, civilization, and religion. The lack of provinciality denotes a lack of colour.—*Spectator*.

The lives of the lesser squires and yeomen, like those of the merchants in provincial towns, mean much in the development of a country.—*Notes and Queries*.

I have often wondered why the larger movements of history have never been localised, so that we may know, all along the centuries, what was happening near a given place at a given time.—JOHN DERRY in the *Sheffield Independent*.

It is these local objects and scenes, and other far less romantic things and places, teeming with the annals of history, and lying unheeded about everyone's homes, that are the best starting posts of all historical study.—*Quarterly Review*.

Amongst the handmaidens of History, Topography is entitled to take a high position because, to use the baldest language, no historical or biographical fact can be so clearly understood as when the locality in which the incident occurred is brought before the actual eye of the student.—*Athenæum*.

Genealogical inquiries and local topography, so far from being unworthy the attention of the philosophical inquirer, are amongst the best materials he can use ; and the fortunes and changes of one family, or the events of one upland township, may explain the darkest and most dubious portions of the annals of a realm.—SIR FRANCIS PALGRAVE.

There is a good deal to be said for the plan of focussing history upon a small spot. The history of a country, of a nation, is apt to overwhelm one by its vast complexity, and only in its great crises does it forcibly appeal to the imagination. But the history of the district, of a parish, or a city, continuously interests and furnishes a series of vivid scenes to those who have the gift to see them.—*The Times*.

Is there in all England a village of any antiquity, without a wealth of association all its own, linking its name with that of some person or event of renown?—a village that has never had a battle fought in its neighbourhood, sent forth a great man from its midst or received one into it, nor in any way contributed its thread to the fabric of our national history? It is hardly possible.—EBENEZER DOWNING in the *New Liberal Review*.

PREFACE

It is not pretended that this is a complete and formal
history of Norton. Such a work would have needed
the application of some local scholars who are unhappily
no longer alive; or, amongst living men, the labours
of an accomplished antiquary like Mr. Sidney Oldall
Addy, M.A., a man not only equipped with the necessary
scholarship for the search and understanding of ancient
muniments, but endowed moreover with the essential
attachment to this alluring region; for more than
scholarship merely goes to the making of the best local
history, just as more than dry erudition went to Green's
imperishable story of this realm as set forth in *A Short
History of the English People*.

History cries aloud for competent scholars who will
be content to work in obscure corners, puzzling over
field names, spending laborious days amongst wills,
charters, rolls of inscribed sheepskin, parish registers,
churchwardens' accounts, and old, old documents " dim
as dreams," listening amongst aged people for words and
place names rapidly becoming obsolete, trying to solve
the riddle of prehistoric man, and doing other arduous
work, for it is premature to generalise until we have
attained to Aristotle's " accumulation of instances," until
every village, every moor, every country side, every
manuscript and book has been compelled to yield its

story. There are hoards of documents concerning Norton in public places and in private hands that have never yet been published nor even examined, and if this book shows some young scholar with means and leisure and with his life before him that the history of Norton is worth his while, that the history of most villages is worth his while, it will not have been written in vain.

Meanwhile then let it be understood that this is not such a book written by a scholar for scholars. It has a more homely intention, and if it finds its way to the firesides of Derbyshire and Hallamshire folk, and helps to round off in an agreeable way some of the days spent in the work of forge, factory, mill or counting-house, or gives point to country rambles, it will not have missed its mark. It is such a book as I should have liked when I began to find that all history was not made at Court, nor in London, nor in the House of Commons, nor upon far-away battlefields, nor embodied in school books ; and so, if this volume should happen to do the service to some studious youth of indicating that there are wider intellectual possibilities and deeper interests at his own doors than he had suspected, in that too *Chantrey Land* will have found some justification.

There is perhaps a further excuse for this book. A time may come when Sheffield will absorb Norton. Though not over the best seams the place is yet upon the coal measures, and apart from this the population presses. We have only to think of what has happened to a valley which Sir Walter Scott was able to call " that pleasant district of merry England which is watered by the river Don," to understand what may be the fate of Norton ; and if such a future of defilement and devastation awaits Chantrey's country, then no time is to be lost in recording some of her charms before they disappear, in hearing her story while she has still the power to tell it, before Sheffield reaches this, its southern horizon, bringing the same blight that the city has spread east and west along the Don, once flowing in a most lovely valley that has since been blasted into a long-drawn horror of confluent damnation.

As Norton is to-day so once were Attercliffe and Neepsend, and even Mexborough ; and so recently as the period in which this book has been in progress have there been changes in the neighbourhood that make some of its passages a tribute to what has been rather than a description of what now is. This being so it is manifest that a generation will arise glad to know what Norton was like in an earlier day than its own. To our descendants Charles Ashmore's sketches will make a special appeal, for he has haunted the lanes of Norton too long to have missed the spirit of the place, and we shall all join in the unavailing regret that Heeley, Neepsend, Attercliffe and many another place had not its Charles Ashmore too before the work of Hallamshire was done by coal, when windmills waved their arms upon her hills, and waterwheels thumped in all her valleys.

Many of us appreciate now the work of Joseph Hunter and of his successors who have written of Hallamshire, but in the future, when Sheffield, as large now as London was in the Stuart times, shall have blotted out her green borderland as London has done, when Ecclesfield is as Camden Town, when Mawfa Lane has been macadamised, Gleadless has been Peckhamised, Norton Brixtonised, and Cold Aston is as Upper Tooting, then will our descendants turn to these writers just as we turn with avidity now to the chroniclers of old London to read how bygone citizens enjoyed their summer holidays amidst the rural joys of Clerkenwell,

how turnips were grown at Hornsey, strawberries in
Holborn, how martins built their nests in Fleet Street,
how the harvest was reaped in the golden cornfields of
Southwark, and how cattle pastured once in the pleasant
meadows of Bermondsey.

For many reasons then it has seemed there was a
function which one who has loved the groves and fields
of this country side might well perform in the weav-
ing together into one available whole the discoverable
allusions from widely sundered books that long have
been out of print, and from manuscripts that lie in
murky closets and obscure corners,

> . . . to knit again
> This scatter'd corn into one mutual sheaf.

It may be, however, that we shall miss our mark, for
artist and author alike are conscious of being curious
survivals that ought to have perished with the Dodo
and the Great Auk ; hopelessly old-fashioned people
given to pottering about ancient churches and halls,
browsing about libraries and picture galleries and poring
over old books, living all the time in an alien age when
the great desire is not to examine things at all but to
fume past them as quickly as possible. I am told that
since this book was commenced some impatient people,
not content with tearing past objects on bicycles and in
motor-cars, have with a perverse ingenuity invented air-
ships that they may fly far over the tops of everything !
Chantrey Land has not been written in this evasive mood ;
not in this spirit of feverish adventure have these pages
been prepared, for Midas, in goggles, and in a whirl of
dust and smells, could dash in at one end of Chantrey's
country and be out at the other end in fewer minutes than
we have needed years for the assimilation of the spirit

of the place, and even now we could go on to the end
of our lives without persuading Norton to yield up all her
secrets, without prevailing upon her to make known all
her enchantments.

It has been stated that this is not a history of Norton,
and it remains to be confessed that neither does the
closing chapter constitute a complete account of Chantrey.
All that it has been possible to do in this book, where
so much else was to be done, has been to look at the
great sculptor in relation to Norton, where he was born
and spent his boyhood and where his body now lies
buried.

Finally, however, let it be said that if there are some
who could have brought more learning to the writing
of a book upon Norton, there can be but few who have
more tender memories of rambles in all weathers and
seasons and times of day and night amongst its lanes
and fields, amongst its halls and cottages ; and even yet,
in memory at any rate, the storm-cock that sang there
in the oak-tree top can make himself heard above the
roar of the London streets ; always may the spirit cloister
itself from the dust and heat of crowded thoroughfares in
the cool sequestered recesses of Norton church yard, and
the vivid life and unrest of the largest city in the world
can never dim the recollection of tranquil hours that have
been spent within the bounds of Chantrey Land—of
Chantrey Land the well beloved.

HAROLD ARMITAGE.

FIELDHEAD,
EASTHOLM GREEN,
LETCHWORTH,
HERTS.
1910.

CONTENTS

LIST OF ILLUSTRATIONS

IN COLOUR

LINE DRAWINGS

b

PLATES

CHANTREY LAND

CHAPTER I

NORTON CHURCH

DURING a walk from the Sheffield side of Chantrey's
country to the old church at Norton, the saunterer,
having crossed the fields that lie between Norton Lees
and Norton, passes at last through the long line of trees
of Summerhouse Wood that dominates the prospect here ;
and he becomes conscious of a change in the character
of the scenery ; for Bunting Nook, the lane that leads
him through this array of trees, instead of being high and
exposed, like neighbouring lanes, is sheltered by oak and
yew, by beech and sycamore ; and it runs deeply, between
banks, under the wall of Norton Park. Here, in summer,
he finds a place of retreat from the heat that parches the
plain he has just traversed ; and in winter he has a refuge
from the piercing winds that sweep across this bleak
tableland. There is a transition from cottages to halls ;
the trees grow with greater luxuriance, as though their
roots were in a kindlier soil ; and if on the way here he
has seen manifestations of ignoble and squalid lives, yet,
now that he has reached the land upon the south of this
frontier of trees, it is possible for him to forget what is
sordid in human ways of living, in an atmosphere where
everything seems gracious and debonair.

Bunting Nook, delightful lane, conducts us past the
Grange to the church, obviously ancient, but not mentioned in Domesday Book. This does not prove there
was no church here then, because it was not the function

of Domesday Book to mention all the churches, but at the time of the survey much of the country here seems to have been woodland. We are prevented from assuming too readily that there never has been a Saxon church at Norton by a piece of evidence that has remained when more recent things have perished, for near the west wall in the church yard, behind Chantrey's tomb, is a stone shaped like a coffin lid, with old and rude incisions of a Greek cross and the symbols of the five wound prints. The lid seems to be Saxon, and if it is then we have in this fragment Norton's oldest relic, a survival which may indicate that here was holy ground even before the advent of the Normans, with possibly a house of prayer, though it might be only of wood and thatch as churches were sometimes in Saxon days. We know, however, that Norton had a church when between 1172 and 1176 Robert FitzRanulph, lord of Norton and of Alfreton, founded the neighbouring abbey of Beauchief, for he bestowed this church of St. James upon the abbey.

In the early days of Norton church, and until the dissolution of the abbey, it was always a regular canon of Beauchief who officiated at Norton, and he resided here permanently. One of these canons, John Greenwood, *alias* Sheffield, became afterwards Abbot of Beauchief, and happened to hold that office when the day of dissolution came.

The Parliamentary Commission of 1650 reported that in this year the incumbent of Norton was "Mr. Kellam Mainwaring, who hath formerly been sequestered in another countye, and is scandalous"; but the scandalous Mr. Mainwaring was preceded by a long list of vicars whose characters we may suppose to have been exemplary seeing that we know nothing more of them than their names, and so far as antiquaries have been able to wrest these from oblivion the list runs :

— Henry de Tresk.
1325. Thomas de Alfreton, Canon of Beauchief.

1349. Thomas de Tykhull.
1351. William de Melbourne.
1369. Robert de Bobenhull.
1380. Thomas de Dronfeld, Abbot of Beauchief 1399-1413.
1425. Geoffrey Harnesby.
1431. John Sheffield.
1432. John Tanden.
—— William Kychyne. Was at the Visitation of the Abbey in 1475.
1490. John Croke. Sub-cellarer of Beauchief Abbey in 1482 ; sub-prior 1488, and attended next three Visitations as Vicar of Norton.
1510. John Sheffield, *alias* Greenwood, Abbot of Beauchief from 1519 to Dissolution in 1536.
1519. Thomas Gilberte.
1547. Michael Brothwell.
1554. Thomas West.
1558. Roger Watson (for Geoffrey Blythe).
1561. Henry Taylor.
1614. Richard Edwards.
1650. Kellam Mainwaring.
—— Jeremiah Scholes.
1663. John Harpur on the ejection of Jeremiah Scholes.
1667. Samuel Trickett.
1710. Cavendish Nevile.
1750. George Wombwell.
—— Robert Robinson.
1763. Peter Robinson.
1812. Henry Pearson.
1844. Henry Hollingworth Pearson.
1888. George Walker Hall.

Henry Taylor was vicar for more than fifty years, and the registers from their beginning until 1614 are in his handwriting. Belonging to the period when Richard Edwards was vicar is an interesting piece of Norton church lore, the endorsement upon a writ of summons issued from the Consistory Court at Lichfield, on February 28, 1615, and addressed " *Georgio More, generoso et Phillippo Gill.*" " To the churchwardens of Norton," runs the document.

At Norton Vicarage

" The next Saboath or festivall day after the recept of these l'res [letters], you are to signifie unto the parishoners that the reverend father in God, the Lord Bishop of this diocesse, by vertue and force of the Kings Majestie's writt to him, hath sequestred all manner of tythes, oblations, fruite, and commodities belongyng unto the vicaredge of Norton, for that the tenthes due out of the said vicarage to his Majestie are behind, and not payde for the time within mentioned. And therefore you must require every parishoner to pay to you all their tythes, oblations, fruite, and profits remaynyng in their hands unpaid, and due to the said vicarage, and the same you must collect, gather, and receive, and in your hand fast keepe, as you will answer for the same at your perill. And furthermore you must appear before the said reverend father, or his Commissarie, in that behalfe, in the Cathedrall Churche of Lichfield, in the Consistorie there, upon Wednesday, the 10th of Aprill next, betwixt iv and vj of the cloke in the fore noone, and then and there make and yeld up a faithfull accompt what you have done in the premiss', uppon paine and perill that may ensue."

NORTON CHURCH

The scandalous Mr. Mainwaring was followed by Jeremiah Scholes, or Scoales, who happened to be vicar of Norton when the Act of Uniformity of 1662 was passed, when about two thousand ministers resigned their livings. Jeremiah Scholes resigned, with many others in Derbyshire, and with the whole of the clergy in the neighbouring city of Sheffield, an act that has given him a place in Edmund Calamy's chronicle of the doings of the ejected ministers, so that we may read there that " he was born in *Salford* near *Manchester* in *Lancashire*. When he was Ejected from his Living, he remov'd to his Native Place, and liv'd on his Estate. He was very Industrious in his MASTER'S Work, and preach'd as he had Opportunity. He was wont to take much Delight in Days of Prayer and Humiliation, in which he was often charg'd by his Bretheren with holding out too long ; tho' he was usually pertinent and acceptable. He was an upright hearted Man. He dy'd *Apr.* 27, 1685. Æat. 56. He left a Son behind him in the Ministry, among the Nonconformists."

In the continuation of this work it has been written that, " Whereas it is said at the End of the Account of Mr. JEREMY SCOALES, that *he left a Son behind him in the Ministry, among the Nonconformists :* Let it be added, that his Name was *Nathanael,* and that some Account of him may be met with in Mr. *Tong's* Life of Mr. *Matthew Henry,* p. 279." Following this clue it will be found that " in the 10th of *October,* 1702, Mr. *Henry* very much laments the Death of Mr. *Nath. Scoles* of *Macclesfield,* of whom he says, ' I hear that my Worthy Friend and Dear Brother, Mr. *Scoles,* died last *Friday* ; *he* was almost three Years younger than I, a very ingenious Man, a florid Preacher, and very serious and affectionate in all his Performances ; he met with Affliction in his Marriage, which occasioned some unevenness in his Temper, but he was a Man of true Piety and Integrity ; he died of a Palsy, in Complication with other Distempers ; his Afflictions had broken his Spirits very much, the Lord prepare me to go after. His Father was a Learned Godly Minister in *Manchester.*' "

To Samuel Trickett's memory is a stone in the belfry, and his sermons were published with biographical matter by the late Archdeacon Blakeney of Sheffield. He is mentioned often in an article on the Wirksworth Classis, 1651–1658, by Dr. Cox in the *Proceedings of the Derbyshire Archæological Society*, Vol. II., 1880. Trickett's son became rector of Aston, and descendants were living in that part of South Yorkshire in 1863.

Trickett was succeeded at Norton by Cavendish Nevile, vicar for forty years, a Master of Arts and a Fellow of University College, Oxford. At Holbeck, near Leeds, lived the Neviles, a branch of the old and illustrious family whence were derived the Earls of Westmorland and the Marquis of Abergavenny. Further back the family was in Normandy, and a Gilbert de Nevile is said to have been one of William the Conqueror's admirals. The Neviles are now of Skelbrooke Park in Yorkshire, but for generations they were at Chevet. Many of Nevile's ancestors are buried in the parish church of Leeds ; but he wished to be buried at Norton, and so he lies here with his old parishioners in the eastern portion of the church yard. No longer may the inscription on his tombstone be read ; but according to notes made by John Daniel Leader, before the words had been worn away they told that he was " a Pius, charitable and truly honest man. His piety and generosity were conspicuous in the extensive neighbourhood wherein he lived. His tender regard for every branch of his afflicted family must with gratitude be remembered, and for the poor their increased misery will but too well remind them of a deceased friend and protector."

There is still in the library at Norton Vicarage a collection of old books which belonged to Cavendish Nevile, who bequeathed these volumes to his successors, the vicars of Norton, during their vicariates.

From the Neviles, themselves connected with the

Bullocks, the owners of the advowson, we pass by an easy transition to the Robinsons—Robert and Peter— because they were connected with the Neviles by marriage. One of Peter's sons married a daughter of Daniel Holy, a name associated closely with Norton history. Afterwards the family became connected with Daniel Brammal of the White House, Brammal Lane, Sheffield, who helped Sir Francis Chantrey, one of whose first attempts at portraits in oils was a painting of a son of Peter Robinson, vicar of Norton.

The Vicarage
NORTON

The Rev. Peter Robinson died in 1811, and the Rev. Henry Pearson, LL.D., who married Miss Harriet Wilson of the snuff-mill family, was appointed in his place; and Thomas Asline Ward, thinking of Mr. Piper, Nonconformist minister, and other friends at Norton, wrote in his diary: "I know the new Vicar tolerably well, and fear he will not prove a great acquisition to our friends. He is a little, pale man, very unassuming, rather silent, and a card player. I should suppose he is rather fond of reading, but such anti-Jacobin orthodox books as would be uncongenial with Piper's turn of mind. Yet I do not think him illiberal, and the two ministers may perhaps contrive to visit each other once in six months. Mr. Pearson keeps very choice wines in his cellar, and loves to treat his friends with the richest and rarest, though I believe he is not himself a bon-vivant. Mrs. Pearson is a woman of very little energy and mind."

Mr. Pearson was patron of the living, for he had purchased the advowson from Cavendish Nevile, who sold the rectorial tithes to the Shores and other land-owners.

A son, Henry Hollingworth Pearson, succeeded his father as vicar of Norton, and Mr. Addy remembers this second Mr. Pearson as a scholarly man who preached model village sermons, which, had they been written, would have seemed like essays from Addison's *Spectator*. His clerk was old Tommy Lee, the shoemaker, a man with a very sonorous voice, and a story of vicar and clerk, still remembered in Norton, relates how Mr. Pearson having allowed his beard to grow during an absence, re-turned and preached from the text " Be of good cheer : it is I ; be not afraid," whereupon a titter went round the church. " What were the people laughing about ? " he asked when he returned to the vestry, and the clerk replied impatiently, " Laugh ! they might well laugh. Whatever did you take a soft text like that for ? "

In those days the pulpit was a " three-decker," a combination of pulpit, reading-desk and desk for the clerk, an office that remained with the Lees for two centuries.

Associated too with Norton for some years as curate was Mr. Pearson's brother, William, in whom there arose some curiosity concerning the antiquities of the place, as his letters to his brother show.

The present vicar, the Rev. George Walker Hall, M.A., came to Norton as curate in 1884, and was inducted to the living on the resignation of the Rev. H. H. Pearson in 1888. It seems in character with the antiquity of the church and parish that only three changes in vicars have taken place during the last hundred and forty-eight years. The present vicar was appointed Rural Dean of Dronfield in 1908, and a Surrogate for the Diocese of Southwell in 1909.

The vicarage, near to the church, is one of the engaging features of Norton, its gable overlooking a goodly growth of trees and flowers. Cavendish Nevile added to it and built the library, where his initials may be seen still. A petition of 1723 says of Nevile that he " hath expended

near £500 of his own money in building a new vicarage " and other buildings.

It is near to this old church and vicarage that Norton is at its best. Here we realise that the place has a charm to stir the artist, to move the poet, to win affection, and few things can be more delightful than to approach its grey walls in their setting of elms and beeches, yews and cedars, to listen to its cawing rooks, to see its homely tower, its embattlements and pinnacles, sun-dial, gable crosses and window traceries, after a walk along the dusty roads to this place, either from the direction of Greenhill or of Gleadless. It has indeed all the welcome qualities for which we look in a village church, and thus many a local artist has a drawing of this comely building in his sketch-book, and paintings of it appear often in Sheffield exhibitions.

When Dr. Cox visited the church in the seventies of last century, he made a painful ascent of the tower to look at the bells, by means of internal ladders, from which many a rung was missing, and he arrived at last at a small trap door through which he passed with difficulty, the clerk cheering him with an account told with much gusto of a fat man who stuck there and was not easily set free. The bells he found were six of the year 1810, cast by James Harrison of Burton ; but this was not the first chime the tower had known, for when in 1808 a subscription was raised for the new one, that cost about £130, there was a stipulation " and old bells given in." Now the bells have been recast and two added to complete the octave. The tenor bell weighs sixteen hundredweight. This work of overhauling the bells was undertaken, at a cost of £500, as a public memorial to Mr. Francis Westby Bagshawe of the Oakes and of Wormhill, who died in 1896, and the chime was dedicated upon the Christmas Day of that year. The clapper of the old tenor bell is used to keep open the church door, and it has been inscribed by Mr. Hall, the vicar, with a verse :

I Rang for the Living,
I toll'd for the Dead,
I gave the First Greetings
To those who were Wed,
And still in God's House
I now stand at the Door
To open its Portals
To Rich and to Poor.

In addition to the verse the clapper is inscribed " Clapper of old tenor bell recast 1811, removed from the belfry 1896."

The clock in Norton church tower has been there since 1869, when it was bought for £60, and an older clock that had been in the tower from 1818 was sold to Holmesfield for £5 ; but Norton had a clock before 1818, as is shown in the drawings by Grimm and Malton.

In an old oil painting and in a lithograph, both at the vicarage, and also in one or two of a number of steel engravings published by Messrs. Rock & Co. in 1860, sometimes printed upon the illustrated notepaper of that time, steps are shown running upwards at the western side of the porch as indicated in Charles Ashmore's sketch. Other external features that have disappeared are revealed in a reproduction in this book of an engraving by Basire executed for Samuel Pegge's work on Beauchief Abbey. The author, whose book was published in 1801, says the plate was engraved "from a drawing by the late Mr. Grimm, now in possession of Cornelius Heathcote-

From an old Painting
in the possession of
the Rev G. W. Hall.

Rodes, esq., of Barlborough-hall, who was so obliging as to communicate it." The plate was printed afterwards in the *Gentleman's Magazine* [Vol. 88, January—June, 1818, p. 497].

In Malton's drawing, engraved by Middiman, which has been reproduced in this book, we see the church again, but subsidiary to a representation of the Hall, and so lacking many details. This engraving was published in 1793 as one of the plates in the *Copper Plate Magazine*, and so it represents the church nearly a hundred years before Street's restoration.

Until Street's rearrangements, the doorway of Norton church bore traces of mutilation, and the side pillars were of wood, but a careful restoration was achieved here. When Grimm made his drawing, probably at the end of the eighteenth century, the entrance was very curious and primitive. The porch does not project quite clear of the church on both sides as is usual in porches, for it is a western continuation of the south aisle, an added bay of that feature transformed into a vestibule by enclosing walls. You enter the porch under a graceful pointed arch, but the portal of the church itself is round-arched, a scrupulous reproduction by Street of an original Norman doorway. The portico has a vaulted roof and shelters six old grotesque stone corbel heads, besides a number of ancient gravestones that formerly have occupied other positions. More old gravestones have been fixed in the belfry, and some originally in the church are now in the church yard.

In the Porch
Norton
Church

Readers of *The Hall of Waltheof*, by Mr. Addy, will remember with regard to the porch the story of the child found there one winter's morning. His parents were never discovered, and the poor little lad whose coming into this world was so little welcomed was baptised Daniel Denial, a name which has survived in this neighbourhood.

When we enter the church we see what is believed to be some late Norman building, although it approximates to the Early English style that followed the Norman. This transitional method of building is to be

seen in a particularly interesting arch under which we
pass from the nave to the belfry in the tower. This is
ancient architecture, and good of its kind, and though
other parts of the tower have been rebuilt there has been
little or no meddling with this tall, graceful feature of
pure pointed Norman of the middle of the twelfth
century, when the earlier Norman rounded arches were
giving place to this later pointed mode. The arches in
the nave belong to the same period, but in some of these
there have been modifications for the insertion and afterwards for the removal of unsightly galleries. Two early
Norman responds may have survived from an older
church that was wholly Norman. The inference drawn
by the Rev. T. W. Norwood, M.A., vicar of Wrenbury,
at his visit in 1889, is that the church was built, or
rebuilt, by Robert FitzRanulph in the pointed form
of the Norman style during the reign of Stephen or
Henry the Second, that is about the middle of the twelfth
century. His interesting notes appeared in the Norton
Parish Magazine in September and October, 1889.

The five pointed arches of the northern side of the
nave are on round piers ; the three similar arches and
the round arch of the southern side are upon octagonal
piers, and so the arrangement is no longer like the pre-
restoration condition of the nave described by Dr. Cox.

Now all the arches in the nave are pointed except one,
that upon the south side nearest the chancel arch, which
is round and terminates in a corbel stone carved into
the form of a head. Under this corbel is a niche, and
in the niche was once the figure of a saint. Dr. Cox
thinks that here very probably stood at one time a side
altar. Near the niche is a hagioscope, or " squint," an
opening in the wall to allow worshippers who sat behind
the wall to see through to the altar.

Very little Early English architecture is to be found
in the fabric of Norton church, but there seems to be
no doubt that the archway leading into the chancel, a
wide arch of graceful proportions, belongs to 1220, or

INTERIOR, NORTON CHURCH, LOOKING WEST.

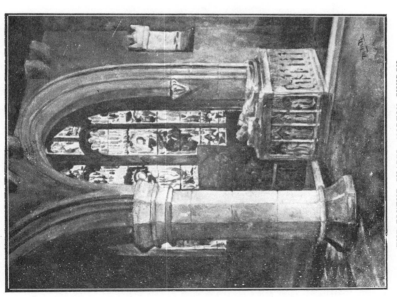

THE BLYTHE CHAPEL, NORTON CHURCH..

thereabouts, when the Early English style was in its perfection. If, however, the student of Gothic architecture is unable to study many original details of this period in the structure of the church itself, he will find in the stone font a rare and beautiful manifestation of its charm when applied to accessories. Early English fonts are uncommon, and thus the font at Norton has achieved fame far beyond the bounds of this parish ; and many who have never been to Norton are acquainted with its form from engravings in works on ecclesiology. There is a sketch in pencil of it amongst the manuscripts at the British Museum, with measurements, by Samuel Lysons. The Rev. T. W.

The Font at Norton

Norwood in his notes is especially enthusiastic about this " incipient Early English font " and says it is " perhaps the most instructive, as well as the most beautiful thing in Norton church. . . . There cannot be imagined a more instructive study of *first Early English* than this rare font combines in its construction ; and of course, to look on, it is of the utmost grace and beauty of form."

The basin of the font is supported by four groups of pillars, three pillars in each group, and one of the spaces between these clustered shafts is filled with the dog-tooth ornament as it is called sometimes, and the other three spaces have the nail-head ornament. The basin itself is ornamented with arcades, one on the top of another ; on the north side is an angel's head with wings ; on the south there is some of the carved foliage of the kind associated with Early English architecture, and on the west side a head and more foliage. Attention, however, is drawn to the east side, upon which, in bold relief, there has been carved a salamander, a kind of nondescript lizard with humped back, twisted and forked tail, two curious little legs, far back upon his body, a pair of wings, and two rather long ears. The meaning, as suggested by those who have pondered these things, is that the salamander has been selected because of the belief that it lives in the fire, and thus suggests both the Devil and his environment ; and it has been pilloried upon the font with upturned baleful Satanic face, to witness in disgust and loathing the dedication to Christianity of each child that is brought to be baptised. The sentiment seems to be that embodied in the old-folk speech : " He hates it as the Devil hates holy water." There are not many fonts which have this feature of the salamander, and Norton has one of the most striking examples.

Of the Decorated period of architecture Norton has nothing to show, and the remaining parts of the church are either perpendicular or debased. The windows in the south aisle are latter-day insertions by Street. In 1852 Sir Stephen Glynne, who visited many churches, made some notes here too that are in St. Deiniol's Library, Hawarden. Whereas Mr. Norwood thought the arches in the nave late Norman, Sir Stephen considered them Early English " with circular columns almost Norman " ; but they were built at a period when no very clear-cut dividing line can be drawn between the two styles.

There are many memorials in Norton church to people who will be mentioned in chapters that follow, but others have been removed, as may be discovered by reference to the notes taken here by Reynolds and by Richard Bassano, whose inventory is in the College of Arms. Bassano came here in 1676 on one of those heraldic visitations made at that period to see who had adopted arms to which they had no right, and Reynolds, whose notes are in the British Museum, was in Norton nearly a hundred years afterwards.

Brasses have been removed from the church, and the coats-of-arms from the east window concerning families now long forgotten in Norton, the Caltofts, the Weldons, the Zouchs, Bassets, Aylesburys and Chaworths. Here is now a modern window with glass by Frampton. One of the brasses which has disappeared—haply it has been sold to a tinker like many another—was one in

memory of a daughter of "Leonard Gyll, Gentleman, who married Major Spencer of Attercliffe." This lady died in childbirth, and, as the manner was, the brass represented her with her baby in her arms. Reynolds says that Leonard Gill himself had a brass, and he allots one also to John Parker of Norton Lees and his wife; "in the south ale are two flatt stones but the brasses are rend of," he writes. There are stones in the church yard now that apparently have been in the church and have borne brasses.

When the church was overhauled in 1881–2 there was a stone, now in the porch, but then under the altar, beneath the east window, which records the burial of a woman standing upright instead of in the usual recumbent position. The elegiac couplet at the end of the inscription is obscure.

In puncto hujusce superficei per-
pendiculari mortalis pars Barbaræ Lee
uxoris Iohannis Lee filiæque Iohannis
Lees generosi de East Retford con-
tinetur quæ non tam ætate quam virtute clara hujusce mundi fruitionem
deseruit vicesimo secondo die Octobris
anō dom̄. 1670 ætatis suæ 28.
Prima sui breviter gracilis pars
defluit ævi,
Iuxta distilans, igne premente,
liquor.

Amongst more recent memorials is a mural tablet and an angel window to the late Mrs. Hall, the wife of the present vicar, in whose memory too the martyr figures were added to the pulpit. These figures were carved by Mr. Advent Hunstone, whose picturesque workshop at Tideswell, which looks like a drawing by George Cattermole, is known to many who tramp about Derbyshire.

The remodelling of the interior of the church was compassed by George Edmund Street, R.A., the architect of the London Law Courts, who died in 1881, while his work at Norton was in progress. In his memory his widow presented Norton church with its lectern. If Street's alterations here removed some features that had become familiar, they revealed others that had been hidden away for many years until they had been forgotten. To clear out one gallery was to open a west window in the tower, and to disclose, moreover, a very important feature that had been bricked up—a pointed arch separating the tower from the nave. When the galleries had been put in the church about seventy years before the advent of Street, the capitals of the pillars in the nave had received very rough treatment, and the flue of a stove had been run through the moulding of the tower arch. Another feature that was uncovered was a very interesting Selioke memorial that will be mentioned when an account of that family is given in connection with Hazelbarrow Hall where the Seliokes lived. In addition to opening the western tower arch, an original feature, and to clearing out the ugly galleries, which were later intrusions, Street replaced the arches that, as Dr. Cox rightly conjectured, had been moved to make way for the galleries, and he exposed once more the old oaken roof that had been hidden behind a commonplace plaster ceiling.

In 1882 Mr. Addy saw over the chancel arch distinct signs of gilding of a character rather refined, patches of rich blue colour and gilt stars upon it ; and under the plaster in various parts of the church passages from the Bible in large black letters in Old English characters, the date being apparently about the time of Queen Elizabeth. Some years before the restoration of the church took place there was a large oil painting of the Royal arms, occupying nearly the whole of the space between the top of the chancel arch and the roof.

Chained to a screen between the chancel and the Blythe chapel are still two copies of *The Beauty of Holiness in the Common Prayer as set forth in four sermons preach'd at the Rolls Chapel by Tho. Bisse, D.D.*

Altogether, Norton church is full of interest, and if the ecclesiologist, the architect and the antiquary find many manifestations that deserve patient study, people who have not made historical, artistic or technical subjects their special care will find here all the welcome attributes of an old, well-cared-for village church, mellowed by time and pleasing to the simple and to the learned alike. Here too, as in other churches, we are made aware of a sharp separation from the world outside ; we experience the sense of projection to another time, to another atmosphere, deep mystery, perfect silence and peace, the consciousness of profound emotions induced by our surroundings, and yet not to be explained by facts of rule and measurement, a sense of beauty, of retreat from the fever and the fret, from the ugliness and perversity of so many things upon the other side of these walls ; and so in our goings to and fro upon the dusty highway, as we bear the burden and heat of the day, we may be thankful for such cool sanctuary as is afforded in the quiet nave and chancel of this old village church.

CHAPTER II

A FEATURE of Norton church, the Blythe chapel, built of magnesian limestone in the late Perpendicular style, is an eastern continuation of the south aisle widened. A similar continuation of the north aisle forms the vestry. A south door, closed by a wall in 1881, led once from the church yard into the Blythe chantry chapel, so that it was possible to enter without passing through the church, a usual arrangement. The doorway, flanked by small buttresses, is shown in Grimm's drawing, and also in engravings of 1860. On each side of this portal was also a large buttress, and though the door has gone and the small buttresses, these large buttresses remain, severally bearing a carved shield, that upon the western buttress showing the arms of the Blythes, "three roebucks trippant," as the quaint terminology of heraldry has it, that upon the western one revealing nothing now, for it had been defaced even before the visit of Bassano, though Trickett, the vicar, told him that upon this other shield had been wrought the arms of the diocese of Coventry and Lichfield, a very likely circumstance as the sequel will show. Reynolds too noted these shields, and saw the Blythe arms, but added of the second shield "the other too much worne with wett and weather and not to be taken, but traditionally as the parson, Mr. Tricket, gives an account are the armes of Litchfield and Coventrie."

The monument to perpetuate the memory of William Blythe and his wife that still stands in the Blythe chapel,

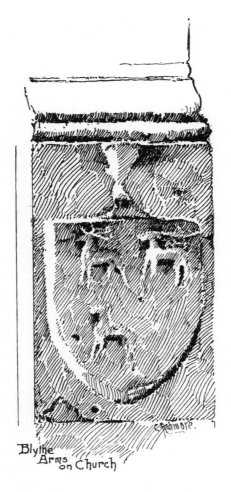

Blythe Arms on Church

is a dignified memorial shaped in alabaster. Upon slabs of this material recline the effigies of the pair, and although the tomb has been broken, scratched and cut, and though its once re-splendent gold and colour have departed, yet its glories have been dimmed only and not extinguished, for we can still enjoy its congruous proportions, its restraint, its quiet beauty that make it so perfectly appropriate for its solemn purpose. William Pearson, once curate at Norton, writing to his brother the Rev. H. H. Pear-son, said "the tomb once was in the centre of the chapel, but was removed about a cen-tury ago I think, when the Offleys and Bag-shawes got a faculty for turning the chantry into burial vaults."

The effigy of William Blythe with its long robes and full sleeves takes us back to the reign of Henry the Seventh. The figure has no hat and its head rests upon a cushion, its feet upon a dog. Under its right arm is a bag or scrip. Blythe's wife is clad in a close-fitting robe, and she wears that head-dress with falling lappets which antiquaries associate with the close of the fifteenth century.

Upon the sides of this monument figures have been carved standing under "elaborately crocketed canopies." Thus the northern side has seven figures representing angels holding shields before them, but they have suffered much from the Goths and Vandals. When Dr. Cox came here, the other side of the tomb was almost entirely hidden by an elevated mass of masonry which covered the Shore vault ; but this tomb of the Shores is one of the features which have disappeared, and thus it no longer obstructs the view, so that some of the coats-of-arms upon the Blythe monument may be deciphered still. On the north side are some indications of the coat-of-arms of the Austens of Birley, the family from which the dead lady was derived, accompanied

Worn Shield on Church

by arms of the see of Lichfield, and of the Blythes. Upon the other side of the tomb there are further evidences of " the boast of heraldry, the pomp of pow'r " in some fragments of the arms of the Blythes, and of those of the see of Salisbury. The Rev. H. H. Pearson, the vicar, told Miss A. M. Blythe Robinson, a latter-day representative of the family, that Chantrey himself said it was the Blythe tomb which kindled his taste for sculpture, a fact unknown to John Holland, one of Chantrey's biographers, for he does not mention this tomb as amongst the works that he suggests might have influenced Sir Francis in his youth. There is a piscina in the Blythe chapel, and the roof is the original oaken tie-beam roof, and though it shows signs of wear and tear not all the old features have been effaced. The bosses were carved with Alpha and Omega, I.H.S., a rose, the arms of the Blythes and the letter B.

At Norton Lees the family of Blythe held property in the fourteenth century, that is as early as the reign of Edward the Third, for John de Blithe received a grant of land there, at " Le Lyes," as the deed has it, from William Chaworth, lord of Norton, in 1376. Mr. Edward Lawrence Ireland Blyth says the deed covering this grant was handed to William Shore along with many others, when Shore purchased the property from Benjamin Blythe in 1753, and it seems to be the one now in the British Museum, the ink brown with age, but the words still readable, for it is in wonderful preservation for a document more than five hundred years old. It tells us that " Sciant, &c Ego Wills Chaworth Dns de Norton dedi, &c. Johi de Blithe heredibz t assign suis dno mesuag' in le Lyes in poch de Norton cu t'is boscis p'tis pastur t cu omibz alijs ptin t pficius p'dca mesug' quoq modo ptinent vid illud mesuag' in qº idm Johes nunc manet t aliud mesuag' vocat Coliteland [highland] Hend t tenend p'fato Johi heredibz t assign suis, &c. Hijs testibz Thom. P'ker Willo Selliok Ade P'ker Robto Aleyn Thom. Birchehed Joh. Brian t alijs Dat. apud Norton die Dnica px post festu Sci Marci Euangelis anno regni Regis Edwardi t'cij post conquestu quadragesimo primo."

During the reign of Henry the Fifth, William Blythe, John's descendant, lived at Norton Lees. Of his eldest son John and of his younger children, Elizabeth and a child whose name has not survived, we are told nothing ; but his second son William, whose monument we see

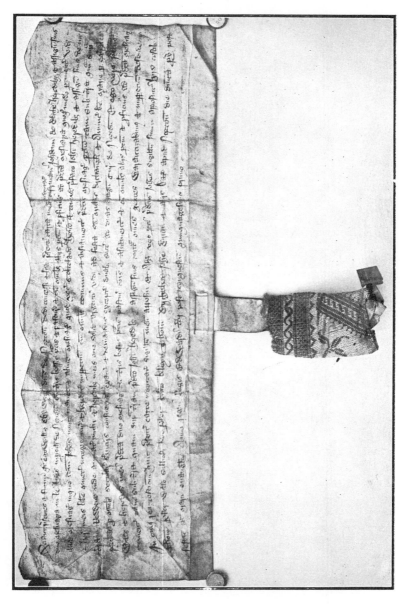

A GRANT OF LAND AT NORTON LEES IN 1376.

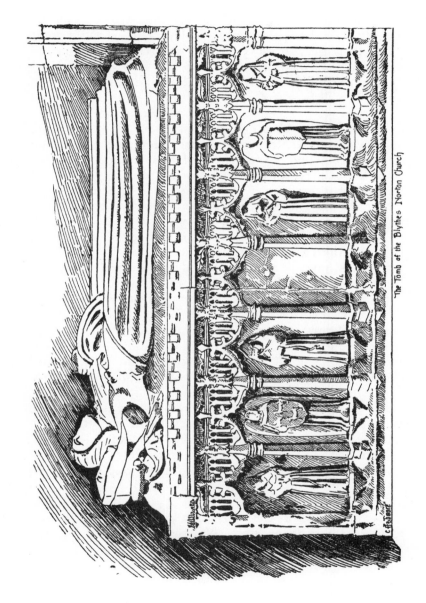

The Tomb of the Blythes Norton Church

25

now in the chantry chapel at Norton, married Saffery,
daughter of John Austen of Birley, and he had a grant
of arms in the year 1485, during the reign of Henry the
Seventh, confirmed in 1566. Mr. Lloyd Simpson, related
to the family, has kindly supplied me with a copy of the
grant, which runs :

To all true Christien people. . . . I John More
otherwise called Norroy principall Heraulde and Kinge
of Armes of the North partie of this Realme sende due
and humble recommendacion. . . . Equitie woll and
reason ordeyneth . . . and therefore I the said Kinge
of Armes . . . ascerteyned that Willm. Blythe of Norton
in the Countie of Derby hath longe contynued in Vertue
. . . and for the remembrance of his gentlenesse vertue
. . . by the vertue of myne Office . . . I the said King
of Armes have devysed ordeyned and assigned unto and
for the same Willm Blythe for him and for his poste-
ritie the Armes hereafter following That is to say he
beareth Ermyn three Roe Bucks Goules armed Gold and
also his Creast a Roo heod as aforesaid rased of three
poyntes in a Wreath Ermyn and Goules, a Garland
of Lorey [laurel] aboute Necke, graunt to the said
Willm to have and to hold the same Armes and Creast.
. . . In witness whereof I the said Kinge of Armes have
sette to my Seale and Signe Manuell at London the
xvii day of February the furst yere of the Reigne of
our Sovereigne Lord King Henry the seventh.
Ratyfied by Willm Flower als Norroy Kinge of
Armes the xi of December anno 1566 under the Seale
of the Armes of the Office of the sayd Norroy.

It was two of the sons of this William who have
conferred distinction upon Norton, for, passing for the
present Thomas and Roger, the older boys, and Richard
the youngest, we have of the family of five the two
remaining sons John and Geoffrey, both of whom became
bishops. Geoffrey it was, indeed, who founded this

chantry and erected this monument in the chapel here at Norton. Some writers have said that the mother of John and Geoffrey Blythe was a sister of Thomas de Rotherham, Archbishop of York. Both Hunter and Swift, however, competent local authorities, state simply that William Blythe's wife was a daughter of Austen of Birley ; but the explanation seems to be that she was a half-sister of Thomas de Rotherham. To-day we associate Birley with a coal mine, but at an earlier time the place was known more widely as a spa with a mineral spring. In the time of Austen it would be a remote country place, with no anticipations of coming griminess. From a letter discovered in the Tower of London, but written at Derby on June 25, 1545, it is to be inferred that Birley Grange, which belonged to the monastery at Louth in Lincolnshire, was inhabited by the Austens, and that they had also a house at Langley, four miles from Derby.

There is another link between the Blythes and Archbishop Rotherham in that they had the same tutor ; and those who have read Thomas de Rotherham's will, of which one of the executors was Geoffrey Blythe, "dean of my cathedral church at York," may recall that in an allusion to Rotherham he says there came to the old town a teacher of grammar "by I know not what fate, but I believe that it was by the grace of God he came thither, who taught me and other youths whereof others with me reached higher stations."

Hunter has written that "among those who, having been initiated into good letters at Rotherham, under this good schoolmaster, attained afterwards to eminent stations in church and state, were probably the three Blythes of Norton, two of whom became Bishops."

John Blythe received further education at the University of Cambridge, and indeed in 1488 was the warden of King's Hall there. This, however, was not his first appointment, for already he had been archdeacon of Stow and archdeacon of Huntingdon, then a prebendary of Lincoln and of York, and later archdeacon of Richmond in Yorkshire. Still rising in the world, John Blythe of Norton Lees was made Master of the Rolls ; and soon afterwards he reached the summit of his career, for in 1494 he was consecrated at Lambeth as Bishop of Salisbury. He was also Chancellor of the University of Cambridge.

At the festivities when Henry the Seventh created his son Duke of York, John Blythe took part in the pageant, and we are told that " this precession was the best ordred and moost preysed off all the precessions that I have herd of in England." Blythe was also at the great feast held upon the same occasion.

Another proceeding which would add to Blythe's glory was that by which during his episcopate, in 1496, the islands of Jersey and Guernsey were taken from the see of Coutances and added to that of Salisbury, until in 1499, the year of Blythe's death, they were finally included in the bishopric of Winchester. He was also Chancellor of Ireland.

Blythe was buried at the back of the screen and high altar that terminated the choir in Salisbury cathedral. As his tomb lay north and south instead of east and west he became known as the " thwart-over bishop," though his body under the tomb really lay in the usual position. To have placed the body north and south would have been a revolutionary departure from usage. In James Linacre's notes concerning William Booker of Lees Hall, buried 1856, he writes in surprise, " This stone lies north and south." During the alterations in the cathedral in the eighteenth century Blythe's tomb was removed to its present position at the northern end of the great transept.

Geoffrey Blythe also, the younger brother of John, rose to high places in church and state. He was sent to school at Eton, and in 1483 proceeded to Cambridge University, where, like his brother, he became warden of King's Hall, a post vacated by John in his brother's favour a year before his death. Having taken a degree as Doctor of Laws, he left the University and became prebendary of Strensall in Yorkshire, and later archdeacon of Cleveland. Next he was appointed treasurer of the church of Sarum, was rector of Corfe in Dorsetshire and had the prebend of Sneating in the church of St. Paul. Subsequently he was admitted Dean of York. He was further archdeacon of Gloucester, Master of King's Hall, Cambridge, archdeacon of Sarum and prebend of Stratton in the church of Sarum.

Not only was Geoffrey a great churchman, but also a diplomatist, and in 1502 he was sent by Henry the Seventh on a special embassy to Ladislaus the Second, King of Hungary and Bohemia, and on his return in 1503 was appointed Bishop of Lichfield and Coventry, a post he retained until his death nearly thirty years later.

A few years afterwards he was accused of treason, but he cleared himself, and letters patent for his pardon were granted, and, honours still accruing, he was appointed lord president of the Welsh Marches.

Geoffrey Blythe is said to have died in London, and he was buried in Lichfield cathedral before the image of St. Chad, one of his predecessors in the see. A monument erected to his memory has been destroyed long ago. It is believed that he was buried in the north choir aisle, not far from where Chantrey's statue of Bishop Ryder is now, so that Norton is well represented there after all ; but his monument at one time stood in the other aisle of the choir.

In his will he gave legacies to his cathedrals of Lichfield and Coventry, to the church of Norton here, and to that of St. Chad in Shrewsbury. Eton College, King's College, Cambridge, and King's Hall also benefited under his last testament. Amongst his bequests to King's College was a great standing cup, gilt, with a cover, which had been given to him by Ladislaus, King of Hungary. He gave also a similar cup to Eton College.

Before his death he had built houses for his choristers at Lichfield cathedral, and he gave to King's College a gilt mitre for the barne bishop, a pair of great organs, a rochet of the best cloth for the barne bishop, and a banner of the Assumption of the Blessed Virgin. He with his dean and chapter collected all the statutes of the cathedral of Lichfield and had them confirmed by Cardinal Wolsey when Wolsey was Papal Legate.

In Thoroton's *History of Nottinghamshire*, with additions by John Throsby, 1797, there is a hint of the " much would have more " spirit, in a reference to Geoffrey Blythe. We read there that " by an inquisition taken 15 June, 5 Henry the Eighth (1513) after the death of Sir Raph Langeford, knight, it appears that he by his deed dated 14 Jan. 2 Hy. 8 did enfeoffe Anthony Fitz-Herbert sergeant at law, by covin and deceit between him the said sir Raph, and Galfr. bishop of Coventry and Lichfeild, to defraud the king of the custody of divers manors in Derby. Nott. and Lincolneshires, of which he otherwise had died seized, viz. in Derbss the moyety of the manors of . . . including moiety of the manor of Norton." The effect of this deed would be to convey manors to Anthony Fitz-Herbert which should have gone to the King ; but we have not Blythe's own comments upon the transaction.

The Rev. William Beresford, of Leek, has written that Geoffrey Blythe was popular at Lichfield for his gifts to the minster. He gave also little silver images of St. Catherine and St. Chad, and delighted the hearts of the canons by dissolving Fairwell Nunnery and bestowing its goods upon them. In return they bound themselves to say an obit for him every year. Mr. Beresford says that in 1510 Blythe was a prisoner in the Tower of London.

Although he does not seem to have done the work willingly, it was expected of him that he should stamp out the Lollards. At Maxstoke Priory he held the Court of Heresy, and it may be that local readers of Foxe's account of the martyrs have overlooked that Geoffrey Blythe is pilloried amongst the persecutors of those who suffered at Coventry. In Blythe's Court most of those who were condemned were permitted to save themselves by abjuration. Later, however, at Coventry, there was a more serious case. Catherine Joan Warde, or Washbury, was unable to conform to the orthodox theology of her time, and though Blythe did all he could to put off the evil day, yet he was at last compelled to hand her over to the Sheriff to be burned.

The work of the diocese was done by suffragan bishops, for it is clear that Blythe could have spent but little time in Lichfield, and if he can be charged with absenteeism and pluralism he seems also to have been guilty of nepotism. There is an old proverb which says " Well's him and woe's him that has a bishop in his kin," but with a relation of Geoffrey Blythe it seems to have been principally " well's him."

Cole, the antiquary, has many notes concerning Geoffrey Blythe, a rough draft of his will, and other matter of interest ; and he has interpolated an extract from Ashmole's *History of the Garter*. "In 1504 the Cardinal of Rouen sent as a Present to King Henry 7 the right Leg of the Martyr St. George, by an Abbot of the Order of Augustine, near Meaux, his Chaplain. This Relick was solemnly received at the Palace of Greenwich by the Choir of the Royal Chapel there, with the Bp. of Lichfeild, attended by many of the Knights of the Garter & carried in Procession to the King's Chapel, where the King received it, and offered it upon the Altar, the Bp. of Lichfeild singing Mass upon the occasion."

Already have we seen John Blythe walking in a procession, and we are permitted a glimpse of his brother Geoffrey in a similar situation, for Cole has recorded that " in *August* 1757 making a visit to my esteemed & worthy Friend, the rev: *John Allen, S.T.B. Senior Fellow of Trinity College in Cambridge, & Rector of Torporley in Cheshire*, at the last mentioned Place I took an exact Copy of the Arms, Names, Titles & Description of Dress, of all *the Lords, spiritual and temporal* who compose a *Procession* to the *Parliament* in the 3d. year of *King Henry the 8th*. It is curiously depicted on a Roll of

Parchment many yards long and about a Foot wide : it lively represents the *King* & his *Nobles* walking in *Procession*, each dressed in his proper *Parliamentary Habit*, with a *Shield of Arms* over each Person's Head & a *Label* or *Scrole* above that, with his Name and Title at length." In this procession was Geoffrey Blythe, Bishop of Coventry and Lichfield, and the roll to which Cole refers belonged to John Arden of Yorkshire and Cheshire, who had it with his estate from his cousin Sir John Crewe of Torporley. It was purchased for the British Museum in 1858 at Sotheby's at the sale of Lord Alvanley's library, and so the Museum has both the roll and Cole's copy. We may not rely upon the roll for a portrait, because along the whole length of the document the faces are alike and it is probable that the intention was to give no more than the order, arms and dress ; and with regard to the arms assigned on this roll to Geoffrey Blythe, Cole mentions that they "are different from those which I have seen in a beautiful and curious manuscript in vellum belonging to Trinity College, Cambridge, where his name and arms are enrolled among the benefactors to that society, he having been formerly of King's Hall now included in that college."

By the side of the bishops march heralds in their coats of France and England. The heralds are drawn like dwarfs, the better as Cole supposes to show the figures of the principal persons in the procession.

Here in Norton, the act of Geoffrey that interests us most is that he founded this chantry, and caused this beautiful tomb to be built in honour of his mother and father, believing that in this little chapel, away from the noise and strife of the world, away from "covin and deceit," prayers would ascend daily for evermore for the repose of their souls. In the year 1524 he agreed with the parish to give ten marks for the purpose of keeping up a stock of ten kine, in consideration of a little croft on the west side of Norton green, on which he built the "mancyon house" for the chantry priest.

GEOFFREY BLYTHE IN A PROCESSION OF 1511–12.

The document recording the agreement is one of the manuscripts at Norton vicarage, and a copy appears in Mr. Addy's book on Beauchief Abbey. The general reader would find its terms and its irritating contractions very tedious, but its effect was that the Abbot of Beauchief Abbey and the Vicar of Norton agreed, Geoffrey Blythe Bishop of Lichfield assenting, that there shall be a stock of ten " kye " perpetually upholden at Norton vicarage " to ye use and behowfe of ye seid vicar." He was to buy " x kye with ye some of x marks " provided by Geoffrey Blythe for " a lyttyl crofft, on ye west syde of Norton Grene," upon which Geoffrey Blythe had built a chantry house. The vicar might have the ten cows himself " or put them to hyre, or to thalves "—he who kept the cows was to have half the milk—" to ther most prophect." If the vicar allowed the number to fall below ten, then the Abbot of Beauchief was to withhold the " corrody " of a weekly supply of nine gallons of ale and nine keyst of bread. The cows were to be branded with the mark of the monastery, " ye bryn of ye sed monastrie of Beawchef."

As some writers have said that the chantry chapel was built in this little croft, it is necessary to repeat that the chantry chapel is in the church itself, at the eastern end of the continuation of the south aisle, and that it was for the priest's house that Geoffrey needed the " lyttyl crofft on ye west syde of Norton Grene." Dr. Cox thinks that not only did Geoffrey Blythe build the chantry chapel and the priest's house, but at the same time restored the church throughout.

The chantry chapel and the tomb remain, but authorities do not agree concerning the fate of the priest's house. Some say it was used as an ale-house and pulled down by Joseph Offley. Others say Samuel Shore demolished it after Chantrey's father had used it as a joiner's shop. A tradition is that the present Chantry House, standing on the road side a little south of the church, and inhabited until recently by Mr. Charles

Jarvis Collier, occupies its site and may embody some of its materials.

In one of the Rev. William Pearson's letters he wrote that " no doubt Chantry Croft in Holy's Park was part of the ground allotted for the maintenance of the priest, and very likely Mr. Mason's old house just opposite might be his residence." He added : " I remember finding among the old documents at Norton (unless I am dreaming) one that conveyed the gift of the Chantry Croft (which you know now forms part of Norton House grounds) for the use of a priest who should say masses for the souls of some one or other, I don't remember who, but would not this be the Blythe family ? " A map prepared in 1737 by Joseph Dickinson, the forerunner of Fairbank, shows that a field known as Chantry Croft was a strip of land along Norton Lane, forming now the western fringe of Norton House park. The same map indicates that some buildings, since removed, stood at the southern end of what is now the garden in front of Norton House. Asline Ward mentions in his diary that " Mr. Samuel Shore invited me to the Chantry House, as the Cottage on the Green is called. The effect is little injured by the enclosure of the green. The Shores lived in the Chantry House while the Hall was being altered." Ward and his sweetheart thought they would like to live at Norton when they married, and Samuel Shore promised to reserve a cottage for them which they thought " the snuggest house in Norton," opposite Mr. Read's and a little below Mr. Shore's. A chantry house is mentioned in the Registers from 1654 to 1741.

Mrs. Sterndale's references of 1824 are puzzling. In any case she cannot mean the chantry chapel when she tells us of " the venerable Chauntry, standing a little aloof, beneath the oak of ages, with the attractive cottage at its termination, over-canopied with lofty trees, and enclosed in verdure." The reader might think this referred to the priest's house but for the further allusion to " the ancient chantry-house, that a few years ago was in existence." However, some of these references may be to a house, mentioned in the next chapter, which stood a little way south of Norton House.

The process of dissolving chantries followed the exploitation of the monasteries, and was perpetrated partly in the reign of Henry the Eighth and partly in the reign of Edward the Sixth. Of this chantry at Norton the chantry roll shows at the time of its dissolution Robert Aleyn was chantry priest and " Will. Blythe the patron thereof keypth." This Robert Aleyn, the priest who found his occupation gone, obtained a pension from the Exchequer of £41 5s. 6d. in the time of Philip and Mary, who were Catholics, but another entry records " Robert Alen for pension for ann £5 6s. 8d. in arrears for half a year." The William Blythe mentioned on the roll was a nephew of Geoffrey Blythe.

With regard to further transactions in land left for the endowment of the chantry priest, Mr. Robert Eadon Leader has kindly supplied me with a copy of a document addressed " to all the faithful in Christ, Edward Pease and James Wilson, of London, greeting." It goes on : " Whereas Edward the sixth, King of England, by letters patent under the Great Seal, dated 28 Aug in the third year of his reign gave and granted, amongst other things, to us, Edward Pease and James Wilson, all that house and capital messuage lately belonging to the Chantry of Norton, co. Derby, with all the edifices &c., with the appurtenance, situate and lying in Norton aforesaid, late the property of the now dissolved Chantry of Norton, now or lately in the tenure of Robert Alen, priest, to have and to hold to us and our heirs &c., for ever, as fully and freely as any cantarist or incumbent of the said chantry ever had or held it, to hold of the said King, as of his manor of East Greenwich, in Kent by fealty only, in free socage, and not in chief, for all services or demands due to the said King.

" Know ye that we, the said Edward Pease and James

Wilson, for a certain sum of money paid to us by Jeremiah Blyth, of Norton, Gentleman, have given and granted to the said Jeremiah Blyth all the said house and capital messuage lately belonging to the Chantry of Norton, to have and to hold to him and his heirs. . . .

" Moreover know ye that we have granted to him the rents, reversions and services aforesaid, from the Feast of St. James the Apostle in the said 3rd year of the King's reign. . . . Dated 20 June, 4th Edward VI." (1550).

The two bishops were the shining lights of the Blythe family, but many others of the line have been distinguished. Robert, their cousin, was Abbot of Thorney Abbey, and sat in the convocation concerning the divorce of Henry the Eighth. John Blythe of this family was first Regius Professor of Physic in 1540. Another Geoffrey, a nephew of the bishops, was Doctor of Laws, and held many church appointments. Richard Blythe, a younger brother of the bishops, married Katherine Birchett, of Birchett near Dronfield—whence the Blythes of Birchett, who owned the manor of Dronfield until Charles Blythe sold it to Andrew Morewood of the Hallowes in 1660. Blythe asked however to be released that he might sell the manor to Francis Burton, and Morewood consented.

Many years ago there was an alabaster slab to the memory of the Richard Blythe who married Katherine Birchett on the floor of the chancel of Norton church. The Reverend Thomas Halladay, a Nonconformist minister, a particularly good friend of Norton historians, whom we shall meet again, was curious about this slab and had it cleaned carefully, but too late for the complete reading of its inscription, which asks for prayers for the souls of Richard Blithe and Katherine, of Birchett, his wife.

> Orate pro animabus Ricardi Blithe et Katharinae uxoris ejus qui quidem Ricardus obiit xxiiij die . . . vicessimo quarto . . . pp . . . Amen.

The will of a Richard Blithe Mr. Addy found at Lichfield, and he reproduced it in the introduction to his local glossary. It runs :

In the name of god Amen. The thridd day of Aprill in the yere of our lorde god m.dxxiiij^ti. I Rich*ard* blythe of norton in the Countie of Derbie, gent., hole in mynde and memorie, louyng be to god, entendinge the welth of my soule and my goods trulie to be ordered and disposed after my decease, bequeth my soule to allmyghtie god and our ladie saynt mari his blessyd mother and all the companie of heuen, and my bodie to be buried wi*th*in the chapell of Saynt Katherin newlie buylditt at norton &c. It*em* I bequeth to my mortuarie, as the custom is, and to the churche of norton vjs. viijd., to the abbot and couent of beacheff vjs. viijd., to eyther of the cath*edral* churches of Coue*ntry* and lich*field*, xijd., to the rep*ar*aci*on* of the high ways wi*th*in the p*ar*ishe of norton xxs. It*em* I will that my wyff and children haue & enjoe the porci*ons* of my goods as they [*sic*] law will by the orderinge of my executor. The residue of all and sing*u*lar other my goods I wyll that they be at the disposici*on* of the Reue*r*end father in god lord Geffry by the grace of god busshop of Coue*ntrey* and lich*field* whom I make and ordeyn my executor. These being wytness : Sir Thomas gilbert, vicar of norton, John Rop*er*, priste, Robt. Clarke, priste, Richard malu*m* [Maleham] giuen at norton the day and yere abouvesayde. [Proved at Lichfield by the executor aforesaid, 4th Aug., 1524.]

The Blythes were connected by marriage with the Seliokes of Hazelbarrow Hall, with the Kirkes, Bullocks and Eyres, and naturally there are many references to the Blythes in the Norton Registers and in those of Dronfield. Amongst the burials in the Norton Register may be seen an entry which tells us that on " July 31 1601 Anthonius Blythe de Byrchett p'ce de Dronfield armiger sepultus fuit in capella ecclesie parochiali de

Norton adjuncta tertio die junii in nocte." This is a local example of the old custom of the solemn burial by night, with torches flaring, a usage which had once a great vogue, though it was ridiculed by Pope, who wrote that

> When Hopkins dies, a thousand lights attend
> The wretch, who living, saved a candle's end.

Members of this family rented land and a mill from the monks of Beauchief Abbey, so that the accounts of the revenues of that foundation contain frequent references to these Norton people.

They emerge again during the period of the Commonwealth, but no longer in association with the church. Still a junior branch of the family remained at Norton Lees. In 1646 a resolution was adopted by the House of Commons that Sheffield Castle should be made untenable, and in the next year another resolution was passed for the "sleighting" and demolishing of it. This led to the issuing of a notice concerning the demolition, signed by the William Blythe of that day, a commander upon the side of the Parliament in its struggle with the Stuarts. He obtained a free pardon from Charles the Second, and died in 1665, his memory still kept alive in Norton by an old gravestone in the church porch.

Early in the eighteenth century the family had not become reattached to the church that had nourished the earlier members of the line so generously, for the Rev. Samuel Blythe of Norton Lees was a Nonconformist minister at Attercliffe. His father had a special licence from Charles the Second to celebrate divine service in his own house. Of Samuel's sons, Benjamin Blythe of Derby sold the Norton Lees estate to William Shore in 1753, and Benjamin's brother Samuel, born at Norton Lees, was a Unitarian minister at Birmingham and a friend of Dr. Priestley. Since then there have been members of the family in nearly every part of the world.

Some of the members of the family have omitted the final *e* in the spelling of their name.

There was a John Blythe canon of Beauchief in the fourteenth century. It is probable he belonged to this family. A Blythe of the eighteenth century is supposed to have been eaten by cannibals in Caffraria. Sir Arthur Blyth held office in the Government of South Australia. When he returned to England he became Agent-General for South Australia in London, and was made K.C.M.G. and C.B. A Neville Blyth also bore office in the Government of South Australia. Charles Berry Blythe had very exciting adventures in Buenos Ayres. Thomas Creswick, R.A., the famous Sheffield artist, was related to the Blythes. Robert Brittain Blyth, born in Birmingham in 1784, was very active in the agitation in favour of the Reform Bill of 1832, and the family was represented too at the gathering in Birmingham to celebrate the centenary of the birth of Dr. Priestley. Amongst the toasts was one to the memory of the Rev. Samuel Blyth, his affectionate colleague, and to this toast responded Samuel's grandson, George Blyth. Benjamin Hall Blyth, born in 1819, became an eminent civil engineer, engaged particularly in railway work. He had great mathematical ability, and when he was about six years of age, while he was walking with his father, he calculated mentally his age in minutes. It was found his calculation was correct, and that he had allowed for two leap years. A Blyth went to Madras as a missionary, and the Rev. Alfred Turner Blyth was a Unitarian minister at Chesterfield until about 1860, when he joined the English church. He became curate of Staveley, and afterwards had the livings of Scarcliffe and Langwith. He died in 1886, his coffin was made by the village carpenter who refused to accept payment, and his body was carried to Langwith churchyard by local farmers and their sons. The life of William Ellis, the founder of the Birkbeck Schools, was written by E. K. Blyth, a member of this family. Blyths were in the Boer war of 1900, and some went who never have returned.

Local readers of *The Story of My Life*, by Augustus
J. C. Hare, coming upon a reference to a Miss Isabella
Barr Blyth, who was "gentleness and sweetness itself;
every one loves her," may like to know that she was of
the Norton family. A William Blythe occupied an old
gabled house that used to stand in the Sheffield market
place. He died there in 1811. A daughter married
Mr. George Wells, solicitor, "whose grandchildren are
still amongst us," as Mr. Robert Eadon Leader has
recorded already.

At Cold Aston two brothers of the Blythe family lived
in one house. They were millers, and rented the old
Abbey Mill at Beauchief. One of the brothers dying
was buried in his own grounds. Their house still stands,
occupied by Mrs. George Greaves, and one of the
buildings bears on a stone in the wall the letters and
date

I.B. A.B.
1672

In 1900 the family reached the sixteenth generation
from its Norton representative of 1376, in the birth of
little Margaret Joyce Blythe, whom we, who love the
place so closely associated with her forbears, may wish
all the happiness that would be consonant with such
names as those of Joyce and Blythe.

CHAPTER III

NORTON LEES

IT would be unpardonable to leave the Blythes without reference to that charming and antique house at Norton Lees which enjoys the repute of having been their home. Though no known ancient document connects the Blythes with this house, the tradition is so positive that the place is called the Bishops' House. Connected specifically the Blythes are, however, with a house, now destroyed, that stood once at Norton ; but the Norton habitation belonged to a later time than the one at Norton Lees, because it has been suggested that Geoffrey built the house at Norton for his parents, who would presumably quit Norton Lees to occupy their new abode, leaving others of the family behind them here. William Pearson, once curate at Norton, writing to his brother Henry, the vicar, says : " The Blythes lived once in an old house just in front of Mr. Holy's [Norton House] near where the yew tree now stands. Mr. Read used to have a picture of the remains of it. It was pulled down some forty or fifty years ago." Again, the Rev. Henry Pearson has a note that the Blythes lived in an old house pulled down by Mr. Read in front of Norton House near an old yew tree. Another branch lived at Norton Lees, in the chamber of which is their coat-of-arms in plaster over the fire place.

Thomas Asline Ward mentions the Norton habitation of the Blythes, for in an allusion in the autumn of 1809 to Norton House, where he used to visit John Read, he

Oak Carving In the Bishops' House, Norton Lees

says : " The prospects from it will be greatly improved by taking down the old houses in front, which will be done in spring.　One of these will be much regretted by Chantrey ; and you will, I dare say, join in the regret. He has frequently admired and sketched it.　A Bishop Blythe, who is said to have been born at Norton, is reported to have erected it for the residence of his honest but homely parents."　Thus apparently the house was removed in 1810.

Mr. Addy has a water-colour drawing of an old timbered house which, before it was destroyed, stood opposite the south front of Norton House.　Probably this is the house mentioned by Asline Ward, and it may be one of those enumerated by Mrs. Sterndale in the quotation from her book which appears in the previous chapter.

No longer may we see the Blythe coat-of-arms in the Bishops' House at Norton Lees, but " W.B. 1627 " carved upon some old oak remains to this day strong evidence in support of the popular tradition.

There was a time when many more trees grew round Norton Lees, and indeed we see a much more generous growth of foliage in the photograph of the Bishops' House, taken probably no longer ago than the sixties,

HOUSE (DEMOLISHED 1810) FORMERLY NEAR NORTON HOUSE.

THE HOME of the BLYTHES

43

by Theophilus Smith. John Holland has referred to Norton Lees as being remarkable for a fine avenue of sycamores, and Mrs. Sterndale notes that the place was surrounded by adjacent woods.

Between the time of Smith's photograph and the period at which the Corporation of Sheffield secured the old house the timber in the gable had been bodged with transverse planks, not at all in keeping with its style ; but the gable has been altered to its more pleasing original appearance, a happy restoration.

Edward Blore made a beautiful drawing of the house for Rhodes' *Peak Scenery*, and a reduced reproduction appears in this book. A coarser, inferior engraving from a sketch by Blore appeared also in the *Northern Star* for February 1818, and this, together with a short note that accompanied the plate, drew a letter upon the Bishops' House from a correspondent, M.M.M., of Sheffield, that appeared in the magazine for May of the same year. It is probable that this was written by Mrs. Sterndale, for some parts of the communication are repeated in her *Vignettes of Derbyshire*, issued in 1824. She refers to " the large barns on its west, their whole structure being wood, except a low stone basement, and their principal support, deep flat beams of oak, naturally carved, of which each pair seems to have been sawed from one tree ; they spring from the ground and form a bold gothic arch overhead." Continuing she tells us that "with that consideration with which our forefathers attended to the warm comforts of their habitations, the house fronts a rising hill to the south, whilst its north aspect was sheltered by native woods, whose junior descendants form a fine colonnade, that protects and screens the venerable building ; from the west winds, that are most prevalent, the huge barns were a strong barrier ; and on the east, an antique yew, still standing, was one perhaps of many more, that formed the ornamental shade of the place. Thus guarded on all sides, and warmed within by immense fires, which the abundance of fuel supplied and the large

THE BISHOPS' HOUSE, NORTON LEES, IN 1823.

P. 44]

hearths and wide chimneys admitted, the original inhabitants felt not the seasons' difference." Surviving
internal features of the house are a draw-well, a buttery-
hatch, old oak panelling and an ornamental overmantel.

The Blythes were not the only people of note connected
with this place. In the reign of Edward the Third land
at Norton Lees was assigned to Roger de Gotham in

An Overmantel
n Bishops' House

consideration of his valour in fighting for his king at
the siege of Calais in 1347. Roger was followed by
Thomas de Gotham and Adam de Gotham, and in 1352
Adam de Gotham was a witness to a deed in which
Thomas de Chauworth, knight, Lord de Norton, grants
to John Tynet and Isabella his wife, all the lands which
were sometimes Robert Loucok's, and a piece of land
called Harecrofte in Norton. The other witnesses were
Robert Seliok, Adam Parker, William Hervy and John

Aleyn. Others of the line too were ot Norton Lees, unless Robert has been miswritten for Roger, for a note amongst the Harleian manuscripts shows that "to Thomas, son of Robert Gotham, Thomas de Alfreton, Baron, gave land in Norton Lees." At length, however, the male line ends, and we have Elizabeth, sole daughter and heiress, who lived in the time of Henry the Fourth. She married Thomas Parker, of Bulwell in Nottinghamshire, whence came the long line of Parkers, so intimately associated with Norton. How high the Parkers rose in the social scale is shown by an entry in the Norton Registers of July 19, 1609, which tells us of the baptism of John, son and heir-apparent of John Parker, of Lees, armiger, who had married Maria Mason, for it is added that the sponsors were Gilbert, Earl of Shropshire, John, Lord Darcie, and Lady Cavendish, wife of Sir Charles Cavendish. Long before this, however, Parker had be-

come one of the most familiar of Norton names,
cropping up in many parts of the parish.   For instance,
there is the evidence of documents that there were
Parkers in this district in 1342, and five years later the
name is mentioned in association with Norton people,
for there is a reference to John Parker in the will of
Thomas de Chaworth, lord of the manor here.   In 1352,
as we have seen, a Parker witnessed a grant of land in
Norton from Sir Thomas Chaworth to John and Isabella
Tynet, and there are many other transactions in which
we see the Parkers taking a share.   In 1448 too there
is a reference to their connection with Norton Lees, for
Thomas, Robert and two Johns were on a jury in an
inquiry at " Leghes, in dominio de Norton," respecting
the obstruction of a lane in this parish.   The record of
the proceedings, sealed by Robert Rasyn, the seneschal,
tells us that the inquisition was held in the lawful court
of John, Archbishop of York and Cardinal of England,
one of the feoffees of Thomas Chaworth, knight, and
others, upon the oath of a jury of Norton people whose
names are given.   A quarrel had arisen concerning the
lane between the tenants of the lordship and William
Blythe, a tenant of the Abbot of Beauchief Abbey, and
the finding of the jury was that the lane, which had been
obstructed by a hedge, was an ancient lane of the breadth
of ten feet, and led from the mill towards the South Field
and the Church Field, and also into a lane or gate called
Lydgate, and that it should thereafter be opened, as it
had anciently been, for the use, convenience and great
ease of the neighbours dwelling there.

Again, in 1471, there is mention of John Parkar, of
Leys, and another reference is in an award by Sir John
Chaworth and Sir Philip Draycot concerning a dispute
between a Parker and a Selioke.   It is a long and tedious
document, but those who wish to read it will find it in
that valuable repository the *Reliquary* (Vol. V. p. 113).
John Parker of Norton Lees, with John Lynacre, a name
well known here, Robert Eyre and Edmund Levett

were arbitrators in a local dispute in 1476, as their award
amongst the Foljambe manuscripts shows.   In 1580
John Parker of Norton Lees sold land to Thomas
Littlewood of Stannington, tanner, and to others.
Amongst the standards recorded to have been borne
by gentry in the time of Henry the Eighth is one of
" William Parker de Norton Leys, Darby."   John
Parker, late of Hemsworth, died in 1607, leaving Lees
Hall, mills and other property, including " Highley
milne " (Heeley mill) and Hemsworth Hall.   High in
High Ley has become Hee, just as a few miles away we
have High Lane pronounced Hee Lane.   In 1615 the
will of John Parker of Norton Lees asks that he shall be
buried with his ancestors in Norton parish church.   He
mentions water-wheels and a scythe wheel, and leaves to
his son John the gilt bason and ewer which his godfather
Gilbert, Earl of Shrewsbury, gave him at his " baptizinge,"
when he is 21.   To " my very loving brother Mr.
Francis Parker " he gave " a ring of gold set with a ruby,
which I have usually worn."   There is an inventory of
his goods at Lichfield.   Still other references are to the
Parkers living at Lees Hall, occupying " sithe or cuttler
wheels," and holding house and land from Charles Blithe
of the manor of Norton.

In his survey of the manor of Sheffield in 1637, John
Harrison reports that " Mr. Parker payeth yearly for the
streame of Heeley corne mill viii^d," and upon the general
question of the local streams says " these Rivers are very
profitable unto ye Lord in regard of the Mills and Cutler
Wheeles that are turned by theire streames, which weeles
are imployed for the grinding of knives."

There was a John Parker of Norton Lees in the time
of Henry the Fourth.   He married Helen, daughter of
Roger, or Robert, North, of Walkeringham in Nottinghamshire, who was the ancestor of the Earl of Guildford.
John's eldest daughter Margaret married John Selioke of
Hazelbarrow Hall, Norton, and both of the Seliokes and
of their home much will be written presently.   Margaret's

brother Henry was Groom of the Bed Chamber to Henry the Eighth, and brother William, Yeoman of the Pantry or Sewer to the same monarch. Brother John held the same office for Queens Catherine and Mary. In the succeeding generation also a Margaret Parker married a Selioke. Barbara, a daughter of the William Parker who has been mentioned as Yeoman of the Pantry, who had land at Norton Lees and also at Luton in Bedfordshire, married John Wickham of Enfield in Middlesex, and was the mother of William Wickham, born in 1539, Bishop of Lincoln, and afterwards of Winchester, but not from that circumstance to be confounded with the great William de Wykeham. He preached the funeral sermon on Mary Queen of Scots, at Peterborough.

There was a William Parker of this Wickham family Under Sheriff of Derbyshire at the end of the sixteenth century, and a John Parker married Barbara, daughter of Sir William West, who had some of the Beauchief Abbey lands. Their son John married Mary, daughter of William "Masoun" of Egmanton Hall in Nottingham- shire, a marriage that explains the Mason connection with Lees Hall, and when Parker died his widow married Humphrey Cardinal of Hornby, whose name occurs in the Norton Register as living at Lees Hall. Some sub- sequent marriages also bring us into touch with Lees Hall. John, the son of the Parker and Mason marriage, married Anne Lynacre, who married a second time Thomas Woolhouse of Glapwell, and Elizabeth, a daughter of the Parker and Mason marriage, wedded John Cave of Pickwell, Leicester. Anne Parker of the Parker and Lynacre union married Francis Barker of Dore and Norton Lees, a union to which further allusion will be made. Then a Thomas Parker married the daughter and co-heiress of John Hobson of Cambridge, who has attained immortality as the man who originated " Hobson's choice."

A Robert Parker of the Norton Lees family was cup- bearer to Queen Catherine, wife of Charles the Second,

4

and his brother William Parker commanded a company of Foot in the service of Charles the First and Charles the Second. He was present at the battles of Hopton Heath, Marston Moor, Naseby and Worcester, and, taken prisoner in the Isle of Sheppey, he suffered much for his loyalty during the time of Cromwell. Later we have John Parker, Deputy Teller of the Exchequer, and his brother Sir Thomas Parker, Sergeant-at-Law, who became Chief Baron of the Exchequer.

A daughter of this Sir Thomas Parker, Martha, was married to Sir John Jervis, the admiral, who was created Earl St. Vincent. Chantrey made a sketch in crayon of Earl St. Vincent and an excellent bust. When Lady St. Vincent died Chantrey wrought a beautiful monument in her memory, so that Norton stands associated with the stern old warrior in another way beside the family connection.

Still another distinguished member of the Parker family was Sir William Parker, G.C.B., Admiral of the Fleet. Both Nelson and St. Vincent agreed that he was a first-rate officer.

The crowning glory of the family, however, is Thomas Parker, Lord High Chancellor of England, created Earl of Macclesfield November 5, 1721, "silver-tongued Parker," who reached to dizzy heights and plumbed also some profound depths of disgrace and misery. His father descended from a younger branch of the Norton Lees Parkers. His son George, the second Earl, was the learned mathematician and astronomer who compassed our adoption of the Gregorian style of reckoning time— the New Style.

Later Parkers, too, were distinguished. Edward Parker, Captain in the Royal Engineers, was killed in the battle of Orthez in 1814, and members of the family have been in the navy in our own days.

Whitley Hall, between Barnes Hall and Ecclesfield, about half a mile from Ecclesfield church, belonged at one time to a branch of the Norton Parkers, one of whom had his name carved there : " 1584 William Parker made this worke."

In following the more illustrious Parkers, however, we have rambled far from Norton Lees, where the transition from the Parkers to the Barkers remains to receive more than a passing allusion. The Norton Register shows that Ann Parker, baptised at Norton in 1629, married Francis Barker of Dore, a member of an old family in these parts. An ancestor of Francis Barker married a daughter of Thomas Fanshawe, a local family that has become famous. Ann, Francis Barker's daughter, married John Cave and lived at Lees Hall. Left a widow, she married John Bright of Brincliffe, the member of another wealthy local family. Their son John gave bells to Dronfield church in 1730. Robert Barker, a son of Francis, baptised at Norton in 1660, became Remembrancer of London. Another Robert, a descendant, fought in the Manillas, and was afterwards made a baronet. At Bolsover he married Anne, the only child of Brabazon Hallowes of Dethick Hall and Glapwell, and died in 1789 leaving no children. The Barkers are said to have been the builders of Totley Hall. In Bolsover church are memorials, noted by Bassano, of the last of the Barkers, with heraldry of Parkers, Barkers, Gothams, Hallowes and Woolhouses. Lady Barker, widow of Sir Robert, heiress of Brabazon Hallowes, was buried at Bolsover in 1806. Bolsover inscriptions mention Lees Hall, the home of the Parkers and the Barkers, a house, however, which is not to be found in the cluster of dwellings at Norton Lees where stands the Bishops' House, but must be sought less than a mile away along Kidnapper Lane. From Heeley it is approached from Gleadless Road by Cat Lane, once beautiful with wild roses, and leading through more woodland than it knows now, for Carr Wood is but the ghost of its old self. In place names "cat" is often a corruption of "coed," a wood, so that in this case we should have Wood Lane, a most appropriate name. Cattle Lane is another suggestion. Glover gives Lees Hall as one of the places at which coal has been worked, but this must have been long ago, for no traces remain. Lees Hall, too, seems to have had its ghost story, for John Holland has the lines

> Forgetful of thy haunted glen, Lees Hall!
> Through which we hasted homeward.

My own recollections of Lees Hall are associated entirely with the dwelling there of the Butchers, Samuel and Henry, bachelor brothers. Samuel, unable to walk, was driven to Sheffield occasionally, but Henry was a robust virile man, with ruddy face and black hair, who stalked vigorously about his fields and woods, not ill-natured with peaceable people, but ready with a few short and sharp expletives for those whom he found relieving his fields of their turnips, his hedges of their stakes, or otherwise encroaching upon his rights. Farming near a large industrial centre is not an experience that tends to philosophic calm. About the house itself, however, in those days it was a rare event to see any one. Always it seemed there like a country Sunday afternoon. Invariably was the door open, and a carefully polished old chair stood in view, but nobody ever seemed to come through the door, nobody ever seemed to sit in the chair. Surely never was such a home of quiet as Lees Hall in the seventies and eighties. There was ever about the old place an atmosphere of dignity and decorum, a silence broken only from time to time by the barking of a great black dog that challenged passage along the path between the house and the stack yard. When I try to recall the place I think of its austere and solemn front and air of aloofness, of its gables with their ball finials, its pond where the ducks loved to swim and to "swattle" in the mud, its old cart shed that had, and still has, an ancient carved stone bearing the word "Pax" and the date 1732 built into its front, its green croft and the lime-tree near the stile under whose branches it was such a delight to lie through a long sultry summer afternoon listening to the

LEE'S HALL

comfortable murmur of the bees amongst the sweetly scented blossoms. Away to the east were delightful views of Hang Bank Wood, the "Cuckoo," where the old box mangle did some of Heeley's mangling, Buck Wood, Newfield Green, Hurlfield Hill, Myrtle Springs, Gleadless, a lovely world for a boy to wander in, and old

Old Stone at Lees Hall

woods, now there no longer, with delightful brooks, a picture at every turn, and about Whitsuntide with the young yellow leaves and the tender greens above and the bluebells below a beauty that might well move an artist or a poet to tears.

To allow the memory to range amongst these scenes is to recall many other features that are there no more and some that still remain. Away at Newfield Green is "Old Collis'" cottage, Addlington's farm and the old home of the Misses Brownell, from which they used to issue sedately with "Owd Thompson," their ruddy white-haired coachman.

Luke Brownell, of Newfield Green, scythesmith, has the distinction that he paid the largest apprenticeship premium ever received by the Cutlers' Company of Sheffield. The premium was for his son Peter, who in 1807 was Master Cutler.

It used to be possible to see an occasional cock pheasant in Hang Bank Wood, and I remember an odd larch tree there that used to come into leaf before the other trees— a harbinger of spring. This curious name Hang Bank occurs in a slightly modified form in Harrison's survey of Sheffield made in 1637, for Harrison mentions a pasture that "abutteth upon Newfield greene North and a Common called Hanbanke South." A picturesque feature of the Brownell's house is the ivy-covered dove-cot, and I once had a talk with a man at Ridgeway who told me that when he was a boy he and his father planted the ivy round the building, and he was proud of its luxuriant growth. Away behind is Buck Wood that has hidden tragedies, and was not to be traversed at night for fear of the ghost of a man who had hanged himself there.

Lees Hall to-day, occupied by Mr. W. Clarke, has so far come into touch with the world that it is connected with the throng of Sheffield by a telephone, but this hint of modernity cannot hide the essential antiquity of the delightful building, a fragment probably of a much larger hall. Indeed some have arrived at the conclusion that the pond occupies the depression made for the cellar of a more ancient and widespread building. Internally, rooms panelled with oak and an old oaken staircase are amongst the interesting features of a hall that has many elements to excite our curiosity and to attach our affections.

It is possible to compile a list of people who have lived at Lees Hall by extracting all the references to the place amongst the baptisms, weddings and deaths at Norton church, where there was a Lees Hall pew. It does not follow that this yields a complete list, but it furnishes many names, and confirms some of the statements made already concerning the Parkers and the Barkers. Lysons says that Francis Gregg of the Ilkeston family once lived at Lees Hall, but Gregg does not seem to have left any records amongst the baptisms, marriages or deaths. The poll book for the election of 1734 gives John Challiner of

Lees Hall; but he may have been the owner without being the occupier.

In 1626 Humphrey Cardinall, gentleman, was at Lees Hall, and in 1659 "Sellbee Massonn," attorney-at-law, whose wife was Margaret Barker. A year later the occupiers were Francis Barker and Mistress Ann, his wife, and they were still there in 1671; but by 1673 John Cave, gentleman, was installed there. His wife was the daughter of Francis Barker, and when her husband, John Cave, died, she married John Bright of Dronfield. In that way we have the Brights, a great local family, at Lees Hall for a time. Then in 1689 William Wastnidge is there, and still there in 1691; but two years later Edward Greenwood, gentleman, occupies the Hall. Edward Greenwood married Beathea, daughter of Andrew Morewood of the Hallowes. He was buried at Wentworth in 1733, and later in the same year their son, Morewood Greenwood, was buried too. Beathea's mother was Mary Spencer, daughter of William Spencer of Attercliffe Hall and lord of the manor of Darnall. Benjamin Eyre comes next in the Norton Registers. Widow Brearley was at Lees Hall in 1703, but it is necessary to be cautious in assuming that all who are given in the Registers as being of Lees Hall were the occupiers of the Hall itself, for labourers and domestic servants, or even people living in neighbouring cottages, are sometimes given as coming from a hall. Thus in the Norton Register there is a scythe finisher of Norton Hall, and another workman of the Oakes.

Ralph Clay was at Lees Hall in 1707, and he was still there in 1719 when he went to Hemsworth. At this time what we know as Fawcett's farm was called sometimes Lees Hall farm and sometimes Cock Shout House —Cockshutts as we write the name now. Thomas Pashley was there in Mr. Clay's time. Following Ralph Clay came John Lowe, but at the same time a George Bramall, gentleman, has incidental mention. Lowe, however, was there in 1721, and still there in 1742. Clay

and Lowe seem to have exchanged farms—Lees Hall
and Hemsworth. Gamaliel Edgbarrow was at Cockshutts, and then Robert Merill, followed by Nancy, his
widow. Thomas Ellin was at Lees Hall in 1747 and in
1767, and he was followed by James and then by John,
who was there in 1771. During this reign of the
Ellins there are mentioned also Thomas Bagshaw, John
Marshall, Arthur Spyth, John Hollinworth and Mary
Webster, but these probably are subsidiary characters.
An entry in a memorandum book kept by Thomas
Ellin gives " May the 15 1762 Thomas Rodger has don
18 days worke of mosing at Newfield Green." In his
glossary of local words Mr. Addy says this was putting
moss under or between slates, and he adds that the
Baslow parish register records the burial, July 21, 1708,
of Edmund Littlewood of Totley, moser, killed by falling
from Bubnell Hall. In his book on the evolution of the
house Mr. Addy gives another example, from an old bill
for the building of a house in Sheffield : " Payd in parte
of a recconing for mossing of and slating my howse xxs."
Architects tell me that in old houses the stone slates are
found often to have been laid upon hay or straw, as well
as upon moss.

The Ellins came from the neighbourhood of Ponte-
fract, and were engaged here supplying stone for slates
and other building stone with the Duke of Devonshire as a buyer. An entry in Ellin's memorandum
book runs : " John Holingworth indebted to Thomas
Ellin for a Barjan of slate whish he had on me £1."
Thomas married a daughter of the house of Brownell,
of Newfield Green, and we need not be very imaginative
to picture the lovers signalling to one another across the
valley of the Meersbrook, for the houses are in sight of
each other. Their sons were John and James, and some
of their descendants are in the Sheffield cutlery trade to
this day. Thomas was Master Cutler, and presided over
the first feast in the new hall, and Ellin Street in Sheffield
was cut through land belonging to the family.

After the Ellins came John Butterill, in possession in 1774 and 1777. Robert Booker is next, bringing us down to 1808. A Mr. Senior kept Lees Hall until Robert Booker came of age, and Robert and John Booker went to school at Norton, where Robert quarrelled with young Bingham, the son of a Quaker. A friend of Bingham implored him not to fight with Booker, who he said got too much beef to allow of any hope of his being conquered by Bingham, but young broad-brim was undismayed. His blood was up; a whole shambles of beef could not cow him. He said sententiously "A bellyful is a bellyful, and I will fight him." So the fight was arranged, a desperate " turn up," and

> Round lugs and ogles flew the frequent fist.

The sequel was unexpected, for in spite of all his beef young Booker went down before the blows of Quaker Bingham.

Related to the Bookers, who had many connections in this district, were their successors, the Butchers. A Directory gives Mrs. Benjamin Butcher at Lees Hall in 1864, and Samuel and Henry many of us remember. One day at Lees Hall the death of Mrs. Butcher was expected hourly. Her sons were there, and the doctor was in attendance. Presently she awoke out of a sleep and said she was hungry. Her dainty fancy was a glass of beer and some bread and cheese. The doctor declared such a diet most unsuitable, but as the end was so near she might be humoured. They would see she would not touch the food when it was brought. At the sight of the beer and cheese, however, Mrs. Butcher sat up and proceeded to eat a hearty meal, and so far from being dead in a few hours, she lived for four more years.

Upon the side of the Hall where the old enclosed garden lies, the Harehills rise, and here is a way to Norton that leads to Norton Backmoor. Then beyond the Harehills is Cockshutts farm, associated for more than one generation with the Fawcetts, and there will be many people still alive who remember the old grey donkey that used to issue every evening from Fawcett's farm with two well-scoured barrels, with shining hoops and glittering brass taps, hanging pannier-wise across his back. Fawcett's donkey was the most loveable of a loveable species, and the people of Heeley were very fond of him and gave him tit-bits or put roses in his head-band. Quite a series of donkey boys came and went during the many years that this old

Old Cottage At Cockshutts Farm
Norton Lees

donkey was growing grey in the service of the people of Heeley, but the one I remember was a Sydney Dodd— Sid Dodd as the name became amongst the boys of the place—who sometimes permitted me to ride upon this patient beast when the milk barrels had been emptied. One of the traits that endeared Neddy to the people of Heeley was the undeviating regularity of his habits. Not only did he appear at the same point at the same time each evening, but he knew his stations better than the milk boy, and seemed to stand even in the same footprints every evening. In Artisan View was a tall iron pump, and each night he took up his position with his head nearly touching this and his body at right angles to the kerbstone, never varying his position as it seemed by a hairsbreadth. In the early eighties he died, and so a looked-for and familiar feature disappeared from Cat Lane and from the Heeley streets.

When I was a boy I was sent to Fawcett's farm for a sitting of eggs, and while I was waiting Mr. Fawcett, the father of the present tenant, undertook, in his kindly way, to tide over the interval by a chat. "And what are you going to be when you leave school?" he asked. "A reporter," I replied, for having literary leanings I had hit upon this occupation as a means of gratifying them, much in the same way, I suppose, that the boy became a butcher "because he was that fond of animals." Mr. Fawcett looked at me aghast. If I had said I was going to be Lord Chancellor he could not have been more amazed at my effrontery, and so, taken a little off his guard, he said, with a puzzled look, "But I thought they had to be varry intelligent to be reporters." Mrs. Fawcett seemed to think this might give me pain, and, coming to the rescue, gave me the benefit of the doubt by exclaiming, "Howd thi noise wi' thee ; happen he is intelligent!"

The term Cockshutt implies a broad way or glade in a wood through which woodcocks and other birds might dart or shoot so as to be caught by nets stretched across the opening. "They are taken by nets, in cock-shoots," says a writer of the seventeenth century. Hence it is held that properly the word should be Cockshoot. In literature the term is found as early as 1496. In 1601 we are told that "a silly honest creature may do well to watch a cocke-shoote, or a limed bush," and there are many similar later allusions. It is likely, too, that the poets mean the hour when the woodcocks "shoot" or fly when they refer to the twilight as cock-shut light,

or time.   Shakespeare uses "cockshut time," and Ben
Jonson has

> For you would not yesternight
> Kiss him in the cock-shut light.

Other poets have similar references, and even so
recently as 1868 Henry Kingsley could write : "It was
getting dusk, cockshot time as they would have said at
Sheepsden." They would have used the same word at
Whitby.

There is another Cockshutts farm near Beauchief
Abbey, a Cockshot Lane near Stannington, a Cock Shutts
Wood near Dore, Upper Cockshutt and Nether Cockshutt at Walkley, Cockshutts Lane at Oughtybridge,
and the name occurs at Thorpe Hesley and near Pits-
moor. There is Cockshot Hill near Bristol, and in many
other parts of the country the name may be found. In
1584 land at Norton is mentioned, including "Cockshut
fylde," apparently not far from Norton Hall, and in 1606
Gabriel Parker of the Oakes, in Norton, conveyed to
John Frecheville of Hazelbarrow some land in which were
"Cockshoote Banck, Cockshoote Bank Spring," and other
fields. Even when a place has been cleared of trees
and covered with houses this name has survived in some
districts, to speak to us of woods and glades where now
we may see naught but courts and slums. The name
Cockshutts has become also a personal name, as place
names are apt to do.

A number of references to the old family of Foljambe
owning land at Norton Lees might be cited. One is an
entry in the memorandum books of Arthur and George
Mower of Barlow Woodseats, in which we read that
"Mr. Foljambe, of Moorhouse, has entred covenant with
Thomas Rowland to pay to him of Whitesunday three
hundred and four pounds in the parish church of Eam
[Eyam], between the hours of nine and three at afternoon, the which day shall be in the anno Dom. 1580, or
else Norton-lees is gone from him."

Interesting mention of Norton Lees occurs in an unexpected place. To light upon a book entitled *The Still Life of the Middle Temple* is not to suspect any allusions to a place so far away ; but it happens that the author, W. G. Thorpe, who has since died, was a native of Norton Lees. He tells us he was descended from an old family hardly above yeoman rank, but domiciled for some five hundred years at a small village on the borders of Derbyshire and Yorkshire called

Norton Lees. He mentions the Blythes, and adds, " I have still the old oak chair—inscribed I. B. 1660 ; it came to us from him in 1677—which old John Blythe had made to commemorate the Restoration." This chair is now at Balham, near London, in the possession of Mrs. Thorpe. Francis Thorpe, member of the High Court of Justice, was of this family, and Mr. Thorpe informs his readers that " my people had fallen from their once high estate, and had migrated from Gleadless, four miles off, upon the disgrace of Sir William Thorpe,

Lord Chief Justice in 1350, and the sentence of death, afterwards commuted for a fine, which beggared him." He adds that a Thorpe was a priest amongst those who followed Wycliffe, and one Godfrey Thorpe remembered the Highlanders passing south to Derby in the 'Forty-five. He told the story to an uncle, who told Mr. Thorpe in 1833, so that three lives covered nearly 150 years.

Mr. Thorpe goes on to say that " one of our nearest neighbours was a clergyman, who fancied his own knowledge of horseflesh, and thought much of a butcher's cob which brought out the meat-supply from Sheffield. A purchase was arranged with the owner for a reasonable price, and the parson rode his new mount to his daily duty as master in the Grammar School; but the animal had lost all its fire, neither whip nor spur would get it out of a shuffle, while jibbing and buck-jumping brought about one or two spills. The butcher was appealed to, and he in turn called his boy and asked him what it all meant.

" ' He's all right, sir, if you'll only carry the basket.' "

At first I thought this anecdote must be of one of the vicars or curates of Norton, but Mr. Thorpe wrote probably of the Rev. Percival Bowen, M.A., Master of the Sheffield Grammar School, for he lived at Norton Lees, and so would answer the description as being "one of our nearest neighbours." Mr. Thorpe wrote another book, *Middle Temple Talk*, which contains his portrait, and the family is still represented here, for Dr. J. F. Thorpe of Endcliffe Hall Avenue, Fellow of the Royal Society, the " Sorby Research " Fellow at the Sheffield University, is his son, and his second cousins are Mr. and Mrs. F. C. Wild of Whirlow Court. Their sons are Mr. F. C. Wild, junior, of Gladstone Road, Ranmoor, and Mr. F. D. Wild of Norton Grange. The author of *Still Life in the Middle Temple* was born at Thorpe House, built in 1829, now occupied by Mrs. Hall; but once standing upon this site was an older house of which no drawing seems to have survived.

Hunter has a note about a Mr. Bowker, topographical writer, a grandson of a person of that name who lived at Norton Lees. In 1846 there was living at the Bishops' House William Beck, who had Chinese and other curiosities there; but most of us associate Norton Lees with the Aldersons, connected with the family of Lord Salisbury, the Cockaynes, Farmer White, the Featherstones, the Beverleys, the Listers and others, and will remember Mr. Welby at the Hollies before he went to Norton House. Altogether, with the Blythes, the Parkers, the Barkers, the Thorpes and such families, though Norton Lees has dreamed its days away for so many years environed by an atmosphere of more than ordinary tranquillity, the lark in the air, the scent of the gilly-flowers and of the honeysuckle about its doors, yet have its sons at times been fired with the ardour and the movement and colour of a world not bounded by its circumscribed horizon, and those who have sprung from this peaceful place have had much at stake in the great issues that have been decided in the distant places of the earth.

CHAPTER IV

MEERSBROOK

THE timbered house of the Blythes at Norton Lees is one of the features of the Meersbrook Park estate, once belonging to the Shores, but now the property of the neighbouring city of Sheffield. The stream in the valley is the Meersbrook, a tributary of the Sheaf, and the dividing line here between Yorkshire and Derbyshire. "Mear," indeed, is an obsolete word which indicates that we have reached the border of some division of territory, the term having been obtained from "mœra," an Anglo-Saxon name for a boundary, as in Meersick, a boundary stream. In a deed of 1507 land is mentioned as "meryed and staked," and in 1725 a croft near Campo Lane in Sheffield is described as "meared and staked out." There are reasons, however, which deter the cautious philologist from concluding too hastily that the name has been derived from "mear," even though this brook is not only the division between counties, but between the ecclesiastical parishes of Heeley and Norton, between the diocese of York and the diocese of Southwell, between the province of York and the province of Canterbury, between parliamentary divisions too, and until a few years ago between Norton and the borough of Sheffield. Then, too, Joseph Hunter has written of "the Meersbrook or boundary-brook now separating the counties of York and Derby, but heretofore performing a much more important office—marking the separation between Northumbria and Mercia, and doubtless also between Maxima and Flavia Cæsarienses."

There is a Meerbrook near Wirksworth, and Meerbrook three miles from Leek in Staffordshire. Mear Oak
divides Sheffield from Wadsley, and there is Meerbrook
between Norton and Eckington; and yet, in spite of these
and other seeming good reasons for a derivation embodying the boundary idea, something is to be urged in favour
of a derivation from " maes " or " meuse," a river of
meadows, a name that would connect us with a noble
European river, and with Mesham, Maesbury, Masbrook,
Masborough and such places. Farmer White, and other
old people of Heeley, always pronounced it Mezzbrook
or Messbrook ; and though this pronunciation was regarded as a vulgar degradation of the name, it may be
that in this case, as in others, they were right, and,
uncorrupted by books and arbitrary spelling, perpetuated
truly the ancient appellation.

In William Harrison's delightful description of England written for Holinshed's *Chronicle* in 1577, with an
" especial eye unto the truth of things," he tells us of
a stream that flows " by west from Gledles, called Mese-
brooke, which diuideth Yorkeshyre from Darbieshyre " ;
and our local John Harrison, who surveyed the manor
of Sheffield in 1637, says that Sheffield extends " unto
Messebrooke next Derbyshire, being the south side of
Heeley." A description of Sheffield in the *Gentleman's
Magazine* for 1764 gives " Mazebrooke, two miles to the
south " of Sheffield ; and an indenture dated August 21,
1744, and made between John Hatfield of Laughton-
en-le-Morthen and George Hobson of Heeley, miller,
mentions some property " situate and being in the parish
of Norton aforesaid, near unto a brook or rivulet called
Mäsbrook, otherwise Mazebrook, which divides the said
parish of Norton and the town or vill of Heeley."

There is an earlier reference to this brook in a grant of
land to Beauchief Abbey made between 1162 and 1183
by Robert FitzRanulph, lord of Alfreton and Norton.
Other land was granted, " and also the field of Hugh,
near Meresbroc, with one toft in Leis "—Norton Lees

probably. "Mere" may mean also a lake or a marsh. "Maes" is Welsh for field.

Possibly this stream, over which even the coy halcyon once darted, boasts no more fish to-day than a few belated "Billy-loiches" and somnolent "bull-heeads," to adopt local rather than scientific terminology; but the Meersbrook once harboured many a lusty trout. I remember the thrill I had when, as a boy, with a home-made rod of hazel, I drew one from under the elder tree at the bottom of Mr. Alfred Dyson's garden; but the doings of many of us of lesser note must pale before the achievements of another, for a large number of these trout, especially from the higher reaches of the Meersbrook, in the region of Hang Bank Wood, must have found their way into the frying-pan of a redoubtable boy who shall not be betrayed in these pages, and many a gamekeeper and many a farmer would have been appeased if he could have come to sufficiently close quarters with that dauntless youth, to have given him a taste of what John Bunyan once called "a grievous crab-tree cudgel." If half the imprecations had been fulfilled which they called down upon his retreating figure as it disappeared over a wall or through a gap in a hedge, the last flash of the corner of his shirt protruding through torn trousers serving to recall the white of a rabbit's tail as it takes to its burrow, or if a tithe of the "vivisectionary threats" that were uttered had been executed, his plight would have been pitiable indeed. If ever there was a bad boy who didn't care, here he was; and by all the portentous warnings that have ever been enunciated in Sunday-school books, he ought long ago to have come to some disastrous end.

However, he has lived to make his peace with farmers and gamekeepers, has attained a staid middle age and has children of his own. Moreover he is an instructor of youth, so that the mention of his name might undermine his discipline; for probably none of his pupils will ever guess, as he stands gravely before his school, that it was not an uncommon occurrence for him in his own boyhood to appear in class, upon a hot afternoon, fresh from one of his trout-tickling expeditions—for he used neither rod nor net—with fishy hands and with half a dozen spotted beauties tied in his red pocket-handkerchief—itself a spotted beauty—lined with grass. When William Petch, the headmaster of the neighbouring school at Heeley—still at his post, with Mrs. Petch there too—had business in another part of the building, this precocious sportsman would unfold his treasures, and they passed from hand to hand in a way that was not conducive to clean copy-books ; or, taken by the tail, they might be flapped jocosely in the face of some unwary and industrious boy "that pored upon a book," with all that pleasantry and fine discernment of subtle humour which is the heritage of schoolboys. Should the master's eye wander in our direction, the fish were hustled unceremoniously under the desk amongst the books "with great privacy and speed," as with solemn faces we seemed deeply absorbed in the involutions of compound proportion. When at last the trout had been examined, handled, sniffed, admired, their weight estimated to the fraction of an ounce, their owner was permitted again to "lap 'em up" in the red handkerchief with the grass, and the end of these denizens of the Meersbrook was as a relish for their captor's tea.

Without knowing it, we were pioneers, and liable to suffer all the disadvantages of pioneers if we had been discovered. To-day natural history lessons have attained all the dignity of a place in the curriculum ; but we had to study trout furtively and in uneasy snatches amidst more arid studies of gerunds and infinitive moods. However, I am sure the schoolboys to-day do not enjoy their overt natural history lessons as much as we did our covert ones, associated as they were with careless, happy days, when the sun shone on Hang Bank Wood and made " the netted sunbeams dance" on the " sandy shallows " of the Meersbrook.

The school will be closed in 1914, and Mr. Petch will retire—the only master the place will have known, for he opened it. The institution recalls many incidents that must not be lingered upon here, including that awful day of judgment the annual inspection, when our shortcomings, which were manifold, were revealed in noughts upon the Government schedules. Upon that dread morning my mother undertook the responsibilities of my toilet herself, and plastered my hair down vigorously with a hard brush, remarking the while that there was a good deal in looking like a sharp lad, with an emphasis upon the "looking" which was not to my taste. Mothers on these occasions saw that more than the mere faces of their offspring had been washed ; they made sure that there did not remain round their necks that dark low-water mark which spiteful Barnsley folk have called a Sheffield necktie.

In those days there was at this school as a pupil teacher a youth studious as I remember him, but not studious of the subjects prescribed by the Education Department ; a great reader, but not of text-books that had reference to matters sanctioned by " My Lords," and now an acknowledged authority upon the subject of birds, to whom many compilers turn for their material. Charles Dixon has spent almost the whole of his life in that study of natural history which had its small beginnings here by the Meersbrook. He has visited most parts of the British Isles, and at St. Kilda he discovered the wren that is peculiar to that place. In Northern Africa also he found rare birds and new species, and for five years he co-operated with the late Henry Seebohm in a great work on British birds. Migration has been his special study ; new theories and new laws he has promulgated, but not one of these things has blotted out the memory of his early days on the banks of this once enchanting stream.

I remember being saluted by a " view Haloo " as I was crossing the little wooden bridge which then spanned the Meersbrook at the western end of Rushdale, and looking

aloft saw Charles Dixon lying along a bough away up
the tree with a book which probably had no reference
either to algebra or syntax.   Here was he in the favourite
haunt of his boyhood, and after many years and wide
travel he has touched lovingly upon this homely place in
some of his later writings.   For instance, referring to the
shrubbery in Meersbrook Park in his *Annals of Bird Life*,
he tells us that " one of these noble shrubberies with
which I am specially familiar stands on a gently sloping
hillside in Derbyshire, almost within sight of the flaming
furnaces of the Sheffield steel-makers," and much of his
first book, *Rural Bird Life : being Essays on Ornithology*,
published in 1880, was written in this very shrubbery.
When the work was issued Charles Dixon planted a tree
there in honour of the event, and his fame came to the
ears of Farmer White, who asked him, " Charley, what is
this Ornithowlogy ?   Is it a new religion ? "

Recalling early days in *Annals of Bird Life*, published
in 1890, he laments the destruction of Rushdale and
Meersbrook, and exclaims : " My ruined aviary !   No
other rural spot has ever yet been able to console me for
its loss.   I knew every tree and bush, and bird and beast
within it, and loved them all!"   Again, in *Among the
Birds in Northern Shires*, he mentions " once picturesque
Meersbrook," and tells his readers of the birds he found
there.   " Fortunately all bird-life here was respected ;
every species was safe and welcome within this fair
domain ; it was a sanctuary, a place of refuge for all birds
irrespective of their ill-deeds, their bad or shady characters.
No gun was ever fired within the sacred fences, and the
birds could live their happy lives in peace. . . . Those
who remember the quaint old village of Heeley (now, alas !
a suburb of Sheffield) in the days before the railway, when
the mail-coach passed through twice a day and caused the
only commotion, when the old flour-mill, driven by water,
with its tree-surrounded dam, stood where the railway-
station does now, may perhaps recall the matchless sylvan
beauty of Meersbrook, the Banks, and the old hall at

In Old Rushdale.

71

Norton Lees." Most people who are fond of country life enjoy Charles Dixon's books, and Heeley people may well regard them with pride as well as with pleasure.

Rushdale, through which the Meersbrook runs just before it enters what was once Meersbrook Park, used to be a glen of unusual beauty, with such oak trees as Chatsworth or Sherwood might show, but not many nearer places. Reuben Hallam, the author of *Wadsley Jack*, pays a tribute to Rushdale and to old Heeley generally in the entertaining opening of his story *T'Days ov ahr Fathers*. Charles Dixon remembers the beginning of the end in Rushdale. In the spring, when the tender greens and yellows of the young leaves began to appear, the woodmen came one morning, a fateful day, and took off the bark for use in tanning, a purpose which demanded that the trees should be stripped when the sap was in them. To those who loved these beautiful old oaks it was like standing helplessly by while your friends were being skinned alive, and there they stood white and stark in the pageant of summer and on until the following autumn, when old Oates and his son Jonathan came to fell them. Oates was a clever woodman, and could bring a tree down, up hill or down hill, on a steep bank or on a level, to within a few inches of the place in which he declared beforehand it should lie, so that afterwards it might be hauled away with a minimum of trouble.

Before it was built upon, Rushdale was regarded as a kind of " No Man's Land," or " Jack's Land," as the old term was, by all except Farmer White, who, as he paid rent for it, thought perversely that he was entitled to secure and maintain control of this outlying territory ; but never were his efforts crowned with success, though sometimes boys who played cricket there paid toll with their waistcoats when the voluble old man made a raid from behind a hedge or tree and caught them unawares. His language on such occasions was noted for what Huxley would have called its " damnatory prodigality," and he was full of threats to " summons yo' oop." Yet was his bark worse than his bite, and he would yield the "little weskit" with unexpected readiness when he was asked to do so. He was indeed quite willing to live at peace with his neighbours if they would but "let him a-be"; and Charles Dixon, whom the Milners allowed to ramble all over Meersbrook Park, had full permission also to study natural history in the fields of Farmer White. This land had been cultivated too by White's father, one of the last in this district to wear a smock-frock, though I can remember a boy wearing one at Heeley in the early seventies. His name was Childs, and his father, who worked on Memmot's

Farmer White's House.
Norton Lees

farm at "The Cuckoo," lived in an old cottage under a pear tree near the top of Alexandra Road.

If Farmer White came from his grave now he would lose his way should he try to find Rushdale, for where once grew these old oak trees and lovely beeches, melodious with the songs of thrushes and of blackbirds, we see now the "tuneless groves" of drying clothes, sheets and blankets, shirts and pinafores, mingled with what an irreverent parodist of Gray once called "the short and simple flannels of the poor." Down the dale echoes the clangour of the bell of a new school, and where in days that are gone beyond recall we had the scent of the wild rose, arises now the pungent odour of a pickle factory. So rapidly in these times does civilization advance ; so breathlessly do "improvements" crowd upon us.

Meersbrook and Heeley are invariably the themes of our conversation whenever I happen to meet Charles Dixon in London. His memory goes further back than mine, to days before the advent of the railway. He remembers when gipsies camped in fields off Thirlwell Road, when old Rushby wore a smock-frock, knee-breeches and blue stockings. In his early years there was a toll-bar in Well Road, and the well-head was green with ferns and moss. A *Directory* of 1864 calls this Townwell Street. Old Naylor kept the post office, near the bottom of Well Road, and used to go down to London Road to take and receive letters when the coach went past. This operation was performed deftly without any stopping of the coach, for Naylor caught the letters that were thrown out and threw in the letters that were going away, to the admiration of the boys who assembled to watch the performance. Opposite the bottom of Well Road was a dam and a flour mill, its site now occupied by the Midland Railway, just as higher up the Sheaf Valley Beauchief Station stands upon the site of the Hudcliffe grinding-wheel dam. An old-fashioned little shop at the southern corner of Well Road, with a liberal frontage for the display of wares, was occupied by Joseph Lancaster, a saddler, who sometimes speculated in the carcase of an old horse, whose hide he would tan for himself. For one of the processes he used the dam that was conveniently just across London Road. Over the Sheaf, at the bottom of what until recent years was Sheaf Street and is now Gleadless Road, was a stone bridge, whence the loiterer might see pleasing views of cornfields and wooded hills, meadows, and, under alders, enchanting pools where the trout leapt for the May fly.

It was indeed early on a fine May morning that Ebenezer Rhodes came this way to write his last tour for *Peak Scenery*, and he mentions "the little village of Heeley," the river Sheaf "babbling and sparkling amongst shades of elms, poplars, and alders." In those days Little London Dam was very much larger, and Rhodes's reference is to "a noble sheet of water, of many acres."

Presently Rhodes went to Smithy Wood, and it happens that when Smithy Wood was devastated I contributed an article upon the subject to the *Sheffield Telegraph* of March 20, 1901, and as in Greece in olden times it was decided that a man may once say a thing as he would have it said, but that he cannot say it twice, I will reproduce the contribution, the proprietors of that journal having kindly given their consent.

"To have spent one's childhood on the green border-land of an expanding city," runs the essay, "is to have rendered oneself, unconsciously, a prey to future in-felicity; for few men are so devoid of sentiment that they can witness, without a pang, the spoiler's invasion of the fields and woods that they have associated always with the happiest hours of their childhood and of their adolescence. In all of us there is awakened a conscious-ness of sadness when we find that the homes of strangers have been built upon the garden where we first knew the scent of the wallflower, and when we find that the stream in which we caught our first trout has now become a victim of pollution. Men not yet middle-aged remember the last of the Cutler Wood before the ground was crushed and burned into bricks; and now, further up the once charming valley of the Sheaf, a similar piece of woodland has disappeared for ever. Ebenezer Rhodes, in one of his tours, 'passed through some sweet scenery about half a mile from Heeley, at a place called Smithy Wood Bottom.' Many who knew Smithy Wood in its best days will regret the need to remove it. Here, on

a summer afternoon, one might lie under an oak and
hear the pleasant sound of cool waters : the lazy lapping
of the wavelets amongst the reeds, the hollow-sounding
water-wheel, and, a little further away, the brawling of
the river Sheaf. In this lotus land even the thud of the
tilt-hammer seemed to come with a softened effect upon
senses that had been soothed by the other elements in
this dreamy scene and time. Many, we say, will remember such afternoons, but few, we think, will know
that Smithy Wood Bottom once won a memorable notice
from an artist of national reputation who died a hundred
years ago. Edward Dayes, touring through Derbyshire
on his way to see some of the Yorkshire scenery, came
upon 'a romantic place called Smithy Wood Bottom'
which he singled out specially as a scene that had
impressed him. It was the evening of a fine summer
day when he walked here from Beauchief Abbey. The
details of the scene were lost in the twilight, and Dayes
saw, with his artist's eyes, the beauty and the grandeur
of the great masses. He was no mean judge of scenery,
as his pictures show ; and his luminous skies, and the
effect of atmosphere in his works in water-colour, had a
great influence upon the early pictures of Girtin and of
Turner. Dayes, who was born in 1763, also engraved
in mezzotint, painted miniatures, and during one period
he was known for his historical pictures packed with
well-drawn figures. After all, however, it is as a painter
of landscape that most artists will like him best. He
painted scenes in the Lake District, in Wales, and in
various parts of England, as only a true lover of nature
could have painted them ; but with the artist's feeling for
beauty he had also the artist's liability to melancholy, and
he died by his own hand in 1804. He praised one of
our own beauty-spots, and for that reason alone Sheffield
people will not wish that his name shall be forgotten in
our midst."

Smithy Wood, and Saint Anne's Well at its foot, knew
James Montgomery the poet, and indeed it was during

a walk here that it occurred to him to write _The Molehill._
Some of its lines were composed while he still lingered
in the wood.   Here too came Mrs. Hofland, who
declared that " Meersbrook is a lovely place."   She took
her stand at the top of Smithy Wood, and, recalling a view
in the Don Valley, wrote : " Yet surely this is not so
beautiful, or grand, as the view on the Chesterfield road,
a little way above Heeley, where an amphitheatre is open
to the eye, comprehending an expanse of rustic and sylvan
scenery of that description which delights not only the
senses, but the heart ; wide farms backed by distant
moors, springing coppice, green lawns, neat cottages,
comfortable houses, ancient mansions, the simple church
of Ecclesall Bierlow, and the shining reservoirs of water
in the valley below you, altogether give a scene so gay,
various, and interesting, that I cannot help preferring it to
every other around us."

If Mrs. Hofland could take her stand at the same point
to-day, she would see but a dreary, depressing scene of
ugliness where once she found such beauty and such
charm.

When we reach The Oakes at Norton, we shall have
more to say about the Reverend William Bagshawe ; but
anticipating that time we may give now an extract from
his diary which mentions Meersbrook and connects it
with Smithy Wood.   The entry belongs to the year
1793, and upon March 19 William Bagshawe " went
with Mr. Shore to Meersbrook.   The Walks extremely
well laid out.   The wavy line has just the bend it ought
to have, in my opinion.   Do not greatly admire the walk
through the dell, nor the full view of Sheffield from an
opening in the shrubbery.   From Meersbrook we proceeded to Skelton Mills, at the bottom of Smithy Wood.
Mr. B———n can there make at his forge [which possessed one of the earliest specimens of the tilt-hammer],
with two men, about twelve or fifteen dozen of scythes
in the course of the day.   At a common smithy two
men can only make about half a dozen scythes a day,

i.e. prepare them for the grindstone.   The axle-tree of the wheel at Smithy Wood forge is remarkably strong.   It was purchased very cheap for £40.   The tree of which it was made grew in Welbeck Park, and T. B. says was well worth £80.   The two men at the forge gain 15*s.* per day between them, if they work hard."

Smithy dams, before the era of steam, when wind and water turned the mills, formed valuable property, as the valleys that radiate from Sheffield testify to this day ; and in Harrison's survey of the manor of Sheffield are references to the utility of the Hallamshire streams.   In 1496 the Abbot of Beauchief Abbey leased a smithy dam to Roger Eyre, who lived probably at Bradway.

John Holland came also to Norton by way of Meersbrook in 1862, but not along the Chesterfield road as Ebenezer Rhodes did.   He seems to have come up Break Back, or Huckle Back, as an older generation called it, "to Norton Lees, remarkable for a fine avenue of sycamores, but more, for an admired specimen of a timbered house."

Meersbrook Park has suffered many changes since John Holland saw it in 1862.   "Among our crew," wrote George Little in his *Life on the Ocean*, " there were a number of musicians who had formed themselves into a kind of band, and although their music was not as ravishing as it might have been under other circumstances, yet it afforded exquisite enjoyment to those who had never heard better."   This passage, seemingly so irrelevant, suggests the case of a generation that knew not the older Meersbrook Park, in pre-tannery days, and even later.   When Miss Shore was there she would not allow a twig to be broken nor a bird to be molested ; but those who never saw Meersbrook at its best will not be conscious of what has been withdrawn.   Like George Little's sailors, they have " never heard better " ; but while in a mood of thankfulness for small mercies we who have " heard better " may be grateful for the little that has been saved of Meersbrook Park, even though

that little has been hedged about by an irruption of the
ignoble slop-kitchen and midden style of architecture that
has become customary in these parts since the district
began to " improve " as the phrase is, since Heeley began
to enjoy the pleasing introduction of urban amenities
amongst her cow-trodden rurals, yet those who can
remember the Park when it was a country retreat will
never cease to lament the features and landmarks that
they will look upon no more, except only in their mind's
eye.   Its pond, with its water-lilies, tench, perch and
water-hens, its noble chestnuts, oaks and beeches, its
great hawthorns with their may-bloom, its trout stream,
its cawing rooks flying homeward in the evening, its
picturesque farm buildings as we used to see them from
Thirlwell Terrace (which had then a rookery of its own)
on a morning of May or June when the beech-leaves
were still young, and the magnificent view the Park once
commanded in the direction of Nether Edge, across the
more extensive Little London dam, another haunt of the
water-hen—all these are interwoven too intimately with
my own early associations to allow me ever to mention
the place, however incidentally, without some little tribute
of passing allusion, " without the meed of some melodious
tear."   No, we are not ungrateful, and certainly the
Ruskin Museum, that gem amongst the museums of the
world, is a great acquisition, and the Bishops' House
too ; but we do not wish to witness the blotting out of
beauty in the woods and fields in order that we may
see it in galleries, and we prefer the wild flowers in
the hedges to the *hortus siccus* in the museum.   Thus
those who recall the older Meersbrook Park, when they
tell themselves the truth, confess that they found more
delight looking over the fence when it was private than
in walking in it as it is to-day ; and there are people alive
who went with more zest into the rookery when they
were liable to be chased back by the men-servants of the
Milners with the dread Grayson at their head than now
that they may go there by right, none daring to make

them afraid. Such as these find it difficult to come into any kind of reconciliation with the hard, ugly lines of the ill-built, ill-arranged barrack-like houses cutting abruptly across the flowing shapes of Nature's lovely sculpturing and softened forms, or with the hideous cold blue slates and raw red bricks obtruding their screeching discords before the gentle contours of the wooded slope. Their sense of the congruous is offended as when they see the vulgar minstrels of the beach going through their rude gambades with the sea and " its drowned empires and forgotten lores " for a background ; they receive the same kind of shock as if they were to witness a rowdy invasion of the people from Hogarth's *Gin Lane* into Watteau's *Bal dans une Colonnade*. However, we must not linger here to cry over spilt milk. The ruin has been wrought ; the place is bare and trampled and bereaved of most of its trees, its oaks killed by the smoke, and for the quiet and beauty we once enjoyed around Meersbrook Park we must hasten now " to fresh woods and pastures new."

I remember the last of a pleasing custom which obtained at Meersbrook House during the days of the Milners there, a custom possible then with a smaller Heeley. Just before Christmas the boys who presented themselves at the house received from the gardener a bundle of holly, bright with berries, mixed with other evergreens for Christmas decoration. At the garden door there was a long line which grew shorter as one lad after another went home triumphantly with the generous supply of " pricking " for the cottage walls.

The Milners, before they came to Meersbrook, were long associated with Burton Grange near Barnsley and with Thurlstone. Then they went to Attercliffe when the place was a village, and there Gamaliel Milner, J.P., had his rural retreat at Attercliffe Hall. Gamaliel has been a favourite Christian name in the family since the Stuart period, and the Vicar of Stannington, the Rev. Gamaliel Milner, is of this family. William Pashley

Milner was at Meersbrook succeeded by his son, William Aldam Milner, who is now at Totley Hall. It was while he was still here at Meersbrook that he married Miss Roberts of Queen's Tower, and Lower Heeley broke out into bunting on the wedding day.

The Milners, however, were not the builders, nor the first habitants of Meersbrook. We owe Meersbrook to one Benjamin Roebuck, to whose initiative Sheffield owed also one or two other things in his day. An article on Sheffield in the *Gentleman's Magazine* for 1764 enumerating the large houses runs : " Broadfield, a mile and a quarter to the South, Mrs. Shore's ; Mazebrooke, two miles to the South, Mr. Roebuck's."

John Roebuck, a manufacturer of Sheffield, had a number of capable sons. There was Dr. John, born in 1718, eminent in the world of science, whose life is given by Samuel Smiles in *Industrial Biographies*, and by Lord Somerville in the *Transactions of the Royal Society of Edinburgh*. It was Dr. John Roebuck who founded the Carron Iron Works in Scotland. He engaged also in speculation in coal fields, some of which eventually brought him low. One of his brothers was Sheffield's first banker, and then there was Benjamin, a merchant, who built Meersbrook House. In Sheffield the Roebucks were the first to open trade relations with the Continent.

Dr. John Roebuck had a son, Benjamin, Paymaster-General of the Forces of the East India Company at Madras. Another son, Ebenezer, was in the civil service in Madras, and he is particularly interesting to local people as the father of John Arthur Roebuck, the distinguished representative of Sheffield in Parliament during so many years. Ebenezer's wife was Zipporah Tickell, daughter of Richard Tickell the poet and pamphleteer of the period of Fox and Sheridan, a descendant of Addison's friend Thomas Tickell, author of *Colin and Lucy*, a touching ballad, and the subject of one of Dr. Johnson's biographies. A daughter of the Benjamin Roebuck who

6

built Meersbrook married Colonel Fenton, who seems to have lived at Meersbrook for a time.

In one of John Arthur Roebuck's letters there is a reference to Meersbrook. Roebuck was in Sheffield in 1849 when ". . . a Mr. Fenton, a reverend curate of Norton, came to claim cousinship with me ; his father, Colonel Fenton, having married Miss Roebuck, the daughter of Benjamin Roebuck of Meersbrook. He told me that I had a family vault in the parish here, if I was at all particular as to my lying when the time comes. I thanked him for his information, but said I was careless of the whereabouts when that time did come." When Roebuck died in 1879, he was buried at Bushey in Hertfordshire. Roebuck, however, knew the place, for Asline Ward has an entry in his diary that " Mr. Roebuck has been visiting at Meersbrook. I do not know how he became a visitor to the house of his ancestors. Miss Shores are enlarging the front where was the entrance door opposite the Little London Dam."

Meersbrook House passed from the Roebucks to the Shores, who, like the Roebucks, lived to suffer financial reverses. Of this family, however, more will be told when we come to Norton Hall. After the Shores came the Milners, and on April 15, 1890, Meersbrook was opened formally by the Earl of Carlisle as the Ruskin Museum of the Guild of St. George, a museum which hitherto had been at Walkley, another Sheffield suburb.

It is not the function of this book to describe the contents of the Ruskin Museum, congenial as that task would be to one who owes so many days of delight to its founder, amongst whose works in the grimy old reference room of the Sheffield Free Library I have spent many delightful hours ; but it happens that a sketch by Turner now in the museum has a very intimate connection with this locality. In 1797, when he was twenty-two years of age, Turner was tramping or driving about the country for the publishers, making drawings of towns and buildings and landscapes for the illustrations of books.

He took the coach into Derbyshire, carrying two sketch-books. Both these books are now in the National Gallery collection, and have been examined recently by Mr. A. J. Finberg, who has been arranging Turner's sketches. There are two drawings of Winfield Manor, then comes a church with a tall spire on a hill which in virtue of my local upbringing I was able to identify for the authorities as Dronfield ; then a drawing of Rotherham Bridge with the chapel on it, one of Conisborough Castle, views of Doncaster church, views of the ruins of Ponte-fract church, and drawings of the chapel on the bridge at Wakefield.

The drawing of Sheffield, however, may belong to 1793, when Walker, the publisher, is said to have sent Turner into Derbyshire and into other counties to make topo-graphical drawings ; and whether in search of a suitable point from which to sketch the town the artist toiled to Sky Edge or panted up Shirecliffe is not recorded, though the drawing itself tells that the choice fell ulti-mately upon this, the Heeley and Norton side of Sheffield. Coming by coach from London the view Turner has given would be almost the first glimpse he would have of Sheffield as he reached Meersbrook Park, and it may be that he knew by instinct he was not likely to find a better general view than this with Shirecliffe and Wincobank Hill for background. An engraving from Turner's sketch appeared in *The Itinerant*, a publication reissued in 1798 as *The Copper Plate Magazine, or Monthly Cabinet of Picturesque Prints ; consisting of Sublime and Interesting Views in Great Britain and Ireland, Beautifully Engraved by the most Eminent Artists from the Paintings and Drawings of the first Masters.* Malton's drawing of the Hall and Church at Norton is in the same work.

Philip Gilbert Hamerton, writing in 1879, has told us that in 1798 " the plates of Sheffield and Wakefield appeared in *The Itinerant*, two towns which were less unpicturesque then than now. Both of them have good scenery very near at hand, but they have been spoiled for the painter by their very prosperity during the last seventy-five years. It was part of Turner's professional business at that time to illustrate towns, and he had done a good deal in that line, no doubt very conscientiously, but his tastes were already too exclusive for him to settle down to a regular trade of that kind."

The copper plates were found about fifty years afterwards by Thomas Miller, and in 1854 he republished Turner's work with some engravings from Girtin's drawings under the title of *Turner's and Girtin's Picturesque Views Sixty Years Since*, a book issued again in a third form as recently as 1873.

Miller wrote an account of the town, but with a number of mistakes with regard to local names. He says the view is taken from Derbyshire Lane. " The valley shown in the engraving is now built upon, the glimpse obtained of the river Porter long since shut out by houses ; and, with the exception of the churches, the whole scene has undergone a mighty change. The moor, rising in the background, was then covered with golden gorse and purple heather, and abounded in grouse ; but as the buildings drew nearer to their ancient haunts, they took wing and flew away in search for other solitudes : the hills on which they once nestled are now covered with the villas of the wealthy manufacturers. But, perhaps, the most striking feature of the engraving is the entire absence of those tall chimneys, which form such prominent land marks in most of our manufacturing towns in the present day."

John Britton possessed the original drawing, and after passing from owner to owner, Sheffield appropriately bought it from Mr. Ward of Richmond. In a sketch-book which Turner used in 1829–30, there is a sketch-map showing the relative positions of Sheffield, Hathersage, Castleton and other places.

A more pleasing picture of Sheffield from Meersbrook is one of 1826 by Thomas Christopher Hofland, a work reproduced as a print. David Martin gave us " A View from the South Side of Heeley Tilt Mill Dam, one mile south of Sheffield," engraved in 1791. Another view of Little London Dam was contributed by R. Bonington of Nottingham, the father of Richard Parkes Bonington, in 1801. It was reproduced in aquatint by S. Alken and gives prominence to Mount Pleasant, now the Girls' Charity School, a house built by Francis Hurt, who married a daughter of the Renishaw house of Sitwell and so became Francis Hurt-Sitwell, the ancestor of the Sitwells of our own times. Here was entertained William Henry West Betty, Young Roscius, when, thirteen years of age, he played at the Sheffield theatre, and he flew his kite in the neighbouring fields that are to-day packed with houses and traversed by streets. Little London Dam is further the subject of a sketch by delightful old Christopher Thomson. This and Martin's engraving are in the High Hazels Museum at Darnall near Sheffield, with other local prints and drawings.

Not many years ago there passed away, after a life of struggle and poverty, a true artist whose fame is likely to increase as his rare qualities of heart and hand become more widely known. Sheffield has been and still is peculiarly favoured with artists of real distinction, and Read Turner will hold his place amongst the best. More than once he painted the dell in Meersbrook Park, and one of his water-colour drawings of the subject belonged to the late Mr. Young Mitchell. This picture and Godfrey Sykes' painting of the Meersbrook pond were taken to America by one of Mr. Mitchell's sons, but lately they have come back, and are now in the possession of other members of Mr. Mitchell's family, who own also Read Turner's picture of a Meersbrook hayfield.

Meersbrook has still another claim to hold us upon this side of Norton in its proximity to the road hence to London along which the coaches used to run before the Midland Railway gave more speedy access to the Metropolis. To-day this road runs by the western boundary of the park, and on its way to Norton Woodseats leaves the park at the bottom of steep Derbyshire Lane, now bereft of its tall old holly hedge ; but at one time the road from Sheffield to London came through Lower Heeley, as it does now ; then when it had reached the point occupied by the lodge of Meersbrook Park, it went hence to Derbyshire Lane in a line very much nearer to Meersbrook House than the present road. At that time steep Derbyshire Lane formed a part of the road to London, and it was continued through what is now Norton Park and Cold Aston to Little Norton. When Meersbrook Park became the property of the city of Sheffield new paths were made in it, and the workmen came upon this old road buried under the turf. Near it was a constant spring of good water, where probably many a bygone wayfarer upon this once dusty highroad has obtained refreshment.

In the offices of the County Council at Derby is the plan of a divergence showing the old road from Norton past Meersbrook House to Sheffield, starting from Derbyshire Lane upon the other side of Cliffe Field, so that though in our own time in going down Derbyshire Lane from Norton we should have Cliffe Field on our right, under the old state of affairs it would have been on our left. The plan shows a pond and a well a little below Cliffe Field. The order for the divergence which accompanies the plan is dated September 11, 1802. It states that the change is made " so as to make the same more commodious t᷍ the publick," and is signed by Josh. Jebb, Sitwell Sitwell, William Chambers Bagshawe and William Allwood Lord, all justices sitting at a special sessions held at Meersbrook.

In James Linacre's notes we are told that " by Cliff Field old road was a little old house covered with ivy. John Linacre's first wife was working it on white silk stretched on a frame when she died." One of Fairbank's plans is of a turnpike road instead of Derbyshire Lane, that is the road through Woodseats, and it is dated 1797.

THE POND, MEERSBROOK PARK, IN 1858.

Daniel Paterson's *Roads of Great Britain* gives particulars of the route from London to Leeds, showing a few of the local points that the coaches passed : Chesterfield Church, Whittington Common, Dronfield Church, Little Norton, Heeley Turnpike, cross the River Sheaf and enter Yorks, Sheffield. Many will remember the toll-house at Heeley, standing where the Meersbrook flowed under the road, and local schoolboys will detect the great Paterson—the Bradshaw of the pre-railway era —tripping upon a point of geography, for it is not the Sheaf but the Meersbrook which here divides Yorkshire from Derbyshire.

Near this point, where once it was possible to lean over a little bridge to gaze into the clear, cool waters of the stream, gathered here into a little pool, overhung by great trees, stood the house occupied by the late Mr. Young Mitchell, at that time the Headmaster of the Sheffield School of Art, a former pupil of Ingres in Paris; and his son, Young Mitchell, who afterwards died and was buried at sea, remembered watching out of the nursery window a number of elephants from a strolling circus taking their morning bath in the Little London Dam opposite, at that time open to the road. Another story of the place relates to an old woman who lived in a cottage where the railway bridge stands now, opposite the bottom of Albert Road. She refused to leave her house, and it was not until she awoke one morning to find the workmen were taking off the roof that she could bring herself to believe in the reality of the railway. Godfrey Sykes was a teacher at the Sheffield School of Art in Mr. Mitchell's time, and he painted a picture of the pond in Meersbrook Park surrounded by trees. This pond was used afterwards by the proprietors of the tannery for tan pits, and the trees, blackened and dying, became a pitiful spectacle. Now even the tannery has been removed, and houses have been built upon its site.

In the art world, too, Meersbrook is associated with a greater designer than Godfrey Sykes, with Alfred Stevens, who ranks with the foremost. Again the connection was brought about by Mr. Young Mitchell, for, just before the famous exhibition of 1851, the principal designer for Messrs. H. E. Hoole & Co., of the Green Lane Works in Sheffield, went over to a rival firm, and Mr. Hoole, thus left in the lurch at a most critical epoch, asked the advice of Mr. Mitchell, who promptly recommended Stevens, at that time a visitor with him here at Meersbrook. Stevens, who had already designed for Messrs. Wolstenholme of Sheffield, cutlery manufacturers, and for the Bradburys, silver manufacturers, went to work at once, assisted by Henry Hoyles, Godfrey Sykes and Reuben Townroe, with the result that Messrs. Hoole & Co.'s exhibits mark an era in English design, and were at the time the talk of the world. In his book on Stevens, Hugh Stannus says that this great artist " often walked out in the evenings and on Sundays to see his friend Mitchell, who lived in a pleasantly situated cottage in a corner of Meersbrook Park, the seat of Miss Shore. Mrs. Mitchell was in a decline ; and during one of the late summer afternoons he painted her old dog ' Ben ' to amuse her, as she lay propped up on the couch. It had a favourite place on the wall of the Park, whence it would observe all that went on ; and Stevens, finding a blank canvas and seizing the colours and brushes of Mr. Mitchell, who was absent at the School, painted the portrait . . . there and then."

The sketch is very clever, and suggests that if Stevens had been apprenticed to Sir Edwin Landseer, as had been contemplated before Landseer's premium was found to be too high for the resources of the Stevens, the popular painter of animals would have had a formidable rival. In the background the glorious trees of Meersbrook have been indicated, with a great beech tree especially prominent. Mr. Mitchell's house was not in Meersbrook Park, but on the Yorkshire side of the Meersbrook.

Hugh Stannus goes on to tell us that " Mrs. Mitchell had become weaker, and in the winter was confined to the bed from which she never again rose ; and Stevens on

one of his day visits in the early Spring of 1851, sitting
by the fire, noticed the refined character of the wooden
mouldings ; and remarked on its suitability for decoration
in the Angelica Kaufmann and Cipriani style.   Mrs.
Mitchell showed an interest in it ; Mr. Mitchell brought
his paint-box, and Stevens commenced and completed the
figure-subject . . . in something less than four hours,
the ornaments and mouldings being painted subsequently."
After describing the design Stannus adds " the only pity
is that, some years ago, it had a bad quarter of an hour at
the hands of a charwoman armed with soap and water."
This design, reproduced like the portrait of " Ben " in
Stannus' biography, is now in the possession of Mr.
Mitchell's son, the Rev. F. G. Mitchell, Vicar of Wendy
in Hertfordshire.

Stevens paid friendly visits to the Sheffield School of
Art, and two of its pupils, Ellis and Townroe, helped him
with his famous Wellington monument, now, unfinished,
in St. Paul's Cathedral.   Sykes became celebrated in connection with South Kensington, and his design for the
cover of the *Cornhill* magazine, made fifty years ago, still
stands, when many contemporary magazines with a
similarly high literary standard have been whelmed in
the flood of lower-grade snippet literature.

CHAPTER V

THE Blythe chantry chapel in Norton church, by causing us to follow the fortunes of the Blythe family, sent us to Norton Lees, and so to Meersbrook, away from the heart of the place, to which, however, we now return ; and, sitting in the church yard upon a summer afternoon in what seems to be the greenest and coolest place in the world, on the steps of this worn cross that the moss, the lichen and the grass have invaded with such persistence, the saunterer becomes conscious that an ancient country church yard, burial place though it is, is not wholly, even if it is at all, a place of lamentation. The dead here are skeletons at nobody's feast, and the gossip that goes on after service on Sunday is not less cheerful for the presence of these tombs, or of these mounds that speak to us now of nameless sleepers. Here, many years ago, I came with other children to puzzle over the inscriptions on the stones, trying in antiquarian rivalry who could find the one that bore the oldest date ; and those who were born here and are no longer children still come to " hearken after the memory of their ancestors," to grope amongst these hallowed memorials of the past in an endeavour to make them tell their tale. " So it is," as Hazlitt has reminded us " that in early youth we strain our eager sight after the pursuits of manhood ; and, as we are sliding off the stage, strive to gather up the toys and flowers that pleased our thoughtless childhood."

It is, too, as men are " sliding off the stage " that they come to notice there, commanding all, is the clock in the tower, the sun-dial on the wall, doling out the seconds, measuring the years of the villagers, beating out the little lives of men, so unresting, remorseless, that in some moods they dare not think of these things for fear of those haunting lines :

> The numbered hour is on the wing
> That lays thee with the dead.

Norton church and church yard convey the impression of the touching unity of village life, of people beginning, continuing and closing their existence in one place. Here the little villager was baptised ; here later he was confirmed ; here, as likely as not, he fell in love with his sweetheart as in her Sunday gown she came to service or lingered afterwards in the church yard. To this place, made holy ground already by so many associations he came to be married, brought here his children to be christened, or, unhappily, to be buried. To this place the old villager knew he would be borne at last to add his dust to that of his forefathers, and for the rest we may wonder with Emily Brontë how any one can ever imagine unquiet slumbers for the sleepers in this quiet earth.

Thus has it come about that church yard and church have touched the villager at many points, and he feels about "God's acre" as Nathaniel Hawthorne felt when he wrote of " the deep and aged roots which my family has struck into the soil " and of that ancestor of his own whose " descendants have been born and died, and have mingled their earthly substance with the soil, until no small portion of it must necessarily be akin to the mortal frame wherewith, for a little while, I walk the streets." It is true that a country church yard like this is permeated through and through by human traditions of a most tender cast extending far away into the " dark backward and abysm of time." The witchery of the Gothic archi-tecture in the background, the most wondrous and moving kind of building of any that has been yet devised, the "solemnities and ceremonies," the requiems, the stately diction of the prayers that are read at the graveside, the deep-toned music that wells through door and window during service, the mournful knolling or joyful pealing of the bells, or even the very silence of the place, its sanctity, its immutable calm and deep peace, the drowsy cawing of the rooks—all these and many another more intangible, more evasive element have gone to the making of what we feel, but cannot utter, as we sit in the old church yard at Norton enjoying its more than ordinary tranquillity in a few quiet and meditative hours after the harsh noises, the unrest, the dust and the struggle in the town, and here at Norton no less than in Greece might Byron have written

> Where'er we tread 'tis haunted, holy ground.

Seeing that a church yard is the place in which the most poignant miseries are suffered that humanity is ever called upon to bear, it is strange that the prevailing note here should be one of such complete peace ; but an old church yard has this character in contrast with a new cemetery where nature has not yet had time with moss and lichen to mitigate the starkness of the gravestones, wrested but recently from the hill sides, nor to round their sharp raw edges. There, in many a place, the earth has been but newly violated and the grave is such a thing of yesterday that Spring, as Thackeray once wrote, has " scarce had time to spin a coverlid for it." Mourners too still come and go with wreath or cross and with all the signs of recent grief and weeping. On the other hand an old church yard like this at Norton has more to say of wounds that have been healed by time, of the sleep that rounds our little lives, and it seems to speak quietly of repose. Here we feel that not only are the dead at rest but those also who have sorrowed for them, that indeed, as Wordsworth has written,

> consolation springs
> From sources deeper far than deepest pain.

So profound is the effect that the church yard has made upon the " sentimental attachments " of the people that nothing else can take its place, and again and again it has appeared in art and in literature, in innumerable pictures, poems and prose, and notably in the immortal elegy of Gray written with relation to a church yard that has many features in common with this at Norton.

In Norton church yard the earth is deep under its mantle of grass which is everywhere green and kind to the eyes. Long ago even these tombstones of the Barbaras, Deborahs, Dinahs and Dorothys of a past time have become so grey and green with lichen and moss that they scarcely strike a new note among the grass and clover, which, with the trailing ivy, straggle over their edges. Indeed much of the beauty of the place comes from its unity. The church yard is a harmony in green and grey, without a harsh note anywhere, and the shadows of the yews, the limes, and of the holly trees and cedars keep the place so cool that the grass holds its dew all through the hottest day.

Upon the northern side of the church yard there has arisen in recent years a Celtic cross of Aberdeen granite whose warmth of colour comes out with peculiar glow in showers of rain ; but even while we admire we regret the cause of this addition, for it marks the grave of the wife of the present vicar. It is fitting, however, that she should lie here, her grave to be seen from the windows of the vicarage in which she passed the fifteen years of her married life, and her monument a conspicuous feature in the midst of those who remember her as an embodiment of cheerfulness and daintiness when she moved to and fro amongst them with a smile and kind word for all. On the roadside at Hemsworth is a well-proportioned and ornate drinking trough to her memory, and we have seen already there are memorials in the church itself as well as this cross that stands in the church yard.

Full of sacred memories as is this quiet harbour by the dusty roadside, it has its odd side too, as we find if

we read the inscriptions on the tombstones. Even the
scythe-maker, so heedless of grammar and of other incon-
sequent things, goes down before the scythe-bearer, as is
shown by the epitaph on Mark Tyzack, of Four Lane
Ends, blacksmith, buried in 1795.

> My Scythe and hammer lies reclin'd
> My Bellows too has lost their winde
> My Iron is spent my steel is gone
> My Scythes are set my work is done
> My fires extinct my forge decay'd
> My body in the dust is laid.

This epitaph, however, is not peculiar to Norton
church yard. It appears also in the church yard at
Felpham in Sussex, upon the gravestone of a village
blacksmith, with the word " sledge " where " scythe "
is in the Norton version. The people at Felpham have
attributed the composition of the inscription to William
Hayley the poet, who is himself buried at Felpham.
Thus it may be that the Sussex village is the place whence
the epitaph has spread to all parts of the realm, for, with
minor modifications, it may be read at Holmesfield, a
few miles away ; Hexton in Hertfordshire ; at Sutton
in Surrey ; on the tomb of a Southwark blacksmith ; at
Longnor ; Alderley in Cheshire ; at Malton in Yorkshire ; Chipping Sodbury in Gloucestershire ; Aldfield
near Fountains Abbey ; and no doubt at many another
place.

There is another odd and rather daring inscription at
Norton ; for notwithstanding that Gray has asked, in-
credulously, can " flatt'ry soothe the dull cold ear of
death ? " there has evidently lived one in Norton who
was willing to try, though his rhythm can scarcely be
described, even by the most charitable critic, as being of
a particularly soothing sort. The stone bearing this
inscription is north of the church, and it was raised to

the memory of Mary, the wife of Joseph Greaves, who died, nineteen years of age, in 1822.

> Heaven did thy lovely presaunce want
> And therefore did so early thee transplant
> For meaner souls he could delay
> Impatient for thine he could not stay.

We " meaner souls " who are left alive have some compensations ; but we respect our betters, and having bowed before the tombstone of Mary Greaves, whose " lovely presaunce " was needed so urgently for the completion of Paradise, we may proceed to explore the remaining parts of the grave yard.

Tragedy too has claimed its place in this hallowed ground. Charles Glover, of Holmhirst, seems to have been murdered when he was sixteen years of age, on July 5, 1846, and his epitaph tells at once of his fate and asks for the forgiveness of his murderers.

> In evil hour I fell, oppressed with pain
> By bloody-minded men untimely slain
> O may they find through Jesus crucified
> That mercy their rude hands to me denied.

Holmhirst is the name of a farm to the west of Norton Woodseats.

There are many thrilling stories of the body snatchers in this district, and the theme is one that tempts to a digression ; but in addition to the tales of incursions upon other church yards, like the lonely one at Holmesfield, Norton had its experiences too of the resurrectionists, the " stiff lifters " as people given to slang used to call them. In Norton was a woman whose every joint was double, that is it would bend both backwards and forwards with equal ease. Her name was Susan Wilcockson, she lived at Cliffe Field, and the doctors regarded her with curiosity, desiring a nearer acquaint-

ance both when she was alive and also when she died.
At her funeral Mr. Herbert Rhodes of the post office,
who, more than eighty years of age, has survived to our
own time, remembers that a conveyance was passing to
and fro while the service was being read, and two hours
after it had been buried the body had gone ! Mr. Rhodes
recalls that sixty or seventy years ago it was usual
for the friends of those who had been buried to spend
several nights in the church yard to keep watch and ward
over the graves of the departed.

There is an idea amongst Norton people that Mary

Wilcockson's skele-
ton is now at the
Sheffield Medical
School ; but the
reply of a leading
doctor of that city,
of whom I made
inquiries, was that
" to use Post Office
phraseology, if Mary
W i l c o c k s o n ' s
d o u b l e - j o i n t e d
skeleton ever was
in the Sheffield
Medical School, it
has ' Gone ; left no address ' or is ' Not known.' " He
assures me that the Professor of Anatomy there knows
nothing of Mary's remains, and that neither he nor the
Professor ever saw a skeleton with double joints.

Norton, distinguished in this respect amongst neighbouring parishes, has been able to retain the ruins of its
church yard cross, its old shaft and worn, mossy steps
enduring to arrest the eye amongst the tombstones.

In the engraving which appears in Samuel Pegge's
book on Beauchief Abbey, published in 1801, an engraving reproduced in this book, the cross occupies a
position near to the place in which now we find Chantrey's

NORTON CHURCH AND HALL, ABOUT 1800.

tomb, that is a little to the south of the church tower; so that either Grimm, the artist, did not draw the cross where he found it—not a likely circumstance in his case—or it has been removed since. Then, as now, it lacked its arms. Reynolds has a reference to the cross in his notes, remarking that it is "a fair cross of Greeces."

It is quite in keeping too with what we should expect of Norton church yard that we find there three ancient yew trees; and these send our thoughts far backward to times of unknown antiquity, and raise questions that have never yet received final settlement. Mr. Edward Snelgrove, B.A., our local student of plant lore, tells me that all the Norton church yard yews are female trees. In Reynolds' notes the reference is to "two large ewe trees, the one especially a very fair one."

Many have asked why a yew tree is found in nearly every church yard, and manifold are the reasons that have been suggested; but as one authority is almost certain to be contradicted by another of equal erudition, it is not easy to see precisely how far we have got in this matter; yet whatever antiquaries may have to say upon the subject, and what they and the poets have written constitutes a literature in itself, the picturesque aspect of the yew, its beautiful deep green leaves, its plumy sprays, murky shadows, bright red berries, the beautiful tints of its trunk are sufficient to justify its presence in the church yard; and, after all, whatever were the original reasons for its introduction, it may be that when those reasons could be pleaded no longer it was retained for its beauty, and because people had become used to seeing it in association with church and church yard.

The yews are not the only trees that grow in and around Norton church yard, for there are cedars, limes, beeches, elms, Irish yews, and two Jerusalem hollies, one on the north and the other on the south of the church, planted by the Rev. H. H. Pearson. It will be

7

noticed that the one upon the south thrives very much better than the one upon the north.

The stocks used to be on the green just outside the church yard gate, and when they were no longer used they were buried. No one knows where they lie, or the present vicar would have had them exhumed and set up as an interesting relic. Cold Aston had stocks until 1835. Some villages in this district still have their stocks, and there are people alive who can remember those who were last imprisoned in them.

CHAPTER VI

THE OFFLEY MYSTERY

A PRIVATE door leads from the church yard to the Hall, and to an older Hall upon this site, represented in Grimm's drawing, belongs a family romance, a ghost story meet for telling in the light of the Christmas fire. Even deprived of their supernatural elements, the incidents are of more than ordinary interest.

When this moving story opens in the middle of the eighteenth century the Offleys were in residence at Norton Hall. The estates of this old and renowned family had been increasing during many generations, and it was indeed a valuable heritage that fell now to the lot of Edmund Offley, at that time but six months more than eighteen years of age, when, on September 3, 1751, his father, Joseph Offley, died at the age of 49. The Offleys were not robust, there was consumption in the family, and already Edmund's mother had been dead for some time, so that of this family there remained now Edmund and his two sisters, Urith, fourteen years of age, and Hannah Maria, eleven. Mary, another sister, had died in infancy.

The Offleys were Nonconformists, and had a chaplain of their own, the Rev. Daniel Lowe, the master of a flourishing school at Norton, held in a large and pleasing house, now known as the Grange, built specially for him by Mr. Joseph Offley, whose monogram may be seen still upon the ceiling of the hall there ; and Edmund having received the rudiments of his education from Mr. Lowe,

99

was sent in 1748 to Dr. Doddridge's famous institution at Northampton. Edmund Offley was also for some time under the care of a Mr. Stubbs, a dissenting minister at Lichfield. The father, when he died, appointed John Rotherham of Dronfield, and with him Godfrey Heathcote, a solicitor of Chesterfield, as guardians, and these gentlemen decided to send Edmund Offley to pursue his studies in Scotland, as was customary in those days when the English Universities were closed to dissenters. A decision not to be explained so easily led them to appoint for Edmund, as private tutor, a Church of England clergyman, the Rev. James Reed, and he and his pupil lived together for some time at York before they proceeded to Scotland. Young Offley detested Mr. Reed, and one of his grievances against his tutor, a sufficiently irksome one to a youth anxious to move in aristocratic circles, was that he was wholly unacquainted with the usages of polite society, and Hunter says that the two had several rough verbal encounters. Offley urged his guardians to provide him with another tutor, " for it is next to an impossibility for me to bear him any longer, his behaviour is so exceedingly disagreeable." In a later letter he urges again concerning Mr. Reed " that he may be removed from about my person at the expiration of the year, otherwise, perhaps, I may find myself under the necessity to do a thing I do not care to mention." Was this thing he did not care even to mention the very thing he actually did with such disconcerting results ?

Meanwhile young Offley had made the acquaintance of the Rev. George Carr, a native of Newcastle-on-Tyne, but since 1737, and until his death, the minister of the English Episcopal Congregation in Edinburgh ; and Mr. Carr offered to receive Offley into his house and to superintend his studies. So matters stood when another incident arose that precipitated the quarrel. Young Offley had with him an old servant who had been with his father, and Reed expressed his intention of sending this servant back to Norton, though Offley was opposed to this arrangement, and seemed to fancy that the servant was being sent home to spread there an unfavourable account of his life in Edinburgh. However, the servant journeyed to Norton in spite of Offley's opposition, whereupon Offley posted after him a long letter to his guardians in which he discussed very naively the charges which he assumed would be made concerning his goings on in Edinburgh. One of these he thought would be that he spent too much time at the billiard table, and he acknowledged that he had gone to the billiard-room very frequently, but he urged in extenuation that he had not lost so much as ten shillings during the time he had been in Edinburgh. Moreover he excused himself that he had gone to play billiards the more frequently that he might escape from the disagreeable company of Mr. Reed, and he urged further that he had now made the resolution that he would go to the billiard-room no more. "Another possible objection that Mr. Reed's artifice may suggest, is that I have too great a regard for a young lady at Mr. Carr's ; but I can hardly allow myself to think that Mr. Reed can be capable of suggesting such a falsity, for I give you my word and honour that I never had nor will have the least intention to make my addresses there."

He thought that the profusion of his entertainments might be another charge, but he conceived that the entertainments he had given had been no more than a suitable return from a gentleman of his station and fortune for the civilities he had received. It might be that Mr. Reed would allege his letters had not been written by himself ; he admitted that he had been assisted, but that the sentiments had been all his own. Mr. Reed might complain too that he had paid no regard to his instructions, which he willingly admitted to be perfectly true. In this letter he also informed his guardians that since he left Mr. Reed he had put himself under the care of Mr. Carr, and was intending during the winter to learn the French language, and to prosecute such studies as Mr. Carr should recommend to him with greater application than he had ever shown before.

On November 18 he wrote again that the Duke of Argyll had taken cognizance of the matters in dispute between him and Mr. Reed, and had expressed a strong opinion condemning Mr. Reed, and approving of the steps Mr. Offley had taken. The Duke had been of late, he says, very particular in his attentions to him, and had written to the guardians, giving his opinion of the whole case. Mr. Offley adds that the Duke had highly approved of his choice of Mr. Carr for his tutor. The Duke was also strongly against the removal to Aberdeen which had been suggested by the guardians, and advised Offley to remain in Edinburgh for the winter.

Before the Duke's letter had reached the guardians they had written again to Offley by the return of his servant. The letter, says Hunter, contained matter very distasteful to him, which he attributed to Mr. Reed's misrepresentations. He told the guardians in his reply that the Carrs "are incapable of dishonest designs, and above the mean and sordid views they are accused of." The letter contains also the following remarkable passage which has a significance that will be understood presently : " As Mr. Carr seems to be the principal object of resentment, I must do him the justice to declare that the proposal I formerly mentioned proceeded solely from myself, without the least means on his part, and that he has often proposed to release me from any promise, and frequently spoke lightly of it, as a subject of amusement and entertainment ; which with the most just character given of him by the Duke of Argyll is sufficient for his vindication."

By the same post the guardians received a letter from Mr. Reed : " Yesterday morning I had the pleasure of seeing John Rhodes return ; and about eleven o'clock went to wait upon Mr. Offley at his new quarters, where we found a good deal of difficulty in being admitted to the interview ; for his master and mistress keep him very close, and suffer nobody to speak with him but trusty friends. As soon as he had read the letter, he told us plainly he did not intend to stir out of Edinburgh till he was of age : that if his guardians should come over, he knew very well they durst not touch him, and that they should likewise bear their own expenses, for as he should not send for them, so he should never suffer any such thing to be charged to his account. On Thursday seven-night, his friends sent him to the Duke of Argyll for a warrant for me for taking him by the collar. The Duke indeed did not grant one, but sent such a harsh letter unsealed, as I never received in my life ; and when I waited upon him I found him so exasperated both against tutor and guardians, that he would scarce so much as give me leave to speak. Every body is amazed, confounded, and struck dumb at this treatment ; neither could I possibly account for it till a certain gentleman yesterday unravelled the whole mystery, which I shall acquaint you with the first opportunity. Mr. Offley has dismissed John, and taken a boy about twelve years old. He has bought him a frock, and ordered him a livery. His counsellers, you may perceive, are determined to clear the coast in order to have fair play. There was to be a meeting of them last night, when your and Mr. Heathcote's letter would be critically examined. I shall set out for Dronfield to-morrow morning ; and intend to be with you about Thursday or Friday next. I am in great distress, you may be sure ; for never was any man's character so sacrificed to the resentment of an obstinate fool."

The guardians dismissed Mr. Reed, asked Offley to retain Rhodes and to leave Edinburgh for Aberdeen. He refused to keep Rhodes or to leave Edinburgh, where " at leisure hours I have access to the best company of this place, to which I was at once introduced by the favour of his Grace the Duke of Argyll, at the election of Lord Cathcart to be a Peer of Scotland."

No further letters have survived. Edmund Offley attained his majority in February or March 1754. On August 21 he died. The news of his unexpected demise created a great sensation here in Norton; but quickly following upon the heels of these tidings came the much more startling tale that as soon as he had come of age he had cut off any entail upon the family property; that a few months after having done this, that is on June 21, he executed a will, of which he made Mr. Carr, with whom he had lived now for two years, the sole executor, and gave to him and to Mrs. Carr the whole of his real estate of £2,000 a year, together with his personal estate, of which even the household furniture was estimated to be worth £10,000. Then two months after the execution of the will he had died, far away from his friends, and in Mr. Carr's house! Could suspicious circumstances go further than these?

Edmund Offley's cruel acts were hotly denounced in all these halls and farms and cottages, where nothing but pity was expressed for the two beautiful and amiable girls who had been deprived so wantonly of their inheritance. The gossips charged the Carrs with having influenced young Offley by deep-laid schemes, and added that to make the booty more certain, to secure it earlier, when they knew the will had been completed, they had administered a draught of poison. To bring the excitement to a climax, it needed only the story that spread wildly from house to house that the gardener upon the day during which Edmund Offley had died in Edinburgh had seen his ghost enter the hall at Norton, and had thought at the time that it was indeed his master who had returned.

No one seemed to know what to do, but at last neighbour Robert Newton of Norton House, a few hundred yards from the Hall, volunteered to go to Edinburgh. He obtained from Offley's guardians the power to act. At first they hesitated, but soon they yielded, and placed the management of the business in his hands. He secured next, for his travelling companion, John Girdler, Joseph Hunter's grandfather, who often was with him both on his travels and at home. Girdler had only a few hours' notice, and was not told of the place to which they were going, nor on what business; but this was unfolded to him after a call for a short consultation with Mr. Shore at Broadfield, a house since pulled down which stood off Abbeydale Road. Then he was told also that Newton had arranged the whole plan of campaign, and that though Girdler was to hear all the negotiations, he was to take no part in them. His rôle, indeed, seems to have borne a resemblance to that of the churchwarden :

> To eat and drink and pay nowt,
> To hear and see and say nowt.

The couple travelled in a carriage, for this was long before the advent of the railway, and at Ferrybridge on the Great North Road they met a funeral party, with Offley's corpse, on its way to Norton that the body, having lain in state in Edinburgh, might be buried in the family vault. " Mr. Newton, who had a very commanding figure, assuming his most dignified air, and producing the paper of authority which the guardians had given him, so awed the persons who had care of the body, that they consented to let it remain at the inn till Mr. Newton should return from Edinburgh and give further directions concerning it."

Upon his arrival in Edinburgh Newton went to see a solicitor, and then proceeded to the home of Mr. Carr. He was admitted at once, and was allowed to enter upon the business. With Carr sat a lawyer, but Newton was accompanied only by Girdler, and the conference continued for several hours. Newton, as Hunter has recorded, urged that the will could not be valid, and that young Offley could never have had such complete control over the property as was assumed in this testament to turn it from the natural course of descent. He dwelt upon the certainty that every effort would be made to recover the estates, and reminded Mr. Carr that the girls had some very powerful friends who would afford them all the means that might be needed to defeat a purpose so unjust and cruel ; and that he, for his part, having a large unencumbered estate, would carry the cause through every court that was accessible ; so that, if they persisted in holding the estates, it must be with the certainty of years of disquietude and the most harassing opposition. He set before them the extreme hardship of the case and the obloquy which always attaches even to parties perfectly innocent of anything wrong, who yet are seen in the possession of that which is theirs only by an act of caprice and injustice. He showed the peculiar aggravations in this case, where the young man had lived in their house, had made the will while living there, no friend being cognizant of the act. Hunter heard that Newton went so far as to say that the most rigid inquiry would be made into the circumstances under which the will was executed, and also into the manner of the death ; and he urged in a very forcible manner how much better it would be for them to possess a few thousands unquestioned and in peace, rather than the larger fortune which would come attended with contention and anxiety, and probably with obloquy, for the remainder of their days.

At the close of the first day's conference Mr. Carr had consented to relinquish all claims under the will, and to accept £5,000.

At this stage Girdler showed some signs of satisfaction ; but Newton by a significant look reminded him that he was to take no part. He told Carr that he could never consent to yield so large an amount, and that if it were insisted upon the negotiations might be considered at an end, that he should leave Edinburgh the next morning and consult with other friends of the family on what should be done. Neither Mr. Carr nor the lawyer showing any disposition to reduce the amount, Mr. Newton took his leave ; but when he had reached the door he returned into the room as if he had suddenly recollected a circumstance of very minor importance, and coolly inquired if they had any directions to give respecting the corpse. Mr. Carr immediately expressed his persuasion that it was already buried, when Newton related for the first time how he had stopped the procession at Ferrybridge, and that the corpse was then there awaiting examination. " This," says Hunter, " I have heard represented as the master-stroke of Mr. Newton's diplomacy. He immediately left Mr. Carr's house, and it was supposed to be the effect of this stroke which led Mr. Carr to desire a second interview."

At this next meeting the terms on which Mr. and Mrs. Carr agreed to relinquish their claims were soon settled, the sum agreed upon being £2,000 according to Mr. Shore, though in the legal instrument £3,940 is the amount mentioned. The agreement was put into proper form, and the will was delivered to Mr. Newton, who left Edinburgh without delay. When they were seated in the carriage Girdler is reported to have said, " Now I hope you are satisfied with yourself," when Newton threw up his hands and exclaimed with the greatest enthusiasm, " Well, Jack! This is worth living for ! "

Young Offley's body was brought forward to Norton from Ferrybridge, and it was interred here on September 24, 1754, that is more than a month after life had left it, and when already his carefully elaborated designs had been frustrated. Hunter makes no mention of an opening of the body, and it may have occurred to the reader as a strange circumstance that no allusion is made to such a proceeding ; but it seems possible that an examination of this kind was made, because Mr. Addy, writing to me upon the subject, states that " with regard to the Offley affair you may like to know that when Norton church was ' restored ' in 1882 the family vault was opened, and in it was noticed a leaden casket inscribed with the words 'The Bowels of Edmund Offley, Esq.' Evidently his remains had been submitted to chemical analysis. I had this information from the Rev. H. H. Pearson, Vicar." The present vicar, the Rev. G. W. Hall, had the same information from Mr. Pearson. It may be, however, that this evisceration was no more than one of the operations in the process of embalming the body for its lying-in-state and long journey from Edinburgh to Norton.

Soon afterwards legal sanction was obtained for the compromise arranged by Newton ; but it is probable that if the Carrs had been more obdurate and mercenary the tangle might not have been unravelled so easily, for though Offley's testament was written in his own hand-writing, it was yet the work of a more powerful head than his. An eminent lawyer to whom he applied refused to make the will when he heard that Offley had sisters in England, but it is clear that Offley managed to obtain professional assistance somewhere, for as the will was drawn most deftly and conformed to all the legal formalities, it may be presumed that though the hands were the hands of Esau, yet was the voice the voice of Jacob.

Many people at the time of these occurrences tried to account for Offley's perversity. It is easy to understand his desire to startle his guardians ; his treatment of his sisters is the puzzle. Hunter draws the inference from some lines written upon him that before Offley went to Scotland he was uncorrupted and amiable, that there he fell into evil companionship, was extravagant and gay, and that he was very much the dupe of an artful and designing woman. Mr. Shore speaks of him in more gentle terms, representing him as being " rather of a fickle and capricious disposition, and his great failing was his suffering himself to be influenced, without due con-sideration, by those he was with at the time. From these causes must have arisen his injustice to his sisters, who were most amiable young ladies and had never given him the slightest cause of offence. That Mrs. Carr, as an artful woman, might gain such an ascendency over him as to induce him to make the will he did, was very probable from the weakness of his character, in being so soon led astray by those he associated with. Had his father lived to have continued him in the society he then had, and to have settled him with some discreet companion in marriage, who might have rivetted his affections, he would probably have made a respectable figure in life, as he was not otherwise deficient in abilities. He wrote a good and sensible letter on business, and I recollect the late Mrs. Sparrow of Wincobank having mentioned that on the death of his Father, she was sent for, as a friend and relation to regulate what was to be done on the occasion, and on the Sunday evening Mr. Edmund Offley enquired of her, if they should not have the servants in to Family prayers she . . . replied by all means, and on their assembling, he prayed extempore with such propriety on the melancholy occasion as to excite both her admiration and astonishment."

Mr. Fletcher of Coventry, a Nonconformist minister born in the neighbourhood of Norton, used to say it was a question with him whether the future career of Mr. Offley would have been worthy of his family and name, or the contrary.

There was much indignation here at Norton and in other parts of Derbyshire when it was known what young Offley had attempted, and the Duke of Devonshire declared chivalrously that he would spend £10,000 rather than the daughters of his old friend Mr. Offley should be despoiled of their inheritance.

This Offley incident was the basis of a story in *Illustrations of Human Life*, by Robert Plumer Ward, whose son was elected as one of the Members of Parliament for Sheffield, but the author departed so far from what really happened that when Ward's story was published many thought a true account should be issued, whereupon Joseph Hunter, the historian of Hallamshire, wrote *A True Account of the Alienation and Recovery of the Estates of the Offleys of Norton in* 1754, a pamphlet published in 1841.

A point of importance with regard to Newton's share in the Offley case is raised by Hunter, who found the following information in a postscript to a letter added by the Rev. Mr. Haynes, who was a dissenting minister in Sheffield : " Carr, whom your brother mentioned above, has sent to compromise matters with Miss Offleys, being conscious that iniquitous reason of the young man's leaving him his estate must appear with a bad face in any court of law, especially of equity."

" It appears from this," says Hunter, " that there was some special reason for the bequest to Mr. Carr inserted in the will ; what it was I never heard. But the point to which I intended especially to draw attention is the information here given that negotiations for a compromise had been thus early opened by Mr. Carr. This may have been but one of the floating rumours of the day. It is, however, information well worthy attention, as, if the fact were so, it makes all that followed more simple, consistent, and in a manner easy ; and, above all, it accounts for the ready access which Mr. Newton had to Mr. Carr, and the willingness of Mr. Carr to enter into conversation with him on the subject, instead of referring him to his solicitor. It takes away, however, much of the heroism of Mr. Newton's conduct, though it may not in reality diminish much the value of his services ; the difference being great between going with a certainty of meeting a decided opposition on every point, and going to meet one who, strong in legal right, has yet intimated a willingness to have a subject such as this discussed on moral as well as legal grounds."

In Ward's story we have two Scotsmen who came from Edinburgh to take possession of Norton Hall for

CHARLES ASHTON, D.D.

SAMUEL PEGGE, LL.D.

ROBERT PLUMER WARD.

THE REV. GEORGE CARR.

JOSEPH HUNTER, F.S.A.

JOHN HOLLAND.

P. 110]

McSweeney, who had poisoned young Offley, an incident which may have been founded on the fact that a young man in Sheffield wrote to his sister that " Poor Mr. Offley left all that ever he had to one Carr of Scotland. There were two men came to Norton, and told Richard [the gardener] that Mr. Offley ordered them to look at the gardens and the house, and particularly the hall. But it was lucky that Mr. Rotherham had ordered him to let nobody look at the house ; and when they heard that they cursed very loudly. They also asked where Miss Offleys were ? He said, at London. They said they were in bad hands."

In addition to Hunter's account of the case there is a manuscript narrative drawn up by the Samuel Shore (son of the Samuel Shore of Broadfield mentioned by Hunter) who lived afterwards at Meersbrook and married Urith Offley. Mr. Shore records that " Mr. Newton gained much credit and reputation among the lawyers at Edinburgh by the manner in which he accomplished his generous, arduous and benevolent undertaking, and the gentlemen of the law at Edinburgh with admiration frequently made enquiries after him for some time after this event. This being about the time that Richardson [another Derbyshire man, Mr. Shore might have added] published his novel of Sir Charles Grandison, Mr. Newton had the appellation bestowed on him by several of the English ladies. Indeed that accomplished Hero of a novel, Sir Charles Grandison, could not, even by Richardson, have been made to execute this friendly and generous action with more virtuous energy and propriety than was in reality performed by Mr. Newton on this interesting occasion."

Mr. Carr had been living in Edinburgh since the year 1737. He was a native of Newcastle-on-Tyne, and was born in 1704–5. His education he received at St. John's College, Cambridge, where he took his degree of Bachelor of Arts. He returned to Newcastle, went into holy orders, and in 1737 was appointed senior clergyman of

the English Episcopal congregation in Edinburgh.
Edmund Offley in his letters spoke in very high terms
of Mr. Carr, both as to his intellectual and moral qualities, and urged upon his guardians the propriety of
formally placing him under his care.   Sir William Forbes
of Pitsligo, baronet, whom Sir Walter Scott laments in
the introduction to the fourth canto of *Marmion*, was for
many years a member of Mr. Carr's Edinburgh congregation, and after Mr. Carr's death he published a
collection of sermons from Mr. Carr's manuscripts, pre-
facing them with a short account of his life and character.
In this account he says of him that he was more studious
of displaying, through the whole course of his life, the
meekness and humility, the mild virtues and gentle spirit
of the gospel, than ambitious of acquiring honours,
wealth, or fame.   When Sir William Forbes published a
Life of James Beattie and had again occasion to mention
Mr. Carr, he wrote : " Every word he uttered, every
doctrine he taught, every virtue he recommended, came
strongly enforced by the purity of his morals, and the
exemplary piety of his blameless life.   With all the good-
breeding of a gentleman, he was a cheerful, entertaining
companion ; and though his manners were most irre-
proachable, they had no tincture of either rigour or
austerity."

Dr. Beattie himself writing in 1776, the year of Mr.
Carr's death, says : " I am no stranger to Mr. Carr's
character, whose death, though I had not the honour
of his acquaintance, was a real affliction to me ; for I
have long considered him as one of the most valuable
men of the age.   I have heard him preach, and admired
his gentle and pathetic eloquence.   But to his merits as
a preacher, great as they were, the lustre of his private
character was still superior.   The death of such a man
is a real loss to society."   And finally, the congregation
of which he was the pastor caused to be cut upon a
monument which they erected to his memory the following inscription :

Near this Place are deposited,

THE REMAINS

of

THE REVEREND GEORGE CARR,

Senior Clergyman of this Chapel ;
In whom
Meekness and Moderation,
Unaffected Piety
and
Universal Benevolence,
Were equal and eminently conspicuous.

After having faithfully discharged the duties
of
His sacred Function
During thirty-nine Years
He died
on the 18th August 1776,
In the 71st year of his Age.
Beloved, Honoured, Lamented !

His Congregation,
Deeply sensible of the Loss they have sustained
By the Death of this excellent Person,
By whose mild yet pathetic Eloquence,
By whose exemplary yet engaging Manners,
They have been so long instructed in the Duties,
and
Animated to the Practice
of
Pure Religion,
Have erected this Monument,
To record
the Virtues of the Dead
and
Gratitude of the Living.

8

No one would accept the inscription upon an eighteenth-century tombstone as conclusive evidence of the excellence of a man's character. Oliver Wendell Holmes has written that "I should like to see any man's biography with corrections and emendations by his ghost," and Guy de Maupassant has a gruesome story "La Morte" in *La Main Gauche* in which the dead rise and correct their epitaphs with sufficiently grotesque results. They erase the list of virtues attributed to them and substitute all manner of contemptible vices and crimes, and the man who has spent the night in the cemetery to be near his buried mistress and to weep upon her grave learns for the first time that she died of a cold caught in stealing secretly in the rain to visit another lover. In the case of Mr. Carr, the evidence of Sir William Forbes and the evidence of Dr. Beattie harmonise with the testimony of the tombstone. Even Mr. Newton came away from Edinburgh impressed by Mr. Carr's obvious good character, and tried to dissipate the prejudice that had grown up against him. Mrs. Carr he did not see, but he understood that her reputation was that of an ambitious, artful, insinuating, designing woman. This may be added for the comfort of those whose method of discovery lies in the formula *Cherchez la femme*, though it need not be forgotten that amongst Newton's perversities was a general dislike of women.

A portrait of Mr. Carr was published with his sermons, and those who look at it may well believe that all the virtues inscribed upon his tombstone were his in life. A face more unlike that of a murderer or of a man moved by money greed it would be difficult to find, or a man more unlike the vulgar McSweeney, the Surrey-side stage Scotsman portrayed by Plumer Ward.

Mr. Carr died suddenly while he was preparing to conduct service at his church. Mrs. Carr soon followed him, and they left no children. Some years after his death, when his sermons had been published, they gave such great comfort to an unnamed admirer that he wrote to ask if Mr. Carr had left any widow and children not provided for, and in this case offering to make provision.

It remains only to add that the elder of the two sisters, Urith Offley, was married five years after the death of her brother to Samuel Shore of Meersbrook. The younger sister, Hannah Maria, became the wife of Francis Edmunds of Worsborough in Yorkshire. In the partition of the estates, the manor, hall and park of Norton, with much other property, were assigned to Mr. and Mrs. Shore, who resided at Norton until the death of Mrs. Shore. Mr. Shore was High Sheriff of Derbyshire in 1761. After the death of Mrs. Shore Norton became the residence of her son, Mr. Samuel Shore, on whose death it passed to his son, Mr. Offley Shore; but the story of the Shores must be reserved for a subsequent chapter.

CHAPTER VII

LORDS OF THE MANOR

THE Offleys were not the first lords of Norton manor. Other families had lived at the Hall before they came. Indeed the earliest of all known references to the ownership of Norton is that contained in the will of Wulfric Spott, so that the allusion goes back to the year 1002, to a time more than nine hundred years ago, and to a period nearly a hundred years before the Battle of Hastings. Wulfric Spott, a Saxon noble, appears to have been an officer attached to the court of King Ethelred the Second. Some say he was Earl of Mercia, and Shaw, the historian of Staffordshire, seeks to identify him with Alfric who betrayed his king. It has been said that he was killed by the Danes at Ipswich in 1010 and his body was buried in the cloister at Burton Abbey. He did not bequeath Norton to the Abbey at Burton-on-Trent, as some authors have said, but to Ufegeat, in order that Ufegeat might be in a better position to befriend that foundation.

⁊ ic gean Ufegeate ðæs landes æt Norðtūne.
on þ gerād þ he freond ⁊ fultum þe betere sy
into þære stowe.

I give to Ufegeat the land at Norton, on condition that he may the better be a friend and support to the convent.

The reference in Domesday Book to Norton, translated from Latin into English, gives :

NORTON HALL, 1910.

The Land of the King

SOKE.—In Tupton and Norton are two bovates of land for taxation. To these sochlands belong seven acres of meadow. Wood, for pannage, five leagues in length, and three leagues in breadth. Of cleared land there are sixty acres.

The Land of Robert de Busli

MANORS.—In Norton Godeva and Bada had twelve bovates and a half and eight acres of land. There is land for two ploughs. Three villanes have one plough there. Ingram holds it of Roger. Formerly it was worth twenty shillings ; now, eighteen pence.

Thus Domesday Book shows that in the reign of Edward the Confessor Godiva and Bada held the land here. Yeatman says that Earl Morcar and the Countess Godiva held Norton before Roger de Busli. In the time of William the Conqueror, Ingram, Ingelram, or Engelramus held the manor, not direct from the King, but from the great Roger de Busli, for the manor of Norton, with that of Alfreton, was held of the honour of Tickhill, and had to render suit and service to the court there.

Following Ingelram came his son, Ranulph de Alfreton, whose reign at Norton belongs to the time of Henry the Second ; and he was succeeded by his son, Robert Fitz-Ranulph, the lord who founded Beauchief Abbey, where he lies buried, with his son and grandson too. He it is to whom the building of Norton church has been attributed. Robert Fitz Ranulph, and the family to which he belonged, were in favour at the court of Henry the Second. His father was known as Ranulph the Sheriff, for he was Sheriff of Nottinghamshire and Derbyshire, in those days combined into one administrative area. This office was held also by his brother, Sir William, and Robert himself had the post for four and a half years.

Indeed this place of honour was in the family during the whole of Henry's reign.

Another Robert de Alfreton, his grandson, gave to Beauchief " all that land which Helias de Trouey held of him." Where the land is does not appear, but Helias was from Troway, a neighbouring hamlet. Robert gave to the canons also, in addition to other territory, some land " near the small stream, which runs from the abbey to the larger brook, called the Scheve, on the north." The small stream itself seems to have been called the Sheyne or Sheene, as written in a paper stating the bounds of the lordship of Dore in the time of Edward the Sixth.

The line of Ingelram failed at last to produce a son. Thomas, Lord Alfreton, the great-grandson of the founder of Beauchief, died, leaving neither son nor daughter, in 1269, during the reign of Henry the Third, and one of his sisters and co-heiresses, Alicia or Einecia, marrying Sir William Chaworth, Lord of Marneham in Nottinghamshire, there came a change of dynasty in the rulers of Norton, though not in the heraldry, for Chaworth assumed the arms of the De Alfretons ; and while Alicia de Alfreton married Sir William Chaworth, her younger sister, Johanna, or Amicia, as some say, married Robert, son of Richard Lathom, of Lathom in Lancashire, and so became the ancestress of the Earls of Derby.

Chaworth family history, which comes down to our own times, reaches back also to a very far-off antiquity, carrying us beyond the battle of Hastings to the old castle of Chaources, now Sources, not far from Le Mans. When the Chaworths had crossed the Channel they were lords of Ogmore and Kidwelly, in South Wales ; but they still held the Château de Chaources in Maine. The ruins of Kidwelly Castle in Carmarthenshire, admired by the historian Freeman, are now amongst the possessions of Lord Cawdor. In the church of Neuvillette, near the Château de Sources, is a thirteenth-century tomb supposed to be that of a Chaworth. An heiress of this house married Henry Plantagenet, Earl of Leicester, nephew of Edward the First, and so became the mother of the "Good Duke" of Lancaster, and ancestress of Henry the Fourth. Amongst the many places which the Chaworths owned was Rawmarsh, near Rotherham. Recently many particulars of the Chaworths have been collected by Mrs. L. Chaworth Musters of Wiverton, who has contributed them to the *Transactions of the Thoroton Society*, Vols. VII. and VIII., 1903–4. Mr. W. P. W. Phillimore includes this family in his Nottinghamshire pedigrees. The Chaworths, as early as 1260, had a park at Norton, and no man might hunt there under a penalty of £10. Even then they had held it so long "that the memory of man runneth not to the contrary." In 1330 inquiry was made how it was kept, and the jury returned a favourable report.

Thomas Chaworth, who belongs to the reign of Edward the First, was a very generous benefactor of Beauchief Abbey, to which he gave the whole of Greenhill and land at Norton Woodseats, Bradway and other places. His generosity extended also to Worksop Abbey. Another Sir Thomas Chaworth, a descendant, having erected a windmill at Cold Aston, and the canons at Beauchief representing that it was to the prejudice and detriment of their mill at Norton, he gave it to them on condition that he and his heirs should grind their corn there without payment.

Some of the wills of the Chaworths have been preserved, including the one of Sir Thomas. "In the name of God, Amen," it opens. "In the year of our Lord 1347, I, Thomas de Chaworth, the elder, knight, make my testament as follows : In the first place I give my soul to God and the Blessed Mary, and my body to be buried in the church of the Blessed Mary of Beauchief, in the choir, before the altar, near the tomb of Sir Thomas, my grandfather. My will also is that my old palfrey walk before my body, in the name of my Principal, with its armorial trappings." In those days it was usual for some piece of personal property to be given at the time of the funeral to the priest of the parish in which the death occurred. This gift was selected from the principal or most valuable property of the dead man, and came in time to be spoken of familiarly as the Principal. Continuing, the will says : " And because the expenses of the day of my funeral, both with regard to my body and the distributions to be made to the poor, cannot, for a certainty, be ascertained, I ask and humbly beseech my executors to give me an honourable burial, out of the proceeds of my chattels, such as becomes my condition and my knighthood. I give to my son John 10 marks. I give to Johannah, my daughter, 100s. I give to my daughter Alice 100s. I give to Thomas, my son, of Marnham, 10 marks. I give to John, the son of Matilda Capsi, 100s. ; and to Alice, his sister, 100s. Also I give to William Stevens, my chaplain, 40s. I give to Henry, the chaplain of Osberton, 20s. I give to Simon de Skeffington, Robert of Medeburne, and Robert Martin, of the same place, 20s. apiece. I give to John, the son of Idonea, of Medeburne, 20s. I give to John, the son of Emma le Parker, of Medeburne, one mark. Also I give to Richard Miri, my chamberlain, my best bed, with all its hangings, and one mark. I give to Richard Rounill, my second best bed, with all its ornaments, and 20s. Also I give to Adam Tony, of Medeburne, and to each of my servants at my several manors, one mark each. I give to the several officers of my household, viz. my butler, gatekeeper, baker, cook, and huntsman, one mark each. Also I give to the eight chaplains to celebrate for my soul, and the souls of parents and benefactors, for the space of two years, four score marks, each of them taking five marks a year. Also I give to the convents of Grey Friars, Augustinian Canons, and Carmelites at Leicester, Nottingham, and Derby, to each convent half a mark. Also I give to William Allibon, of Medeburne, and all my pages and footmen, half a mark each. Also I will that the debts which are owing to the abbot and convent of Beauchief, under the will of my lord of Chaworth, that is to say, 40 silver pounds, be paid without gainsaying. Also I will that my debts be paid out of my own chattels, and if anything shall remain undisposed of, I will that the same be distributed to priests and poor men to pray for my soul. In order that my testament may be faithfully carried out, and that the will, which I have duly expressed in my lifetime, may be accomplished, I appoint as my executors," and here follow their names.

When the line of the Norton Chaworths ended in a daughter Joan, or Johanna, she married John Ormond, or Urmon, probably of Irish extraction, who lies buried in the chancel of Alfreton church. In this way the name of Chaworth, so far as this Norton branch is concerned, was absorbed by the Ormonds, but the family survived in Nottinghamshire, where Mary Chaworth inspired a lifelong and unavailing passion in Lord Byron. Upon the female side the family is represented by the Earl of Meath.

There were three daughters of the Chaworth-Ormond marriage. The eldest, Joan, married Thomas Denham, Dynham or Dinham, of Eythorp in Buckinghamshire, natural son of the last Lord Denham, by whom she had several children. Her husband died and she then married Sir Edward Greville, and, surviving him, married Sir William Fitzwilliam, whom also she survived, though she does not appear to have married again.

The second daughter, Elizabeth, was the first wife of Sir Anthony Babington of Dethick in Derbyshire, and so became great-grandmother of the Anthony Babington who lost his head in plotting in favour of Mary Queen of Scots. During his intrigues he needed money and sold land at the Herdings, in Norton, to Robert Holland, at that time vicar of Sheffield.

The third daughter of John Ormond, Anne, married William Meryng or Mering of Nottinghamshire.

The manor was held now in two parts, the Denhams

holding one and the Babingtons the other. The Denhams' part passed by sale successively to the Bullocks, the Eyres and the Blythes, and to the Blythes came eventually the other portion in 1587. Then Charles Blythe, who held the whole manor, sold it to John Bullock, already a large landowner here. So it passed to William Bullock, who was born in 1617 and died in 1666. The Bullocks were associated long with Norton, Unstone, Darley Abbey, Derby and other parts of this county. They built Unstone Hall and their arms appear over the doorway. In Rotherham church too their arms may be seen, and an alabaster monument to John Bullock is a most interesting feature of St. Alkmund's church in Derby. The Bullocks intermarried with other local families, the Poyntons of Bradway, the Fanshawes and the Morewoods. By their loyalty to the Stuarts the Norton branch of the Bullocks became impoverished.

There is evidence that under the Commonwealth William Bullock suffered for his loyalty to the Stuarts, afforded by a list of knights and gentlemen of Derbyshire who compounded for their estates in 1655 by a payment of a tenth of their value. Bullock's name appears as having paid £40. Such men as Bullock were known as "delinquents," and to their wealth the supporters of the Parliament turned to defray the expenses of their struggle with royalty. There is also an intimation, derived from Pegge, in one of Hunter's notebooks at the British Museum, that William Bullock left his wife and son "in great distress." This wife was Sarah Gill, of Lightwood in Norton, a member of a family we shall meet again.

A conspicuous memorial of the Bullocks is the monument, with its two heads of cherubs, upon the north side of the chancel in Norton church. It has remained when others, including one of John Bullock, have been removed. This monument was erected in memory of William Bullock and his son John, and the inscription, of pathetic import, tells us that

Hic juxta situs est Wilhelmus Bullok de Norton
in agro Derbiensi Armig.

Virtute, et ingenio præcoci, primâ statim juventute,
In coll. D. Johan. apud Cantabrig. electus est Socius.
Belli autem Furore á musis mollioribus rapide divulsus,
Regijs partibus contra rebelles cum primis se devovit,
In quibus pertinaciter cum ultimis fortissimus stetit.
Cum Ser$^{mo.}$ Car. 2do. redeunt illi etiam res suæ familiares,
Diu in perduellium manibus sequestres, et misere attritæ.
Nec minus jam pace, quam bello olim clarus, et utilis,
Deo scilicet, ecclesiæ, et regi tenaci proposito ubiq Fidelis,
Quicquid, quæq, postulet necessitudo, ad amussim perfecit.
Charus maritus ; indulgens ; pater ; dominus facilis ;
Comes Facundus, et gratus ; amicus certus, et integer,
Patrem secutus est Filius unicus Domus spes ultima,
Johannes Bullok in Coll. D. Johan Cantab$^{r.}$ noviter ascitus,
Variolis abreptus in ipso juventutis Flore, cum jam spem
     daret,
Se Patrem vitæ instituto, virtute, et moribus referre.
Vidua, utrinq. orba, et ipsa assiduo dolore pene confecta,
Hoc utrisq, et toti Familiæ, hic simul sepultæ, posuit
     monimentum.

$$\text{Obiit} \begin{cases} \text{Pater} \begin{cases} \text{Mar. } 7° \text{ Anno} \begin{cases} \text{Ætat suæ } 50° \\ \text{Salut } 1666. \end{cases} \\ \text{Filius} \begin{cases} \text{Feb. } 27° \text{ Anno} \begin{cases} \text{Ætat suæ } 19° \\ \text{Salut } 1682. \end{cases} \end{cases} \end{cases}$$

Mr. Addy's translation of this inscription runs : Here
lies William Bullock of Norton in the county of Derbyshire, esquire.   For his good qualities and talent early
displayed he was chosen Fellow of St. John's College,
Cambridge, at a youthful age.   But swiftly torn from the
gentler Muses by the Fury of war he was among the first
to devote himself to the King's side against the rebels,
remaining on that side with the utmost fortitude and endurance to the last.   On the accession of his Majesty

Charles the Second his estate long sequestered in the
hands of enemies, and miserably impaired, was restored
to him also.   Nor was he less eminent and serviceable in
peace than he had formerly been in war.   Everywhere
faithful to God, the Church, and the King, with steadfast
purpose, he did perfectly whatever necessity called upon
him to do.   He was an affectionate husband, an indulgent
father, a kind master, a witty and pleasant companion, a
sure and unchanging friend.

His only son, John Bullock, the last hope of the house,
newly admitted to St. John's College, Cambridge, was
snatched away in the very bloom of youth by small-pox,
when he was already giving promise of resembling his
father in mode of life, virtue, and manners.   His widow,
bereaved of both, and herself almost worn out with grief,
hath erected this monument to them both and to the
whole family here buried together.

Died { The father { March 7 in the year { of his age, 50 ; / of salvation, 1666.
The son   { Feb. 27 in the year { of his age, 19 ; / of salvation, 1682.

Mr. Addy writes of the inscription : " I have not
altered the punctuation, which in several places is inaccurate."

William Bullock is said to have been educated at
Ashbourne, under Mr. Mounteney, but Mr. H. C.
Fanshawe has found his name on the list of scholars at
Repton.   He was admitted a pensioner of St. John's
College, Cambridge, in 1635, when he was seventeen
years of age.   He became afterwards a fellow, but was
ejected from his fellowship in 1644.   The founding of
the Knights of the Royal Oak was contemplated, and
amongst the names of those suggested for admission to
the order was that of Colonel William Bullock, the value
of whose estate was then £1,000.

The Bullocks had the advowson of Norton, and if we

follow the line upon the female side it carries us forward
to Cavendish Nevile and on to the Robinsons, vicars of

The Bullock Tomb in NORTON CHURCH

Norton, and so to the Holys and Brammals, all associated
most intimately with this place.

When the Bullocks were in difficulties they mortgaged

Norton to Cornelius Clarke, a descendant of a family
that had been settled at Ashgate, near Chesterfield, since
Elizabethan times. It was a member of the Clarke
family who was the first Mayor of Chesterfield. The
Clarkes were very wealthy, and Cornelius Clarke left
much for charitable purposes in North Derbyshire. His
tomb, though not in its original condition, may be found
still in the Blythe chapel in Norton church. When
Reynolds made his notes in the eighteenth century he
recorded that " in the south-east end of the Chancell is
a quire lately made, and by the south wall is a raised
monument of fine stone of 4 feet high and upon it a large
black marble on which is engraven

Here resteth ye body of Cornelius Clarke, Esq. who
departed this life ye 18 of June 1696

ÆEtatis suæ 64
Æternitatem Cogita.

Upon the wall above it is cut in stone a Bear rampant
collored between three mullets. Crest upon a wreath on
a Helmet a Lion rampant collored and chain'd holding a
battle axe in his paws."

No longer is the tomb raised ; but the inscribed slab,
much worn, is level now with the floor of the Blythe
chapel, and the rampant bear has been affixed to the
south wall.

Cornelius Clarke had no children, and much of his
wealth went to his sister Ursula, who married Stephen
Offley, so adding a part of the Clarke accumulations to
the heaped riches of the Offleys. Another of Clarke's
sisters married a Nevile.

In a previous chapter we saw the male line of the
Norton Offleys end abruptly and ignobly ; but Edmund
Offley does not well represent the people whose name
he bore. In the *Genealogist* (New Series), vols. xix.
and xx., 1903, 1904, is a comprehensive account of the

family, with many particulars of the highest general interest, some of them compiled from a delightful old manuscript. The pedigree goes back to a John Offley, the father of a William Offley, twice Mayor of Stafford and a Sheriff of Chester in 1517. Sir Thomas Offley was Lord Mayor of London in 1556. His tomb is in the church of St. Andrew Undershaft, in London. Hugh Offley, Sheriff of London in 1588, was the great-grand-father of the Stephen Offley who married Ursula, the sister of Cornelius Clarke of Norton. From the great Sir Thomas descended the John Offley to whom Izaak Walton dedicated *The Compleat Angler.* This John Offley married Anne Crewe, daughter and heiress of John Crewe, of Crewe. Their son John took the name of Crewe, and a descendant became Lord Crewe, from whom the present peer has descended. Some of the Offleys were connected with Norwich. Joseph Offley, Bencher of the Middle Temple, Member of Parliament for Rye from 1698 to 1703, died "at his lodgings in Kentish Town," and made his cousin, Stephen Offley of Norton, son of his late cousin Robert Offley of the city of Norwich, merchant, his heir. This Stephen Offley, woollen draper, St. Paul's Churchyard, married at Chesterfield, in 1635, Ursula, daughter of Ralph Clarke of Ashgate, and eldest sister of Cornelius Clarke of Norton Hall. They had a son, Robert, and when Cornelius Clarke died this Robert entered into his possessions, which included the Hall and estates at Norton.

The eldest son of this Robert, another Robert, was killed by a fall from his horse in August 1699 at Hazel-barrow, where he had been to see his sweetheart Margaret Wingfield, and he was buried in the vault at Norton. One of his brothers, Stephen, thus became the heir. Stephen was High Sheriff of Derbyshire in 1715, and died at Norton when he was fifty-six years of age on October 1, 1727. His portrait used to be at Norton Hall.

One of Stephen's sons was another Stephen, a physician

The elder son, Joseph, born December 1, 1702, married Mary Bohun of Beccles. He died September 3, 1751, when he was forty-nine years of age, and was buried at Norton. The children of this marriage were Edmund, Mary, who died young, Urith and Hannah Maria, so that we are back again upon familiar ground, for the fortunes of these children have been told in the previous chapter.

Urith Offley, as we saw, bestowed her hand and the Norton estate upon Samuel Shore. He was a descendant of an old Sheffield family of tradesmen and bankers, which, after great prosperity, came to financial disaster by the failure of its Sheffield bank in 1843. A Sheffield man who had a few thousands in the bank used to say, " I would not trust the Bank of England ; but I am all right with Parker, Shore & Co." His idea was that the Norton estate alone was security sufficient. Shores of the same family were amongst the gentry of Derbyshire in early times. John Shore of Derby was knighted by Charles the Second after the Restoration, for the Shores had suffered losses for their loyalty. The Sheffield branch came from the Darley Dale Shores, who migrated first to Dronfield, and lovers of Wordsworth may have read the sonnet relating to a tradition of Oker Hill in Darley Dale, which opens with the lines

'Tis said that to the brow of yon fair hill
Two brothers clomb . . .

These brothers are said to have been Shores, and the elder one was the ancestor of Lord Teignmouth, who thus represents a branch of the same family as the Sheffield Shores, and bears the same arms.

The story of the two brothers embodied in the sonnet was told to Wordsworth by a fellow traveller upon a coach, but a more prosaic account of the planting of the trees, still known to some as Shore's trees, was that a William Shore placed them there to represent himself and his wife, and as a memorial that all the land that could be seen from this eminence had belonged to his family.

Of the Sheffield Shores there was a succession of Samuels, one of whom bought Meersbrook from the Roebucks. This Samuel died at Meersbrook in 1785. It was his son, another Samuel, who married Urith Offley and went to live at Norton Hall. The Shores had also a branch at Tapton, in Sheffield, where lived William Shore from whom descended Florence Nightingale, whose name was Nightingale and not Shore by the accident that her father, William Edward Shore, assumed the name of his maternal uncle, Peter Nightingale, whose wealth he inherited. Samuel Shore quitted Norton Hall for Meersbrook on his second marriage, though he left his son there. He was High Sheriff of Derbyshire in 1761, took an active and useful part in public life, and fought the powerful people who were opposed to making the river Don navigable. A militant dissenter, he retired from the magistracy when Parliament refused to repeal the Test Act. He died at Meersbrook, ninety years of age, and lies buried at Norton. His son, still another Samuel, lived at Norton Hall, which he rebuilt in 1815, and he was High Sheriff in 1832. He had eight children, including six daughters, and not one of the girls married. His brother, Bohun Shore, a lieutenant-colonel, died unmarried at Meersbrook in 1840. Shores generally live long, even when they seem frail, and so Florence Nightingale, who was not robust, reached her ninetieth year before the end came in 1910. In her case there are traditions of old age on both her father's and her mother's side.

One of the Misses Shore, probably Elizabeth, had literary and philosophical enthusiasms, and when she went to pay afternoon calls took with her Dugald Stewart's *Philosophy of the Mind,* from which she read extracts to the company. She founded a manuscript periodical, *The Gleaner,* to which the ever-obliging Montgomery sent contributions.

9

There was an unfortunate incident at Norton with regard to Miss Maria Theodosia Shore. She died in 1855 at Meersbrook, and the vicar, the Rev. H. H. Pearson, being away from Norton ill at the time, the curate in charge, the Rev. Thomas Townshend Sale, M.A., kinsman of a very popular Sheffield vicar, refused her Christian burial in the family vault of the Shores in Norton church on the ground that she was a Unitarian, with the result that the interment took place in the Sheffield cemetery, where also afterwards some of her sisters were buried, for there was then no cemetery at Norton. The idea of a Shore being shut out from Norton church of all places stirred much angry feeling and bitter resentment, and so the "churlish priest" who had refused Christian burial to this representative of the line of a much-respected old family connected so closely with the parish came in for some "vivid abuse" and some condemnatory letters in the newspapers. Mr. Sale acted no doubt from conscientious motives, but the vicar himself said that, had he been at home, he would not merely have permitted the burial, but would have read the service. All the same Mr. Sale was a curate after Mr. Pearson's own heart, for it was of him he used to say, "I once had a curate for sixteen years, and I had a horse for the same length of time. The curate left, and the horse died, and I have never had a horse or curate to suit me since."

A gruesome story is told of another lady of the house of Shore being buried unwittingly in a trance. Her tomb was rifled for the sake of some rings she wore that had been buried with her, and the removal of the jewels caused her to wake. Variants of this story have been told of so many families that there is no reason to give the tradition credence. Generally it is the cutting off of a swollen finger to secure a priceless ring that awakens the cataleptic lady.

The last of the male line to live at Meersbrook was Offley Shore, the brother of the Misses Shore. He shared in the troubles of the family, for he was forty-six years of age when the bank failed in 1843, and selling his Norton estates, he removed from the neighbourhood of Sheffield, and died at Mickleover House in Derby. He has been described as a man of kindly disposition and retiring habits, and he was much beloved by all who knew him. In religion he was a Unitarian and in politics a Liberal. When there was proclaimed inoculation for the cow-pox, afterwards abandoned for other forms of vaccination, Offley Shore of Meersbrook was one of the first to venture upon a trial of this suggested preventive for small-pox, and vaccine was obtained from Dr. Jenner.

Joseph Hunter, the historian of Hallamshire, pays an eloquent tribute to Offley Shore and to his father, Samuel Shore, in *An Historical Defence of the Trustees of Lady Hewley's Foundation and the Claims upon them of the Presbyterian Ministry of England*, published in 1834.

In connection with one of the Norton Shores there is a diverting story that George the Third, taking the air on the beach at Weymouth, saw some children playing in charge of a nurse. "And whose children are these?" asked the King good-naturedly. The nurse curtseyed and replied, "May it please your Majesty, they are Mr. Shore's of Norton, near Sheffield." "Ah, Sheffield! Sheffield!" exclaimed his Majesty, as he continued his promenade. "Damned bad place, Sheffield!"

After Offley Shore and his sisters, come numerous other Shores, the descendants of the Norton and Meersbrook family, now living in other parts of the country. One of the later members of the family, Offley Bohun Shore, wrote *Domestic Medicine: Plain and Brief Directions for the Treatment Requisite before Advice can be Obtained*, a work that was published in 1867. Although yearly their ranks are growing smaller there are people still alive who remember the Shores of Norton, and always they speak of the family with respect. Mr. Rhodes of the Post Office, who in his younger days paid a visit to the Shore vault, remembers how kindly the family at the Hall treated

the poor, and how generous was the dispensation of milk
and soup ; and now, when in the literary journals we see
the name of Teignmouth Shore, who was editor of *The
Academy* during one of its brilliant and reputable periods ;
when in the church journals we read the name of the Rev.
Thomas Teignmouth Shore, M.A., Canon of Worcester,
Chaplain-in-Ordinary to Edward the Seventh, formerly
Honorary Chaplain to Queen Victoria, once curate under
Frederick Maurice, and writer of well-known books ; and
when in the military journals the name of Major Offley
Bohun Stovin Fairless Shore, a distinguished soldier who
was in the Boer War, and has won a number of the
honours which soldiers prize, then do our thoughts revert
to Norton, to Meersbrook, or to that Bank Street in
Sheffield which it was proposed to call Shore Street,
and which even now owes its name to the early operations of this family, a street where the house of Shore
knew prosperity, and where, during some dark days
that are now passed, it knew temporary humiliation
and defeat.

After the Shores there came to Norton Hall, not as
the lord of the manor, but as a tenant, James Yates, M.A.,
who afterwards went to Lauderdale House, Highgate.
One of his hobbies was the study of science, and he was
an advocate for the introduction of the decimal system of
weights, measures and money. "I recall with pleasure,"
wrote John Holland, "his urbane, hospitable, and intellectual intercourse with his neighbours of all classes ; a
pleasing instance of which, enjoyed in company with my late
friend James Montgomery, is recorded in the Memoirs of
that poet." These memoirs show that on May 12, 1846,
"James Yates, Esq., the President of the Sheffield Literary
and Philosophical Society, having invited the membe s
to Norton Hall, Mr. Holland accompanied the poet
thither. . . . The evening passed very pleasantly ; Montgomery staying all night, according to previous arrangement. On entering his bedroom . . . he was impressed with
likenesses of the Misses Offley, through whose family the

estate came to the Shores ; and with one of their singular benefactor, old ' Squire Newton,' as he was called, the veritable hero of Mr. Plumer Ward's interesting story of *St. Lawrence*, in his *Illustrations of Human Life*."

On one of the occasions that Montgomery visited Norton he bought a bullfinch from a poor man who had taught it to whistle the sprightly air of *Jockey to the Fair*, as well as snatches of other tunes. The two stanzas at the opening of his poem *The Grave* were written when the bullfinch died, to be buried with it. Another stanza does not appear in the published version. The bird was sealed in a paper coffin with the verses and buried in Cook Wood. It had been a great pet and companion, and when it died the poet tried to teach another bullfinch with a flageolet, but did not succeed.

James Yates was a friend of Joseph Hunter, and when Hunter died Yates wrote an interesting and sympathetic account of his career in the *Unitarian Herald* for May 18, 1861. He connects us also with John Britton, the accomplished author of many works on antiquities, architecture and topography. Britton sends Yates a copy of the engraving of Norton Hall, from Malton's drawing, and he writes that, " As promised I send a print of Norton Hall, which, I suppose, is the place of your residence, and which I certainly should be much gratified to see, both on account of your society and to witness some of the far-famed Derbyshire scenery : but alas ! my time is to be fully occupied with hard work, I suppose to the ' *finis* ' of the lot of life. . . ."

While he was at Norton, James Yates came to know a local geologist of world-wide fame who has died but recently, for as a young man Dr. Henry Clifton Sorby, born in 1826, used to come to Norton Hall to go upon geological expeditions in these parts with Yates, and no doubt many of the quarries and cuttings hereabouts have resounded with the strokes of their hammers as they pushed their investigations into the coal measure rocks of Norton, or wandered further afield to explore the millstone grit, the limestone and the Yoredale rocks of other parts of this varied county.

The reasons for the little mark that Yates has made upon Norton and upon the memories of its inhabitants must be found in his short stay, in the fact that his ancestors were not here before him, nor descendants after him, and in. his own modesty; for if it comes to personal accomplishments, lasting work and intellectual force James Yates is probably the most distinguished man who has ever lived at Norton Hall. He was descended from Liverpool people, and was born in 1789 at Toxteth Park in that city, where his father was a Nonconformist minister. Having received some education from a tutor, William Shepherd, himself a notable Liverpool man, he went to Glasgow University, then to Manchester College, and afterwards to York, where like Joseph Hunter, and at the same time as Hunter, he fell under the influence of Charles Wellbeloved the antiquary. From York Yates went to Edinburgh University, then back again to Glasgow University. He became a Unitarian minister, though he was not ordained, and he took an active part in Unitarian organisation. Birmingham was one of the places at which he preached, and resigning his post there at the end of 1825 he retired. Two years later he went to the University at Berlin as a student of classical philology. We find him in 1832 the minister of Carter Lane Chapel, Doctors' Commons, London; but soon afterwards he retired from the ministry. Interested in most subjects, Yates wrote pamphlets and books, and contributed many papers to the proceedings of learned societies. He was one of those who entered the fray in which Samuel Shore was involved concerning Lady Hewley's bequest, and towards Smith's *Dictionary of Greek and Roman Antiquities* he contributed the drawings for half the woodcuts, and he wrote one-eighth of the text, in many ways displaying his minute and accurate learning. He was a member of the Royal Society, a fellow of the Linnæan Society and of the Geological

Society, Secretary to the Council of the British Associa-
tion and to the British and Foreign Unitarian Association,
President of the Sheffield Literary and Philosophical
Society, and connected with other kindred associations.
One of his brothers founded the Literary and Philo-
sophical Society of Liverpool.

Although nature had not conferred upon him a commanding presence, yet he was dignified, a good talker,
deliberate, calm and impressive, caustic occasionally, and
with a well-stocked memory to draw upon. His own
way of living was simple as became a scholar who has
other pleasures than those of ostentation and of the table,
but he was profuse in his entertainment of others, and
intellectual people were pleased with an opportunity to
see him in his own house in the midst of his splendid
library and surrounded by works of art and antiquity.

His death took place at Lauderdale House, now included in Waterlow Park, on May 7, 1871, when he
was eighty-two years of age, and he was buried in
Highgate cemetery. His widow survived, but they
had no children ; yet the line is not extinct, for James
Yates had distinguished brothers, one of whom gave to
Liverpool the Prince's Park, and these left children to
continue the honoured name.

At the sale by auction of the Shore estates in 1850
the Hall received no bid. Afterwards Henry Wilson,
the snuff manufacturer, educated at Norton, contemplated
purchase, but Charles Cammell secured the Hall, and was
living there when John Holland visited Norton in 1862.

Charles Cammell had no patrician ancestors, and inherited no wealth, but he managed to accumulate in his
own life more than many lords of the manor had received
from a long line of ancestors. He was born in Hull in
1810, and as a boy was apprenticed to an ironmonger
there. In 1830 he migrated to Sheffield with four or
five pounds of his own, and worked as a commercial
traveller—an occupation in which he was so successful that
in 1837 he went into business for himself. The tide of

railway enterprise was just setting in, and it carried Charles Cammell to fortune. His difficulty was not to obtain orders, but to execute them with sufficient rapidity. In 1845 where now stand the Cyclops Works were meadows and a very occasional cottage, but Cammell's establishments spread until in one place or another they occupied nearly sixty acres. He had an idea of a mausoleum in his own grounds, but when he died in 1879 was buried at Hathersage, and old Norton was represented at the funeral by the Rev. H. H. Pearson.

Bernard Cammell, a son of Charles, lived here too for some years after the death of his father. He was an accomplished painter, and I recall a portrait of remarkable power which he sent to one of the annual exhibitions of the Sheffield Society of Artists.

The Cammells were followed by Mr. John Sudbury, who within six months sold the estate to Mr. W. F. Goodliffe, a Nottingham manufacturer, from whom the old place was purchased by its present occupier, Mr. Bernard Alexander Firth, a son of the late Mr. Mark Firth, who was a steel manufacturer in Sheffield, at Norfolk Works, one of the establishments at which the age of steel manifests itself in operations of quite colossal proportions, in works that have spread over many acres. He was mayor of Sheffield in 1875, and in that year entertained the Prince and Princess of Wales (whom we were to know later as King Edward the Seventh and Queen Alexandra), when they came to open Firth Park, which Mr. Mark Firth had given to the town. Prince Leopold also was the guest of Mr. Firth at Oakbrook, when he visited Sheffield to open Firth College, another of Mr. Firth's many generous gifts to Sheffield. Mr. Bernard Alexander Firth has been at Norton Hall since 1902.

Just as there has been a succession of inhabitants at Norton Hall, so also has there been a series of habitations. How many homes may have occupied this site is a matter for conjecture, nor is it known in what shape they confronted the wayfarer as he went past this place; for the

first hall of which any pictorial representation has survived
is that which serves as a background in a portrait of
George Chantry, huntsman, of Cold Aston, though the
artist has probably exaggerated its height and made it
look more formidable than the case demanded, for he
has perched it on a mound which does not exist, and has
given an air of Conisborough Castle to the place.   Samuel

Shore of Meers-
brook told
James Mont-
gomery that
Chantry the
huntsman lived
in the time of
Stephen Offley,
a n d possibl y
also in the days
of his uncle,
C o r n e l i u s
Clarke. Cor-
nelius Clarke
died in 1696,
and S t e p h e n
Offley in 1727,
two dates that
give an idea of
the period of
this picture at
the Hall.

Entrance to
NORTON
HALL

A later drawing is one by Samuel Hieronymous
Grimm, who died in 1794, and his sketch was published
in 1801, in Pegge's work on Beauchief, and later in the
Gentleman's Magazine. He shows the old Hall to have
been a bold conception, executed with vigour. High
lights and deep shadows would be the attributes of its
beetling front, both in sunlight and in moonlight, and
probably it would be much more arresting and effective
than the insipid designs of so many latter-day architects,

with their shallow, smooth-rubbed façades, without contrast of light and shade, reminding one of weak faces that have no eyebrows. In this older part there was upon the ceiling of one of the rooms the date 1620. There is, however, a reference to a hall at Norton earlier than 1620, for it is set forth in an indenture of 1584, during the reign of Elizabeth, between Anthonye Babington of Dethick and John Bullock of Darley, that, in consideration of £400, Babington conveyed to Bullock a manor house " knowen by the name of Norton Hall."

It is not likely that even this would be the first hall of the lords of the manor of Norton.

In his history of Chesterfield the Rev. George Hall says that Norton Hall " was one of those picturesque old mansions of our country gentry of the higher order, of which so few now remain. Some portions of it were of very high antiquity. Others were probably built about the first of the Stuart reigns ; and some of the best apartments were added by the Offleys. There was a fine old entrance-hall, and in this the Nonconformists of Norton, and the neighbourhood, were accustomed to assemble for public worship, during greater part of the last century."

In 1815 Samuel Shore rebuilt the Hall, and the newer building was resented by Chantrey, who exclaimed in his pointed way that it was " a packing-box with windows in ! " The comments of Ebenezer Rhodes, who gave a detailed account of Norton Park, are more staid. At the time that he wrote the fourth part of his *Peak Scenery*, published in 1823, he tells us that Norton Hall had been rebuilt recently, and he adds that when the father of the Mr. Shore who occupied it at that time first possessed it the hall was an ancient stone mansion, its principal front having a projection at each end and a recess in the centre. Rhodes had before him at the time that he wrote the engraving from Malton's drawing, published in 1793, which has been reproduced in this book. Commenting upon this engraving he says : " The

NORTON HALL AND CHURCH, 1793.

P. 138]

front of the old building is exhibited, together with the
whole of the western wing which was erected by the late
Joseph Offley Esquire, who had it in contemplation to
rebuild the remainder, and convert the whole into a
modern mansion.   This, however, was reserved for the
present proprietor, Samuel Shore Esq., to accomplish,
who has not only carried the plans of his predecessors
into execution, but has greatly extended and laid open
the grounds about the house, and formed the whole into
a range of beautiful park scenery, which is adorned with
seats, alcoves, and occasional poetic inscriptions."

These changes at Norton did not pass without comment
in Asline Ward's diary, for this diligent chronicler,
writing in 1812, says that " Mr. S. Shore has begun to
take down the old parts of his house nearest the Church,
and nearly all the building is to be levelled with the
ground, and the new part added to the opposite end.
It will thus be improved for quitting, as it were, the
Church ; and the latter will be a better object in the
scene when less crowded by buildings."

In this book has been reproduced a lithograph of
Norton Hall as it appeared about thirty years later.   The
drawing was prepared for those who were interested in
the sale of Norton Hall when it was offered in 1850
by Joseph Nicholson, the Sheffield auctioneer, and it
was kindly lent for the illustration of *Chantrey Land* by
Mr. J. J. Greaves, of Messrs. Nicholson, Greaves, Barber
& Hastings.   It will be seen that the artist has not
forgotten the deer, and this recalls the fact that in the
early part of the fourteenth century there were in Derbyshire about fifty-four deer parks belonging to monasteries
or individuals, and one of these was at Norton.   According to Lysons it was still a deer park in 1817, when it
belonged to Samuel Shore, junior.   The features of the
hall and park at this time included the entrance supported
by four columns that we see to-day, the private chapel
near the hall, a gamekeeper's house, great oak trees,
about two hundred acres of park and woodlands, sheets

of water and a walled garden of one acre and a half.
Many of the household treasures of the Shores were
dispersed by the sale that followed their troubles ; but
a hint of the magnificent appointments of Norton Hall
at that time may be gained in a glance at a huge oval
mirror, handsomely mounted in a gilded wood frame,
elaborately and beautifully carved, which adorns now the
staircase at Barbot Hall, the residence of Mr. W. T.
Freemantle.

Some of the features we see now at Norton Hall are
due to Charles Cammell, and these include a stately
dining-room, a billiard-room and a colonnade. When
the Cammells left Norton the Hall was allowed to fall
into disrepair, and a dark age came for the old place ;
but Mr. Firth had the dining-room panelled in oak, and
so gave it its present dignified appearance, and generally
he stopped the downward tendency and made the old
Hall quite worthy again of its interesting traditions.

Asline Ward mentions in his diary a pleasing dance
at Norton Hall in the time of the Shores, when the
pupils from Mr. Piper's school were present. Hunter,
naturally, remembered particularly a large room which
was for some years hung round with painted coats-of-arms
that had been given to the Offleys and to the Shores
after the funerals of the neighbouring gentlefolk. They
included arms of the Pegges, Bagshawes, Rotherams,
Wingfields and others.

In John Holland's time there was a tradition of a
George Chantry, huntsman for the Offleys at Norton
Hall, and Holland mentions a note in the handwriting
of Samuel Shore, from which it seems that this man had
a voice like a bull of Bashan, and could make himself
heard from Norton Hall to Cold Aston. Holland adds
that in 1850 there was still in Norton Hall a full-length
portrait of this stalwart retainer, whom he has described
as good-looking, with black bushy hair, a large hat, and
bands like a clergyman. In one hand he holds a long
staff, and with the other he caresses a couple of hounds.

GEORGE CHANTRY, HUNTSMAN, AND BROWNELL, WHIPPER-IN.

p. 140]

Beside him stands a kind of satellite, a squab, dwarf-looking fellow, with a hare on a stick over his shoulder. In the background is a view of the old Norton Hall. In a letter to James Montgomery, which may be the note mentioned by Holland, Samuel Shore of Meersbrook calls this Chantry, Francis. He wrote: " There is a large, full-length picture upon wood at Norton Hall, of a Francis Chantry, who is said to have been huntsman to Mr. Stephen Offley, and possibly of his uncle and predecessor, Cornelius Clarke. He is said to have been a yeoman, with some landed property. He appears to have been a tall man : there are in the picture some favourite hounds, and a little man who was the dog-feeder. This Francis Chantry is said to have had so strong a voice, that [living at Coal Aston, a distance of about two miles] he could stand on the hill near his residence, and shout so as to make the dog-feeder and keeper hear him at Norton Hall, when he wanted the hounds to come that way. He was apparently a foot-huntsman, as was then the general practice."

When the Shores left Norton they took this picture with them ; but quite recently the Mr. Offley Shore of our own day has returned it to the present owner of the Hall, Mr. Bernard Firth, and so, happily, the old portrait has come home again. The inscription upon the picture is " Chantry, Huntsman to Mr. Stephen Offley. Brownell, Whipper in," and apparently the portrait was painted about the beginning of the eighteenth century, the age of Sir Godfrey Kneller. In many ways it is a picture of unusual interest, and a reproduction appears by kind permission in this book.

George Chantry was not the only Cold Aston worthy with a powerful voice. Mr. Addy was told by his mother of one Sam Priestley of the same place, who had sold a bull to the Duke of Devonshire. The bull was so unruly that nobody could subdue him, and at last an appeal was made to Sam, who went to Chatsworth and overcame the animal simply by shouting him down.

He came back to Cold Aston with his rent reduced, and,
" elevated " probably to a state of more than market
merriness, he could be heard crossing Greenhill Moor
roaring " Victory ! Victory ! " with a voice of brass.
Then there are those cognate stories of another Sam—
Sammy Slack of Tideswell, the famous bass singer—who
on hearing that his powers had been commended by
George the Third, replied with a grin, " Oh, he wor
pleeased, wor he ? Ah ! I knowed—I knowed I could
dow't." Once after a carousal Sammy went to sleep
in a field, when a bull came and turned him over ; but
Sammy waking, roared in the animal's face with such
effect that the bull fled in terror. Another odd collo-
cation of Derbyshire bulls and bass singing relates to
" Jemmy Queer," a Hathersage character at one time
in great request at races, fairs and wakes ; and even for
a time a famous singer in London. He also, full of ale,
slept in the open air ; and a bull roaring, caused Jemmy
to dream that he was engaged in one of his many bass
singing competitions in the village alehouse ; and when
the bull tossed him into the next field he remarked
merely, " Well, tha may be a good bass singer, but tha
canna call thisen a gentleman." It is a singular circumstance that Lucius Junius Moderatus Columella, a Roman
writer on husbandry who belongs to the first half-century
of the Christian era, should have some allusions to this
influence of the voice upon animals ; but in his great
work *De Re Rustica*, expounding " of what size and
plight of body the slaves must be, which are to be
assigned to every particular work," he says that the
" genius or disposition of the mind, though necessary in
a herdsman, or in one that labours with oxen, nevertheless is not enough, unless the hugeness of his voice,
and the bulk of his body, make him formidable to the
cattle " ; and in another place he advises of oxen, " Let
him rather terrify them with his voice than with blows."
In a tenth-century manuscript in the British Museum
a slave is made to say that he has for comrade " a boy

driving the oxen with an iron goad, who also is hoarse with cold and shouting."

One of the lakes in Norton Park served once for a scientific experiment. Asline Ward records that " Dr. Davis flatters himself that he has invented a mode of propelling vessels which will render horses needless in towing them on canals, and may perhaps be applied successfully to larger ships. It was suggested by observing, in a dream, the manner in which a fish used his tail. He has laboured at it for several months, and flatters himself with such success that he has entered a caveat in the Patent Office, or even taken out a patent. He tried the apparatus on Mr. Shore's pond. There were three kinds of fishes' tails—elastic and non-elastic, double and single, etc. They moved the boat with tolerable velocity, but not superior, if equal, to the rate at which oars impelled it, and in consequence of not being strong enough, some of the apparatus broke. I was not much astonished at the effects, nor augur very valuable improvements."

Asline Ward's gloomy auguries were fulfilled, for the results of the doctor's researches were loss of practice and impaired health.

At the Hall is a fragment of inscribed stone whose origin is not known. It was discovered serving as a flagstone in the courtyard at the back of the house, and may have been brought here from some demolished building in another part of the country. What is left of the inscription runs :

. . . Late Earl of Oxford to Thos. Parker the present possessor And his Heirs for EVER (out of Compassion to his being A dark Man) in 1729. Mr. Hubbard Steward and Witness to the Gift.

In Ireland it is usual to call a blind man a dark man ; Milton uses the word in this sense, and upon the same point Dr. Bradley, in his Sheffield days, made a communication to the *Sheffield Independent* that is very apropos. "I was quite mystified the other day by the sentence 'I always serve them that are dark.' The statement was made as an explanation why the speaker found it convenient to carry some coppers in her pocket, and simply meant that she always gave to a blind beggar when she saw one. I had met with the use of 'dark' for blind, and seem to have some recollection of the phrase 'serving beggars,' but the combination of these two curious idioms in one sentence had a very enigmatical effect."

Down in the rookery in the Hall grounds, near the garden, may be seen still the traces of a cemetery for pet dogs used by former residents. It is near to what is known as the Temple, a small, old semicircular building with columns in front.

The manor of Norton was extensive, and whereas some parishes contain parts of more than one manor, Norton included not only the whole parish but also Cold Aston in the parish of Dronfield. There were two great courts held for the manor of Norton at Michaelmas and Lady Day, when deeds were enrolled and signed, but it is not known where the court rolls of Norton now are, though those of Holmesfield are still safe, and the Duke of Rutland has the manor rolls of Baslow in his keeping; but there are those who hope that the Norton rolls may be found again, because they were in existence towards the end of the eighteenth century and there is no evidence that they have been destroyed. Mr. J. D. Leader used to say he thought they would be found at the Hall, and in Pegge's work on Beauchief there is a reference to some of the manor rolls being in the possession of the Shores, but so far they have not been recovered. A manuscript list of the manors of Derbyshire was presented by Mr. Harrington Shore to Mr. G. H. Marples of Thornbridge Hall, near Longston, about 1892. He had found the list in the muniment room at Norton Hall on the death of his father, Mr. Offley Shore, when he was examining and sorting his deeds, and the questions

arise, were the manor rolls there too, and into what
category were they " sorted " ?   Not for the bonfire
let us hope ; but it is disconcerting to be told that after
the crash of 1843 the Shores had a cart body full of deeds
burned in the saddle-room at the Hall, though a few
were saved by William Swift the genealogist.   It is a
pity that all the documents were not handed to him, for
he would have made the right use of them.   He was
assistant distributor of stamps in Sheffield, but his hobby
was family history, and his knowledge was both wide
and deep.   He was born in 1818, and dying in 1874
was buried in Norton cemetery, where there is an
appropriately unobtrusive and tasteful memorial.   A son
who was deaf and dumb lies there too, and upon the
occasion of his interment a lady amongst the mourners
mentioned to the superintendent of the cemetery that
the boy was deaf and dumb, whereupon, with the true
North-country readiness for a joke, even upon the grimmest
occasions, he replied " This cemetery is for nobody else,"
and the mourner, in no mood to detect double mean-
ings, nor expecting them at such a time, looked round
aghast that there should be so many gathered together
in one cemetery who had been unable to hear or speak.

Nearly thirty years ago Mr. Addy sought diligently
for the Norton rolls, but without success.   Mr. Charles
Jackson of Balby, Doncaster, wrote to him at the time
that Mr. Hunter said once there was a vast number of old
deeds and papers in boxes in a hay-loft at Norton.   He
called it " a singular and beautiful collection," and he
only obtained access to it in 1848, when it was entrusted
to Mr. Samuel Mitchell, after the Shores' misfortunes.
" Ubi nunc ? "

Mr. J. D. Leader made another attempt to discover
the rolls in 1881 by inserting a notice in the *Sheffield
Independent* (April 7) asking if " any one can give information as to where the ancient Court-rolls of the
Manor of Norton, near Sheffield, are now to be met
with ?   The late Mr. Hunter, in a memorandum he has

left, states that there was once a large collection of con-
veyances respecting Kilnhurst (and perhaps other places
also) which were in several boxes in a hay-loft at Norton
Hall. These, he says, were placed by Mr. O. Shore's
assignee in the hands of Mr. Samuel Mitchell, at whose
house he (Mr. Hunter) saw them on August 8, 1848.
Does any one know what further became of these ? "

Pegge made use of the court rolls when he traced the
descent of the manor, and Mr. Addy says that much of
Dr. Pegge's information seems to have been sent to him
by the Rev. T. Halladay. Now there is much for which
we have to thank Mr. Halladay. He read the rolls of
the Norton Manor court, and compiled a skilful summary
of the entries, so that though the rolls themselves have
disappeared we are not in Egyptian darkness concerning
their contents.

When James Pilkington, Unitarian minister of Derby,
wrote *A View of the Present State of Derbyshire, with an
Account of its Most Remarkable Antiquities*, which was
published in 1789, he stated that " the rev. Mr. Halli-
day [Halladay] of Norton, who has examined the
court rolls, has been so obliging as to furnish me with
the following particulars, which he has extracted from
them." The particulars furnished by Halladay, which
appear also in *A New Historical and Descriptive View of
Derbyshire from the Remotest Period to the Present Time*,
by David Peter Davies, Unitarian minister for Belper
and Milford, published in 1811, show us that "Formerly
two great courts were held here regularly every year.
The principal business transacted on these occasions was
examining into, and punishing offences, by which the
inhabitants of the manor were or might be injured.
The following in particular are noticed : incroachments
upon the waste, altering water courses, neglecting to
scour or cleanse ditches, turning a scabbed horse on to
the common, shutting up a bridle road, giving an account
of wafes and strays, examining those who brewed or
baked for sale without a license from this court and

NORTON HALL, 1850.

P. 146]

amercing them for such offences, fixing the assize of bread
and ale, and also the price of the latter (which appears
about the thirty-fourth year of queen Elizabeth to have
been one penny per quart), and fining such as broke the
assize. Two men were sworn in as frank pledge, two as
tithing-men, and one as constable for the year ensuing.

"Two ale tasters were also appointed at the court ;
and it appears, that there were brewed in the parish love-
ale, help-ale, and unwholesome-ale, for all which fines
were levied. Those who had committed an assault, and
drawn blood, were fined separately for each offence.
Some also were fined for carrying staves or clubs, lodging
suspicious persons, and remaining in alehouses after eight
o'clock at night.

"The inhabitants of the parish were also obliged to
make two butts to shoot at, and keep them in repair
under certain penalties ; and to provide their sons and
men servants with bows and arrows, as late as the thirtieth
year of queen Elizabeth. The stocks were to be kept
up, and every gap in their fences to be made up before
Lady Day.

"In the thirty-fourth year of Queen Elizabeth upwards of one hundred and thirty suitors were amerced
for non-appearance, and other offences. Of this number
were eleven brewers for selling ale unlawfully, and twenty-
one persons for playing at unlawful games, as huddlings.
If a frank pledge neglected to appear at court heavy
penalties were inflicted.

"There is no appearance of cock-fighting, horse-racing,
throwing at cocks, no cards, or dice, nay what is more
wonderful, no ducking of witches, or even a ducking
stool is noticed."

I have tried to discover what was the nature of the
game called huddlings, but I have not been successful.
Etymologically the word is related to rough embracings,
disorder and general confusion, and this, coupled with
the command for discontinuing the game, points to something perhaps not very edifying.

CHAPTER VIII

OLD NORTON HOUSE

PLUMER WARD, far as he strayed from history in most matters concerning the Offley case, seems to have given an accurate account of the appearance of the old Norton House, since demolished, at the time that Robert Newton lived there. " It is surrounded with high walls," he says, " towards the road, so that you can hardly see it ; and this with a mere wicket for a gate, makes many a man pass it without curiosity thinking it a common grange. But it is pretty though gloomy within."

Hunter, too, agrees with Ward that Norton House was in those days "a gloomy abode : the garden, being inclosed with high stone walls, which half blocked up the windows on one side of the house, obstructing the passage of the light, which had at last to make its entrance through apertures of but small dimensions." He shows, however, that afterwards " it put off all its gloominess, and the light of heaven and a more uniform and liberal hospitality were freely admitted within its walls." In another place Hunter says it was an excellent specimen of the house of the gentry of the age of Charles the First, and Mr. Addy's recollection is of a large and beautiful old mansion : " Norton House is a solemn-looking old-fashioned building," writes John Holland in *Sheffield Illustrated*, and in his book on Chantrey he mentions " the venerable ivy-covered front of Norton House." When he had occasion to write of the place in 1862 he called it " a substantial . . . stone building, of plain archi-

Old Norton House
from a Drawing
in the possession of E.M.E WELBY, ESQ.

tecture, embosomed in trees." Thomas Asline Ward wrote " Old and handsome, it seems to combine strength and utility," and Mrs. Sterndale writing in 1824 tells us that " the bright ivy and gadding woodbine clothed the gables and gateway of Norton House, the old elms throwing their shadows on the green below its windows."

There has been general agreement that Norton House was built by the Morewoods. A memorandum of the Rev. H. H. Pearson mentions that the house was built in 1623, and that two oak trees were displayed over the north door. This tends to confirm the idea of the Morewood origin, for the oak trees form a prominent feature in their coat-of-arms; but at any rate Leonard Gill added to the Morewood fabric even if he was not the founder of the house. Of the Gills and Morewoods, however, nothing is said here because their family history is set forth in the next chapter, seeing that they were at the Oakes before their names were linked with Norton House.

Later, Norton House was owned by Samuel Hallowes, sheriff in 1674, and a county magnate with a long descent and a coat-of-arms. The Hallowes family inherited the riches of the Woolhouses of Glapwell, who had added to their belongings the estates of conspirator Babington of Dethick. There was a Samuel Hallowes of Hallowes, in Dronfield, and it was his grandson, Samuel, who was at Norton House. He went hence to Nottingham, and is buried in St. Mary's church there. A descendant, Thomas Hallowes, married Lady Catherine Brabazon, daughter of Chambre, fifth Earl of Meath, and of Juliana, daughter and heiress of the Viscount Chaworth. The last of the line, Ann Hallowes, married Sir Robert Barker, who was mentioned in connection with Lees Hall. She lies buried at Bolsover.

After Hallowes came Alexander Radcliffe, who belonged to an old family that had derived its name from Radcliffe, near Bury, in Lancashire, a family in which Alexander was a favourite Christian name. A Radcliffe accompanied Edward the First in his wars in Scotland; another was in the French wars with Edward the Third. Richard Radcliffe was slain in Ireland, and two of the family died together in battle in Flanders. Their sister Margaret, a favourite maid-of-honour of Queen Elizabeth, died of grief for their loss. Later, still another Radcliffe was killed in Irish wars, and Sir John Radcliffe met a similar fate in the Isle of Rhé in 1627. Robert Radcliffe, born in 1650, married Anne, the only surviving daughter and heiress of Rowland Eyre of Bradway. He was killed in a duel in 1685. The Alexander Radcliffe of Norton married Elizabeth, the daughter of John Bagshawe, and their son Robert married Margaret, the only daughter of Adam Bagshawe of Wormhill. The Radcliffes were connected with the Byrons of Newstead and with the Earls of Sussex and other families of rank. Children of the marriage of Alexander Radcliffe with Elizabeth Bagshawe were baptised here at Norton, Anna in 1700 and Elizabeth in 1701. Five days later Elizabeth was buried, but another Elizabeth was baptised in 1702 and Frances in 1703. For many years the Radcliffes have been connected with Fox Denton Hall in Lancashire.

Alexander Radcliffe was succeeded by the Bramhalls. About 1712 John Bramhall sold Norton House to John Wingfield, at that time living at Hazelbarrow Hall less than a mile away. When John Wingfield bought Norton House, he left Hazelbarrow as a residence for his son, Storie Wingfield, and having lived at Norton House for about twenty years he died in 1732, eighty-one years of age. As he had survived both his sons the estates at Norton became the property of his grandson Robert Newton, the hero of the Offley affair, then nineteen years of age. Newton received also Bradway Hall, and Hazelbarrow. He was the only surviving son of Mr. Wingfield's eldest daughter Margaret, who had married Mr. Newton, of a Mickleover family. She had been engaged to Robert Offley of the Hall, but he was killed by a fall from his horse after a visit to her at Hazelbarrow.

Young Newton at the time of his grandfather's death was in the dissenting academy at Findern, near Mickle-over, where, as at Norton, the spread of Nonconformity had prevailed; and though we met him in a previous chapter as the hero of the restoration to the Offleys of their ancestral acres, yet in his own home we may well seek closer acquaintance, especially as he was what is known in these parts as a " character." At the time that he went to Edinburgh on behalf of the Misses Offley he was forty-one years of age, and in the full vigour of his manhood. In 1745 he raised a troop of horse to defend George the Second against the Stuart rising. In the following year he was High Sheriff of Derbyshire. He was in Edinburgh with his friend Girdler when the battle of Prestonpans was fought, and rose early to go to see the fight. In Plumer Ward's story of the Offley alienation Newton is an introspective and apathetic recluse, but he was not so in actual life. Friends came from Sheffield, jolly parties, and in writing of old Sheffield doctors Mr. R. E. Leader has told us that " the earliest mention we meet with of Mr. John Hussey, apothecary, is in 1738. . . . He was ever a welcome guest at Norton House, one of ' the jovial debaters,' including John Girdler, Hunter's grandfather, and others, who met there round the convivial table of Robert Newton."

Hunter, controverting Plumer Ward's description, does not deny that Newton had some peculiarities, and heard that he had an extraordinary aversion to receive ladies at his house, which extended itself even to ladies the nearest in blood to him. He adds that Newton was perhaps too self-indulgent in his little whims as he grew old. He never married, and applied himself closely to the management of his own affairs, and particularly to the acquisition of land. He had more than one Chancery suit, and did not leave all the fighting to the lawyers. He employed the learned Dr. Pegge, rector of Whittington, to compile the genealogies of his family and those of the

Wingfields, Stories and Clarkes, and of the people of Norton Hall. Of Newton's letters Hunter says they are lively, full of pleasantries, and sometimes display an exuberance of high spirits. They were gay, cheerful, jocund letters, and Hunter might have added that upon occasion they were coarse as well. In 1874 Dr. Julian Hunter, the historian's son, writing from Bath to the *Sheffield Independent*, said : " I have a bundle of letters addressed by Mr. Robert Newton, of Norton House, to Mr. John Girdler, of Low House, in Sheffield Park. They are in Mr. Newton's racy and scarcely decorous style. . . . After having scandalised successive generations of our family for a hundred and twenty years the worst of the old fellow's letters have recently undergone cremation at my hands. If modern society in Sheffield can bear a few Shandean facetiæ, I will, if you please, send you a few samples of Mr. N.'s style." The editor did not please.

One of the founders of the English Unitarians was the Rev. Theophilus Lindsey, who had been an Anglican clergyman until his opinions changed. Then he resigned his living at Catterick and came to poverty. Writing of this period his biographer, Thomas Belsham, says that " Dr. Priestley and Dr. Price were active and zealous friends. Samuel Shore, Esq., then of Norton Hall, now of Meersbrook, in Yorkshire [Derbyshire], whose name ranks high among the advocates for civil and religious liberty, the patrons of truth and science, and the friends of pure and practical Christianity, called upon Mr. Lindsey with a present of a hundred pounds from a friend whose name was then concealed, but since known to have been Robert Newton, Esq., of Norton House, whose delight was to spend the income of a large estate in doing good in the most private manner possible, and from the shade of retirement to scatter blessings upon his fellow-creatures. To this princely donation of Mr. Newton, Mr. Shore generously added a very liberal present of his own ; and to the end of Mr. Lindsey's

life he continued the warm personal friend, and the firm
and liberal supporter of him and his cause."

Mr. Belsham supplemented this by adding a letter
from the Rev. W. Turner, of Wakefield, to Mr. Lindsey,
written on June 14, 1777. "Robert Newton, Esq., is
a near neighbour to Mr. Shore in the same village, aged
about sixty-six or sixty-seven, and a bachelor of large
fortune. I have known him since the year 1732, when,
and for two or three years afterwards, we were fellow-
pupils under Dr. Latham, at Findern, near Derby. His
mother lost her husband when she was pregnant of this
son, and gave so much way to grief for that event as
was supposed to have an ill effect on the constitution of
her child. He has always had very weak nerves and
uneven spirits, but generally a prevailing hypochondria.
For many years past he has been telling his friends that
he should soon give them the slip ; but in the mean time
he has looked well and grown bulky. When any extraordinary case, particularly for the service of his friends,
called for it, he could exert as much vigour, activity, and
resolution as any man."

Mr. Turner then gives an account of Newton's efforts
in frustrating the attempt to alienate the Offley estates, and,
continuing, writes: " Mr. Shore says, Nature formed him
for a soldier; and that as a commander, and especially as a
partisan, he would certainly have distinguished himself.
When younger, he made little of riding from his own
house to Scarborough in one day ; supping, and perhaps
dancing there till midnight with a party of his friends,
and would then remount and return next day. Like
sudden excursions and returns, to and from London,
Bath, Bristol, and even abroad, were common with
him,—and all the while he was *dying*. From all the
above circumstances you will easily conclude he must
have had some humours, and even whims ; but they
have always been very innocent, and only laughable. He
has always been very steady in his friendships, of which
Mr. H., a Dissenting minister at Mansfield, who for

many years has been his most familiar friend and companion, both when at home and in many of his excursions, has had, I doubt not, ample experience.—So much for your generous back-friend Mr. Newton, who, as a friend of mine said of another person, delights to do such extraordinary good deeds and nobody must know ! I need not caution you not to draw the curtain behind which he chooses to conceal himself."

When the Nonconformists attempted to establish a

Norton House

large institution for education at Hackney, Newton contributed £500, and at his death he left money towards the erection of a chapel at Norton for the Nonconformists who had been accustomed to meet at the Hall.

Although Hunter is gentle in his treatment of Newton in his account of the Offley incident, he was not blind concerning Newton's shortcomings ; for though Robert came out of that affair with flying colours, as Hunter was careful to show, and remains the hero of the event, he had the faults of his time and class : purse-pride, tyranny, greed, bigotry, coarseness, and the other evil characteristics of the eighteenth-century squire as portrayed by Henry Fielding. " He was," says Hunter, " a somewhat intolerant politician. My grandfather having said in a moment of dissatisfaction with some public measure, that it was indifferent to him whether a George or a James, or a Charles, were on the throne, this sally produced a coolness, a remonstrance, and almost a rupture." Writing in 1858, seventeen years after the publication of his account of the Offley case, Hunter says that " in respect of Mr. Newton I think I am warranted in putting on paper a few remarks on his character, finding it to be so untruly represented by Mr. Belsham, and, I believe, generally misunderstood. Mr. Belsham says that he spent the income from his large estates in private acts of benevolence. This is quite untrue ; he was constantly buying land to near the end of his life, adding farm to farm, and left a vastly increased estate to his heirs. As to his acts of private benevolence, I suspect they would be found so *exceedingly private* that it would require a glass of very strong optical power to discern them."

Girdler was a grocer in Sheffield, and a farmer in the Park, and the Samuel Shore who married Urith Offley said Newton was the ruin of Girdler by frequently tempting him away from his business, a neglect of his affairs he was not rich enough to commit with impunity. While Girdler was alive Newton professed great esteem for Mrs. Girdler, but when she was left a widow with four young children he took no further notice of her. He became morose with his relations, particularly if they were not well off, and pressed a creditor named Baker so hard as to cause him to commit suicide. A man who had been carousing with Newton at Norton House was thrown from his horse at the gate and so killed. One of the Roebucks used to vituperate Newton, who, he said, had cheated him about a horse ; and Hunter has added that Newton was the father of many illegitimate children in Norton.

In a reference to Sir Francis Chantrey's father, Holland

gives us incidentally a glimpse of the character of Newton, for he tells us that the elder Chantrey " sung a song, told a tale, or bandied a joke but too cleverly for his own welfare. The public-house was not far off ; and still nearer was the hospitable residence of ' Squire Newton,' among whose eccentricities was a too frequent preference of the hilarious frankness of persons in a grade of life below his own, to the more formal intercourse of the neighbouring gentry."

John Read, a tenant of Newton's at Norton House, used to tell how Newton's gardener went to his master and said, " It's a boy, and they have called him Robert Newton." This was the announcement of the birth of Robert Newton Shawe, of Kesgrave Hall. Newton replied, " And he shall not be called Robert Newton for naught." He was not, for he inherited great wealth under Newton's will. It is related that Newton went in shabby clothes on a cart-horse to the sale of an estate. One of the company desired the auctioneer to dismiss him, but the auctioneer said the sale must be open to all. Newton outbid everybody, giving more than its value for the estate, and, pulling out of his pocket a bag of money, offered to pay in full then and there.

Although Newton's conversations and letters were not always edifying, he seems to have endeavoured to compass a "good end," and to have tried to make amends in his will, for he left money for the improvement of morals, with the solemn injunction that the boys taught under his endowment " should be instructed how heinous the vices of swearing and lying are, and the threatening and punishment against swearers and liars in their Bibles, and they should be punished severely if guilty thereof after a second admonition ; and, if they should not be reclaimed by frequent admonition and correction, that such children should be turned out of school, and their places supplied."

There seem to have been books at Norton House in Newton's day, as may be inferred from a reference in the

Life of Montgomery. Gales, Montgomery's master, was a printer, bookseller and auctioneer ; and Montgomery wanted to read the books which passed through his hands, but they were sold too rapidly to allow this. He specially regretted not being able to read the books of the Rev. John Bullock, sold at Ashford-in-the-Water, Mr. Greenways, of the Manor House, Dronfield, and Robert Newton's at Norton.

A later resident of Norton House was John Read, descended from Northampton people and connected with Peterborough. He married Ann, daughter of Joshua Turner of Sheffield, and amongst their children were Joseph Read of Wincobank and John Read, who afterwards left Norton House to go to Derwent Hall. The elder Read lost a daughter at Norton, for the register records the burial on August 11, 1797, of Catherine his child, and Read himself was buried on February 7, 1803. Something of the style of living at Norton House of the younger John Read may be learned from a demand note for assessed taxes made upon him, in 1810, showing that he was taxed for fifty windows £37 6s. ; inhabited house duty (on £20), £2 5s. ; four domestic servants, £10 7s.; one carriage, £11 5s. ; five horses, £25 15s. ; other horses and a mule, 14s. ; four dogs, £2 6s. ; armorial bearings, £2 8s., a total of £92 6s.

This John Read and Sir Francis Chantrey were close friends, and Read accompanied the great sculptor upon his Italian tour. John's father was one of the first to introduce the refining of precious metals into the town of Sheffield. He had a knowledge of chemistry, and by great industry and perseverance managed to accumulate a fortune. Upon the demolition of the Duke of Bedford's mansion in Bloomsbury, Chantrey's friend, then a boy, accompanied his father to London to purchase the gold ceilings from which he recovered the gold. He went to the House of Commons, and witnessed the dramatic incident of Burke crossing from one side of the House to the other, when the great orator closed his ears with his hands, like Christian flying from the dissuasions of his family.

Read, a very hospitable man, bought some of Chantrey's early work, and had many pictures and books at Norton House, as Asline Ward's diary indicates, for Ward came here in 1818 to "survey the treasures of his library." In 1826 Ward dined here with the Reads of Wincobank and with Poole the painter. There were dances at Norton House in Read's time, and when Edward Blore, the artist, came to Norton he stayed here with Read. Probably this would be when Blore made a drawing of the Bishops' House at Norton Lees for Rhodes' *Peak Scenery*, one of the chief ornaments of the work, a beautiful plate full of artistic qualities and deep feeling. Later, Read moved to Derwent Hall, which he had bought, but there misfortune came, and he died, 85 years of age, in 1862, at Rycroft farm, near Dore, to which he had retired when dark days came, when the lean years followed the years of abounding prosperity.

Next to Read as a resident in Squire Newton's old home comes Thomas Beard Holy. Daniel Holy of Sheffield had a son, Thomas, a button manufacturer of the middle of the eighteenth century, and a grandson, another Thomas, of Sheffield Moor, a merchant, and a great buyer of land. This Thomas married Elizabeth Beard of Glossop, and their only son was Thomas Beard Holy of Norton House, who married a daughter of Jonathan Alderson, Rector of Harthill.

The Holys were in the very forefront of the Methodist movement in Sheffield in its earliest and troubled days, when Wesley and his followers had to face infuriated mobs, and when a Methodist, merely because he was a Methodist, went in great peril of having his head broken. According to William George Thorpe, in his *Still Life in the Middle Temple*, tradition says that one of the principal residents of Norton, Mr. Holy, was given to great hospitality to the Wesleyan ministers, and as one of them was walking through Sheffield after one of his dinners a button flew off his waistcoat, and knocked down a little boy. The family is represented now by Miss Holy of Leamington.

For what we know concerning Norton House we owe much to one J. S. (Dr. John Sykes of Doncaster), who upon October 2, 1877, wrote a long, valuable and interesting letter to the *Sheffield Independent*, a journal which under the Leaders contained a place for reference to local antiquities. We wish there had been more people of the " J. S." kind, so that fewer old buildings might have been removed without a good friend to tell us of their glories. " As this old mansion is now in the course of demolition," writes J. S., " and will shortly be among the things which have passed away, it may not, perhaps, be uninteresting to some of the readers of your *Notes and Queries* to receive a parting notice of it.

" Understanding that there was much about the place not unworthy of observation, especially in the way of ancient woodwork, the writer, with several friends, paid a visit to it on Friday last, September 28, but unhappily a day too late to see the dining room panels attached to its walls.

" The house is a very substantial, well-built structure, of the early part of the 17th century, with a few windows inserted and other small alterations made about a century later. It consists of a body with projecting wings, and was evidently erected as the residence of a family of good position. It has an entrance hall of good size, panelled throughout, but not in a very rich style, and various rooms below and above of goodly dimensions, but somewhat low. The principal of these is the dining room already alluded to, which is on the first floor. Here the panelling, of which we saw specimens which had just been stripped from its walls, was of very good and rich character, and strongly resembled that still remaining in the old dining room at Carbrook Hall. We understood that it had been sold for £500 to a person from Lancaster. The ceiling of this room is in six compartments, and of fine, elegant stucco work, each compartment varying. On the chimney piece in one of the rooms is the figure of a Saracen (perhaps intended as a crest), with the initials L. E. G., and the date 1623. The same figure, with like initials and date, appears repeatedly on the conductor spouts of the western end of the house. The spouts are partly gilt, and of extremely good character. The initial and date in all probability will lead to the knowledge of the time of the erection of the house and the name of the builder. This latter, it would seem, is not a Morewood, as Lysons suggests, but Leonard Gill, who married Elizabeth, the sister of Bishop Saunderson, at Blythe, October 13, 1607 (see Hunter's *Hallamshire*, Gatty's Edition, p. 399). Edward, the eldest son of this marriage, took as his first wife a daughter of Stephen Bright, of Carbrook, and this connexion may well account for the great similarity of the panelling of the dining rooms of the two places, which very likely were designed and executed by the same artists. Though Norton House was erected before the civil wars, and was possessed by a family of stout Parliamentarians, it does not appear that it suffered any aggression in those troublous times. It was reserved for a later day for its inhabitants to be brought into suspicion and danger for their political opinions, for it is stated that during the revolutionary period of the latter part of the last century it was searched, to the great annoyance of its then owner, Mr. Newton, under the authority of a warrant from the Secretary of State, certain supposed dangerous characters having been suspected of hiding there. Before taking leave of this venerable mansion one cannot but express a regret that it should be deemed necessary or desirable to demolish it, especially as it is so well and substantially built that it might be restored at a very moderate cost."

Amongst the Rev. H. H. Pearson's notes upon Norton House is one that, in the dining-room over the fireplace, was the family crest, a kneeling figure surrendering his weapon, evidently the Saracen of "J. S." The legend connected with the figure is that when the Moors occupied Spain an ancestor of the Newton family encountered and overcame in battle one of the Moorish princes, who, to save his life, surrendered his sword, and from that time the family adopted this subject as its crest. This seems to suggest that Newton made some alterations in the house and did not leave it as he received it from the Wingfields.

Leonard Gill, mentioned in a document published by Mr. Addy as possessing a lead mill or smelting house at Totley, resided here, and the letters "Le. G." were inscribed on a finely decorated mantelpiece of the best apartment. Gill had a shot manufactory at Greenhill near Norton, through which, in 1626, he incurred the suspicions of the Privy Council. He carried on a manufactory of shot along with John Bloodworth, a silkman of London. Mr. Addy can remember when a shot tower still stood at Greenhill.

Norton House had a handsome entrance hall ten yards square with black oak panelling and screen, and the dining and drawing rooms were each ten yards by seven yards. There was an outer court, with cottages for servants and other buildings, and with its park and half-acre of walled garden the estate included more than forty acres. In Rhodes' day there was on the lawn near the front of the house a fine old oak tree that had been struck by lightning.

On May 26, 1868, when Thomas Beard Holy had been living there about thirty years, Norton House was offered for sale by auction in Sheffield, but was withdrawn at £5,000. On June 2, however, it was offered again, and was bought for £10,000 by Charles Cammell, who was already at Norton Hall. He had the old place demolished; the oak, with "Le G 1623" upon it, was bought for Derwent Hall by the Duke of Norfolk, and in place of the old Norton House there arose the Norton House we know to-day, occupied by Mr. Edward

NORTON HOUSE, 1862 (DEMOLISHED 1878).

Montague Earle Welby, Barrister-at-Law, a member of an old Lincolnshire family, and the fourth son of a baronet. He has been tempering justice with mercy since 1874 as Stipendiary Magistrate for Sheffield.

By the kindness of Miss Holy it has been possible to include in this volume a representation of the old house, from a photograph taken in 1862. By that time the west wing had been spoiled, for bay windows had been thrust upon it, but as there had been no meddling with the east wing, it is easy for us to restore the house, in our mind's eye, to its original state ; and we see at once that its style, Renaissance, Jacobean, Palladian, corresponds exactly with the date, 1623, carved upon the interior oak. In that year James the First had only two more years to live; and two years before 1623 Inigo Jones, the student of the Italian Palladio, the exponent in this country of the Renaissance style that reached its culmination a little later in the work of Sir Christopher Wren, had completed the banqueting hall of the Palace of Whitehall. Compare the central door of old Norton House with the features of the London palace and it will seem as though Inigo Jones had been to Norton, and so, adapting a time-honoured exclamation, we may say verily " Italy has crossed the Alps ! " Such a doorway, too, was amongst the last fragments that remained of old Rotherham College.

Those who remember Aldwarke Hall, on the Don, in one of the most beautiful bits of beech and river scenery in England, now despoiled, will be struck with the remarkable resemblance of Norton House to that old home of the Foljambes and the Walkers.

For the representation of the back of Norton House the reader will be grateful to Mr. Welby, who very kindly lent a contemporary pencil sketch of the place. Both photograph and sketch are very precious now that the old place can never be seen again.

CHAPTER IX

OAKES-IN-NORTON

THERE was consonancy in naming the house and the park upon the eastern side of Norton "The Oakes" or "Oakes-in-Norton," for stately examples of the royal tree abound here, and they remind us that this district is famous in the matter of great oak trees, as we may find in Harrison's survey of the manor of Sheffield, Evelyn's *Sylva*, Hunter's *Hallamshire* and other books. Already has reference been made to the Meersbrook oaks, and to those of Rushdale, and we shall see the remains of some very large oaks too when we come to Hazelbarrow, just outside this park ; but for the present we may admire these at "The Oakes," which give such grateful shade upon a summer's day as we recline to listen to the cawing of the rooks that have here one of their numerous Norton strongholds. In winter, too, Norton has nothing to show that is more impressive in its grandeur and solemnity than these dark and mighty trunks and limbs, lifting themselves in the silence of the gloaming between us and the white sheet of frozen snow and the grey sky ; and many a saunterer, many a lingering skater on this lake has witnessed sunsets of remarkable splendour here, for the view is unstopped, mile after mile, towards the west, where the sun sinks behind the lonely Derbyshire upland of gritstone and of heather sending its beams across this lovely park.

At such a time we seem to have here precisely those elements that stir the most profound emotions of men

and women who love rural life and scenery. The park
and surrounding fields covered with snow, the soft yellow
light stealing from the windows of the ancient home there,
under the great oaks, telling of the comforts of the hearth
to those who still loiter outside. Hovers not here the
spirit that Washington Irving sought to embody in *Old
Christmas*? Do we not feel in this place at such a time
what Randolph Caldecott felt when he made his charming
drawings? In Norton, surely, Randolph Caldecott might
have found his delightful backgrounds, Addison might
have written *Sir Roger de Coverley*, Washington Irving
Bracebridge Hall, or Thomas Gray the elegy that will last
as long as the English language.

In James Linacre's notes there are references to changes
that have taken place here, for he says there used to be
two old houses in the Oakes park called Moorhouse
Lands Houses that stood not far from Magathay, near
the pond which is now surrounded by trees, and that
were taken down early in the nineteenth century. In the
principal lake at the Oakes used to be many perch, and
an old poacher was wont to boast in the "Bagshawe
Arms" in the presence of the gamekeeper that he should
have as many as he pleased and they would never catch
him. I am told they never did.

The Georgian, neo-classical appearance of the house is
due to the modifications made by Sir William Bagshawe,
who came into residence there in 1801, during the reign
of George the Third. The hall he remodelled was a
seventeenth-century mansion, and some of the mullioned
windows marking that interesting period in architecture
may be seen still in the stables. It may be that a yet
older house stood upon this site. The terrace was
designed by Chantrey, who gave to Sir William its decora-
tive urns.

Beautiful iron gates are amongst the treasures of the
Oakes. These were made of metal obtained upon the
estate, presumably at Delve's Wood, where traces of
mining operations may be seen still, and the gates are

said to have been cast here too. The larger gates bear
the arms of Bagshawe, impaling the arms of the Simpsons
of Babworth, a charming place near Retford. Richard
Bagshawe married Mary, daughter of John Simpson of
Babworth and Renishaw. The smaller gates have the
initials of Richard Bagshawe.

In our own generation we associate the Oakes entirely
with the Bagshawes, and find it difficult to believe that
any one else ever lived here ; but they were preceded by
the Morewoods and the Gills, families linked with the
Bagshawes in the far-off times.

The known pedigree of the Morewoods goes back
to the reign of Henry the Sixth, when a William Morewood of Bradfield emerged from obscurity as the plaintiff
in a law case concerning land in that parish. Anthony
Morewood of Hemsworth bought Alfreton from Robert
Sutton of Aram in 1629, and some years later conveyed
Hemsworth Hall in Norton to John Urton *alias* Steven
of Lightwood.

In 1615 there were baptised at Norton the Morewood
twins, Rowland and Anthony, the sons of this Anthony
Morewood of Hemsworth. Rowland died unmarried in
1647, and Anthony lived at Hazelbarrow and was Sheriff
of Derbyshire in 1649. He had a daughter Anne who
married the Hon. Alexander Stanhope, son of the Earl
of Chesterfield. She died before she was seventeen years
of age, yet had already borne him a son, though the
child did not survive her. Such early marriages were not
uncommon then. Henry the Seventh was born before
his mother had completed her fourteenth year. Anthony
Morewood, the father of the twins, had a brother John,
from whom came another Rowland Morewood, who
married Mary, the daughter of Leonard Gill of Norton.
Their son John was Sheriff of Derbyshire in 1677 and
received a grant of arms in 1678. His first wife was
Elizabeth, daughter of Edward Gill of Carr House,
Member of Parliament, and commander in the Parliamentary army, who will be mentioned again presently.

The descendants of John's brother Samuel are connected with Norton, and another brother Joseph was of Hemsworth, and dying in 1714 was buried in Norton church. "Here is deposited in good hope of a glorious resurrection ye mortal yet precious part of Joseph Morewood of Hemsworth, gentleman, that earnestly holy, humble, conscientious, and circumspect Christian, whose immortal and most precious part was translated from this world to the far better country on the 28th March . . . ætatis suæ " (the date is obscured by a stone). Samuel's daughter Martha was married to William Scriven of the Herdings in Norton. The Morewoods were connected also with Dronfield and with Alfreton; and in 1657 they built Hallowes Hall, a picturesque old place near Dronfield, placing their initials over the doorway. As we saw in the previous chapter, some have thought they built the old Norton House.

A number of generations of Gills, whose name was pronounced with the " G " soft as in the liquid measure, had been nurtured near the place where now stands the Oakes, though at an anterior period they seem to have come from Sheffield and to have settled at Norton during the reign of Elizabeth. Some think the family is a branch of the same stock as the Gells of Hopton.

Ann Gill of Lightwood married William Blythe of the Norton Lees family, who bought much land at Lightwood from John Parker and others. Ann was buried in 1596-7. Her father was the John Gill of Lightwood who contributed £25 towards the defence of the country against the Spanish Armada; and his son was Edward Gill of Norton, who was the father of Leonard Gill, whom we met at Norton House. Leonard married a daughter of the house of Saunderson of Blythe in Nottinghamshire, and had a son named Edward, who has been mentioned as the father of the Elizabeth Gill who married her cousin John Morewood. Edward married Elizabeth Westby of Carr House. This Edward Gill was an officer in the army of the Parliament, in the struggle with the Stuarts, and was for some of the time Governor of the Sheffield castle. He lived, not at Norton, where he had been baptised, but at Carr House, near Rotherham, which had been the home of his wife before their marriage, for she was the only daughter, and the heiress, of Henry Westby of Carr House, another of Oliver Cromwell's officers, and a descendant of an old family associated with Ravenfield, Firsby, Howarth Hall and Gilthwaite—all places near Rotherham. Carr House still stands upon the Greasbro' road, but now on the verge of some of the most depressing of the Don valley's mean streets. The Gills of Norton and the Saundersons of Blythe seem to have been on very friendly terms, for there is still another marriage between the two families recorded in the Norton Register in 1604 : " William Saundersonne of Blythe, yeoman, and Anna Gill of Norton, daughter of Edward Gill, yeoman, Oct. 29."

To Henry, the second son of the Gill and Westby marriage—" my much honoured friend "—was dedicated part three of *Trading Spiritualised*, by William Bagshawe, the Apostle of the Peak, who wrote, " Can I ever forget the encouragement which my ministry met with in times sufficiently discouraging at the beloved Oaks ? " The tradition is that when the Apostle of the Peak came to the Oakes he preached in what is now the drawing-room.

The eldest brother of Henry Gill of the Oakes was Colonel John Gill of Carr House, Sheriff of Yorkshire in 1692. Henry had a daughter Elizabeth, who married Richard Bagshawe, " that worthy Magistrate " of Goosehill Hall, Castleton, Sheriff of Derbyshire in 1721, and so came the transition here at the Oakes from Gill to Bagshawe.

There is an indenture dated April 25, 1603, between George Gill of Hasilhurst, yeoman, Edward Gill of Norton, yeoman, and Philip Gill, eldest son of Edward Gill, on the one part, and John Urton *alias* Stevyn, of

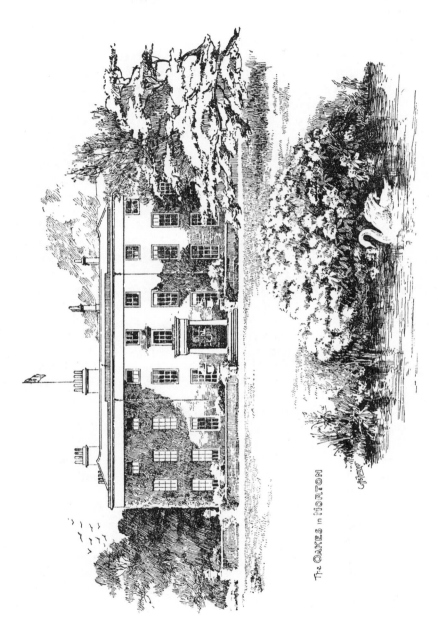

The OAKES in HORTON

169

Lightwood, yeoman, on the other, in which these men agree that all suits between them concerning a right of way claimed by Philip Gill from his dwelling-house unto their close, called Nottrell Place, eastward through a lane called Lightwood Lane *alias* Jacke Lane, shall cease, and that the parties, their and every of their heirs and assigns shall from henceforth continue lovers and friends.

Carrying out the wishes of Leonard Gill as set forth in his will, Edward Gill, his son, granted property for the maintenance of a schoolmaster and for the education of five poor children at Norton.

As a result of the marriage of Richard Bagshawe and Elizabeth Gill three sons of theirs reigned successively here at the Oakes. First came Richard, of Wormhill Hall, Gentleman Usher of the Privy Chamber. Adam one of his sons, who died at the age of seventeen, is described in the Norton Register as a youth of promise. After Richard came William, succeeded by John. Each one of these three, Richard, William and John, died without leaving children, and so they were succeeded by John, the second son of Colonel Samuel Bagshawe of Ford Hall, from whom the Oakes passed to William Chambers Darling. His advent was in this way : when Richard Bagshawe of Castleton married Elizabeth Gill of the Oakes they had eleven children, most of whom died without offspring. Ellen, however, married William Chambers of Hull, a physician, and their daughter Elizabeth married Ralph Darling of Hull, apothecary, by whom she had, with other children, William Chambers Darling, M.D., born in 1771, who inherited the Oakes in 1801. He assumed the name of Bagshawe immediately afterwards and became the Sir William Chambers Bagshawe, M.D., who, marrying Helen, daughter of Nathaniel Ridgard of Gainsborough, was in time the father of eighteen children. It was in 1806 that he was knighted on presenting an address from Derbyshire, of which he was High Sheriff, on the victory of Trafalgar.

During the time that Sir William Bagshawe was at the Oakes the jubilee of George the Third was celebrated " with peculiar hospitality," as the *Sheffield Mercury* has it. " At eleven o'clock Sir William and Lady Bagshawe, with their nine children, followed by a numerous tenantry and their children, accompanied also by the children of the Free School, walked in procession to Church. . . . At the return of the procession to the Oakes, a Royal Salute was given from the terrace by cannon placed there for the occasion ; other vollies were fired by a company of Royal Marines, and there were further discharges from two brass swivels on board a ship on the water in the park." A song composed by Mr. Thomas Wild of Norton Lees was sung by Sir William Bagshawe at a dinner, His Majesty's health was drunk in wine which was as old as the King himself, and in the afternoon the children, who had fed upon furmety, were treated with gingerbread, for which they scrambled. Furmety—Herrick's " all-tempting frumenty "—seems to be neglected now in most homes, a fate surely not according to its merits.

Sir William Bagshawe showed his enthusiasm for this Georgian Jubilee in still another way, for there was baptised during the year of the rejoicings little Georgiana Jubilee, Sir William's daughter. The Bagshawes were connected by marriage with Spencer Perceval, the second son of the Earl of Egmont, Premier during part of the reign of George the Third, and it is said that Perceval offered to make Sir William a baronet, but a consultation between Sir William and his eldest son brought about a decision to decline the title. There were celebrations again at the Oakes upon the passing of the Reform Bill of 1832.

Of Sir William's children, William John, the eldest, was the father of that Francis Westby Bagshawe, born in 1832, whom most local readers will remember at the Oakes, for he died no longer ago than 1896. In 1868 he was appointed High Sheriff of the County, and was also a Deputy Lieutenant. Though he died at the Oakes Mr. Bagshawe lies buried at Wormhill; but through the silent watches of the night before the funeral he lay in a sarcophagus in the Blythe chapel here at Norton amidst surroundings that in life had been very familiar, and full too of the most affecting memories to one who lived often in the past and loved its legacies. The widow of Francis Westby Bagshawe, whose maiden name was Caroline Amelia Cloyne Godwin-Austin, died in 1905 at Cairo, where she had gone in an endeavour to improve her health. Her home before her marriage was at Shalford House, near Guildford. Her sister, Augusta Victoria, married Mr. William Bryan Lushington, second son of the Right Hon. Stephen Lushington, LL.D.

Francis Westby Bagshawe left Trinity College, Cambridge, as Master of Arts, and he was a musician and interested too in antiquarian matters. It was while he was examining Mr. Bagshawe's muniments that Mr. John Pym Yeatman found reference in a document of the time of Queen Elizabeth to very ancient forest rolls of the Peak of Derbyshire, and following this clue was at last rewarded with the discovery of these valuable rolls at the Record Office in London.

Although Francis Westby Bagshawe inherited the Oakes from William John Bagshawe, his father, he was not the eldest son. The heir was William Leonard Gill Bagshawe, who met with a violent and tragic death under circumstances which caused quite a sensation at the time. In his youth Bagshawe was a great favourite at Eton, where his victories on the river were many and brilliant, but were withal borne with an engaging modesty. " Go it, Bags ! " rang along the banks whenever he was involved in a contest. In 1847, in the first heat for the Sculls, Bagshawe's boat sank. He clung to it, swam ashore with it, bailed out the water, and at last coolly set out after the disappearing competitors, reaching the winning post in time to secure a place in the final. When the final came he carried off the prize. At Cambridge too he was counted the best oarsman on the Cam, and it happens that we get a vivid picture of Bagshawe at Cambridge in an article entitled *Memories of Undergraduate-Life at Trinity Forty Years Ago*, by J.S.P., in *Temple Bar*, for May 1887. The writer says " the last story I shall tell is a very sad one of one of the finest young fellows who ever came up to a University. W. L. G. Bagshaw, of Wormhill and the Oakes, Derbyshire, came up a ready-made oar from Eton in my last Term, October 1847. As he was a Freshman, and unknown, he easily got any odds he liked against himself for the Colquhoun sculls, which he won, and also bets to the tune of three hundred pounds. This was rather ' steep,' and was so much talked about that his Tutor most judiciously thought it prudent to get him out of the way—especially as he had kept his Term. So one morning he sent for him, and said : ' Mr. Bagshawe, there's your " Exeat." I think on the whole you had better go down. I dare say you understand why.'

" ' Thank you, sir,' said poor ' Bags,' ' that will suit me all round. I have won the sculls, got my three hundred pounds paid, and now I'll go home and get some hunting.'

" Besides winning the sculls, he had also rowed No. 6 (weight 11 st. 4 lbs.) in the University crew. . . . Poor Bagshaw ! Some little time afterwards, having heard that poachers had planned a raid upon his salmon [J.S.P. should have written trout], he got a body of watchers together and went with them himself in command. A fearful fight took place by the river-side, and in the middle of it Bagshaw was struck down by a blow from behind, fell into the river-bed, and was stamped to pieces by the heavy boots of the ruffians. Such was this fine fellow's tragic and untimely end."

This affray with the poachers to which J.S.P. has alluded was an incident discussed with much animation at the time. Bagshawe, intensely interested in sport, and in the full tide of life, enjoying his pleasures with all the zest of youth, for he was not yet twenty-six years of age, was preserving the fish in the Wye, belonging to Mr. Henry Marwood Greaves of Ford Hall, near his home at Wormhill, between Tideswell and Buxton. He was much annoyed by the depredations of poachers who traversed the stream in the night with spears, impaling the trout, and hour after hour he used to watch the river with gamekeepers and friends when most people were in their beds.

On the night of July 19, 1854, soon after ten o'clock, he left Wormhill Hall with Sir Henry St. John Halford, his brother-in-law, of Wistow Hall, Leicestershire, for the purpose of watching the river. They had sticks with them, an old bull-dog and a life-preserver, but no fire-arms ; and they came to the river at Raven's Torr. A little later Captain Partridge, Mr. Bagshawe's cousin, and a gamekeeper, Jarvis Kaye, left the hall and went to the river at the toll-gate at Miller's Dale.

While Mr. Bagshawe was waiting at Raven's Torr Kaye came to him with a message from Captain Partridge that poachers were coming up the river with lanterns, spearing the trout, whereupon Mr. Bagshawe and Sir Henry Halford accompanied Kaye to the toll-gate, at which they found Captain Partridge and the keeper of the gate. Small as was the party the ardent Bagshawe was eager for the fray, and proposed immediate attack, but was persuaded to wait for assistance. Arthur Duke Coleridge says that " from my experience of Bagshawe's character, I think it likely enough that he was in high spirits at the prospect of a row ; I also think that he would not have hesitated to initiate the fray." How-ever, he consented to run back to Wormhill, mustered tenants and others, eight in all, and with these went back to the river, though not to the place where Captain Partridge and the others were. Without waiting for these he ordered three of his party to cross to the south bank, and he and the remaining four remained upon the north bank. Here the sides of the river both north

and south are precipitous; there is very little space
between the edge of the water and the foot of the
limestone cliffs, and upon this narrow place, in the
gloom of the defile, the watchers lay.

Gradually the poachers drew nearer and nearer, the
lights from the lanterns gleaming, the spears darting
from time to time into the water. When they were
within fifteen yards Mr. Bagshawe rose and cried " Go
into them." Kaye let loose the old bull-dog, and the
attack began, the poachers discharging two guns. Mr.
Bagshawe took off his coat, and having selected one of the
men who had a lantern, and who is supposed to have
been James Walton, went ahead of his men straight at
him. The fight was short and sharp, and precisely what
happened is not known, for it was a struggle in the dark,
all were engaged, and there were no unoccupied spectators
to describe a combat in which it is not certain that some
of the combatants did not hit their friends as well as
their foes.

Milner, another poacher, seemed to be drunk, and,
approaching one of the hall party, he lifted his stick, saying
" Hey up for the best man," but was himself stricken to
the earth. It was said at a later stage Kaye was engaged
with Milner when he heard his master call for assistance.
He could not get away just then, but when he had
succeeded in knocking " Big Ben " down he went to Mr.
Bagshawe, whom he found struggling with a poacher
in the river. He struck the poacher upon his head,
which caused him to release Mr. Bagshawe, and then
he returned to Milner. John Booth, one of Mr. Bagshawe's servants, saw a poacher kneeling upon his master
in the river. When Sir Henry Halford arrived the
combatants had returned from blows to words again, and
thus when Captain Partridge seized Milner, saying " You
are one of those poaching scoundrels ! " Milner replied
merely " You need not hold me; I have had enough."
One of the party said " It's Big Ben," and Kaye coming
up just then said " It's all right, but I fear my master is

badly hurt." Mr. Bagshawe himself, joining the party, said " We have had a terrible business ; they have nearly killed me ; I think they have done for me. Three big brutes got me down in the river and knelt on me. I think one of them must be dead in the river." He asked to be supported, but added with regard to Taylor and Milner, two of the poachers, " Mind, don't let them go." Captain Partridge had handcuffs with him, and was proceeding to put them on the captured men when Milner showed resistance, saying " I will die first ; I am too good blood for that." The two poachers were however secured.

Mr. Bagshawe was assisted towards the hall by his friends, but his head had been battered severely, the base of his skull terribly fractured, apparently with a gunstock, found broken after the fight. His liver also had been ruptured. Suddenly he became faint, his head fell forward, and he was carried home insensible. He never spoke again, and before noon upon the following day was dead.

Turner, one of the gang, was arrested in an upper chamber of a house at Tideswell, where he was discovered lying under a bed without shoes or coat and with a cut upon his head. Two of the others, Walton and Dawson, were apprehended at the bridge at Baslow, and started when they were told that Mr. Bagshawe was dead. At the Bakewell lock-up, however, they said they knew nothing of the affray, though wounds upon their heads seemed to tell another tale.

The result of this lamentable encounter was that seven poachers were charged at the Derby Assizes of July 29, 1854, before Mr. Justice Maule and a jury, with having wilfully murdered Mr. Bagshawe. They were Benjamin Milner, known as " Big Ben," 33 years of age; James Walton, 40; John Turner, 38 ; William Taylor, 50 ; William Dawson, 40 ; Thomas Wilson, 36 ; and Thomas Dodds, 28. A formidable set of men they looked as they stood in the dock to await the result of the trial.

Contrary to all expectations, they were acquitted. It was held that if Mr. Bagshawe had intended to have the men arrested and taken before a magistrate he would have been acting in accordance with the law ; but in this case he was taking the law into his own hands, and went forth to punish the men himself, and not only to apprehend them. Thus the men were not merely resisting apprehension ; they were defending themselves from a savage attack. Moreover, even if it were murder, they must select the murderers and prove precisely who dealt the fatal blows ; they could not involve men who clearly never came into contact with the man who was murdered.

The poachers marched in a triumphal procession with their friends up the Tideswell street, a result which excited bitter resentment amongst neighbouring owners of estates, and amongst Mr. Bagshawe's numerous friends. It was known that the judge, a capable, cynical, caustic and formidable opponent—an "awkward customer" Coleridge calls him—was averse to the game laws, and some who heard his charge to the jury said it was more like the speech of a counsel for the defence. They complained moreover that he never told the jurors what it was manifestly his duty to tell them, that if they did not think the evidence strong enough for a conviction for murder they could convict of manslaughter or of armed night poaching, or even of common poaching Commenting upon this trial in his *Eton in the Forties*, Arthur Duke Coleridge, the clerk of arraigns, who says that Maule was "a special favourite with poachers," has written : " I have often talked with Midland Circuit men who were present at the trial. There was but one opinion among the experts, and this was that the evidence, if not strong enough to warrant the conviction of one and all the prisoners on the capital charge, was quite sufficient to sustain a verdict of manslaughter, and that of a very aggravated kind. From first to last the Judge— a powerful and determined one—was against the prosecution ; it was plain that he meant the accused to escape, and they were acquitted. I think it was Maule's last appearance on any Circuit ; he certainly never appeared again upon ours. His name in Derbyshire *non redolet sed olet*. With all his scorn of popularity-hunting, I doubt if he would have faced another meeting with the gentlemen and magistrates of Bagshawe's indignant county . . . with whom and their descendants the bare mention of Maule's name is to this day 'maranatha.' No one has ever attempted to palliate the Judge's conduct in my hearing."

Many Norton people will remember Jarvis Kaye in later years as coachman to the Cockaynes of Norton Lees. His son, another Jarvis Kaye, died at Norton in the spring of 1910. He was a sculptor, and Mr. Herbert Rhodes, of the Norton Post Office, has a medallion portrait of Chantrey which he executed.

Headstrong no doubt was William Leonard Gill Bagshawe ; but the Empire perchance would have been able to make better use of such delight in adventure, such spirit, such daring and strength, had he lived ; perhaps would have found him foemen more worthy of his steel than poachers, a mightier cause than the cultivation and protection of trout.

Mr. Francis Westby Bagshawe, who now, upon the death of his elder brother, inherited the Oakes, left two daughters, Beatrice Muriel Westby and Gladys Godwin de la Hall. The elder daughter succeeded to the estates at Norton and at Wormhill, and in 1907 was married to Mr. Henry Bradshaw-Isherwood, the elder son of Mr. Bradshaw-Isherwood of Marple Hall in Cheshire, one mile and a half from the Derbyshire border, and he has since taken the name of Bagshawe.

The Bagshawe family is one of the very oldest in Derbyshire, or in the country. In the earliest annals of the royal forest of the Peak they appear in office and seated at Bagshawe. William Bagshawe, the Apostle of the Peak, lived a life resembling that of John Wesley, and in his diary there is a reference to " the beloved

The Oakes
in Norton

179

Oaks," in association with the name of the Rev. Nathaniel
Baxter of Attercliffe, who lived in or near Sheffield, but
who preached at Norton when the Gills lived there.
A well-authenticated tradition has been mentioned already
that Bagshawe himself preached at the Oakes.

Samuel Bagshawe, the second son of the Apostle of the
Peak, and the only son who survived, married the granddaughter of Sarah Westby of Ravenfield Park.

Of William Bagshawe, the eldest son of Samuel, there
will be more to say when we reach Hazelbarrow Hall in
Norton, for he married Mary Wingfield of that place.
Septimus Bagshawe, a younger brother of William, went
to Jamaica, where he held an appointment from the
King, and seems to have fallen into evil ways and upon
evil times before he died, when and where is not known.

Colonel Bagshawe of Ford Hall, Member of Parliament,
was second in command for some time in the East Indies.
At the siege of L'Orient in France he lost a leg. He
lost an eye in India, where he lost also his health, and,
dying in 1762, was buried, like so many other Bagshawes,
in the chancel of the church at Chapel-en-le-Frith. He
had visited the Oakes sometimes and had fallen in love
with his second cousin there, Elizabeth Bagshawe. They
corresponded for years, but nothing came of this letter-
writing, and Elizabeth died unmarried. Colonel Bagshawe was engaged in a disastrous Chancery suit with
Robert Newton of Norton House.

Samuel, Colonel Bagshawe's heir, was a charming boy,
bright and vivacious ; but he became a great spendthrift,
a gambler, an extravagant dandy, and was engaged in
ruinous lawsuits. His younger brother, John, was a
barrister-at-law, and needed all his legal knowledge, for
he was involved in nineteen lawsuits, and won all but
one. He was only four years of age at his father's death,
and was brought up by his relations here at the Oakes.
As we have seen already, he inherited the Oakes upon
the death, without children, of the three brothers Richard,
William and John.

He had inherited a pack of hounds with which he seldom hunted himself, but Mr. Read of Norton House told Mr. Greaves Bagshawe that he remembered them perfectly, and that they went out with two whips who, as well as the huntsmen, were excellently mounted and in handsome liveries. In those days there were kennels not only at the Oakes, where hounds had been kept for more than sixty years, but also at Wormhill and Castleton. At Broomfield Wood, upon the Oakes estate, is a burial ground where bygone horses and hounds have been interred. Asline Ward has recorded that in the year 1804 William Bagshawe's hounds followed a fox into the village of Attercliffe, and into the yard of a public house. Reynard could not be found, and at last the huntsmen withdrew. Next morning when the servant opened the door the fox stole from under the copper and bolted. John Bagshawe once sold a horse to Mr. Robert Gregge-Hopwood, of Hopwood, and then told him he was very venturesome in buying a hunter without making inquiries, to which Mr. Hopwood replied that he had " an innate idea that any horse bred by a Bagshawe must be good." As the groom who took this horse, Herod, to its new home at Hopwood was riding back to the Oakes, and had reached a lonely part of the road, between Disley and Whaley, about five o'clock in the afternoon of a November day, he was attacked by a mounted highwayman who had first passed him with his head down as though he were looking if his horse were lame. Then turning suddenly, " he got me by the bosom," said the groom, demanding " my watch and money. I told him I had not any, but before I could give him much answer, I struck him with the heavy end of my whip in the face, and got clear off without any loss, only my cravat a little torn, but was afterwards very ill frightened." No doubt the groom was glad when he saw the familiar landmarks that told him he was reaching the Oakes at Norton again.

John died unmarried at Staines, at the Bush Inn, on his way from London into Devonshire, on August 21,

1801, and he lies buried at Staines, according to his own desire, though his family thought his body ought to come to Norton.

William Bagshawe, another brother of the spendthrift, was educated partly at Norton. He entered the Church and became curate at Norton and afterwards vicar of various parishes. In his youth he lived with his guardians at the Oakes, and in one of his letters from Manchester Grammar School, written in 1778 to his brother John, he mentions Norton: " . . . I went to Mr. Shore's [Samuel, who married Urith Offley] on the Saturday after you left, a fishing. We caught nothing, but Sam Shore [eldest son of the Samuel just mentioned] had hold of a pike. There was a whole drove of us ; Sir Francis Barnard [who married Amelia, daughter of Stephen Offley] and his two daughters. I was half smitten with the beauty of Miss Julia. Bohun [Shore] and I were on the best of terms."

He mentions the Oakes several times in his diary. At the end of December 1791 the place was almost cut off from the rest of Derbyshire by the amount of snow on East Moor. Upon another day he could not go to Sheffield because of the snow. At Ford Hall he prepared a slope for strawberries, and sent to the Oakes for roots. Then we see him hunting with Mr. Shore near Ridgeway, dining with the Shores at Meersbrook and noting that " political passion " is " less violent." On March 27, 1793, he " walked with my brother to the boring engine." This was at work at the time on Greenhill Moor, where it was hoped to find coal. On September 14 he went from the Oakes to see the first stone of the Sheffield General Infirmary laid.

He married the daughter of Samuel Foxlowe of Staveley Hall, the only sister of General (Foxlowe) Murray of Banner Cross, and she inherited the General's estates. Mr. Bagshawe's daughter married Henry Marwood Greaves of Hesley Hall in Nottinghamshire—hence the Greaves Bagshawes of our own day.

William Bagshawe wrote a book on *Man : his Motives, Their Rise, Operations, Position and Results,* which was published in two volumes in 1833 after having been seen through the press by James Montgomery. "I perceive from the newspaper," says Montgomery to John Holland, "that my old friend, the Rev. William Bagshawe, of Banner Cross, died on Friday ; he was the last of those kind individuals who used to send me a hamper of game in the season ; and this he has done every year since 1833, when I revised his work *On Man.*"

Mr. Bagshawe laid the foundation stone of Fulwood church in 1837, and was asked to perform a similar ceremony for Heeley church on November 4, 1846, but deputed this office to his son-in-law, Henry Marwood Greaves. The opening of Heeley church was made memorable by Vicar Jones' sermon, for he urged that Adam ate of the apple that he might share the fate of Eve, gallantly preferring any consequences to separation from his beloved. Mr. Jones, a shy, retiring man, lived on well into our own days, growing so old in his work that he began to read the baptism service upon couples who presented themselves to be married.

There are many memorials of the Gills and Bagshawes in the church at Norton, and one in memory of a John Bagshawe who belonged to the Great Hucklow branch of this family and who died in 1721 was placed in the Upper Chapel in Sheffield displaying the arms of the Bagshawes. At the Oakes are interesting Gill, Westby and Bagshawe portraits.

Even in the briefest sketch of the history of the people whose name is associated with the Oakes at Norton, and this is but a short account of the families, it would be unpardonable to make no allusion to Edward Bagshaw, a member of that branch of the Bagshawes that had strayed away into Northamptonshire.

Edward Bagshaw became Vicar of Castleton in 1723, and it happens that he used a ledger partly as an account book and partly as a diary between the years 1715 and

1750. Dr. Cox found this book in the library of Mr. Bateman at Middleton by Youlgreave, and edited it for the *Proceedings of the Derbyshire Archæological and Natural History Society* (Volume II, 1880, page 74). He pointed out that we gain from this book a considerable insight into the life of a country parson of the eighteenth century, living in a retired and bleak valley.

Edward Bagshaw came to the Oakes sometimes. On August 31, 1743, the entry is " My son and I dined at Oaks." On September 14, " I went to Oaks, near Norton, in Derbyshire, and took my eldest son along with me." On September 25, " I preached at Norton church, morning and afternoon."

Dr. Cox refers happily to the likeness between the Vicar of Castleton and Goldsmith's *Vicar of Wakefield*, and remarks that " in skilful hands this diary would afford abundant material for a pastoral tale. The Vicar, of family and fortune, deluded by an unworthy London friend into foolish investments until all his patrimony has vanished—his struggles with poverty—his readiness to join in a meal with any of his neighbours—his contracting to be shaved by the village cobbler—the little presents of tea, milk, butter, and hogs' puddings from his parishioners and neighbours—the kindly benefactor who puts his lads into business—the half-crowns he is not too proud to borrow—the eldest son settling down in a draper's shop in the city—the lad's shirts sent home from London to be made—the return of the shirts, with a present to the lad's master, of four tongues and four pots of butter—the daughters sent out as governesses or companions—their illness—the public thanksgiving in the Church—the Vicar's pious thankfulness for his wife's life being preserved when fetching water from the brook —his indulgence in three-halfpence worth of snuff and two-penny worth of tobacco when the lead tithes suddenly increased his income—his enjoyment of the wakes and the children's ' merry-nights '—his patronising the talents of the village caster of accounts—his letting a room in the vicarage as a dancing academy—his humble thankfulness for small gifts from his wealthy relatives—these and a score more of familiar incidents, but all telling a certain tale of pathetic struggle, coupled with Christian courage and cheerfulness, make Edward Bagshaw a very real and a very charming character."

Requiescat in pace says Dr. Cox, and we can all very sincerely echo his words, for through this old ledger we have come to love him and his.

CHAPTER X

HAZELBARROW HALL

THE farmhouse at Hazelbarrow, from behind its three
wind-blown pines, looks down Dowie Lumb towards
Ridgeway ; but in the mind's eye of the student of local
history this farmhouse dissolves and there stands in its
place an ancient hall—"a good old mansion" Hunter
calls it—built on three sides of a square with the pleasing
accessories of grey time-worn gables, dripstones, mullioned
windows, leaded diamond-shaped panes, and substantial
stone chimneys, a place of great enchantment whether its
ample roofs and gardens were under a canopy of snow,
whether the moon shone upon it or whether the mid-
summer sun drawing the fragrance from the stocks and
mignonette was throwing its front into sharp contrast
with the profound shade of its deep recess where the two-
storeyed bay-window stood crowned by its little gable,
meet place for association with the romance of bonnie
Mary Wingfield.

Apparently she was born here, though that is assumed,
for it is not stated in the memorandum which her father
John Wingfield wrote on February 20, 1681–2 : "being
Monday, about eleven o'clock at night" ; but the
register shows that she was baptised at Norton on the
27th of the same month, so that it is almost certain that
she was born in the old Hall of Hazelbarrow.

When the time for Mary's schooling came she was
sent to Mrs. Frankland's establishment near Manchester.
She had a good fortune, considerable personal attractions,

and with her sisters was entitled to quarter the arms of
Plantagenet through the marriage of their ancestor, Sir
Robert Wingfield, with Elizabeth, daughter and co-
heiress of Sir Robert Goushill, a descendant of Lady
Alice Plantagenet, sister and heiress of John, last Earl of
Warren and Surrey. Thus when she left school it was
natural that she should have many .suitors, and she

Old Doorway
and Window
Hazelbarrow

was pressed with many importunities to marry Mr.
Gervas Nevile, of Chevet Park and of Holbeck in Yorkshire, brother of Cavendish Nevile, Vicar of Norton ; but
neither she nor her father could be satisfied that he was
sufficiently religious, and so she, with her distinctly devout
temperament, declined to become his wife.

During this period there was coming to the Oakes
from time to time, to visit his kinsfolk there, that
William Bagshawe of Ford Hall who was born in 1686.
It was not likely that he could come so near to Hazel-

barrow Hall without catching glimpses of bonnie Mary at church, or in other places, and during the winter of 1726–7, fired by a growing affection for her charms and high character, he began to reveal his love.

At this stage it is said that Mr. Wingfield, the prudent father, sent a confidential friend or servant to view the Ford estate, and was so well pleased with the report which he received of it that at once he gave consent to his daughter's engagement. This sending of the friend to spy out the nakedness or plenty of the land at Ford is a curious proceeding, and seems to indicate a lack of communication between the parts of Derbyshire in those days, and no great familiarity between the Wingfields and the Bagshawes. We should expect that John Wingfield would have known many years before of the wealth of the Bagshawes, especially as he had some of the family for very near neighbours; but, like Moses, who sent spies from the wilderness of Paran to view Canaan to see "what the land is, whether it be fat or lean, whether there be wood therein or not," John Wingfield sent emissaries from Hazelbarrow to Ford Hall before he would consent to let his daughter go.

Mary now went to London upon a visit, and while she was there made some of the purchases necessary for her trousseau, and before the end of July the family lawyers were busy arranging the marriage settlements. We are told that Mary was all constancy and meekness, and in one of her letters she wrote of herself, "You may depend upon it that you will find Atlante firm and unmovable as a rock," and when Bagshawe fell ill she wrote in a note that will remind the reader of Dorothy Osborne's letters that "the great trouble I have been in ever since I received your first letter is not easy to imagine, sometimes hoping your disorder would go off, then again fearing its increasing. . . . And this day when Mrs. Sleigh brought me your letter into my room, it was some time before I was able to read it. . . . I am very sorry for the continuance of your indisposition, and do wish and pray for the removal of that and every other uneasiness, if God sees it good, or that He will please to support you, and grant that you may find that as your day is, so your strength shall be. . . . You may depend upon it I shall not be unmindful of my best of friends at the time you mention. God grant that both yours and my troubles may be sanctified to us, and that we may be restrained from fretting ourselves to do evil ; and may we learn obedience by what we suffer, and be better in our spiritual concerns for these rubs and disappointments in the things of the world ; but we should take care that we do not bring troubles upon ourselves, as I really fear both you and I do. . . . I return you a thousand thanks for all the testifications and repeated assurances of your great respect, which I should be the worst of creatures did I not make you a suitable return for. . . . I thank you for the present you are so kind as to send us. . . . My prayer is, and shall be, for the health and prosperity both of your soul and body ; and for a comfortable meeting with her who is yours for ever, M. WINGFIELD."

An entry of her own in a pocket-book recorded that Mary "was married October ye 26, 1727, and came to Ford that day month after, being Thursday." The marriage was at Whittington and not at Norton, possibly because she had rejected the addresses of the vicar's brother.

In her new home Mrs. Bagshawe was kind to the poor, is said to have been more considerate with beggars than was wise, and had such skill in housekeeping that Colonel Bagshawe once wrote, " I think I can say, without flattery or compliment (notwithstanding that the Irish ladies pretend to great elegance), I have not seen so accomplished a housewife as my Aunt Bagshawe in all Ireland."

She paid occasional visits to London, to Norton and to other places, chiefly when her relations were in trouble and so needed her kindness, and in 1732 her sister,

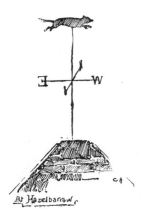

At Hazelbarrow

Miss Ann Wingfield, "a pious Christian lady," went from Hazelbarrow to Ford Hall, and remained there until a short time before she died. Mrs. Bagshawe herself was sincerely religious, and one form her interest in theology and morals took was to make copious notes of the many sermons to which she listened.

It happened, however, that her life was not destined to pass thus peacefully in housekeeping, visits to friends, listening to sermons and such pursuits, for she lived in the stirring days of the '45, and in the long list of Derbyshire subscribers for the fighting of the Pretender are William Bagshawe of Ford, £50 ; Richard Bagshawe of the Oakes, £50 ; Richard Bagshawe, junior, Wormhill, £20 ; William Bagshawe, Castleton, £20 ; Robert Newton, £100, and Joseph Offley of Norton, £100.

Time and the romancers have invested the rising in favour of the Young Pretender with a halo of sentiment, and have given many people a sneaking sympathy with the losing side. The Duke of Cumberland to most is what his contemporaries and Scott called him — a butcher ; but those who occupied these old halls in Derbyshire in 1745, and stood in peril of being despoiled of all they had, may be forgiven for having taken an opposite view of the incident. To them Cumberland came not as a butcher, but as a heaven-sent deliverer.

Upon the approach of the Scottish army there was a terrible scare. Many Lancashire people fled over the heather and gritstone of the wild Pennines, and so Chapel-en-le-Frith, Sheffield and other places upon the eastern side of the mountains were full of excited refugees.

Great anxiety prevailed at Ford Hall, and Mrs. Bagshawe urged her husband to ride with her over the hills to Norton House, then owned by Robert Newton, her nephew, the incoming Sheriff of the county, our old friend of the Offley case.

Mr. Bright of Banner Cross, their kinsman, had removed already to a farmhouse on his property at Scarcliffe, near Bolsover, with his grandchildren—one of whom married Lord John Murray—but William Bagshawe was a deputy lieutenant, and wishing to continue as long as possible at his post replied, " Not until the rebels appear within sight of the house." All the same, he caused some of his horses to be kept saddled and bridled, by night as well as by day, so that if retreat became necessary it might begin without delay, and so the horses remained during two weeks of great anxiety.

How critical was the time is shown by the distress of Mrs. Bagshawe concerning the welfare of her nephews should she lose her life in the impending dangers. Writing a hurried note for her husband on November 25, 1745, she said : " I desire of you, my dear Mr. Bagshawe, that you will please to fulfil my wishes in letting my three nephews have each a thousand pounds at your decease, you enjoying the interest of it for your life. If I live to see these troubles over, I hope to make a will regularly ; if not, I depend on you to do it. . . . To nephew Newton one thousand, to nephew Shawe one thousand and to nephew Wildman one thousand pounds."

However, she did live to see these troubles over. Her mother had died when Mary was young, but her father had lived on till 1732 when he was eighty-one years of age, and was buried at Norton. He gave £200 to be laid out in land, the interest to be given to Norton poor, one year in clothes and the next in money on Michaelmas Day.

The unequal distribution of his property, of which Mary's sister Margaret, the widow of the elder Robert Newton, obtained the largest share, does not seem to have disquieted Mrs. Bagshawe, although it occasioned many heartburnings in the family, and involved all the children in a Chancery suit. It was urged that when John Wingfield was on his deathbed Margaret had pressed him to leave Norton House and the bulk of his property to her, to the deprivation of his other daughters, and for this reason Margaret was very unpopular. Referring evidently to Mr. Wingfield's will, Mr. Bagshawe observed to an old dependent and friend, "John, I had a cartload of money with my wife ; but I expected to have had two." Mrs. Bagshawe, who had no children, died at Ford Hall in 1754, and was buried in the chancel of the church of Chapel-en-le-Frith. There can be no doubt that in her death the county lost a woman of sweetest disposition, untiring industry and the highest integrity. It would be superfluous to say more, for her description is contained in the last chapter of the *Book of Proverbs*.

A portrait of Mrs. Bagshawe remained at Ford Hall until spendthrift Samuel sold it. Fortunately it was restored by a descendant of the purchaser before its identity had been lost, and it used to hang at Banner Cross. It is now amongst the treasures of Mr. W. H. Greaves Bagshawe, and so has gone home to Ford Hall again. There, too, is a portrait of Mrs. Bagshawe's sister Margaret.

Mary's husband, William Bagshawe, was, like the Wingfields, Offleys, Shores and Newtons, a Presbyterian, and hated the religion of the Catholics. In politics he was a Whig, opposed, as we have seen, to the Stuarts, and loyal to the house of Brunswick. Locally he was much attached to the Cavendish family, considering that the nation owed much to this house for its invitation to the Prince of Orange to come to Britain, and for its vigorous opposition to the two Pretenders. When the county was in the throes of a hotly contested Parliamentary struggle in 1734, Mr. Bagshawe rode into Derby with eight hundred followers to vote for Lord Charles Cavendish.

Chivalry is not dead, and thus Mary Wingfield has

Old Oak at Hazelbarrow

193

13

had first place in this chapter ; but the Wingfields were not the first to inhabit Hazelbarrow Hall. In a most interesting article illustrated by reproductions of drawings and of photographs taken by the Vicar of Norton, the Rev. G. W. Hall, Mr. Sidney O. Addy has shown, by means of valuable transcripts of the documents executed between the Chaworths and the De Haselbarrows, that " in the thirteenth century a family called De Haselbarrow lived in Norton, taking their name from the estate in that village on which they resided." He adds that a little to the south of the house is a wood which still abounds with hazels, and he draws the inference that here is the very *hæsel-bearo*, or hazel-grove, from which the name of the place, and then the name of the family, has been derived.

In the fourteenth century there are references to Walter Moriz, or Mores, of Boston in Lincolnshire, in connection with this estate, which he had received from the De Haselbarows, and then it passed by purchase to Robert de Selioke, the representative of a Dronfield family. The name means blessed oak, or holy oak, and there is a Selloak Spring Wood not far away, in Cold Aston. It is clear that there was a place bearing the name of Selioke, for in the Foljambe archives is a transfer of land " in Sellyok and Le Halughys " to Robert de Sellyok, in 1342, and the deed was drawn at Halughes, possibly the modern Hallowes. Some documents which Mr. Addy transcribes give the name De Sellyoke, and in 1346, Del Sellyoke. Birmingham readers will recall their own Selly Oak, and if they know anything of Teutonic mythology will connect the place with the sacred oak of our ancestors. Holyoak occurs in Worcester, near Redditch, and in Leicestershire, near Uppingham. Three oak leaves appear upon the coat-of-arms of the Seliokes, and it may be no more than a coincidence, but here they are, close to Hazelbarrow Hall, the oldest oaks that this district can show. In an article on *The Study of Field Names* in *Macmillan's Magazine*, for April 1889,

Mr. Addy wrote that he has seen the oak leaves on the seals upon Selioke deeds as far back as the fifteenth century.

The Seliokes seem to have been engaged in iron manufacture, and it may be that their purchase of this estate was prompted by their industry. There are indications of this in the fact that the Selioke documents with regard to land here include the right of ingress and egress "as well below as above the ground," showing that minerals were not left out of the reckoning. Coal Pit Wood stands less than half a mile south of Hazelbarrow, there are remains of old coal or iron workings, the coal comes near the surface here, and it need not be forgotten that the lane which conducted us to Hazelbarrow from Norton past Jordanthorpe is called Cinderhill Lane. Already have we seen that the iron gates of the Oakes were made of Norton metal, and Mr. William Fielding, in some draining operations, had to deal with an iron ochre spring near Delves Wood.

In connection with mining Hazelbarrow seems to have drawn the attention of eminent scientists in the seventeenth century, and is touched upon in Plot's work on Staffordshire. John Ray, in his treatise upon the Deluge, says "there is a Sort of Damp which some call a Fire-Damp or Fulminating-Damp, of which I had the first Notice from my honoured Friend *Francis Jessop*, Esq ; *An* 1668. . . . He instances in three Persons that had been hurt by it ; one in the Coal-Mines in *Hasleberg* Hills, who had his Arms and Legs broken, and his Body strangely distorted by it." Joseph Hunter evidently identified this as the Norton Hazelbarrow, as an entry in one of his note-books shows.

The Francis Jessop mentioned here lived at Broom Hall, Sheffield. He was a Fellow of the Royal Society, and in the Proceedings of that society are references to " that Inquisitive and Learn'd Gentleman Mr. Jessop," " the Ingenious Mr. Jessop of Broomhal in York-shire." In 1675 Jessop wrote about " damp " in pits, recording that "a Fellow, they commonly call *Dobby Leech*, is at this day a sad example of the force of one of those blasts in *Hasleberg-hills*, having his arms and legs broken, and his body strangely distorted."

Referring to the Garden Warbler in *Among the Birds in Northern Shires*, Charles Dixon writes that "the bird was first described from an example obtained near Sheffield —possibly in the immediate neighbourhood of Broom Hall—and sent by Francis Jessop to Willughby, the co-worker with Ray nearly a century and a half ago, the latter naturalist describing it in his *Ornithologia*."

For ten generations the Seliokes were here. One of the Seliokes married Margaret, daughter of John Parker of Norton Lees ; another of the family was lord of the manor of Dronfield. A John Selioke married Dorothy Chaworth, and, when she died, Elizabeth Foljambe. In 1546 the Seliokes had some transactions with the Dynhams concerning half of the manor of Norton and other land hereabouts. Some of the Dronfield Seliokes were apprenticed in Sheffield as cutlers; a William Selioke was churchwarden at Norton in 1664 ; William Blythe of Birchett, son of Richard, married one of the Seliokes ; there is a deed in the county archives at Derby which shows that a William Selyocke in 1587 mortgaged "Hasilborowe" to William Dyckenson of Sheffield. Amongst the documents which connect the Seliokes with Norton is one at the Vicarage, and this is given in Mr. Addy's *Memorials of Beauchief*. It states that "in the fourth year of Henry the Fourth on the feast of Palm branches, John Baret de Lyghtwode, and Alice his wife, grant to John de Lyghtwode some land, park, and wood in Southfeld, which had been given them by William Seliok, together with a right of way across the land of Lightwood, as far as Notel Place." In a deed of 1603 this is called Nottrell Place. Another deed consists of an award belonging to 1543 of Sir John Chaworth and Sir Phillip Draycot, knights, arbitrators to settle disputes between John Selioke of Hesilbarowe and

SELIOKE MEMORIAL, NORTON CHURCH.

197

John Parker of Norton Lees, respecting tenements at Gleadless and " that called Jurdanthorpe in the lordship of Norton Lees." In 1546 there was a lease from John Selyoke of Haselborough, esq., to James Castlyn, citizen and mercer of London, of three houses in Hemsworth.

So in one way or another their names appear in deeds and other records and in the Registers of Norton until at length their Norton estates go to other owners and the Seliokes pass away to other parts of the country. Alderman John Selioke was Mayor of St. Albans in 1684, and died in 1709, and there the record of the family seems to end.

In the church here at Norton is a most interesting Selioke memorial. Robert Newton of Norton House told Dr. Pegge that " he once saw under the Haselbarow seat two or three of the Seliokes, in effigy at full length, but they are all now boarded up." Hunter has written that a tomb of a Selioke under a pew was broken up during some alterations ; Mr James Linacre has a note, derived from the Vicarage manuscripts, that when the church was repewed in 1819–20 this stone with its Selioke figures was found. He says the frost began to affect them, and so they were covered again. In 1882, however, during Street's restoration, there was revealed once more the slab of alabaster in which representations of two of the Seliokes had been incised, and though the inscription was imperfect Mr. Addy was able to make out that the figure of the man represented William Selioke who died in 1541, so that the slab takes us further back than the Registers, and he inferred that the figure of the woman was meant for his wife Joyce. By working down on his stomach in the dim light of this part of the church Mr. Ashmore was able at length with much difficulty to prepare from the worn slab the drawing which appears on page 197. Who cut the figures is not known, but grace and piety and much artistic feeling have been embodied in the few masterly lines that have been employed to give us William Selioke and his wife Joyce.

Birds of passage at Hazelbarrow seem to have been Thomas Beverley, and, before him, Cyril Arthington, evidence of whose stay here is found in the Registers, for Beverley had a son baptised and buried at Norton in 1596, and Arthington had a daughter buried here in 1592. There are still people bearing the name Beverley in the neighbourhood ; but the Arthingtons are associated more closely with Arthington, near Leeds, and generally with that part of Yorkshire, many of them distinguished people in Yorkshire history. There is some Arthington heraldry in Ecclesfield church, upon the other side of Sheffield. Cyril seems to have been a favourite name in the family, and occurs in most generations. In the journal of John Hobson of Dodsworth Green there is an entry February 4, 1729–30 : " Cyrill Arthington, of Arthington, esq., is dead of excessive drinking, because he had an heir born." The Arthingtons became connected by marriage with the Fairfaxes, and a Francis Nevile of the same family as Cavendish Nevile married Rosamund, daughter of Cyril Arthington, so that there is a close connection with Norton folk.

The Cyril Arthington who lived at Hazelbarrow married Rosamund, daughter of William Hawksworth of Hawksworth. A member of the Hawksworth family was slain at Musselborough in 1547 ; another, a traveller, was poisoned at Madrid ; and Sir Walter Hawksworth was created a baronet in 1678. Rosamund was a Catholic, and Hunter says she was related to Cardinal Allen, " a fact which is mentioned by the Earl of Shrewsbury when he returned a list of Popish fugitives from the county of Derby. It seems also as if he meant to say that Rosamond was herself a Recusant."

Whether the Earl of Shrewsbury meant to say she was a Recusant or not, she was one actually, for a record of the Derbyshire Recusants in the reign of Queen Elizabeth includes the name of " Rosamond wife of Cirill Arthington," amongst other Norton people.

Hazelbarrow also brings us into touch with the old

family of the Frechevilles.   Beginning with Hubertus de
Rya in the time of William the Conqueror, we come
next to his son, Ralph Fitzhubert, or Hubert FitzRalph
as some writers put the name, in possession of the manor
of Crich during the reign of the same monarch.   A
daughter of this line married a Frecheville, a member of
an old Nottinghamshire family.

Anker, a descendant, brings us a stage nearer to Norton, for he married Amicia, a girl's name which surely
ought not to have become rare, the heiress of the Musards
of Staveley, and Baroness of Staveley.   A Ralph Frecheville was with Edward the First in his Scottish wars,
and was summoned to Parliament in 1297.   A Peter
Frecheville was knighted for valour at Musselborough
in the reign of Edward the Sixth, and another Peter
Frecheville was knighted by James the First at Worksop
in 1603.   The church lands at Cold Aston were given
to Henry, Earl of Cumberland, and sold by him to Peter
Frecheville.   This Sir Peter had a younger brother John,
and it was John who bought land at Hazelbarrow and
married Barbara Eyre of Newbold, Kiveton, and Laughten-
en-le-Morthen.   Of his family of five girls four were
born at Hazelbarrow.   Sir Peter bought Hazelbarrow
from his brother John, and it was bequeathed to Sir
Peter's son John, the most famous member of this old
family.

When the war between Charles the First and his
people opened, Sir John, who was an ardent Royalist,
garrisoned his house at Staveley and distinguished himself
on several occasions, and particularly when, like a hero
of George Meredith, he became "master of an event,"
for he drove some of the Parliamentary troops for shelter
into Mr. Eyre's house at Hassop and took them all
prisoners.   In August 1644, however, his own house
capitulated, and a passage in Mrs. Hutchinson's memoirs
of her husband shows that during the Civil War Frecheville had a narrow escape in 1643.

After Charles the Second had come to the throne he was

made a peer, Lord John Frecheville of Staveley, and he
became governor of York and a gentleman of the Privy
Chamber.   He died in 1681–2, and with him died the
title.   Following the Frecheville family upon the female
side we come to Sir John Ramsden, M.P. for the West
Riding of Yorkshire, and it was from a daughter of the
house of Frecheville too that old Gervase Holles, the
soldier and antiquary, was descended.

The family burying-place of the Frechevilles was at
Staveley, and a handsome monument to Sir John, and

In the Rickyard
Hazelbarrow

other memorials, may be seen there, though some have
disappeared.   The principal branch of the family lived at
Staveley for more than three hundred years, and it was
there that the male line became extinct.

It is believed that Hazelbarrow Hall, which was taken
down about 1810, was built by the Frechevilles, and it
is a fortunate circumstance that drawings of the place
remain.   One, a water-colour, which apart from its
connection with Hazelbarrow is entitled to our admiration for its own qualities as a work of art, occupies an
honoured place in Mr. Addy's library, and that has been
reproduced in this book.   Mr. Addy thinks the water-

colour was made by one of the Misses Pearson of Norton Vicarage, and copied by the late Mr. John Fenney Parkin of Sheffield. Mr. Addy has added that the drawing " shows that the style is Elizabethan or early Jacobean. We may regret that the drawing does not tell us more, but at all events it shows how picturesque the old house was. The right wing seems to contain, on the middle floor, the dining hall, with a window forming a recess for a high table. A survey of 1635, when the Moorwoods became owners, shows that there was a bowling alley, and a conyger or rabbit warren. I have heard that some of the rooms were beautifully panelled, and my relation, James Jenkin, who was born here, and whose family had lived at Haselbarow for about a century, had a huge oak chair which formerly stood in the house. It was very old and massive, and of remarkable appearance."

Concerning this chair, Mr. Addy wrote some years ago that it was of the kind known as a turned chair—that is, its parts had been made upon a turner's lathe, and he referred to it as a great bundle of spindles. In James Linacre's notes, taken apparently from the vicarage manuscripts, he mentions as other internal features an ancient chimney with a window in it and a wooden table fast to the floor.

Another picture of the old Hazelbarrow Hall is a water-colour drawing copied from an oil painting. This water-colour is in the possession of Mr. Rhodes at the Norton Post Office.

In 1635 Lord Frecheville sold Hazelbarrow to the Morewoods of Alfreton for £2,450, and the Anthony Morewood who was High Sheriff of the county in 1649 lived at Hazelbarrow, and one of his daughters marrying Henry Goring of Lyden in Sussex about 1670, Hazelbarrow went with her to the Gorings. Sir Charles Goring, baronet, sold the place in 1671 to John Storie, a lead merchant, Andrew Morewood's partner. The will of John Storie, merchant, of Hazelbarrow, which belongs to 1664, left money for poor boys to be sent to the university and funds for church purposes. He settled money upon the vicarage " for the better maintenance of a Godley Protestant painfull Preaching Minister there for ever," and left means too for the assistance of " the most needful and impotent people of Norton." When the church was restored in 1882, his gravestone was found. It shows that he died in 1674, and there was a brass plate let into the stone recording the death of Storie Wingfield, who died in 1729, and the death of Storie's wife.

John Storie's sister, Margaret, became his heiress, and married Ferdinando Wingfield of Stanley Hall, near Wakefield. Their son John lived here, the owner of the place, and he bought Norton House.

It was one of the many daughters of this John Wingfield, Margaret, who in 1705 married Robert Newton of Mickleover, and so became the mother of Robert Newton, the hero of the Offley will adventure. In the chapter on the Oakes we read a suggestion that she was greedy for land and money, pleading successfully on her own behalf with her dying father regardless of the claims of her sisters. If she desired wealth, she had her wish, and in the memoranda of George Mower of Barley Woodseats we may read that " Madam Newton, of Norton, widow, was taken ill at supper 7 of June ; died next day. . . . Left a son and a great estate in land and money." This son was Robert Newton, and it may be that he inherited from his mother those acquisitive traits that have been mentioned in a previous chapter. It has been shown already that Margaret's sister Mary, who married William Bagshawe, had a very different disposition.

The last habitant of Hazelbarrow Hall who was both owner and occupier was Storie Wingfield, Margaret's brother, who died in 1729. His will, which belongs to 1725, leaves property in Dronfield and Lightwood " to pay yearly to the Master of the free Gramer School of Norton, and his successors, £5 per annum for ever, for the teaching and instructing of ten poor boys of the

parish of Norton at the said schoole, untill such time
as they shall attain their respective ages of 14 years ;
and to pay the residue to an assistant minister to preach
every Sabbath day in the forenoone at Norton Church,
every such preaching minister to be elected and chosen
by the Bishops of Litchfield and Coventry ; the said ten
poor boys to be always chose and pitcht upon by my said
assistant minister and the church wardens of Norton."
The first minister appointed to this church lectureship
founded by Storie Wingfield was named Wood, and he
resigned and went to Edensor in 1762. A very elaborate
pedigree of the Wingfields appears in Thomas Blore's
work on Rutland.

When Robert Newton, the younger, made his will in
1784, he left Hazelbarrow to his cousin, Wingfield
Wildman, the son of his mother's sister Priscilla, who
married William Wildman, a London chemist. " He
describes the property," says Mr. Addy, " as consisting of
about 200 acres, and he expresses a wish that his cousin
would make either Norton House or Haselbarow his
usual place of residence. He goes on to say ' I hope he
will comply with my will and desire. . . . I have heard
him often express a particular regard for Haselborough,
and thought it a very pleasant place, and if he chuses
to live and fix his abode at Haselborough Hall then I
give and bequeath him the sum of £2,000 to lay out and
expend in improvement of the said house and place.'
Further on he gives to Mr. Wildman £5,000 ' provided
he makes Norton House or Haselborough Hall the
principal place of his annual residence.' "

Mr. Addy remembers that on the chancel wall of
Norton church, before 1882, was an old hatchment on
which the arms of Wildman with the escutcheon of pretence for Wingfield were depicted. Beneath was the
motto *In cælo quies.*

Of the tenants of Hazelbarrow there is a note by
Mr. James Linacre that " Mr. Wright lived at Hazlebarrow before Jenkins ; he played a musical instrument.

HAZELBARROW HALL (DEMOLISHED ABOUT 1810).

A friend of Lee the bassoon player." Robert Blackwell was there towards the middle of the eighteenth century, and the Jenkins of Hazelbarrow will be familiar to those who are acquainted with the life of Chantrey. They came from Whiston, near Rotherham, and members of the family are still at Rotherham. Edward Jenkin was at Hazelbarrow until 1810, and he was succeeded by his son James, whose portrait Chantrey painted. Then came his son, another James, who however did not complete his life in the old hall, but died at Magathay. Mary, the sister of this James, was the grandmother of Mr. Sidney O. Addy, for she married Mr. Sidney Oldall, his grandfather, and he thinks that a curious story which belonged really to Tankersley Rectory, but was found attached to Hazelbarrow Hall, must have been imported by her. The story is given amongst the *Yorkshire Diaries* published by the Surtees Society in the journal of John Hobson, of Dodworth Green. Two children and a maid were left at the rectory while the rector was in church, when they were beset by two ruffians who " began to give ill language " and tried to break in. Hot broth flung in one of their faces was amongst the means of defence, and at last the men withdrew. The Hazelbarrow tale, which has some details that are not in Hobson's account, is given fully in Mr. Addy's article *Haselbarow Hall and its Owners*, and some years ago he embodied the incident in a story entitled *Valentine Frankincense*.

The Hazelbarrow property has descended from Dorothy Wingfield, still another of John Wingfield's daughters, in the line that resulted from her marriage with Mr. Joseph Shawe, a Liverpool merchant, and the present owner is Mr. H. N. Cunliffe Shawe, of Weddington Hall, Nuneaton. The present farmhouse looks down Dowie Lumb, but does not present any of the picturesque features which characterized the hall whose site it occupies.

The old farm buildings of Hazelbarrow Hall are still there, wide-spreading and full of interesting details, with ample accommodation everywhere for doves, once such

an important feature of farming that it is said the right
of erecting and keeping dovecotes was a privilege of
manors, rigorously protected by law.   The garden, which
has still a clipped yew, and commands views of the brook
in the valley and of the wooded hills beyond, retains
its ancient boundary wall upon the east, draped with ivy
in parts, foxgloves growing at its base, and a massive
buttress stands at the corner which overhangs the valley.

It is a pity the property no longer includes the old hall,
and the fact that it has gone makes more precious the
time-worn gateway, farm buildings, buttress, and the other
fragments that speak to us now of what has passed from
the earth for ever.

A Buttress
of the Old Wall
Hazelbarrow

CHAPTER XI

THOUGH old Norton Hall, old Norton House, Hemsworth Hall, Suarte Hall and Hazelbarrow Hall have been demolished, with other ancient houses in Norton, Greenhill Hall has been spared, and a delightful place it is with its gables, old chimneys, mullioned windows, and with those other features that distinguish this substantial, satisfying style of seventeenth-century domestic architecture. There is a ghost story connected with the house when the Luptons were living there, a vague tale about a phantom carriage and horses, and an elopement; but the tradition lacks outlines, and Lupton's bull, a terrible animal recalled by Mr. Rhodes of the Post Office, is better remembered as a more tangible and even more terrifying feature of the hall nearly eighty years ago.

Greenhill Hall has an old room distinguished even beyond the other rooms in dignity and interest. It contains a beautiful carved mantelpiece of oak, and in the centre of the mantelpiece a coat-of-arms. All the walls are panelled in oak, with carving over the doors, and carving also at intervals between the panels. The ceiling too is ornamented, one half of it of a different design from the other half. Each window has very small panes of glass, and all are guarded with iron bars. The principal window has a wide seat, and a very romantic touch is imparted to this part of the house by the writing upon

one of the panes of " Leonilla remember Adela July 28th
1786," and upon the next pane of " Adela, Sylvia
and Diana," delightful names in complete harmony with
this noble old building. In the garden is a stone on

which is carved | B. T.E. 1667.

Many will remember Greenhill Hall as the home of
Mr. William Lister, land agent and surveyor, who was at
Greenhill in the fifties, and more recently the Misses Lister
dwelt here and owned the place. After them came the
Crawshaws, and in 1900 the present occupier, Mr. James
Smith Andrew, bought the Hall. It is a great comfort to
know that he appreciates its charms, and that he is not
aching to pull the old place down to build upon its site a
commonplace modern mansion. May he and his successors
continue to see that Greenhill Hall is more valuable than
anything else that could be erected upon its site.

In national history Greenhill Hall connects us with
the Kirkes, and if we examine the pedigree of that family
we come to a time when at Whitehough, near Chapel-
en-le-Frith, there dwelt Arnold Kirke, one of the
foresters of fee in the Peak Forest, and he had three
sons, one of whom, the third, was Thurstan. It was
Thurstan who married Frances Blythe, the daughter of
Jerome Blythe of the Norton family. Anna Blythe, the
mother of Frances, a member of the old Derbyshire
family of Eyre, is described in the Norton Register as
modest, pious and benevolent, and her brother was the
Anthony Blythe to whom allusion has been made already
as having been buried at Norton during the night.
Thurstan and Frances, living here at Greenhill Hall,
had nine children, and the eldest of the family was
Gervase, baptised at Norton on April 16, 1568 ; but he,
for some reason that is not known, was disinherited, and
so, without hope of a fortune from his father, and his
mother dead, he left Greenhill Hall for London, determined
to make one for himself.

Gervase Kirke, like Dick Whittington, became a London apprentice, and afterwards a merchant. For many years he lived in Dieppe, at that time a very important port, trading with England ; and it was in Dieppe that he married Elizabeth Goudon, a merchant's daughter. Born of this marriage were five boys and two girls, David, Lewis, Thomas, John, James, Elizabeth and Mary. Elizabeth married Monsieur Gretuelo of Dieppe, and Mary married John West of Hampton Poyle in Oxfordshire. In the church of St. Aldate in Oxford there is a monument "in Memory of Mistress Mary West, who was the youngest daughter of Jarvis Kirke, of Greenhill, in the parish of Norton, in the county of Derby, Esq., who departed this life ye 8th day of May in ye year of our Lord 1686." Thus is Greenhill linked with the university city of Oxford, and many miles away the monument in St. Aldate's speaks for Norton and keeps its name alive in the centre of learning.

At an early age the Kirkes were in charge of armed vessels that traversed the Channel, trading with London and Antwerp. " The three brothers," wrote Monsieur Ferland, " had contracted a taste for dangerous enterprises, and were respected as very good navigators by the Dieppians, at that time the most skilful and hardy sailors of France." So it was natural when the Company of Merchant Adventurers of London was formed that Gervase Kirke should join, and that his sons should be placed in charge of the ships of the company.

In the year 1627 a combination was organised by Sir William Alexander, Gervase Kirke and others to found a colony in Canada to trade with the natives. The King, Charles the First, granted the adventurers a patent which placed them in complete control, and they might displace the French if they could and seize French and Spanish vessels. Fighting the French, with whom England was then at war, was not the only aim of the expedition, for the licence was for discovery, fishing and trade " on the south side of the river of Canada,"

14

as the patent so vaguely and yet so comprehensively puts it.

In the spring of 1628 the three ships of this expedition set sail from England with Captain David Kirke in command, and meanwhile there was on its way for the relief of Quebec a French expedition under Admiral de Roquement, who, in April 1628, left France with twenty vessels containing stores, food, tools for building, guns, ammunition, ordnance for Quebec and other forts, priests and emigrants, women and children. Four of the vessels were armed.

In Quebec itself at this time the French colonists, worn down with hunger, were ever on the look-out for succour from their native country ; but day after day went by and none came. Many times did they gaze anxiously beyond Point Lévi and along the channels of Orleans for sails from France, but night after night came without relief. The fort itself, built when Champlain, the great Frenchman who was in charge of Quebec, had been away, was badly built by men under no authority and lacking supervision, and it began now to fall about their ears, the superstitious regarding this as a portent of evil.

On July 9, 1628, their suspense was broken, for two men, spent with fatigue, arrived in Quebec after having forced their way through forests and over torrents to the crossing of the St. Charles under the rock. They had hurried from the French farm at Cape Tourmente with the news that an Indian lad had called there to tell them that there were six large vessels in the harbour at Tadousac, commanded by Captain Michel of Dieppe, a renegade Frenchman and " *Calviniste furieux.*" After these messengers had arrived at Quebec there came up the river in his canoe the Indian lad himself, and Champlain, questioning him, was driven by his answers to the unwelcome conclusion that the fleet at Tadousac was not French, nor helpful, but English and hostile.

A couple of Champlain's followers went down the

GREENHILL HALL

211

river in a canoe to learn more of this arrival of vessels. Near the island of Orleans they met two canoes with Indians in them tearing up the river at great speed, and the Indians shouted and waved their hands for the missionaries to go back to Quebec at once. The Frenchmen waited, however, to hear why the Indians were in such great trepidation, and then they saw a woman and child from Cape Tourmente, and, lying in the bottom of one of the canoes, a wounded fellow-countryman, his moustaches burned by the musket which had wounded him, at such close quarters had he been with his enemy. This man they found to be Foucher, more frightened than hurt, who had been in charge at Cape Tourmente, and they were told that twenty men had landed from a small fishing vessel at Cape Tourmente, and as these were assumed to be Frenchmen, and friendly, they were made welcome ; but when they came indoors they opened a violent attack upon the French people, killing, wounding and taking them prisoners, burning their houses, butchering their cattle, and so revealing themselves to be foes.

Champlain found also a Greek, ready to disguise himself as an Indian, who would go down the river, with some real Indians, to act as a spy ; but he too met the fugitives from Cape Tourmente, and so had no need to go further for information.

The truth was that Kirke's expedition had arrived, and after a short stay at Newfoundland it had visited the French settlements. Then a schooner with twenty men had been told off by David Kirke at Tadousac to destroy the farm buildings and to kill the stock at Cape Tourmente. The object of this was to cut off Champlain's supply of meat and to replenish his own. The English tried to surprise the farm, but failing in that, pretended to be friends. The farm buildings they burnt, and they killed the herd of forty cattle, except one cow, which managed to escape into the forest. The people who did not elude the English were made prisoners.

Upon the following afternoon the watchers at Quebec

saw another canoe coming up the river, and as there was so much hesitation on the part of those who directed it, Champlain supposed they did not know the river well and were enemies. He sent men to intercept the canoe, which proved to contain three of the prisoners taken by Kirke at the Cape Tourmente farm, and a few Basque sailors picked up on the river by Kirke's fleet. They bore a very polite letter from Kirke to Champlain calling upon him to surrender, but bad as was his plight the great Frenchman, in terms as courteous as those of Kirke, refused to yield.

Champlain always calls the Kirkes the Quers, and in his letter to Champlain Kirke wrote his own name Quer. Kirke had been known as Quer in France, so that in addressing a Frenchman he had used this form. He had also given carefully the date both in the old style and in the new, not adopted in England until 1752, and this is cited as the earliest instance of the recognition of the difference in an English document.

It is probable that Kirke did not receive Champlain's reply, for hearing that the Roquement relief expedition had reached Gaspé point he would know it was of more importance to attack this than to spend his time upon the people of Quebec, who were not worth powder and shot, as he would have heard from the treacherous Indians. Moreover, he would know that, if he could defeat Roquemont, Quebec would be his whenever he wished ; and if he could not defeat Roquemont, then it would be easier to get away in the open gulf than if he were pinned in a narrow strait, between his adversary and Quebec. Therefore instead of going forward to take the fort from Champlain he went back to grapple with Roquemont.

Roquemont's policy was to save the provisions and relieve Quebec, so he endeavoured to elude Kirke, but he was unable to evade an engagement, and the struggle closed in favour of Kirke, who now decided to leave Quebec until next year and go back to England with his prizes and prisoners, for some of whom he would be able to exact ransom.

When the news reached Paris the French King and his council were furious, and the merchants who had lost their money in this expedition clamoured for revenge. The three Kirkes were carried in effigy through the streets of Paris, to the accompaniment of the tolling of bells, and then the effigies were burnt in the Place de Grève "amidst the yells of an exulting populace."

Already, however, the Kirkes were employing the wealth won in spoils and ransom in fitting out a much stronger expedition. In the middle of March 1629 the new fleet was ready, and the vessels sailed away from Gravesend on March 25. After a short stay at New-foundland, where they were revictualled, they reached Great Gaspé on June 15. Eventually Tadousac became the headquarters of the fleet, and Lewis and Thomas went forward to demand the surrender of Quebec.

In Quebec, in the previous year, Champlain had been left in suspense. Upon his refusal to surrender he had expected to be attacked, but neither the English fleet came to assail nor the French fleet to succour; "no white sail moved athwart the green solitudes of Orleans," says Parkman, and so after their brief spell of hope the colonists went back wearily to their dreary search for acorns and roots. The peas were diminishing. Champlain devised a mill to make them available in more palatable forms. The roots of the plant Solomon's Seal were dried and powdered and made into bread. By bartering skins with the Indians or by other devices they had sometimes a change in the shape of flour, eels, barley, Indian meal and venison; but notwithstanding all their efforts they were so famished that they cared not now whether English or French should arrive if they might have relief from the pangs of hunger and from the tension of suspense.

So matters went on until July 1629, when an Indian eel-fisher told Champlain that three ships were coming up

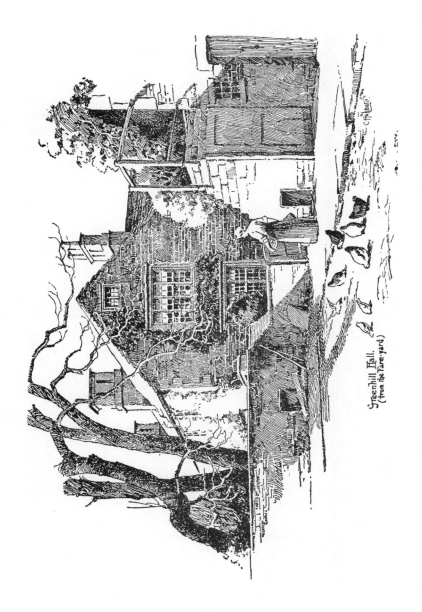

Greenhill Hall.
(from the Farm-yard)

215

the river. Champlain was alone, for his few companions were out fishing or grubbing up roots. One by one this starveling band returned, and Champlain told them the news and ordered them to their posts. The English vessels of this second of the Kirke expeditions arrived at Quebec and anchored in the harbour. A boat flying a white flag steered towards Quebec, and, in response, Champlain caused a white flag to be hoisted in the fort. Then a man came and delivered a very urbane letter, calling upon Champlain to surrender.

Champlain acknowledged that he had received the summons and asked for time to consider. He warned the English against coming within gunshot, and one of his followers went on board to see the Kirkes to ask why in time of peace—for peace had now been declared—they were attacked, an awkward question that received but vague answer.

The French leader had done all that a brave man could do. Beset by Indians, threatened by English, without help from France his cause was hopeless. No good, and very much harm, would be done by fighting. Therefore he surrendered, and on July 21, 1629, Captain Lewis Kirke landed with 150 men, and took possession of the fort. Upon the following day, Sunday, July 22, the English flag was hoisted, and there was a beating of drums and much firing of cannon and muskets in honour of the victory. As Parkman has written, the English flag was planted "where the followers of Wolfe again planted it a hundred and thirty years later." This incident of the surrendering of Quebec to Kirke has been painted by R. Caton Woodville, and reproduced on a postcard by Messrs. Raphael Tuck & Sons.

Champlain is very careful to show in his writings that the Kirkes were very courteous, and he seems very much surprised that an Englishman could be polite and considerate. At last he solved the enigma by attributing this polish to an infusion of French blood. " Lewis Kirke," writes Champlain, " was courteous, having some of the French nature in him, and loving the nation. He was the son of an Englishman who had married a French-woman at Dieppe, so he desired to oblige the French families, preferring their conversation to that of the English, to whom his humour was repugnant."

Parkman says that Lewis Kirke was courteous gener-ally, but showed an aversion to the Jesuits and regretted that their surrender prevented him from battering their house about their ears. He adds that, successful as David had been, he was not satisfied, and " his mood, therefore, was far from benign, especially as he feared, that, owing to the declaration of peace, he would be forced to dis-gorge a part of his booty ; yet, excepting the Jesuits, he treated his captives with courtesy, and often amused him-self with shooting larks on shore in company with Champlain." Kingsford adds snipe, woodcocks and plovers to the list of the victims, and says they killed more than twenty thousand.

Kirke refused to accept Champlain's apartments, but left the Frenchman in undisturbed possession of them so long as he remained in Quebec. This was not a pro-tracted period, for on August 24 Champlain sailed in the *George* with Thomas Kirke to Tadousac. On the way they met a French ship which was discovered to be in charge of the belated Emery de Caen, who was on his way from France to Quebec with stores. He had managed to steal past David Kirke at Tadousac in a fog, but only to fall now a prey to Thomas. After a fight of several hours De Caen lost a mast and was compelled to surrender, and so it came about that Thomas went to Tadousac with De Caen, as well as with Champlain.

David now left Tadousac and went to Quebec for a consultation with Lewis, whom he then left there as a commander. On November 20, 1629, David Kirke ar-rived at Plymouth with his prisoners and prizes, and was assured there, much to his chagrin, that peace had been made between England and France some months before.

After all, the rejoicings of the English at Quebec had

been premature, for the victory turned out to be hollow. About a month after the Kirkes had left England Charles had agreed to restore all forts captured by the English since April 24, 1629, and Quebec was included in this agreement. The King, in great need of money, was pressing for the payment by the French of 400,000 crowns, half of Queen Henrietta Maria's dowry which still remained unpaid. The French refused to pay unless the places taken by Kirke were given back, so Charles agreed to yield Quebec and other French settlements as soon as the money should be forthcoming. He does not seem to have realised the importance of Kirke's victory, and as for the rights of those who had spent £60,000 in winning Quebec, probably he did not consider that a matter in which he had any concern. Everything was to be delivered to the French again, even down to the last beaver skin, and a commission was appointed to discover all that the Kirkes had taken. A warrant was issued to search their warehouses. The Kirkes pointed out that of the 7,000 skins only 1,300 were taken from Quebec, for the others had been obtained in traffic with the Indians. Moreover the French had consumed in food and drink more than the value of all the skins. One of Kirke's captains swore that "there was not in the sayde forte at the tyme of the rendition of the same, to this examinate's knowledge, any victualls, save only one tubb of bitter rootes." Summoned before the Lord Mayor, Kirke was ordered to deliver the key of the warehouse where the skins were kept, but he refused, whereupon the Privy Council gave the Lord Mayor and the Sheriffs the power to break down the door and seize the skins. Kirke and his partners, including one Fitz, a merchant, broke into the warehouse first and carried off the skins, so Fitz was apprehended and taken before the Star Chamber, where he was ordered to be imprisoned until the skins were restored. Thomas Felty, another merchant, says Douglas, was imprisoned in the Fleet prison for stealing some of the skins.

Kirke tried again to persuade the King to keep Quebec, and he enlarged upon the beauty and advantage of this position ; but Charles was obstinate, and the only compensation promised was that Captain Kirke should have £20,000 from the French Government—an arrange-

Old Doorway
Greenhill Hall

ment which ultimately the French repudiated, so that the Kirkes received not a penny for all their expenditure and trouble, merely a grant of honorary additions to their ancient coat-of-arms. David Kirke was knighted in 1633. Lewis was made captain of the *Leopard*, one of the King's ships in the Channel squadron, and he was often engaged in hazardous enterprizes upon this and other vessels. In a tavern affray in which Captain Peter Clarke was killed, Lord Morley and Mounteagle endeavoured to throw the blame upon Lewis Kirke, but unsuccessfully, and Kirke helped to suppress the Irish rebellion. He was dangerously wounded in the attack upon Knock Castle, not far from Trim.

Champlain was reinstated at Quebec, and this great, unselfish and brave man died there upon the Christmas Day of the bitter winter of 1635, when he was sixty-eight years of age. " In a chamber of the fort, breathless and cold, lay the hardy frame which war, the wilderness, and the sea had buffeted so long in vain."

Gervase Kirke, a few months after he had seen his son David return victorious from Canada, died in Basing Lane, London, and he was buried in the church of All Hallows, in Bread Street, a sanctuary that was demolished in 1878. Sir David Kirke, though others had failed to found a colony in Newfoundland, was resolved to attempt the arduous work, and having obtained powers from the King he collected a hundred men, fitted the *Abigail*, and sailed in 1638 to establish himself at Ferryland. " Sir David Kirke," Mr. Henry Kirke has written, " was the right man to colonize a bleak and inhospitable region. Unlike Lord Baltimore, who had been a courtier, and accustomed to the sedentary life and luxurious surroundings of a Secretary of State, Kirke had from his youth faced all the rigours and hardships of a seafaring life ; he was hardened by exposure to all weathers and all climates."

Notwithstanding the injuries they had received at his hands, the Kirkes remained loyal to Charles, and Sir David, unmolested in Newfoundland, flew the Royal Standard over his house and fort during the struggle between the King and the Parliament. Unexpectedly, in the winter of 1655–6, when he was but in his fifty-ninth year, his once robust constitution gave way and he died. He was buried at Ferryland, but no trace of his grave can now be found. Mr. Henry Kirke, who gives many details about the Kirkes in *The First English Conquest of Canada*, says the oldest tombstones in the graveyards do not reach back beyond 1770, and he remarks that as the soil is a loose gravel it falls away year after year, so that little is left to-day of the site of the original settlement. In the year 1880, however, some excavations were made, and amongst the relics that were found was a silver snuff spoon—figured on page 189 of Mr. Kirke's book—of a kind which a few Scotsmen still carry, bearing the initials G.K., the initials of George Kirke, Sir David's son. I remember a Scotsman who used such a spoon, and repeated a kind of grace when he used it :

> This is the benefit of guid snuff,
> It clears the een, and clags the nose,
> And redds the brain as we suppose ;
> So here's to ye a' and up it goes.

When Millais, the artist, was in Scotland he went to church, and was amused to see the old men passing their ram's horn snuff-mulls to one another, and putting little bone spades full of snuff up their noses to keep themselves awake.

While Sir David Kirke was flying the Royal Standard in Newfoundland, his brothers, Lewis and Thomas, had joined the King upon the memorable day when he had hoisted his flag at Nottingham for his struggle with the Parliament. Both brothers fought at Edgehill, and not long afterwards Thomas was killed in a skirmish with the Roundheads. Lewis accompanied the King into the west country, where he bore a part in the siege of Gloucester, and then in the battle of Newbury, in which his services were so distinguished that after the battle Charles knighted him at Oxford, and later conferred upon him the important post of Governor of Bridgnorth Castle. When the cause of the King was lost Sir Lewis, like William Bullock, the squire of Norton, was counted amongst the " delinquents," and he was compelled to pay

£151. At the Restoration he was appointed Captain and Paymaster of the Corps of Gentlemen-at-arms, and dying in 1664 was buried beside his father in All Hallows Church, Bread Street, London.

There was another branch of the Kirkes at Martinside, Chapel-en-le-Frith, from whom has descended the present representative of the family, Mr. Henry Kirke, M.A., B.C.L., F.R.G.S., author of *The First English Conquest of Canada* and of other books, in addition to an account of Lewis Kirke in *A Derbyshire Cavalier*, published by the Derbyshire Archæological Society in 1909.

Dr. James Douglas, in an excellent work entitled *Old France in the New World*, emphasises the fact that David Kirke was a gentleman, and adds that " the Kirkes must certainly, from whatever sources they inherited their fine feeling, have possessed it to an eminent degree."

The stranger passing old Greenhill Hall would receive the impression of a house withdrawn from the busy life of the nation, a remote place ; but to him who knows of its connection with the Kirkes it must always conjure up vivid pictures of stirring actions on land and sea, the thunder of guns, the brisk movement of battle, the life and colour of naval warfare before the age of steam. He will be conducted from this tableland to the abrupt rock at Quebec, " perhaps the most romantic spot in the Empire," round which so many memories cluster, under whose shadow those struggles began that culminated in the decisive encounter in which Wolfe wrested the rock from Montcalm, and so decided whether England or France should be supreme in this part of the American continent ; but though Wolfe must remain, and properly so, the most widely known British hero in connection with Quebec, yet we in these parts must never forget that ninety-eight years before Wolfe was born the fort was won for England by the members of a family whose name is closely linked with the old walls of Greenhill Hall in the historic parish of Norton.

CHAPTER XII

THE REGISTERS

SEVEN volumes constitute the Norton Registers. They go back to the time when the record was kept in Latin, but they are not wholly in that language. The earliest volume is of an unusual and inconvenient shape, 2 ft. 3 in. long and $7\frac{1}{2}$ in. broad, in covers of thin parchment. Some slovenly person of a bygone generation has doubled the book so that the binding and leaves are broken, but the present vicar, the Rev. G. W. Hall, has had the volume cleaned carefully and rebound, so that any further damage is not probable.

Norton Registers take us back to September 30, 1559, the first year of the reign of Queen Elizabeth, and we find many names that now have become familiar in connection with the halls of Norton. One name, however, we light upon for the first time here, the name of the Rev. Andrew Marvell, M.A., of Emmanuel College, Cambridge, the father of the famous Andrew Marvell, B.A., the friend of Milton and Member of Parliament for Hull. This was the father's second marriage, and he wedded Lucy Harris at Norton in 1638.

Entries occur of four natives with the name Godfrey Sykes. They may have been related to Godfrey Sykes, the distinguished artist whom we met at Meersbrook, and whose monument stands in Weston Park in Sheffield, for his ancestors came from Calver, and Godfrey was a favourite name in the family during several generations.

The Norton Registers show that the village, like many

others, had its "dogg whipper," whose duty was "to whip ye dogs forth of ye church." His name was John Morton ; he lived at Backmoor, and his onerous duties do not seem to have affected his health, for he died of old age and was buried in 1743. Many parishes appointed a dog whipper, and a sluggard waker. At Great Ouseburn, in Yorkshire, Dicky Scar was the borough Dog Nawper. One Sunday the dogs evaded him and fought in the church in the middle of the service, when Dicky was surprised into such an outpouring of oaths and curses that the scandalised parson had to bereave him of his office. There were some places in this district, including Dronfield, where the sluggard waker was known as the Knock Nobbler, because he " nobbled," that is, rapped the " nobs " or heads of the sleepers. Abel Bywater, who wrote in the Sheffield dialect, says, " Here's a foine lady cums in, an' nock-nobbler runs up and dahn to foind her a seeat."

It was not a general custom to mention trades in parish registers, though some clerks gave this information. At Stokesley, in Yorkshire, there is a period when in the registers the occupation of the villagers is recorded, and this is the case here at Norton. When he examined the Registers thirty years ago, Mr. Addy noticed that they show a remarkable number of sickle-smiths. There are labourers, charcoal burners, cutlers, locksmiths, wheelwrights and tailors. Cooke Toote of Greenhill was a shotmaker ; and, as Mr. Addy has shown, Leonard Gill of Norton House, and John Bloodworth, had a shot manufactory at Greenhill and in 1626 incurred the suspicion of the Government. Then there are shoemakers, coverlet weavers, dish turners, musical instrument makers, and one " Marya Medley " is described as a " chimni sweeper." A glance down the pages reveals sheathers, bloomers (ironworkers), woodcoliers, nailers, swailors or swailers (travelling traders), leadworkers —one at Greenhill and another at Beauchief—coopers, a puncher from Heeley Bridge Houses, a poynter,

SIDNEY OLDALL ADDY, M.A.

HENRY KIRKE, M.A., B.C.L., F.R.G.S.

LLEWELLYN LLOYD SIMPSON.

EBENEZER RHODES.

GODFREY SYKES.

HENRY PERLEE PARKER.

p. 224]

chapman, waller, smelter, paperman, a silversmith at the Herdings, a worker in leather of Pynfold, "Grennell," a hatter at Gleadless and another at Woodseats, a soaper, a physician at Greenhill, Richard Barten, a scissor-smith at Hurlfield, a whitesmith and a glover at Hemsworth, a tailor and a cobbler at Magathay. George Hobson was at Heeley Mill in 1738, and further back, in 1610, during the reign of James the First, we have "Thomas Milnes, of Hielay Brigghouse, milner of the mylne thear." Richard Revell of Heeley Mill, miller, was buried at Sheffield in the same year. The Willisons were there in 1723. The Registers mention also the hammerman at Norton forge and "Water" Thong, military servant. In 1717 Norton had a Bachelor of Arts for a schoolmaster in the Rev. John Staniland.

The latitude allowed formerly in the spelling of names is well illustrated in the Norton Registers, for in some cases the clergyman or his clerk and the people themselves, upon the same occasion, spell the name in different ways. In addition, however, to these vagaries of spelling, some of the Christian names are curious in whatever way they may be spelled, and are no longer heard. Of curious names or names with eccentric spelling for women and girls are Jamima, Dionisia, Emmota, Emmina, Troth, Juliana, Effame, Emyna, Meriola, Mirialla, Dorcas, Immina, Godith, Batheba, Daybara, Emot, Emat, Emata, Goyse (Joyce probably), Dorcade, Tryphena, Nutty, Goodwitha, Malliana, Malion, Malyan, Emilia, Albenia, Theodosia, Ketura, Katura, Eden, Ephama, Effama, Camdena, Annis, Thamar, Camdama, Comforta, the forerunner surely of one of the two daughters of an eminent cocoa manufacturer whose two girls were known amongst his neighbours as "Grateful and Comforting." Phanney as another way of spelling Fanny occurs several times. Then we have Amia, Emea, Parcilia, Athania, Betty, Molly, Nanny, Faith, Scisilia and Doway. Jana is found as a Christian name, an entry that will recall to some readers that this was the Christian name of Mrs.

Charles Brookfield, a daughter of the Rev. M. Preston, of the Sheffield Parish Church. Her son was the Rev. W. H. Brookfield in whose memory Tennyson wrote a sonnet.

Amongst the men and boys are Elizeus, Elyseus, Emori, Eagidius, Achilles, Ebephanius, Ezechia, Enias, Azarius, Azariah, Amazia, Dionysius, Esaia, Averaye, Isa, Schemuel, Euria, Volintary, Malenus and Eneas. Pengrina is an unusual name, and Pircifaull a curious form of Percival. Robert Knottoo was married here in 1643, but his alien name does not appear to have survived, nor that of Dorothy Spybye, an appellation that suggests inquisitive tendencies, and causes us to conjecture that there may have been a window in Norton as well as " a window in Thrums."

The Register reveals how death dogged a family with singular persistence at Carrfield, once a lonely farmhouse, but now upon the edge of a populous district. Here lived the Oudalls, Matthew and Mary, who lost seven children within a year, and six more in succeeding years.

One section of the Register belonging to the eighteenth century gives the causes of the death of those who were brought to be buried. Some are described as having died from " wearing " or " disease wearing " ; there are very many who succumbed to consumption, and convulsions prevented a large number from surviving babyhood. Some die of old age, one " hanged himself," another was " killed at a Wheel," another is drowned, and in those days of almost universal insanitation and coarse feeding small-pox claimed many victims. Palsy, fever, dropsy, cancer, " quincey," accidents and various causes account for the death of many another, and it makes sad reading that Richard, the son of Ben Rose, died of " grypes."

On May Day, 1651, was buried " A infant, being a boy of a travelling woman " ; in 1811 "a person unknown, who committed suicide at Woodseats " ; Maria Wallis, an itinerant, was buried here in 1669 ; Thomas, unknown stranger, was buried in 1730. Here was interred in 1609 William Brownell, Bachelor of Arts, of Rawmarsh, zealous, pious, learned, and remarkable for his great humanity ; in 1611 Christopher Chapman, of Greenhill, yeoman, an old man at about 100 years of age. Other entries are : Haslam, stranger, pauper, old man, dying at Himsworth ; Thomas Clarksonne *alias* James Clarkson, pauper, stranger, lately inhabitant in the parish of Birstoll, co. York, dying at the home of Eliseus Poynton, of Grennell, yeoman ; Sept. 6, 1594, Pauper stranger, name and place of abode unknown, died at the house of James Bate, where he had been hospitably received ; Feb. 1, 1598, John Mylner, a young man, stranger, sick and dying at the home of William Blithe, of Lees ; March 17, 1598, Thomas Browne, mason, a man of proved honesty and piety, who died at the house of George Gill, in Lightwood ; Sept. 9, 1607, Elizabeth, wife John Brygges, lately of Sutton above Lowne, co. Notts., daughter John Bradell, lately of Whalley, co. Lancaster, Esq. (as is affirmed), deceased, a poor wandering woman who met her death at Jordanthorpe, was buried at Norton ; Aug. 14, 1608, John, son and heir apparent Thomas Hudson, of Sickhouse, yeoman, a youth of zeal, goodness, and humanity, and one who was possessed of no common talent for writing beautifully.

Amongst the baptisms are, 1652, Sarah, daughter of Samuel Heward, being travellers come forth of Peniston Parish ; another baptism is that of John, son of John Nevill, a traveller come from Booton in the Moor, presumably Bolton-le-Moors in Lancashire. A baptism of 1595 reminds us of national affairs, for it refers to the son of " Henry Mylner, soldier serving in Ireland," and there is another reference to a William Shackersley, gentleman, a soldier serving in Ireland, in 1598. He, however, may not have been a resident here. Joseph and Benjamin, and Joseph and Abednego, are twins ; Abraham, Isaac and Jacob, triplets. Belonging to 1582 is the entry of the baptism of " Alice, daughter, Isabella

Newtonne, born at the home of Christopher Chapman of Beauchief. Stranger, unknown traveller at that place."

From 1651 to 1655 many Sheffield children were brought here to be baptised, for at that time Sheffield was going through a period of great unrest in consequence of local operations connected with the great struggle between the Stuarts and the Parliament. Sheffield Castle had fallen to the Parliament in the year 1644.

A number of incidents are indicated by the entries. In 1590 was buried " John, son and heir of Richard Holland, late of Ecclesall, deceased , killed by the fall of a mass of lead, being then the apprentice of Ch. Chapman, of Grennell, yeoman." Then there is " John Allen of Lightewood, woodman at Mackeray, poisoned July 28 [1594], buried after an inquest." A kind of accident familiar to-day in this district is here mentioned as early as 1596, " Andrew Barker, of Norton, labourer in the mine of John Parker, senior, gentleman, killed by a fall of coal which he was working." In 1599 there was buried " John Northe, of Bradway, a youth, who met with sudden death in a wood at Grennell." Another entry tells us that in 1604 was buried " Robert Waddye, lately servant to Mr. Cardinal [Lees Hall] of Egmanton, co. Notts, drowned at Lees." Does this mean an accident with the Meersbrook in flood ? In 1608 was buried " Robert Northe, of Himsworth more side, laborer, killed by a fall from a tree at Wodbent" ; in 1611 Francis Bray, of Eyam, gentleman, killed at Bradway, parish Norton, was buried at Norton after an inquest held as to the cause of his death, and in 1612 Robert Fell, of Dronfield, was killed at Lees.

Children whose parents had not conformed to the marriage ceremony are indicated in various ways. Some are called by the uncompromising name of bastard, others as " being base gotten ", or " unlawfully begotten," and amongst some ingenious adumbrations we have in 1591 the baptism of " Elizabeth, spurius twig, unlawfully engendered between Francis Hynscliff, of Whooleley, otherwise the village carrier, and Alice Mydgelay, who was delivered at the house of Christopher Chapman." In 1730 there is the baptism of Elizabeth, spurious daughter of Martha Hanson, of Hammer; in 1595 the baptism of "Godfrey, reputed son of Godfrey Bowne, of the lately dissolved monastery of Fontanes, Co. York, and Beatrice Wilson, born at the home of Richard Cappes of Beauchief"; Samson, reputed son of Godfrey Fuljamb, of More Hall, Esq., and Jane Warde; and in 1600 Isabella, reputed daughter of Godfrey Fanchawe, of Fanchawe gate, and Anna Wootton, spinster. The English language, and the Latin language too, have had their resources strained for ingenious or evasive methods of indicating illegitimate children, and in other registers than Norton are many quaint terms, amongst them "scape begotten," "love begot" and "merry begot." In the Register of East Woodhay, in Hampshire, is "John filius populi, his mother's name was Elizabeth Carter."

From time to time very old people are mentioned in the Registers, and evidence that Norton folks have lived to a great age is forthcoming from other sources. In 1879 there died at Dore George Fox, a native of Greenhill, baptised at Norton in 1772, who had attained the age of 107 years. Fox, an ardent Protestant, fought in the Irish Rebellion of 1798 as a volunteer, but he was still more remarkable for his great skill in abstruse arithmetical calculations and in the estimation of distances, weights and quantities. It is said that on one occasion he discovered a mistake in the measurement of Dore for the County Assessment, and that this detection of the error saved the parish from the payment of several thousands of pounds. One of his sons became the Beadle for the Cutlers' Company in Sheffield.

Mr. Elijah Wragg of Lightwood, over ninety, has died while this book has been in progress, and to 1910 belongs the death of Mr. Joseph Bingham, born at Sheephill in 1826, in the same house in which his great-

grandfather was born.   Chantrey, as a boy, used to go to
his house, and in his later years Mr. Bingham received
help from the money left by the great sculptor.   Another

Thomas
HIGGINBOTTOM
in his 92ⁿᵈ Year

old Nortonian
who lived to
receive assist-
ance from the
local Chantrey
bequest was
Thomas Hig-
ginbottom,
who helped at
Chantrey's
funeral and
died recently,
ninety-two
years of age.
In the old days
he was a trom-
bone player
at Norton
church.   " I
could blow
now, Mester,"
said he to
Charles Ash-
more, " only
I've none of
these 'ere,"
and he pointed
regretfully to
his toothless
gums.   His
son at Heeley had recently celebrated his golden wedding.
Thomas was under-gardener at the Oakes for a few
years short of fifty, and remembered Chantrey, who used
always on his visits to the Bagshawes .to seek him out
in the garden and have a " crack " with him.   So it

was appropriate that he should survive to receive one of the Chantrey pensions. Now both pension-giver and pensioned, eminent and lowly, have reached the common goal, have received the last thing it was possible for their friends to bestow—a grave.

Ravel Linacre, the brother of James, died a few years ago, ninety years of age, and " Betty " Yates of Greenhill died in 1884 three months short of a hundred years of age. Mrs. Hazard, the mother of the late Thomas Hazard of the Herdings, was more than ninety years old, and no doubt there have been many others as long-lived. Amongst living veterans are Mr. Herbert Rhodes of the Post Office, eighty-four years of age in 1910, Mr. William Fielding, Surveyor of Highways, and Mr. Bullifant of Jordanthorpe, who at eighty does not know what it is to feel tired.

The Norton Postmaster in his 85th year.

Herbert Rhodes.

A parish register is liable to gradual decay, or to sudden destruction by fire. It may be lost, or stolen, or it may be tampered with for family reasons in the manner made known by actual instances and by episodes in stories by novelists of the Wilkie Collins school ; and therefore to have it printed and to have copies dispersed is a praiseworthy thing, for the loss of such a valuable record as a parish register is a most deplorable accident. In the case of Norton, the vicar, the Rev. G. W. Hall, has not only permitted the printing of the Parish Register, so that utter destruction of the record need no longer be feared, but he has borne the whole of the financial burden.   The transcript was made by Mr. Llewellyn Lloyd Simpson, of Littleover, Derby, who has done other work of the same kind, and the three volumes, one of which is an index, were published in 1908, and may be obtained from Mr. Simpson.   The Registers are far from being merely a list of names, and may be studied with interest and with profit.   In the compilation of this book they have been particularly useful, and I have blessed the name of Mr. Simpson very frequently.

CHAPTER XIII

NORTON AND LITTLE NORTON

As might be expected in a country full of " tuns," many of which, presumably, stand to the north of some place or other, or upon the northern side of some manor or estate, the name Norton is of frequent occurrence. I have counted seventy-six, and it is likely there are more. The name is so essentially a village name that when Goldsmith wrote one of his poems and desired to indicate rusticity he called his imaginary place Hogs Norton.

The term " tun " seems at first to have indicated a hedge or fence, and later to have come to mean the land that was enclosed, and when upon this ground buildings began to arise the name " tun " was still applied and so became associated more with the buildings than with the land or the hedge. To-day in many parts of the country a stack-yard is called a barton, and it is suggested that this means the tun or enclosure in which has been stored the bear or yield of the fields, from *bere*, which means barley. In districts that have been peopled by Anglo-Saxons there are many Bartons in the names of places, Earl's Barton and other similar terms. To this day in Lowland Scotland people call a farm house and its outbuildings a toon, and Wycliffe translates Matthew xxii. 5 : " but thei dispiseden, and wenten forth, oon into his toon, another to his marchaundise."

In modern Dutch *tuin* means a garden, and in Germany it signifies a hedge, suggesting the Anglo-Saxon *tynan*, to hedge, which leads to the " hedging and tining " formerly used for hedging and ditching. Latin law terms yield *tinetum* for brushwood.

Even when around the isolated homestead there grew a village the word "tun" still clung to the place, and, growing with the expansion of the village, it grew to have a signification the very opposite to its early association with rusticity, and we behold it now as a town—nay as Town does it not connote London, the largest city in the world?

A Norton Farm Hand

Such are the mutations of meaning through which a little word may move. Seebohm holds that the tuns and hams were generally manors, that they were manors even in the time of King Ethelbert, and probably from the first English conquest; and Dr. Bradley has written that the numerous Eastons, Westons, Nortons, Suttons and Middletons, probably indicated originally the various farms belonging to a single estate.

Orally the word still survives in its application to villages. Many people in Whiston speak of going down the main street of the village as going "dahn t' tahn," and in Thornton Rust, in Wensleydale, with seventy-five inhabitants, the term "town" is employed. A field at the eastern termination of the hamlet is called the Town End Garth.

Already have we seen that Norton is an old village,

and there are some places that have only their ancient annals to recommend them, or memories of beauty long ago destroyed ; but interesting as is the past of Norton, she can still win us by her present comeliness, and she charms those who come here though they have no know-ledge of her bygone days.   The village itself has no river, no mountains, nothing but the primitive charms of fields, open sky, trees, houses and a church ; and yet those who love the country will count it a winsome place, and Ebenezer Rhodes, after all his tours, regarded it as one of the pleasantest villages in any part of Derbyshire.   All beauty is not in height nor in depth, nor in the sensational manifestations of nature.   What grateful pictures did those lovable artists David Cox and Peter de Wint paint of scenery less striking even than that round Norton !

To the homely delights of Norton John Holland pays many a tribute, and says the village "is both interesting and pleasant ; the cottages are generally plain, but being embosomed in gardens, festooned with roses, or overhung with trees, present an unusual air of rural comfort and repose."   In the year 1848 he wrote twenty-one stanzas entitled *A Meditation, on May-Day Morning, in Norton Churchyard*, and he dwells affectionately in that poem upon some of its features.

A Sheffield poet of the early seventies, in *Sheffield and its Vicinity*, does not forget Norton, and exclaims in lines reminiscent of the eighteenth century

> To Norton then, whose sweet Arcadian fields
> Ceres adorns and golden treasure yields.

In Asline Ward's diary we read of Norton as a paradise for lovers, for in July 1813 his sweetheart Miss Lewin arrived to stay with her relatives at Norton Grange, and the lovers strolled to Hazelbarrow, Dronfield, Bole Hill, Bradway, Norton Lees, Greenhill, Backmoor, Beauchief, and often in the grounds of Norton Hall.   Cobnar Hill near Woodseats was a very favourite walk for the view.

During the last forty years the part of Norton round

the church and round the Oakes has changed very
little. On the north she is threatened, for Sheffield, like
the dragon of Wantley, gobbles up its own green
borderland and demands each year its toll of the neighbouring fields ; but so far, though much of Norton Lees
—including once lovely Lees Lane—has fallen, old
Norton has remained unassailed. The parts of the parish
of Norton which slope to the Meersbrook and to the
Sheaf display now those signs of wear and tear and fatigue
which woods and fields show under the pressure of an
overgrown population. The hedges grow thin and
straggling, revealing frequent gaps, the meadows are
trampled, gates are broken, the trunks of the trees are
black and devoid of moss or lichen ; the earth is grimy,
and the fields are crossed by the abhorred cinder paths.
To-day the golf-ball whizzes over pastures where once
flew the cock pheasant, and the raucous cries of football
spectators come now from meadows which lately knew
the fluting of the blackbird.

Many centuries go to the making of a place like
Norton. Hundreds of years are needed to evolve her
architecture, to mature her buildings, to grow her oaks
and yews, to accumulate her traditions and folk tales,
and therefore such places should be valued above price.
Philistines can destroy them in a few days ; no one
can make them in less than a thousand years. " It
might have been sold " was the only aspect that obtuse
Judas Iscariot could understand of the incident of the
very precious alabaster box of ointment of spikenard,
and the school of Judas has multiplied greatly, applying
its narrow and sordid formula on every occasion when it is
sought to safeguard natural beauty from the greedy and
the insensible. Norton " might have been sold" ; some
of it has been sold already, and a day may come when the
rest will go; but for the present the village round the old
church remains, with its peace yet unmolested, its beauty
not only unimpaired but increased year by year by the
growth of its noble trees, so that the native, be he ever

so old, may return even from the ends of the earth to find still at Norton

> . . . Voices of eld,
> The home, the church upon the village green,
> Old thoughts that circle like the birds of Even
> Round the grey tower. Soft sweet regrets, like sunset
> Lighting old windows with gleams day had not.
> Ghosts of dead years, whispering old names
> Through grass-grown pathways, by halls mouldering now.

Amongst its features we must not forget the rooks of Norton. At times it seems as though the place were dominated by the citizens of the " black republics." It is a pleasure to watch them ; there is something soothing about their cawing, and altogether we may count it amongst the many delights of Norton to sit here looking for

> The many-wintered crow that leads
> The clanging rookery home.

Folk lore has been busy with the crows as with other things, and it is interesting to know that "ravens and crows, when they do make a hoarse, hollow, and sorrowful noise, as if they sobbed, it presages foul weather approaching. Crows flocking together in great companies, or calling early in the morning with a full and clear voice, or at any time of the day gaping against the sun, forshews hot and dry weather ; but if at the brink of ponds they do wet their heads, or stalk into the water, or cry much towards the evening, are signs of rain."

The appearance of Norton seems to have been changed very much by the operation of its Enclosure Act of 1803. Under this act about two hundred and seventy acres of land were enclosed. At that time Samuel Shore, the younger, was lord of the manor, and Peter Robinson was vicar and entitled to glebe lands. John Nuttall of Matlock was appointed commissioner to allot the land, and the award map showing how the territory was

shared was drawn by William and Josiah Fairbank
of Sheffield, surveyors.   The earlier enclosures, under
which a farmer obtained his holding in a compact whole,
instead of in widely sundered strips which were inter-
mingled with the land of his neighbour, was an economic
necessity ; but the later sharing amongst the rich of
what were euphemistically called waste grounds, the
partition of the people's commons, the stopping of footpaths, stirred deep resentment which expressed itself in
many ways.   An old folk rhyme laments

> But now the commons are taen in,
> The cottages pulled down,
> And Moggy's got na wool to spin
> Her linsey-woolsey gown.

Then there is the clever epigram

> We send to gaol the man or woman
> Who steals the goose from off the common ;
> But let the greater felon loose
> Who steals the common from the goose.

Writing in 1823, in his *Peak Scenery*, Ebenezer Rhodes,
coming from Heeley to Norton by way of Woodseats and
Bole Hill, complained that Norton " has lost part of its
rural appearance by the enclosure of the many little
verdant spots with which it was once adorned.   The
Village Green, the scene of many a mirthful sport, has
disappeared, and every plot of ground is now securely
hemmed in with fences.   I question not the policy of
such proceedings—they may be wise and useful, perhaps
necessary, but they have devastated many a lovely scene,
and impaired the beauty of many a rural picture."
     James Montgomery deplored very bitterly, in the *Iris*,
in 1828, the ruthless enclosure and stoppage of footpaths
that was going on then around Sheffield ; and Hunter
wrote that " it was a great pity that the Green at Norton,
which was spacious and pleasant, was taken in to the
grounds of the Hall."   Asline Ward, on the other hand,

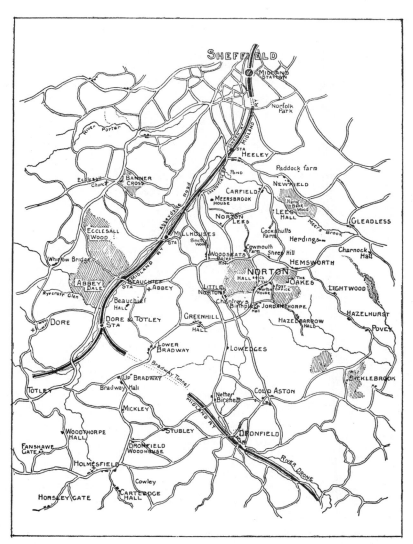

MAP OF "CHANTREY LAND"

239

wrote of Norton that " the effect is little injured by the enclosure of the Green."

Mrs. Sterndale also makes her moan in her *Vignettes of Derbyshire*, and incidentally gives a description of the Norton of 1824. She says " Norton Green *was* surrounded by Norton Hall, Norton House, an ancient chauntry, and the vicarage, forming an area of uncommon beauty and rural accommodation. The church, standing on a gentle rise, forming its southern boundary; and the green, divided by a commodious carriage-road, was partly shaded by a row of fine trees, that screened Norton House from the west winds, and gave sylvan beauty to the rustic lawn ; fronting which, beneath the wall that enclosed the opposite domain, an expansive pool of water dispensed freshness and aliment to man, and all the lower world. Forest trees, shrubs, and flowers, presented themselves in approximation with the different habitations ; and though all was private property, yet their open display was general pleasure. The Virginia creeper, in its varied changes of green, yellow, and red, covered the high square turrets of Norton Hall ; the lilacs and laburnums hung over its walled enclosure above the water ; the elms and yews of the church-yard blended their foliage ; the spreading pear trees, and the starry jasmine, covered the front of the Vicarage, its little court beneath rich in floral beauty ; the bright ivy and gadding woodbine clothed the gables and gateway of Norton House ; the old elms throwing their shadows on the green below its windows ; the venerable Chauntry, standing a little aloof, beneath the oak of ages, with the attractive cottage at its termination, over-canopied with lofty trees, and enclosed in verdure ; and from the midst of all, a distant view of the Derbyshire hills consummated and contrasted the beauty of the scene. Such was Norton Green—but it is such no longer. The enclosure act has changed its appearance. Private convenience may be attained, private property certainly is enhanced, but rural beauty is lost, time-established liberty invaded, benevolent associations banished, and pictorial effect destroyed ; angular walls intersect the once open green, that is now parcelled off to its proprietors ; but it must ever be lamented by those who remember its former interest, that amidst all the territory by which they are surrounded, this little patch of village freedom could not be resigned ; that the right of its possession should have been maintained is allowed, but its privileges and its pleasures should, like the verdant hue of its turf, have been perennial."

Deeds and old maps show that the unenclosed land at Norton was scattered about the parish. A document of 1690 mentions " the Lords wast adjoyninge to the Church yard wall," and maps show commons at the top of Bole Hill, on Back Moor, Cobnar Bank and Magathay Green. Norton Lane from the church to Greenhill crossed a common ; Cold Aston had a large common, and there were Hemsworth Common and other open places. When the coach road crossed Norton Park it ran through common land.

In former years a road had its direction changed by the licence of the king ; but during the reign of George the Third the matter was placed in the hands of the local magistrates, who seem to have been called upon to decide questions of this kind oftener than we should have thought. In an old village like Norton, living its uninterrupted life, it seems as though the roads and footpaths had been in their present places almost from time immemorial, but a footway between Norton and Little Norton was diverted in 1780 ; Derbyshire Lane was diverted in 1803, a footpath from the Chesterfield Road to Hazelbarrow in 1811, and in the same year one from the church yard to Magathay ; still in the same year one from Little Norton towards Greenhill and another between Hemsworth and Norton. In 1816 there was diverted a bridle road passing through the grounds of Sir William Chambers Bagshawe of the Oakes, between Norton and Eckington. The last turnpike trust in Derbyshire created

by Act of Parliament was for the Greenhill Moor and
Eckington Road in 1840.

Norton's most famous road, however, was, as we
mentioned at Meersbrook, the coach road which until the
early part of the nineteenth century passed through Little
Norton, a place then on one of the main routes, but now
left in a quiet backwater of England, with nothing con-
ducting us through it but an obscure footpath, no traffic
upon its road but an occasional slow-moving load of
manure, a hawker's cart surrounded by a knot of women,
or a herd of leisurely cattle.   On some maps Little
Norton is given and not Norton.   So, standing upon
this old road at Little Norton, it is natural that we should
think of those bygone days when the coaches thundered
past on their way from London to Sheffield and Leeds,
or from Leeds through Sheffield to London, on what
variety of errands connected with joy and sorrow we
know not now.   How often then must the quiet of these
fields have been broken by the rousing notes of the
guard's horn!   When the Rev. H. H. Pearson went as
a young man from Norton to Oxford University he joined
the coach on Greenhill Moor, and he used to talk of the
days when the horns echoed and re-echoed upon this still
tableland that has slept ever since while the traffic has
come and gone no nearer than the Midland railway line
through Bradway, Beauchief and Heeley, the people boxed
in their carriages knowing not so much as the name of
Little Norton, for, though it had its place in Paterson and
Cary, it is not to be found in Bradshaw.   For us, however,
this short stretch of deserted road that to-day comes to
an abrupt end at Norton Park, near the village pump on
its patch of green, speaks not only of life but of literature
and art, of old books and old prints of absorbing interest.

If the coaches generally brought life to a village
they sometimes brought death, for here at Little Norton
the child of James Turner was run over and killed
in 1800, and the Eyam Plague in this county arose from
tainted clothing carried in a coach from London.

LITTLE NORTON

243

Fairbank's map of 1804-5 shows the road going straight from Little Norton to the top of Bole Hill, across a patch of waste land, but now road and land alike are merged in Norton Park. In the County Offices at Derby is a document that records the appointment of John Nuttall of Matlock as commissioner in 1802-3, and his decision, in which Joshua Jebb and William Allwood Lord, two justices, concurred, that this road "beginning at a certain Gate near Widow Biggin's House at Little Norton . . . and ending at Bolehill . . . be stopped up and discontinued, the same appearing to me to be useless and unnecessary." If Widow Biggin of Little Norton was ever in the mind to go to Bole Hill she may have thought differently; but probably her views were not considered in the transaction, though after all she had more at stake than the excellent Mr. Nuttall of Matlock, or Joshua Jebb and William Allwood Lord, Justices of the Peace, who did not reside at Little Norton nor at Bole Hill.

At Little Norton was a branch of the Parker family, and the late Mr. Charles Jackson of Doncaster, whose wife was a Parker, collected sedulously the particulars of many deeds having reference to the Parkers of Little Norton, of Norton Lees and of Sheffield too, and these may be found in the *Proceedings of the Derbyshire Archæological Society*, Vol. IV. 23 and V. 30. In 1384, during the reign of Richard the Second, Thomas Parker and Adam Parker are the witnesses to a grant of land in Little Norton from Adam Bate to Hugh del Backhous. In 1471 Roger de Ecclesale conveyed to Richard Bullock a wood called Cangull, in Onston, and amongst the witnesses are John Parkar of Leys and John Parkar of Little Norton. In 1480 land at Greenhill is conveyed to John Parker of Little Norton. A document of 1482 is an indenture between Thomas Chaworth, Esq., lord of Norton, and Thomas Parker for the lease of " Johnsett Woodde " and other land and houses. The wood is mentioned as Chauncit, or John Set, Wood in particulars of sale of

245

1850, where its area is given as 21 a. 0 r. 12 p. In 1493 John Parker of Little Norton was one of the witnesses to a grant of land in le Brendclyf, from William Machon of Halume. Here we have the modern Brincliffe, a suggestion of the origin of Machon Bank and Hallam in another form.

The will of Robert Parker, of Lytyll Norton, belonging to 1535, directs that his body is to be beryed in the parish church of Sant James at Norton. He gives to St. James on lb of wax to be bernt a for hym. I assyne my ferme y^t I have be leyise of the Abbot & convent of Bewecheff to ysabelle my wyffe, & to John my son aft hur decesse, durent my termes. Also, I beyng seke in my bode & whole in my mynd, do testyfy y^t ye lands of my faders y^t they of Ekylsfeld hold wrongfully were gyffen to ye chyrch of Sant James at Norton wher my faders bones lyeth, & y^t was hys last wylle & mynd os I shall make answere a for God at ye dredfull day of dome. The rest of his goods are to be delt amongst my wyff & my chylder. The executors were ysabelle my wyff, John Parker my son, and gylbartt butteler. Mest. John Seleok m^r John Parker, overseers. Witnesses, Sir Thomas gylbart clerk, and others. It was usual then, as we may infer from Shakespeare, to call a clerk in holy orders Sir. Gilbert was chanter at Beauchief Abbey and Vicar of Norton in 1524.

Amongst other deeds connecting the Parkers with Little Norton are Isabelle Parker's will of 1545, and a lease of 1548 from Thomas Babington to Thomas Parker of Little Norton, yeoman, of all that his moyte part and ppartye of all such toftes closes, lands, &c., whyche be sett lyenge or beynge in Lyttle Norton or elsewhere wth yn the lordsyppe of Norton.

William Swift the genealogist gave to Charles Jackson a drawing of the remains of an old house at Little Norton which he made in 1866. The house had two gables and a receding centre, and he thought it might be the home of the Parkers.

A deed of 1605 or 1606 mentions a house at Little
Norton, and refers to a parlour " wherein is a chimney "
and to " three bayes of a new shyfted or builded " house
or barn.   A reference of 1632 gives more details, mentioning " the Hall or Fierhouse [the part of the house
in which was a fire] of the nowe mansion house of the

Birch-House
Farm
LITTLE NORTON

said John Parker the elder in Little Norton aforesaid
with the entry leading into the same, the parlor on
the south side of the said hall, the chambers over the
said hall, parlor and entry, the butter and milk house
adjoining to the said hall, all the outhouses and buildings
standing on the south side of the said fould, the moiety
or one halfe of the kitchen, the moietie or one halfe
of the threshing flore of the barne, and the moietie or

half of all foldes, curtelages, gardeines, and orchards, belonging to the said messuage or mansion house, and eleven closes of land."

The Parkers of Little Norton claimed kinship with the Parkers of Norton Lees. Hunter pushes their pedigree back to a Robert Parker of Little Norton concerning whom we know not when he was born, baptised or buried; but his son Thomas was living in 1547, and Thomas's son John was living in 1583. In the next generation it is possible to find dates, and thus we have another John Parker of Little Norton and Jordanthorpe, yeoman, baptised on September 4, 1575, and buried at Norton on July 17, 1638. He was married three times, and his first wife was Dionysia, a daughter of Thomas Bright of the neighbouring hamlet of Bradway. Her brother was Stephen Bright of Carbrook, the father of Sir John Bright, baronet. John Parker's second wife he found also near home, for she was Jane Bate of Jordanthorpe. Of his third wife we know only that her name was Anne and that she was buried in 1642.

Without repeating the John begat Thomas process all through the subsequent generations, we may pass to the year 1700, when there was born John Parker of Greenhill, who inherited, from John Woodrove, to whom he was related, a house at Intake near Sheffield known as Wood-thorpe Hall, not to be confounded with the Woodthorpe Hall between Totley and Holmesfield. Upon John Parker a grant of arms was bestowed, and he was buried at Norton in 1779. This John Parker had a son whose name also was John, and he was educated at Oxford and became a barrister. For many years he was steward of the manor court at Sheffield, and lies buried at Handsworth. To him was born, in 1772, a son Hugh, who, after having been educated at Cambridge, became a barrister like his father, and like him held the office of steward of the manor court of Sheffield. He married Mary, daughter of Samuel Walker, who from small beginnings at Grenoside passed to greater achievements at

Masborough, and
became distinguished
in the world of iron-
founders as the maker
of Southwark and of
other bridges. It
was in the office of
the Walkers that the
father of Ebenezer
Elliott was employed
as a clerk, and the
father of Ebenezer Rhodes worked for the same firm.
From this Parker-Walker marriage came John Parker
born in 1799. He was educated at Repton, afterwards at
Oxford, and became a barrister. He too was steward of the

manor court of Sheffield, but lived to witness the abolition
of the court in 1847.   When Sheffield, under the Reform
Act of 1832, became entitled to have Members of Parliament of her own, without having to share them with the
West Riding of Yorkshire, Parker, who was a Whig, was
elected with Silk Buckingham.   He was successful in
Parliament, was elected again and again by his Sheffield
friends, became Secretary of the Admiralty and afterwards
Secretary of the Treasury ; but in 1852 he lost his seat to

At Jordanthorpe

Roebuck and Hadfield.   He was, however, made a member of the Privy Council, and lived on until the year 1881,
when at No. 71, Onslow Square, London, he died nearly
eighty-two years of age, leaving no children.
    Almost every feature of old Norton is pleasing to those
who ramble through the place, and the group of cottages
which includes the post office presents a charming picture,
its one clipped yew amongst all this wealth of trees and
flowers reminding the wayfarer of gardening methods now
happily abandoned.   About Jordanthorpe too delightful

peeps of ancient farm houses are seen as we stroll along from Norton Lane to Hazelbarrow. First comes Jordanthorpe Hall, or House, as some call it, the residence of Mr. John Percy Collier, standing back in a lovely little park-like paddock. It is covered with ivy, but a portico stands clear of this green profusion, and the house is one of the most attractive in Norton. Here, cared for by his aunt Linley, Linley Sambourne spent some of his childhood, dreaming probably, but never imagining that before his

JORDANTHORPE HALL

death in 1910 he would leave Jordanthorpe for Fleet Street and Whitefriars to be entrusted with the drawing of the chief cartoons for *Punch*. The Linleys of Norton appear to have been connected with the celebrated Miss Linley, who became the wife of Sheridan; Elizabeth, the beautiful, the talented, the "Maid of Bath," painted by Gainsborough.

Next along the lane come a few outbuildings, and a few yards farther east the birthplace of Chantrey, to which we shall return. It is now owned and occupied by Mr. and Mrs. Andrew, of the same family of Andrew as the one at Greenhill Hall. Mrs. Andrew belongs to the family of Somerset, connected for a number of generations with Bradwell, an isolated village amongst the hills in the

NORTON GRANGE

Castleton region. In the annals of Methodism there the name of Somerset often has honourable mention. A lodge much newer than the house now guards the track to Chantrey's birthplace.

Still a little farther towards Hazelbarrow is a farm

Bullifant's Farm.
(Old Jordanthorpe Hall)

253

house known to natives as Old Jordanthorpe Hall, which is now and for thirty or forty years has been the home of Mr. John Bullifant. One of the features of the place is a cedar brought here in a flower pot by a former occupier named Bingham, and a walnut tree grows upon the north. An old lane, known to the few who know it at all as Rabbit Lane, and said to be an old packhorse track, has been traced to Barlow by Mr. Bullifant. It commences in one of his fields between his farm and the path to Hazelbarrow, and runs into a field between Hazelbarrow and the wood through which we pass to Cold Aston.

A little way past Mr. Bullifant's farm the Jordanthorpe Lane runs into School House

Entrance to
Norton Grange

Lane at right angles, and according to a map of 1737 the field at the right-hand corner, the corner we round if we go to Hazelbarrow, was called Lime Kiln Meadow. There is no lime kiln there now, nor traces of one, so this may be one of the cases in which a field name preserves the record of a forgotten feature. The field at the other corner is called Stony Field, and the one next to that towards Magathay, School House Croft.

A Corner at the Grange

Already incidental mention has been made of one of the most prominent and pleasing of the Norton residences, the Grange, near the church. This seems to be the house which Mr. Joseph Offley built for his chaplain, the Rev. Daniel Lowe, who had a school at Norton. Upon the ceiling of the hall is an ingenious monogram composed of a repetition of J. O. and the date 1744. Joseph Offley died in 1751. In a subsequent chapter we shall see here Mr. Piper, who left Norton in 1843. Afterwards the Gascoignes were here. Probably some alterations were made in 1852, because that date and a shield are on the mantelpiece in the dining-room. The Fishers and the Gladwins too have lived at the Grange, now occupied by Mr. Frank Dickinson Wild, to whom allusion has been made in connection with the Thorpes of Norton Lees.

CHAPTER XIV

CHARLES ASHTON AND OTHERS

ONE of the outposts of the parish of Norton is the hamlet of Bradway, whose name the natives pronounce Bradda, though philologists derive its name from Broadway. In a deed of the year 1280 the road here is called the *regia via*, the King's highway. There used to be a stone cross at Bradway, and what seem to be its remains peep at us now over a wall in the corner of a field. The name Hempyard suggests an industry no longer known here ; the name Bradway Moor Gate indicates wild surroundings, for Bradway is well within sight of the heather. I remember a Bradway man who used to tell weird stories of hobgoblins in the lanes with eyes as big as saucers, of gates that would open of their own accord upon the approach of a minister of religion, of men who died untimely when their path had been crossed by a visionary black cat, of the faces of the dead looking over people's shoulders in mirrors, and other similarly arresting and veracious narratives. In ancient times there was a corn mill at Bradway, "Bradway Mylne," with Thomas Aram as miller in 1562. In 1595 Robert Shepphearde was the miller, and in 1600 Thomas Meller. There was a William Mawer of Bradway in 1426.

Bradway Hall, at one time inhabited by a branch of the old and powerful Derbyshire family of the Eyres, has now upon its site a farm-house. It was part of the estate of our old friend Robert Newton, and passed, with Norton House, to his relations, who still own it. In the church porch at Norton is a memorial, removed from the church during the restoration of 1882, to John Eyre of Bradway, who died in 1664. The Eyres sold Bradway to the Stones, whose descendants in their turn sold it to John Parker for £1,360 in 1761. There were in the hall some armorial remains which Pegge thought might be the arms of the Fitzherberts, but which others considered to be those of the Talbots. Famous local people connected with Bradway are the Brights. Thomas Bright of Bradway settled at Carbrook about the beginning of the seventeenth century, and his son Stephen, baptised at Norton, built or enlarged Carbrook Hall. In 1804 died the Marchioness of Rockingham, the last of the Brights of Carbrook.

These fragments of the old hall at Bradway occupy an exposed corner of Norton parish where the road from Norton to Holmesfield turns abruptly at right angles, changing its direction sharply from west to south. Here, overlooking the grim moors, the hall receives the stringent, salutary winds that stir the blood and brace the nerves, though sometimes as the angry blasts smite this " wuthering " height it seems as though the houses would be torn up by their foundations, the trees by their roots, and under the hedges at Bradway the snow lingers in long lines many days after it has disappeared in the valley of the Sheaf. Much old work remains in the buildings, ancient oak doors, coping stones, and windows. The woodwork is of particularly massive oak, the timber used with a prodigality which is in sharp contrast with the penurious use of deal in those modern farm buildings that are eked out meanly with hideous corrugated zinc. Especially in what is now the cow house do the huge balks crowd upon the sight. In the corn chamber is oak panelling, and one of the bedrooms of the inhabited part of the house has an oak wardrobe built into the wall. In a field belonging to Bradway Hall, and known as Three Nook field, was found an ancient urn in 1783, but it was broken to pieces.

Thus in one way or another it is clear that, undistinguished as Bradway may appear to the supercilious glance of those who flash through it on a bicycle or see it through goggles from a motor car, it has yet something to offer to those who desire to penetrate its reserve and aloofness ; but its crowning glory is that it was the birthplace of the distinguished scholar Charles Ashton, who was born here in 1665, when Charles the Second was upon the throne.   Queens' College, Cambridge, received him in 1682, and he took his degree of Bachelor of Arts and was elected to a fellowship.   For some time he served as chaplain to Bishop Patrick, but was presented to the living of Rettenden in Essex.   He did not stay there long, but soon became the chaplain of Chelsea Hospital.   In 1701 he was collated to a prebendal stall in Ely Cathedral, and was elected upon the following day as Master of Jesus College, Cambridge, so filling two of the vacancies caused by the death of Dr. Saywell.   Before the close of the year he became a Doctor of Divinity, and in 1702 Vice-Chancellor of his University.   His life at Cambridge was the life of a scholar spent in quiet and seclusion.   Not often did he leave the University, and then it was when his duties at Ely called him forth. So in peace he lived until he was eighty-seven years of age, and he lies buried in the College Chapel at Cambridge, away from so many of his kindred who lie buried here at Norton.   Charles Ashton's works are not for popular entertainment.   The most enterprising publisher is not likely to reprint them in any of his " series."   Extracts from his writings are never found in the popular snippet journals.   Ashton contributed to Wasse's *Bibliotheca Literaria* of 1724 an article on *Tully and Hirtius reconciled as to the time of Cæsar's going to the African War* and also an emendation of a passage of Justin Martyr.   He wrote also for Reading's editions of Origen *De Oratione* and *Historiæ Ecclesiasticæ Scriptores*.   Dyer in his history of the University of Cambridge says that Ashton's " edition of Hierocles's excellent commentary on the golden verses of Pythagoras is without his name, or, it should rather be said, with another person's. . . . Mr. Wakefield also has particularly noticed a Tertullian as being replete with notes by Dr. Ashton. I have also myself perused a dictionary marked in the same manner. In 1768 there was issued an edition of Justin Martyr's *Apologiæ* prepared by Frederick Keller, fellow of Jesus College, to whom Ashton had left his papers except his sermons which he destroyed out of the way." At the British Museum are copies of some of Ashton's letters to Dean Moss, and also his additions to Sherman's *History of Jesus College* and particulars he had collected about the University generally.

In his *Literary Anecdotes* Nichols says that " Ashton was one of the most learned men of the age ; his great knowledge in Ecclesiastical Antiquities was excelled by none, and equalled by few ; as by his manuscript remarks upon the Fathers, and corrections of the mistakes of translators, will sufficiently appear. His critical skill in the writers of the Classicks is well known to many persons now living. There were many valuable pieces of his published in the time of his life, but without his name." Ashton seems to have had even more than the modesty usual to scholars, working hard, but caring naught for publicity nor for recognition, bestowing his writings unsigned upon those who needed them, careless who obtained the credit for all this painful research.

A small stone before the altar steps in the chapel of Jesus College, Cambridge, is inscribed :

Car. Ashton
S.T.P.
huius Collegii
per annos L Magister
Obiit
Anno Christi MDCCLII
Aetat LXXXVII.

In the Master's lodge is his portrait by Robert Pyle, which has been engraved, and there are copies of it in the Hall and in the Combination Room. Pyle painted also a portrait of Queen Charlotte. Many of Ashton's books, containing his manuscript notes, are in the College Library.

Robert Ashton, the father of Charles, came to Norton from Scotter in Lincolnshire, and the family seems to have gone hence to Darfield. In Norton church yard is a tomb of the Ashtons with a weather-worn coat-of-arms, and at Darfield there is a memorial with the family arms and a Latin inscription, supplied probably by Charles himself.

Charles's grandfather was Robert Ashton of Stoney Middleton, who was High Sheriff of Derbyshire in 1665. He excused himself from providing the Judge at the Assizes with a carriage by explaining that carriages were unknown at Stoney Middleton because the place was not upon the level but on end. Charles's uncle, Alexander Ashton, lived at Whiteley Wood, near Sheffield, and is believed to have built the hall there. The family seems to have come from Shepley, in Lancashire, and has a pedigree running back to Saxon times.

Ashton is not the only Cambridge scholar from Jesus College whose name is associated with Bradway. The hamlet gave shelter for a short time in our own days to another distinguished if heterodox student from this college and from this ancient seat of learning. Edward Carpenter, M.A., was born at Brighton in 1844, and at Cambridge became, like Ashton, a fellow of his college. A year later he entered the Church, and was for a time a curate under Frederick Denison Maurice. Later, becoming very uncomfortable, and feeling that he " must leave or be suffocated," he abandoned his fellowship and his curacy, and became a University Extension Lecturer in Sheffield. This work did not satisfy his longings for reality, and in an attractive piece of autobiography he has told us of his early desire to write a book " which should address itself very personally and closely to any one who cared to read it," and how "at last, early in 1881, no doubt as the culmination and result of struggles and experiences that had been going on, I became conscious that a mass of material was forming within me, imperatively demanding expression." Later in the article he has added that "the necessity for space and time to work this out grew so strong that in April of that year I threw up my lecturing employment. Moreover another necessity had come upon me which demanded the latter step—the necessity namely for an open-air life and manual work. I could not finally argue with this any more than with the other, I had to give in and obey. As it happened at the time I mention I was already living in a little cottage on a farm [at Bradway near Sheffield] with a friend and his family, and doing farm-work in the intervals of my lectures. When I threw up the lecturing I had everything clear before me. I knocked together a sort of wooden sentinel box, in the garden, and there, or in the fields and the woods, all that spring and summer, and on through the winter, by day and sometimes by night, in sunlight or in rain, by frost and snow and all sorts of grey and dull weather, I wrote *Towards Democracy*—or at any rate the first and longer poem that goes by that name."

Edward Carpenter's attachment to this district had a direct effect upon Norton, for two men young enough and enthusiastic enough to try experiments, Mr. Herbert H. Stansfield and Mr. Hugh Mapleton, after a course of Edward Carpenter and Henry David Thoreau, went back to the land. In 1896, when Mr. Goodliffe had Norton Hall, they rented his kitchen garden and one of his cottages, and grew and sold tomatoes, cucumbers and bedding-out plants. Others joined, and sandal-making and a few more handicrafts were added to the operations. Some of the colonists had long hair, wore sandals and cloaks, sported bare legs on occasion, and were known amongst the villagers, who do not take kindly to innovations, as "the funny fellows in Norton Lane," or briefly as "them fooaks." However, they had youth on their side, and so were able to hold their course at Norton for two years in the old garden of the Offleys and the Shores. When the members separated, four went to the Starnthwaite colony, near Kendal in Westmorland, founded under the influence of Herbert V. Mills' *Poverty and the State.* All are scattered now. Mr. Mapleton is Managing Director of the Nut Food Co. at Garston near Liverpool, Mr. Stansfield pursues sculpture and metal work at Ipswich in intervals of art teaching, another is a chemical analyst in Russia, one is in the Royal Navy and has traversed the world, another is a city sanitary inspector, and still another is in New York, so that Norton from this little social experiment has those who remember her in many parts of the globe.

Belonging to the family of Stones that purchased Bradway from the Eyres was Nicholas Stones, "a most flourishing merchant of Himsworth," who was buried at Norton at the age of seventy in 1676. There is a slab to his memory in the church porch. He left land towards the payment of the vicar of Norton, the schoolmaster, and for the apprenticing of poor boys. A stone in the belfry commemorates others of the family. A descendant, Joseph, lived at Bradway for a time, but bought Mosborough from the Coopers. His wife was Ruth, a daughter of Edward Gill, of Carr House, near Rotherham. It was a later Nicholas, buried in 1691–2, who bought Bradway from the Eyres.

At Bradway we are not far from Stubley, where was born Ralph Gosling, who published the earliest known map of Sheffield in 1732. He was a schoolmaster, topographer and surveyor, and for some time lived at Heeley.

We are also near to Woodthorpe Hall, and so close upon Fanshawe Gate, where there are a few remains, still habitable as a cottage, of one of the homes of the Fanshawes, a family whose name occurs occasionally in

the Norton Registers, and whose fame has spread to
most parts of the King's realm.   Not only is the memory
of the family perpetuated in the name Fanshawe Gate,
but in 1656 Fanshawe Storth was given as the name of
a field near Holmesfield, and there is Fanshawe Bank
at Dronfield.

Even the most casual wanderer past Fanshawe Gate
assumes that some house of more than ordinary preten-
sions has been built here, for there still remain, though

not in their original position, two sets of square stone
pillars that have served for gate posts, one set surmounted
by the pine-cone ornament, the other by pyramids of
balls, and these, like the gate posts we saw at Hazelbarrow, serve for the memorials of a time when a house
stood here that was greater than any we may see in
this place to-day.

Mr. George Adams, who lived at Fanshawe Gate for
six years, and one of whose drawings of what is left
appears in Mr. H. C. Fanshawe's edition of Lady

Woodthorpe Hall

265

Fanshawe's memoirs, told me that some of the materials
of the old house are to be found in the outhouses,
but that no carved wood remains. There used to be
some that had been adapted as a kind of dresser,
but even that has now been taken away. A fine old
arched fireplace with arched recesses on each side had
been masked by modern material. A very massive oak
beam runs across an oaken ceiling. It is a tree so roughly
trimmed that the points at which the boughs branched
out may be seen. It had received the inevitable coats
of whitewash, but these were cleared away by much
patient labour. The Holmesfield Court Rolls allude to
" the parler belowe thentry with the chambers ouer it
. . . the greate barne of the west side the fould."
Again, the arched cellars of Fanshawe Gate remain, and
form a feature of the old place worthy of close examination. Some of them have been built up. Dr. Rooth of
Dronfield, and a former holder of the lease, Mr. Gregory,
explored these, but found nothing more than a few broken
bottles.

In addition to the part used as a cottage there is,
composed of old materials, a tall building of three
storeys to which access may be obtained at two levels,
from a field at the lower level, from a garden at the
higher. Doves seem to have inhabited the uppermost
region, and an interesting feature of this building is a
beautiful round window. Some glass in the windows
is thick enough to resist thrown stones, as a young
man who spent his boyhood there has assured me.

It would be beyond the scope of a book on Norton
to give a complete account of the Fanshawes, and there
is no need to enter into details, for a comprehensive
history of the family will be found in that edition of
the memoirs of Lady Fanshawe that was edited by
Mr. H. C. Fanshawe in 1907 and is now the standard
work upon the subject. Mr. Fanshawe traces the pedigree
back to 1417, when there was living John ffaunchal, for
from 1417 to 1540 the name was spelt ffaunchal, ffaunchall,

267

ffawnchall, Fonchall or Fanchall, and took its present
form about the time that the members of the family
began to occupy the post of Remembrancer. Whether
this place near Holmesfield derived its name from the
family, or the family from the place, is here as in
the matter of other names an open question, though
Mr. Fanshawe thinks it probable the family name was
derived from the place.

Passing over a number of generations we come to
Henry, who, though born here at Fanshawe Gate, went
to London, and obtained a post among the clerks of the
Exchequer, very possibly, as Mr. H. C. Fanshawe has
remarked, through the influence of Sir Christopher
Moore, or More, who was King's Remembrancer under
Henry the Eighth, and belonged to Norton, though
he went afterwards to Loseley in Surrey. Later the
Fanshawes migrated to larger houses in other counties.
The office of Remembrancer to the King, now held by
Master James R. Mellor of the Crown Office, Royal
Courts of Justice, was held by five Fanshawes in succession up to the Civil War and by nine from 1566 to
1716. A Thomas Fanshawe, in accordance with the
will of his uncle, founded the Grammar School at Dronfield, and in these days of celebrations it would not be
amiss if the boys of the Dronfield Grammar School were
marched to Fanshawe Gate upon each anniversary of
founder's day to see what remains of the old home of
the family who established their school. The Rev. John
Faithfull Fanshawe, B.A., was headmaster of Dronfield
Grammar School in the sixties. One of Thomas Fanshawe's daughters, Katherine, married John Bullock of
Norton in 1608, and John Bullock's father was also related
by marriage to the Fanshawes. His son William married
Katherine, the elder daughter of Sir John Wolstenholme,
originally of Cartledge Hall, who in 1619 became the
purchaser of Parsloes Manor House and afterwards of
other estates. An account of the Wolstenholmes is given
by Mr. H. C. Fanshawe, who relates that before the

Cartledge Hall

269

end of the twelfth century the Wolstenholmes were at Rochdale, but about 1450 representatives of this family came to Holmesfield and lived at Cartledge Hall, less than a mile away from Fanshawe Gate. Their name in more recent years has become associated also with Horsley Gate in Holmesfield. In Cartledge Hall is a notable mantelpiece carved to show a picture of the Fall, and there are moulded ceilings with Tudor details. A Wolstenholme went to London during the reign of Edward the Sixth, and obtained a post in the Customs. His son Sir John becoming a merchant prince and farmer of the Customs, grew rich, and one of his many operations was that of supporting Baffin's expedition in 1615, a circumstance which caused his name to be perpetuated in Wolstenholme Sound and in the Cape and Bay of this name in the Hudson Strait region of Canada. He married Catherine Fanshawe, and one of his daughters married William Fanshawe of Parsloes. The Wolstenholmes introduced John Harrison, Lady Fanshawe's father, when he was " a Lancashire lad," into the Custom House.

The most eminent member of the family was Sir Richard Fanshawe, who had a brilliant and eventful career in the reign of Charles the First. He was a soldier, diplomatist and poet. His lady it was who wrote the charming memoirs which would keep the name alive if all else perished. It is a delightful work, embodying a plain tale of human joys and sorrows told vividly, and yet with an engaging simplicity and charm that win our sympathy and even our affection for her who tells us so naively of her experiences. The story is compacted of cruel separations between wife and children, of the death of fondly loved offspring, of perils at the sword's point, grievous losses, storms at sea and shipwreck, painful illnesses, rough fare and dirty lodgings, ghosts, pomp, pillage, plague, scenes of violence, and generally of " wars, excursions and alarms."

So near to us as Tankersley did Sir Richard spend a memorable part of his life as a prisoner of war. In the

summer of 1891 I went there with my good friend
Ebenezer Downing, tramps with whom in Hallamshire
are amongst my happiest recollections, and he wrote a short

The Pigeon Cote
Fanshawe Gate   C Ashmore

account of the place which appeared in the *Sheffield Weekly
Independent* of August 29 of that year.   Sir Richard's
connection with the " groves of Tankersley " finds mention
too in Ebenezer Elliott's poem on *Love*.

Since the end of the seventeenth century the family has contributed a number of members to learning and to the Services.   The Rev. John Fanshawe, D.D. (1697–1763), was Professor first of Greek and afterwards of Theology at Oxford ; 'the Rev. Frederick Fanshawe (1821–1879) was scholar of Balliol and Fellow and Tutor of Exeter College, Oxford, and Headmaster of Bedford Grammar School ; and the present head of the family, Mr. Henry Ernest Fanshawe (*b.* 1844), is Fellow and Tutor of Corpus Christi College, Cambridge.   The gift of Latinity which Sir Richard Fanshawe possessed seems to have reappeared in the family in the nineteenth century, as the second member above-named won the Latin Verse prize at Oxford, and the last was four times Members' Prize-man of the Latin Essay at Cambridge.   In the Navy six members have attained the rank of Admiral or an equivalent rank, viz. Charles Fanshawe (1699–1756), his son Robert Fanshawe (1740–1823), his grandson Sir Arthur, K.C.B. (1795–1864), his great-grandson (son of General Edward Fanshawe, K.C.B.), Sir Edward Gennys Fanshawe, G.C.B. (1814–1906), and his great-great-grandson, the late Commander-in-Chief at Portsmouth, Sir Arthur Dalrymple Fanshawe, G.C.V.O., K.C.B. In the military service Colonel Henry Fanshawe (1756–1826) was colonel in the British Guards and of the 83rd Regiment, and afterwards became General in the Russian service, in which two of his sons (who like himself received various Russian decorations) and one grandson attained the same rank ; his eldest son, Henry Fanshawe (1778–1857), became a Rear-Admiral in the British Navy. Charles Fanshawe (1817–1901), like his father, became General R.E., and Brigadier-General Hew Dalrymple (*b.* 1860) now commands the Presidency District, India. Besides these Colonel Thomas Basil Fanshawe (1829–1905) commanded the 33rd Regiment, and Colonel Robert Fanshawe, D.S.O., at present commands the Oxford Light Infantry.

Among other members of the family may be mentioned

Charles Fanshawe (1740–1814), Recorder of Exeter ; Sir Arthur Upton Fanshawe, K.C.I.E., C.S.I., C.V.O. (*b.* 1848), late Director-General of the Post Office in India ; Herbert Charles Fanshawe (*b.* 1852), C.S.I., editor of the memoirs of Lady Fanshawe ; and Reginald Fanshawe (*b.* 1855), scholar and Fellow of New College, Oxford, and till lately Professor of Classics, University College, Bristol.

In a walk to Bradway we are often near the steep wood at the back of Beauchief Abbey. It is indeed this wooded hill, sheltering the abbey upon its southern side, which is the *bello capite,* or *beau chef,* the beautiful headland from which the abbey has derived its name, and here the monastery lifts what is left of its old western tower in a dale that runs almost parallel with the valley of the Sheaf, a still, pastoral region that has succeeded so far in retaining much of its quiet, remaining to-day a realm of ancient peace remote from the city life, away from the " dust of the struggling outer world." Whether it will much longer remain so is a question to give us pause, for it is threatened by the same doom that is so rapidly substituting ugliness for beauty in the valley of the Sheaf, and not far away there may be witnessed disconcerting tendencies towards the outbreaks of that architectural scarlatina, modified by the cool tints of the blue slate, to which the country hereabouts is so liable, notwithstanding that stone is so plentiful. Since the first words of this book were written hitherto rural Woodseats has more than commenced to emulate Attercliffe, and no one knows how far this kind of blight may spread ; for just as Leeds is catching up to Kirkstall, so may Sheffield surround Beauchief Abbey, and Abbey Lane, in spite of all its wild-rose blooms, may yet become as is Carlisle Street East. Already there is talk of trams, and before the first car runs along this dale its charm will have fled for ever.

Still, no matter what may happen in the future, no spoiler can take away the pleasures so many of us have enjoyed here in the past, not forgetting even the boyish

slides upon the abbey fish-ponds in winter nor the delight of seeing this sequestered place under deep and
unpolluted snow.   Pleasant has it been too in summer to
sketch the great oak in Beauchief Park, or to sit under
its widespread boughs reading *Ivanhoe*, or to watch the
sheep and cows browsing quietly or languorously chewing
their cud ; to drink at the cold spring that runs into its
mossy trough under the trees not far from Beauchief Hall,
itself upon a summer afternoon like a poem by Tennyson ;
to loiter in the cool of Gulley's Wood, where patches of
oak-fern used to grow ; to spy upon the mad gambols of
the water shrews in the little Shene, that runs through the
abbey grounds to join the Sheaf.   In any case these joys
could never return with the same zest, for are they not
associated with

> Dreams that the soul of youth engage
> Ere Fancy has been quelled ?

A whole book would be needed for an account of Beauchief Abbey, yet it is so closely connected with Norton
that it is not to be passed over in this volume and no
mention made.

With regard to the name of Beauchief, there is precisely
the same word in Beachy Head.   In the State Papers of
Henry the Eighth Beachy Head is given as Bechiff,
Bechiefe, Beauchif and Beauchief, " beautiful headland,"
so that it was pure ignorance which added the word
" Head " when it was there already.

A beautiful headland this one at Beauchief truly is,
though its attraction is of a different kind compared with
that of the famous Sussex cape, and here many an artist has
been tempted to take out his sketch book at sight of the
ruin and its lovely surroundings.   Tom Creswick, R.A.,
the Sheffield artist who became known for his beautiful
paintings of English landscape and for his exquisite book
illustrations, made a drawing of Beauchief Abbey ; and
picturesque old Christopher Thomson, who spent his
last years in Sheffield, sketched many of her beautiful

scenes, and wrote that interesting *Autobiography of an Artisan*, painted Beauchief Abbey too, a work now in the possession of Mr. W. T. Freemantle of Barbot Hall. Not only innumerable local artists, but others of national fame who were not, like Creswick, born here, have yet found their way to Beauchief, for here came Dayes, whom we have met already at Smithy Wood Bottom, and he tells us that " four miles from Sheffield, at the sign of the Hammer and Pincers, I turned into an indifferent cross road, which, at the end of two miles of pleasant country, conducted me to Beauchief Abbey, which is situated in a delightful vale, near the northern boundary of Derbyshire. The remains of the Abbey, though inconsiderable, are nevertheless sufficiently attractive to engage attention by the aid of the rich surrounding scenery, the back-ground being formed by bold hills, richly decorated with wood. . . . Beauchief being highly enriched with wood, will afford some excellent studies, in which the building will happily unite."

Dr. Pegge, Mr. Addy, John Holland, James Montgomery, Dr. Cox, Mr. Henry Kirke and others have written of the abbey, but none of the writers who have described it, none of the artists who have sketched it, have seen Beauchief Abbey except as a ruin. This solitary, truncated tower and the relics that still cling to it give no idea of the extent of the monastery, but if the foundations are ever exposed by excavations an abbey, not amongst the greatest, yet one of considerable proportions, will be revealed. The west doorway is of thirteenth-century architecture, the tower itself of fourteenth-century. The portals which now flank the tower are not in their original positions, but were placed where we see them to-day when they were discovered amongst the ruins. They do not appear, for instance, in the drawing of the brothers Buck, of 1727; nor in Grimm's plate of 1785. The doorway upon the north is Norman ; that upon the south, Early English.

Not far from the abbey of Prémontré, the parent

abbey, in France, is the town and abbey of St. Quentin, or St. Quintin ; and it may be that a well near to Beauchief Abbey was known as St. Quentin's well by the canons, for the name seems to survive to this day in the grotesque corruption Twenty Well, or Twenty Well Sick, " sick " being a denomination for a stream.

The lane from Bradway to Dore and Totley railway station, on the Midland line, is known as Twenty Well Lane, and the stream itself that adds the " sick " to the Twenty Well is the one that belongs to the deep valley in which to-day we find the Bradway tunnel between Dore station and Dronfield.　There is a reference to Quintine well during the time of Edward the First, but Mr. Addy has shown in his glossary that an alternative derivation may be from Centing, the son of Centa or Quenta.　In 692 there was in England a man of this name, and there is Centing's tree.

The abbey at Beauchief was founded about 1175 by Robert FitzRanulph, whom we have seen already as lord of the manors of Alfreton and Norton ; and it was dedicated to the Virgin Mary and to St. Thomas the Martyr — that is, to Thomas à Becket, who had been canonised a little before the foundation of the monastery.　Earlier writers upon the abbey—Dugdale and Tanner, for instance—say that FitzRanulph founded it in expiation of his crime in being concerned in the murder of Thomas à Becket in Canterbury Cathedral ; but Dr. Pegge set himself the task of proving there was no truth in this tradition, and though the altarpiece of alabaster that stood in the abbey, and is now in the possession of the Foljambe family, represented the murder of Thomas à Becket and the seal of the abbey bore a similar design, yet subsequent writers also have stoutly resisted the expiation theory.

In the days of the manors vassals were compelled to grind their corn at the lord's mill ; and as the land of Beauchief Abbey constituted a manor, it was natural that the abbey too should have its mills, and indeed it had at least four corn-mills, besides a fulling-mill, and rents

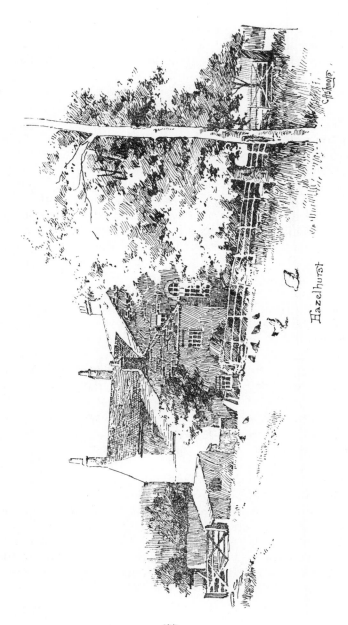

Hazelhurst

277

issuing out of other corn-mills. The first of these mills of which there is any record is that of Hastona, or Cold Aston, which was given to the abbey by William, Baron of Alfreton, apparently about the year 1200. This mill was on the stream at Hazelhurst, near to Cold Aston, and just outside the boundary of Norton parish. Thomas Jones, junior, writing in the *Sheffield Independent* in 1877, says the mill at Hazelhurst was on the brook just at the junction of the three parishes of Eckington, Norton and Dronfield, in the wood lying between Hazelhurst, Povey and Carter Hall farms. He mentions also that the faint outline of the mill-dam and the foundation of the mill might still be traced in his day, and adds that a number of ancient bridle roads radiate from this place, and that the fields on each side bear the names of Mill Meadow, Mill Field and Mill Holt. Still upon the same point there is a note by Mr. James Linacre that the mill "is said to have been near Povey on the stream running through Parson's wood. An old bridle road leads to the site of the mill from Hazelhurst farm."

This mill at Hazelhurst seems to have been moved from the east side of the stream, where it was in Eckington, to the west side, where it was in Norton ; for we read that Sir Thomas Chaworth gave the canons " half a rood of land lying near their mill of Aston, or Hesilhyrst, on the West side of the water-course of the mill, for the purpose of transferring the mill from the East side to the West, for the greater advantage of the mill, to be erected on that spot which Roger Pykard held of him. The canons gave him in exchange a rood of land in Aston-Field."

In the time of Queen Elizabeth there was litigation concerning the mill and the boundaries hereabouts. " Heardinge lane," " Roileswood," " a ryver called Harebeck *alias* Mearbeck," " Whelefeld . . . good and fertile land," are mentioned in the documents, and it is stated that " twoe [mills] are under one roof—one called Parke Mill and the other called Eamylles Sett." Heardinge

Lane is the disused bridle path from Norton to Ridgeway running up the side of Roileswood, now Royals Wood.

About the time of Edward the First, Sir Thomas Chaworth, a grandson of Sir Thomas the great benefactor of the abbey, erected a windmill at Cold Aston, within the manor of Norton. The canons objected to this, saying it was to the prejudice and detriment of their mill at Norton ; and thereupon he gave the windmill to them, on condition that he and his heirs and his family should grind their corn toll free so long as they resided at Norton.

The abbey had also, in addition to the mill at Bradway, another mill, called the New Mill, which is described as being in the parish of Norton, but which, though in the parish, was near to Heeley. At least Mr. Addy takes this to be the case, because, apart from the stream at Hazelhurst, which itself is only very small, there is no stream in Norton strong enough to turn a mill, and because mention is made of Hugh Hanslen of Little Sheffield, who " gave the canons leave to make a dam for their mill, called the New Mill, in his *cultura* de Holleford, so that they might conduct the river Sheaf at pleasure and as was convenient through his alder-plot." As one of these mills was three and the other four miles from the abbey, however, the canons would probably make use of the mill at Ecclesall which was afterwards given them by Robert de Ecclesall. With regard to the fulling-mill of the canons, Ralph de Ecclesall gave " a spot of ground near the river of Schefeld, for the erection of a fulling-mill, with leave to turn the river if necessary; he to have one-third of the profits, and to bear one-third of the expense."

The district of Lightwood, Povey and Hazelhurst, mentioned in connection with a Beauchief Abbey mill, is one of the parts of Norton that have retained their rural character untouched by other influences. In bygone years Lightwood was the home of the Gills and the Urtons, and the place retains an old barn on Fox's farm well

worth a visit for its massive oak roof of the kind represented upon the other side of Sheffield in the Monks'
Barn, near Thorpe Hesley. There is a note amongst
James Linacre's papers which suggests that this barn at
Lightwood was a tithe barn. It stands near to Hell
Clough, often mentioned in old documents, and has
become a dilapidated relic in this lonely place, where the
" moping owl " finds quiet, for the track that leads hither
is grass-grown now and little used. A story connected

Hell Clough Barn

with this crumbling building is that one bitter December
evening a strange man, tall and dour, carrying a little girl,
came this way, and applied for admission at a local inn.
It was in the days of the '45, and as the man was a
Scotsman, he lay under suspicion ; but at length the innkeeper admitted him. He said he was a " luckless laird "
who had lost gold, land, everything except this little girl,
the last of his children. Truly he was a laird ; but he
did not tell that he had himself killed his wife and one of
his kinsmen in a fit of jealousy, and had thus been compelled to flee, nor did he mention that he had taken part

in the attempt to place the Young Pretender upon the British throne.

The stranger stayed from day to day until he had been here for some years. Meanwhile he had bought land down Packman's Lane, and had built for himself a house, this very building now used as a barn, which he opened as an inn that became a favourite house of call for pack-men and for other wandering Scotsmen, some of whom were attracted by the beauty of the innkeeper's daughter, now grown into a most winsome maiden. One Paul was the favourite suitor, and when this attachment was dis-covered by the girl's father he upbraided her so furiously that she swooned at his feet. Just as she recovered consciousness Paul happened to enter, and her father felled him to the ground. The daughter pleaded for him, and at last confessed that he was not merely her lover, but her husband, whereupon the Scotsman drew his dirk and ordered the young man to stand upright. " As lover," he said, " thou hast ta'en a blow ; as husband take thou this " ; and he would have stabbed him had not Paul drawn and defended himself. The two men now fought furiously, their weapons clashing together until the older man fell pierced to the heart, his daughter dying beside him from fright.

Paul fled over sea, and since then the inn, now turned to other uses, has been falling steadily to ruin. The whole story has been told in verse in *Legend and Lyric* by the Vicar of Norton, the Rev. G. W. Hall, in a volume printed for private circulation in 1903.

At Povey lived Thomas Kent, the last heir of an ancient family, who left an only daughter, and she marrying George Sitwell added the land at Povey to the possessions of the family at Renishaw. In 1403 there was a William Povey at Hazelhurst.

Often in Lightwood annals traces are found of the yeoman family of Urton *alias* Steven. It is not known how the name came to take this shape, but the form persists in the Registers, in deeds and upon gravestones.

Many are the references in the Registers to the Urtons,
one as early as 1561, when there was baptised Gertrude,
daughter of Henry Urton *alias* Steven of Lightwood,
yeoman ; and old deeds show the numerous transactions
this family had in local lands.   It may be that a member
of this house is indicated in " John Orton, our canon,
priest, and professed brother," an entry in the obituary of
Beauchief Abbey.   In 1571 Richard Fenton of Doncaster
sold to John Urton *alias* Steven a building and land in
Lightwood and Hell Clough that had been recently occupied by Humfrey Clayton.   In 1546 " Omfraye " Clayton
was occupying the property under a lease granted by
Richard Fenton, who died about 1571, leaving a son
John, who, though a minor, was old enough to be
described as husbandman or labourer.   Thereupon John
Urton *alias* Stevyn, who had now bought the property
from Fenton, agreed to lease this property to John
Clayton, from the Feast of Pentecost, 1576, if Clayton
should be able, of his own proper goods, to enter it ; if
not, then from Pentecost, 1579, if able.   He is not to
assign the premises to any person but his wife, when he
shall fortune to have one, or their children.   However,
nothing came of this lease, and it was cancelled ; but the
relations between Urton and Clayton were not concluded,
for another deed of 1574 reveals that John Clayton,

labourer, of Lightwood, of his free will, hath bound himself servant with John Urton *alias* Steven, and after the manner of a servant with him to dwell, from Michaelmas next, for the full term of four years from this date ; faithfully to preserve his secrets, keep his lawful commandments, and not absent himself from his master's house by day or night without the special license of his master.   Urton covenants on his part to cause Clayton to be taught, learned and made perfect in the arte, craft and occupation of the scythesmith's craft, if he take the same in ; and in due manner to chastise him, finding him sufficient meat and drink, and also paying him 40 shillings yearly.   It was agreed also that as John Urton had some common rights (meanor) at Lightwood, Clayton should have these in consideration that John Urton should at his own cost find and keep Clayton six sheep during the four years.   The deed anticipates that at the end of the four years Clayton will be a workman, and " able to keep whole work "—that is to say, to work and make three dozen of scythes in a whole week, that then he shall work with John Urton, he finding him meat and drink, and also paying £5 a year for his wages, so long as they can agree after.

A further document relating to the Urtons sets forth that, in consideration of a marriage to be on this side and before the feast day of the Nativity of St. John the Baptist, solemnised between the said John Urton *alias* Stevyn, the younger, and Gartrude one of the daughters of John More, late of Ekyngton, yeoman, decessed, the elder John Urton covenants to convey to John Parker, of Norton Lees, gentleman, John Bullock of the Inner Temple, of London, gentleman, Edmund Stephenson, of Gray's Inn, gentleman, John Parker of The Okes, in Norton, William Lee, of Ekyngton, George More of Sheffield, son of Robert Moer, William Moer, of Newbold, James Bullock of Grenehill, yeoman, houses and lands in Lightwood, Herdings, Hymsworthe, and Helcloughe.   This property was to be held for the elder

Urton until the marriage, and indeed until the elder
Urton's death, when it would pass to the younger Urton
and his heirs.   Meanwhile, however, from the time of the
marriage there is to be provided for the younger Urton
and " Gartrude " Moer and their children sufficient meat,
drink and lodging, meet and convenient for their degrees,
in his now dwelling house at Lightwood, if they be contented to dwell in house with him in the said mansion
house at Lightwood ; if not, then a lease to be made to
them of property at Herdings for forty years without any
rent.

Another way of spelling the name is disclosed in a
deed of 1576, in which for £30 Godfrey Foliambe of
More House, Dronfield, conveys to John Orton *alias*
Stevyn two fields called the Byrches in Norton, the town
fields of Hymmysworth, called Whyssenall south, and
other land.   John Stevyn *alias* Urton of Lyghtwood sold
land in 1584 to Anthony Babyngton of Dethycke.   This
deed sets forth that Babington is to have "all his moiety
of trees, woods, and underwoods in a spring or piece of
wood ground, called Rowha Spring and Over Spring ;
parcel of wood ground called Banke Spring ; another
called the Great Spring ; another at the east end of the
said spring called Great Spring ; another called the Carr
Wood, now divided into two several inclosures ; also the
moiety of all the woods and underwood growing in a
spring called Grenewyeffe Spring, now divided into two
inclosures, one in the occupation of Agnes Grene, widow,
and the other of Henry Stevyn, brother of the said John."
Also in 1584 there was a partition of land which had been
held in common between Anthony Babington and John
Urton *alias* Stevyn of Lightwood.   Babington was to
have a close called Woddcrofte, with the house thereon
buylded, in the occupation of Godfrey Atkyne ; a piece of
ground called Woddacre, in Hymsworth field, abutting
upon Oldfield Lume north, Wysnawe Carr west, which last
named land extendeth from Wysnawe Carr to the midst of
a well-spring, or watering-place, in the same Woddground ;

also one little piece of ground in the west end of the
meadow called Carr meadow, meant to be used for a
way or passage for the said Anthony Babyngton to pass
with wayens, &c., and to drive his cattle to and from
Wysnawe Carr.   Urton, *alias* Stevyn, to have one piece
of the said Woddground, called Wysnawe Carr, from the
east end to the midst of the well-spring, or watering-
place ; and, also, one little piece of the Woddground
lying next to the lands of John Parker, called Adkin's
lands, and extending to the meadow called Carr meadow,
and intended to be used as a way or passage for the said
John, for wayens, cattle, &c., from the east end of
Wysnawe Acre ; also, a meadow or pasture called Carr
meadow, except only the little piece in the west end, so
as above alloted to Babyngton.   A covenant by Urton
that he will not, by digging the ground, making a trench,
ditch, or otherwise, draw the whole water of the said
well-spring, or watering-place, from such part of the
Woddground as belongs to Babyngton.   The seal upon
this document was a bird with a long beak.   I am told
that the crest of the Urton family is a hart with an arrow
in his mouth.

One of the most interesting of the Urton archives is
the will of Henry Vrton *'alias* Steven of Lightwood,
yeoman, dated March 1, 1590.   He commends his soul
to God, and his body to be buried in the parish church
or church yard at Norton.   Twenty shillings are to remain
as a perpetual stock to be put out by the Vicar and
churchwardens, and the yearly increase thereof to be
dealt yearly to the most impotent and needy people
of Norton.   Francis, his youngest son, is to have the
house at Hemsworth tenanted by Edward Maln, two
other houses in Hemsworth in the holding of John
Greene and his mother, a smithy there held by John
Barnes, and other property, including land lately purchased from Anthony Babington.   His wife Elizabeth is
to receive the rents to the use and bringing up of his
two younger sons Henry and Francis during her widow-

hood. She is to have one yoke of black oxen and all his husbandry gear, waynes, teames, yokes and such things as boards, fellowes and axle-trees about my house at Lightwood ; one heap of marl to be spread on the land about the house ; one coffer, one presser, and also all the salt flesh in the house ; and one third of all his silver spoons, the rest of these to his two daughters Alice and Elizabeth, equally between them. Furthermore, to his wife, one handiron, one brandreth, and one recontyne of iron, with all other iron instruments belonging to the house fire ; also all the pieces of ground and wood lying and being in Whysnowe and Over Oldfield, and the old close Spring being leasehold, and all his corn in the house and barn, and also growing, and eight mets or strikes of pease " which I lent to my brother John." The testator desires that his son Henry be kept to erudition and learning till he be come to twenty-one years of age ; and that his son Francis be put to such an occupation as he shall be apt to learn. Should his widow marry she is to bestow her legacies upon such of the children as shall stand in most need of them, excepting James and Francis, for whom provision has been made. Francis and Henry are to have one heifer calfe each, to be kept at his house at Lightwood until they have either of them a calf. James is to have all such smithy gear as belongs to one hearth ; Alice, £11 and a cowe ; Elizabeth, £10 and a cowe. In Wensleydale a hook upon which pots may be hung over the fire is called a reccon. This may be the recontyne of Henry Urton's will.

There is a will of 1641 in the British Museum, amongst the Woolley manuscripts. It is not interesting ; but there are many points that make it worth while to reproduce the will, belonging to 1592, of John Urton *alias* Steven the elder, of Lyghtwoode, yoman, " sycke and impotent of bodye, but off good and perfect remembrance." To be buried in the parish church of Norton. To John Urton *alias* Steven the younger, my nephew, and Gartryde, his wife, eight oxen and six kyne, in full recompense of all I owe them, and in performance of covenants in an indenture dated 20th of Jan., 18th of her now Majesty's reign, and made between John Fanshawe, gent., lately deceased, on the first part ; me the said John Urton, *alias* Stephen,

A Quiet Corner at Lightwood

on the second ; and the said John Urton *alias* Steven, my nephew, on the third part.   To Anthonie Urton, son and heir apparent to the said John Urton, *alias* Steven, my nephew, six oxen and six kyne, one waine with wheels bound with iron, three yokes, and three iron trants for the said six oxen to draw with ; also to him three great arkes and three meat bordes, and yet I will they remain as earelomes at my now dwelling house in Lyghtwood ; if he die before he shall be preferred in marriage, then the said goods to go to Edward Urton, *alias* Steven, brother of the said Anthony. To George Urton, son of the said John, £10 when 21. To Ellen Urton and Elizabeth Urton, sisters of the said Anthonie, Edward, and George, twelve markes each, "when matched in maryadge." To every one of the children of my said nephew John, and Gartryde, now his wife, £10. If my brother, Thomas Urton, *alias* Steven, shall survive Elizabeth, now his wife, he to have £4 within eight years after the decease of the said Elizabeth, viz., in the first year, 10s., and so the next seven years next following 10s., if the said Thomas so long live. To Henry Urton *alias* Steven, my nephew, 3s. 4d., and to Francis Urton *alias* Steven, his brother, 2s., and to every of my godchildren, 12d. To Richard Lee, son of William Lee, deceased, £3 14s., which William Lee, of Caldwell, his brother, oweth me, and one yearing heifer calf. To Dorothy and Gertrude, daughters of the said William Lee, 10s. to be divided, and to Alice, wife of John Hewet, 10s. to be dealt amongst her children. To Elizabeth Bower, wife of Robert Bower, 13s. 4d. for her children. To James Lee, brother of William, 3s. 4d., and to Ellen Hold, his sister, 12d. To Anne Bower 12d. Dynis England, 7d. ; Hugh Hopkinson, 12d. " Item I devise and bequeath that my said executors shall, within the space of one year next after my decease, deliver to the hands of church-wardens of the parish church of Norton for that time being the sum of 20s., which sum of 20s. I will, and my meaning is that it shall remain and continue in stock, and the profits thereof for ever, to be disposed to and for the relief of the poor people inhabiting within the said parish of Norton, and by the good discretion of the church-wardens of the said parish for the time being, and of the next of my kindred inhabiting within the said parish of Norton." Residue to my said nephew, John Urton *alias* Steven, and Gartrude, his wife, and they executors. My worshipful friends, John Bullock and John Parker, esquires, and my trusty and well-beloved Edmund Stepheson, gent., William Lee, Arthur Mawer,—my cousin to be supervisors, and they for their pains to have 6s. 8d. Then follow the signatures and names of witnesses.

In 1656 Anthony Urton of Lightwood, gentleman, sold to Thomas Hartley of Gleadless, lands called Middle Birchett near a place called the Herdings ; and in 1669 George Urton, in consideration of a marriage shortly to be solemnised betwixt him and Magdalen, daughter of John Burnley, hatter, of Worsborough, grants to Burnley and John Stacey, a Sheffield butcher, a house at Lightwood in the possession of Thomas Benton, crofts there called East Rycroft, Yewtree croft, fields called Newditch, Carre meadow, the upper Addam lands, Ryfield Pingles, with privilege to draw water at two wells or springs lying near the house, one in the meadow and the other in the paddock, the latter called the Paddock Well ; to the use of the said George and Magdalen for their lives and the life of the survivor.

The Urtons intermarried with the Parkers and with other Norton families, and altogether seem to have been as firmly fixed here, and that too for as long a period, as any Norton people. A memorial of a John Urton, buried in 1645, used to be in the church, but is now in the church yard. In Norton church the Urtons had their own vault and their own pew. No longer has the family any land here, but the present representatives of the Urtons contend that the property was entailed, that the entail was never cut off, and that, as the owner had no power to do more than mortgage his life interest, the Urton houses and acres ought still to be with the Urton family. The only member of this ancient stock now at Norton is a daughter of the late Frank Urton, at Woodseats ; but some are no farther away than Gleadless,

Chesterfield, Holy Moor Side and Doncaster, and others
have wandered away into Canada. Early in its history
the family seems to have been at Lincoln, and an Urton
married a Lister from Newark.

Another family whose name persists all through Norton
history is the family of Linacre. The name occurs
frequently in Norton documents and in the Registers,
and Hugh de Linacre, or Lynakir, witnessed a local deed
as early as 1301. There are many Linacres in North
Derbyshire, and Linacre the scholar is said to have
sprung from Brampton people. Until recent years the
brothers Ravel and James Linacre were well-known
figures in Norton life, and their descendants are still with
us. Mr. James Linacre showed great interest in Norton
affairs of the past, and made many notes concerning
people and incidents and buildings. Through the courtesy
of his son, Mr. H. W. J. Linacre, of Woodseats, I have
had access to these, so that this book owes many things
to Mr. Linacre's recollections and diligence.

Sir William Kniveton seems to have been at Norton
in 1614, and another family that found at least temporary
habitation here was that of the Stringers of Whiston.
The Strelleys, too, afterwards represented by the Pegges,
came into touch with Norton frequently. The Bates
of Jordanthorpe figure often in registers and deeds, and
early in Norton history the name Castelayn occurs sometimes. There was a John Castelayn of " Hymsworth."

A familiar name in the district is that of Mower, or
Mawer, and at Woodseats lived Dr. Arthur Mower and
Robert Mower, authors. Arthur Mower wrote some
stories, *The Welch Mountaineer* (1811), *The White Cottage*
(1817), *Zulneida* (1837), a dissertation on *Delirium
Tremens* (1819) and *On Vocal Music considered as a Branch
of National Education* (1838). Robert Mower wrote a
tract, *A Few Remarks on Present Times*. These works
are not read now, nor is interest in them likely to be
revived.

It may be that the name Mower is but another form

of More, or Moore, for that name too is of frequent occurrence hereabouts. Already have we seen that the Fanshawe family is said to have been introduced to the service of the King by a native of Norton, Sir Christopher More, King's Remembrancer of the Exchequer to Henry the Eighth. One of the Norton Parkers, John, had a sister, Elizabeth, who married Thomas More, son of John More of Greenhill. They had a son John, and it was his son Christopher who held office under Henry the Eighth. He, however, did not continue to make his home at Norton, but bought Loseley Park, two miles towards the south-west of Guildford, in Surrey, and there, in 1562, a mansion was built, on or near the site of an older house, by Sir William More, the son of Sir Christopher. This mansion, one of the architectural features of Surrey, contains ancient furniture, a famous collection of manuscripts and the rooms once occupied by Queen Elizabeth and by James the First.

Sir Christopher More, who thus left Norton to be the founder of the famous and favoured Mores of Loseley, was Sheriff of Sussex and Surrey in 1532–3 and in 1539–40 ; was knighted probably about 1540 ; and was Member of Parliament for Surrey from 1547 until his death, August 16, 1549. He was twice married : first to Margaret, daughter and heir of Walter Mudge of Guildford ; secondly to Constance, daughter of Richard Sackville of Buckhurst, who survived him. When the line of the Mores ended in a daughter she married Sir Thomas Molyneux, whose descendants have borne the name of More-Molyneux. In the Loseley Chapel, in the church of St. Nicholas, Guildford, are the tombs of the Mores, including that of Sir Christopher More, from Norton.

Away from Norton, on the way to Gleadless, we come upon the Herdings, one of the many pleasing features of this parish, an old house covered with ivy and so set upon a hill that it is a landmark for many miles round, perched aloft there above the springs of the Meersbrook

The HERDINGS

A grant of 1320 by Thomas de Chaworth of the Herdings, found by Mr. Addy with Messrs. Marples and Marples, solicitors, Sheffield, gives the old spelling of the word as Heytridding. The name is written in a very old hand, at the back of the deed, " Heardinge," so there is no doubt that Heytridding is the same place. It was anciently of sufficient mark to give its name to a family, as we have in the charter itself William and Robert " of the Heytridding." The grant discovered by Mr. Addy is from Thomas de Chaworth to Alice, the daughter of Agnetis Castelayn of Osberton, and Rose, her daughter, of all that land at le Heytridding which William de le Heytridding sometime held in the soke of Norton, with other lands there. A witness of this transaction, which belongs to the time of Edward the Second, was Dom William de Folkingham, Abbot of Beauchief. In the time of Elizabeth a windmill stood on the hill-top at the Herdings, for during her reign there was a lawsuit about it, and part of the record of the proceedings is a curious drawing of the mill itself. It is a pity such a pleasing feature of Norton is there no longer, but we look in vain in these days for the mill at the Herdings and for

the others that used to whirl their mighty arms at Cold
Aston.   In Sheffield there used to be a windmill where
now stands the Weston Park Museum, and people not
yet old will remember the very picturesque old windmill
which dominated Doncaster Gate in Rotherham.

The family of Rollinson or Rawlinson was at one time
of the Herdings.   Robert was a landowner at Norton in
1633, and was baptised at Norton on April 12, 1582.
He is described in the Register as the son of Jerome
Rawlinson of the Herdings.   The wood northwards
from the house is still known as the Rollinson wood,
" t'Rolli'son " the boys used to call it.

Mention of the Herdings occurs in a deed of 1622.
This document tells that John Bullocke of Darleighe
(Darley), Esquire, dealing with Robert Rollingson, of
Heardinges, yeoman, grants to him in fee of all and all
manner of tithes corn sheaves and blade of corn, hay
money for tithe hay, wool and lamb, woods, herbage, and
all other tithes of right belonging to the rectory of
Norton aforesaid, and due to the said John Bullocke, as

At the
Herdings

Old Cottage at
HEMSWORTH

to his said rectory, out of messuages and lands, &c.,
held by the said Robert Rollingson, which rectory was
sometime parcel of the late Monastery or Priory of
Beaucheiffe.

In 1653 there was living at the Herdings Andrew
Scriven, churchwarden. His children were Ann, William
and Sarah. It was this William who was such a liberal
benefactor to the church and to the poor. His stone was
removed from Norton church in 1882, and is now in the
porch. William Scriven left money for the teaching of
six children, fees for apprentices and clothing for poor
men and women. Latterly the Hazards have been at the
Herdings. The late Mr. T. O. Hazard was born there
and died there, after having spent his very long life at
the place.

The way to the Herdings lies through Hemsworth, a
hamlet whose name Mr. Addy explains as Hemelesworth,
Hemele's farm, and Thomas de Hemilword appears in a
transfer of land executed about 1320. Hemsworth, to-
day a group of farmhouses and cottages, some of them
obviously old, with mullioned windows built up, at the
eastern entrance to the Oakes Park, with the Bagshawe
Arms, the principal inn of Norton, once had also its own
hall and park, both mentioned in the Registers. The

The Bagshawe Arms

family of Stones occupied Hemsworth Hall at one time ; the ubiquitous Parkers also have been here, but at last the mansion became the parish workhouse, housed paupers instead of yeomen, and was taken down in 1802 by Sir William Bagshawe.

The last time I heard the word "scummer" used for a fire shovel was at Hemsworth. A child, two or three years old, staggered out of a cottage with the shovel, and an elder sister exclaimed, " Sithee ! he's getten t' scoomer nah ! "

There was until quite recently a periodical police court held at Hemsworth in a chamber over a stable that might well have recalled the surroundings of Henry Fielding's justices. The Bagshawe Arms is a picturesque inn, the scene of the Norton dinners and other gatherings. The landlord whom most of us remember here was William Fielding, still at Norton, though no longer at the Bagshawe Arms, but Mr. Robert Eadon Leader has kindly supplied me with particulars of an earlier host, George Rogers, a man useful and active in Norton affairs, Secretary of the Farmers' Club and member of a family that produced some well-known organists of Sheffield and Doncaster. His imposing presence won for him the name of "Lord George," and later, a striking white beard added yet more to his distinguished personal appearance. In his youth he was apprenticed to Henry Andrew Bacon when this old Sheffield printer founded the *Independent* in 1819. New proprietors came and went, but George Rogers remained, and, promoted from one post to another for his efficiency, he became foreman, or overseer, in the printing department, trusted completely by the proprietors and respected by the men. His work at the *Independent* office, however, punctiliously as he performed it, was not enough for his exuberant energy. He must needs keep the Bagshawe Arms and work a farm too ! Upon this Hemsworth side of his activities Mr. Leader writes : " I do not know precisely when he went to Norton, combining inn-keeping and farming with his duties at the *Independent* office, but he was there as far back as my memory goes—more than sixty years. My impression is that he took to the Bagshawe Arms in succession to his wife's family, who was, I think, a Broomhead, and Mrs. Rogers very efficiently managed the house while he was engaged in Sheffield or looking after his farm.   It was one of those well-conducted, reputable, old-fashioned hostelries now so seldom met with, and I can remember many pleasant days enjoying its hospitality

At the Back of the Bagshawe Arms

and wandering about amongst the animals and fields of the holding.   In later years I had often to attend the quaint and rustic petty sessions held usually in the club room over the stables, occasionally in the coffee-room, when magistrates like the Bagshawes, Wilson Overend, Henry Boden, Mr. de Rodes and others administered a sort of paternal justice, with a good deal of severity on poachers.

" Mr. Rogers was a capable farmer, snatching early morning hours, before driving to Sheffield, in his fields,

Grange Farm
NORTON

and spending his Saturdays on them, after a brief sleep. For the *Independent* being then published weekly, he was kept at the office until the small hours of Saturday morning. Everybody on the road between Sheffield and Hemsworth was familiar with the figure which rattled backwards and forwards in a gig drawn (for some years) by a fast-trotting pony, Peg, a little mare endowed with an abominably vicious temper but infinite pluck and spirit.

" After leaving the Bagshawe Arms Mr. Rogers lived at a pleasant old-fashioned farmhouse at Lightwood. When Mrs. Rogers died and he retired from the *Independent*, he spent his last years with his last-married daughter, Mrs. Turner of Tapton, Chesterfield."

To follow the lane opposite the Bagshawe Arms past Grange Farm, and so along devious field paths to Ridgeway, used to be a favourite walk of mine. It is a continuation of the path that comes to Hemsworth from Heeley under Hang Bank Wood, through Lees Hall Wood, and up Mawfa Lane past Hemsworth Lumb.

Pursued beyond Grange Farm, the lane conducts us to paths that lead into a region of quiet and beauty, with wooded hills rising from a brook that twists and turns down a pastoral valley. It is now more than twenty years since I saw this particular part of Chantrey's

country, for it lies a little off the beaten track, but I am
always promising myself an attempt to renew the zest
with which I used to roam about this sequestered tract
of meadow, hill and woodland, where it used to seem as
though I might encounter at any moment the spirits of
Gainsborough and of Constable.   On one occasion, with
Willis Eadon, the artist, for companion, I rambled about
this sleepy hollow looking for a subject for a sketch, and we
came upon a delightful old place called Sicklebrook Farm,
on a stream of that name, and this building, from one
point or another, kept us busy for the rest of the day.
Generally, however, the way was down the valley, then
up the hill to Ridgeway, a village whose name has suggested the presence here of a British or a Roman road,
running aloft to evade the floods and the marshes of the
Rother and its tributaries.

LITFIELD
Near
RIDGWAY

CHAPTER XV

BELIEFS AND CUSTOMS

So far in this account of Norton, as was inevitable for a number of reasons, the Anglican Church has held a place of first importance ; but many things fall to be written now concerning the affairs of other communities of religious people. After the Reformation the Catholics of Norton as of other places were made to feel the stigma which Protestants place upon their beliefs and ceremonies, and they were also pleasant to spoil. An account of the " Recusants " which belongs to the reign of Queen Elizabeth shows what money was received for their goods or land, and the record includes the names of " Rosamonde," the wife of " Cirill " Arthington, whom we saw at Hazelbarrow Hall ; the wife of John Dance ; Edmund Eyre ; Henry and Elizabeth Hunter ; and Catherine Marescal, all of Norton. At the Assizes held in August 1682 six Norton recusants were indicted : John Bate, labourer ; Hannah Bate ; John Patricke, joiner ; Elizabeth Patricke ; John Castleton, cordwainer, and Elizabeth Castleton. From Holmesfield there were " Frances " Wolstenholme, yeoman ; Christiana Hattersley, widow ; and John Hall, labourer. So that it is clear that this neighbourhood had staunch supporters of the older religion which has in our time retained so many adherents in North Derbyshire.

The bishops and other leaders of the Church, in the year 1676, were growing anxious about the Duke of York's attachment to the Catholics and were contemplating legislation against Rome. Desiring therefore to know what was the state of affairs in this country upon the point, a religious census of those over sixteen years of age was taken, and from the returns made at this time it appears that in Norton there were 479 Churchpeople, 7 Catholics and 10 Protestant Nonconformists. During spells of toleration the Nonconformists met openly in the homes of members, and the houses in Norton licensed for this purpose were those of Henry Gill in 1689, Mrs. Woods in 1693 and Samuel Blyth in 1714, and the Nonconformists were meeting in houses at Norton also in 1774. At Norton Lees they assembled in the house of Robert Fern in 1689. " There is at this place," says James Pilkington, writing of Norton in 1789, " a society of protestant dissenters of the Presbyterian persuasion. They assemble for divine worship in Norton-hall. As early as the reign of King Charles the Second they performed divine service in a private house. I have seen a license, which was granted and signed by that king for William Blythe to celebrate divine worship in his own house."

Many references have been made in previous chapters to Nonconformist services at the Oakes and at the Hall, and to the prevalence of dissent at Norton in the days of the Offleys and of the Shores, and it is possible now to supplement these allusions by a few remarks upon the Nonconformist ministers. The first of these of whom it has been possible to find mention was the Rev. John Wood, M.A., a native of Chesterfield, Fellow of St. John's College, Cambridge, who died in May 1690. He preached in his own house at Norton after his ejection under the Act of Uniformity, and it is interesting to know that his house was the one mentioned in a previous chapter as having been built in the reign of Henry the Seventh, for his father and mother to live in, by Geoffrey Blythe, Bishop of Lichfield and Coventry. Thomas Rose, ejected from Bloodworth in Nottinghamshire, who preached at the Oakes when Henry Gill was there, was minister from 1690 to 1700, when he was succeeded by the Rev.

Mr. Denton, son of the Rev. Nathan Denton, ejected from Bolton on Dearne. Mr. Denton conducted a service in the entrance hall of Norton Old Hall, then occupied by Mr. Stephen Offley. Next came the Rev. Mr. Lowe, who resided in the Hall and was the family chaplain; and after him, about 1708, the Rev. John Wood, chaplain for fifteen years, the son of the former minister of that name. He died in London about 1723, and after an interval of about a year, when neighbouring ministers officiated, the next two were Mr. Warren 1724 or 1725, probably 1724, who went to Tenterden in Kent, and the Rev. John Holland. John Holland, domestic chaplain to the Offleys, came from Buxton. He married, at Norton, Catherine Clarke, daughter of Samuel Clarke of Chesterfield, who having been one of the King's messengers was distinguished from the other Clarkes by being called Messenger Clarke. Holland died of consumption at Norton Hall on July 1, 1743, and was buried in Norton church, whence his stone with many others was removed at the repewing of 1820. It is now in the belfry. He was followed by the Rev. Daniel Lowe, from Loscoe near Alfreton, who was in charge from 1744 to 1776. He was educated at Glasgow at the same time as Joseph Offley, and he gave place to the Rev. Thomas Halladay, born at Baildon and educated at Sedbergh schools under Dr. Bateman, the last resident chaplain at Norton Hall, for now a chapel was built in the park. He lived in a house a short distance away, and came to the Hall in the morning and evening for family worship. This must have been the Halladay who has been mentioned already as having supplied both Pegge and Pilkington with information about Norton and with having given a digest of the Norton Manor Rolls. He married a wife who had money, one Martha Patrick, whose dower he dispensed with princely profusion, much of it upon a house and grounds at Little Matlock, not far from the confluence of the Loxley and the Rivelin near Malin Bridge. His ambition seems to have been to serve Little

Matlock, quite unconsciously no doubt, the ill turn that unspeakably vulgar Philistines have served its greater namesake. He cut walks in the cliffs, committed other tea-garden futilities, and, according to some contemporary observers, "wasted his substance in paying men fourteen shillings a week for lying on their bellies to plant privet on the ledges" of what he called Cliff Rocher. When the smash came kindly Asline Ward contributed his guinea to the relief fund and attributed Halladay's failure to entering into a cotton manufactory to serve a relation. Halladay did Norton a good turn. He rescued all we are ever likely to see of the manor rolls from oblivion, and he seems to have had scholarly instincts. Let us hope he found that

> When land is gone and money spent,
> Then learning is most excellent,

or that he was able even to say with Crabbe that "Learning is better worth than house or land."

Many years ago, in 1837, and probably for many years after that, saunterers down the Loxley valley would have found, amongst traces of Halladay's sojourn at Little Matlock, this Latin inscription on a house there :

Anno Christi M. DCC. XC. IX.
Thomas et Martha Halladay
sine liberis, ætate provecti, necnon jam nunc morituri,
has construxerent ædes.
Sic vos non vobis mellificatis apes.

Also, cut on a stone over a door,

. . . Nec vos dulcissima mundi
Nomina, Vos Montes, cataractæ, Pascua, Sylvæ,
Rupes atque Cavernæ, anima remanente reliquam
Thomas Halladay 1804.

Both the inscriptions are pathetic, for the first, belonging to 1799, tells of Halladay and his wife, grown old, without children, and with not many years to live, building houses in which neither they nor theirs, but others, will pass their lives, and it seems to them that they are like bees making honey that others will consume. In the other inscription, Halladay invokes the lovely surroundings of mountains, cataracts, pastures, woods, rocks and caves, and says that nevermore will he leave them ; but no long time afterwards poverty forced him and his into less congenial places.

Mr. Arthur Lister, of Oughtybridge, my kinsman, tells me the second inscription is still there, clear as though it were but newly cut. It is over an old doorway on the north side, and what seems to have been the front, of the Robin Hood inn, overlooking a gorge. The doorway is now walled up except a little space at the top filled with panes of glass. The natives say Halladay built the Robin Hood as a private house, and that he built also Loxley House on the opposite hill, and some cottages in the valley. The cottages were swept away in the disastrous flood of 1864, when the Dale Dyke reservoir at Bradfield burst and sent its waters down this valley, drowning 270 people, and destroying most of the buildings. It may be that the first inscription was on these cottages, for it has not been possible to find it. John Holland, in *The Tour of the Don* (1837), says the inscription was upon one of a cluster of dwellings "at the foot of the craggy steep" on which stands the Robin Hood inn. Halladay died in obscurity, in Ireland, after having re-entered the ministry.

The next minister at Norton, the Rev. John Williams, 1804, was tutor to the family of Shore at the Hall, and he was succeeded by Robert Aspland, who remained five weeks only, when he went to Gravel Pit meetinghouse at Hackney and had there a distinguished career, and gave place in 1805 to the Rev. Henry Hunt Piper. Piper, born on August 26, 1782, a native of London, where his father was a builder, was designed for the same business as his father, but manifesting a strong desire to be a minister he was packed off to Hoxton Academy, and afterwards to Homerton. There he began life as a Congregationalist, to which community his father belonged ; but fond of discussions and inquiry he became unsettled, and in time passed through Arianism to Unitarianism, where he remained till the end. His first ministry was at Rochford in Kent, and thence in 1805 he came to Norton to be the chaplain for the Shores, and to be minister in the chapel in Norton Park as successor to Robert Aspland. In this year, too, he married Alicia, the eldest daughter of Samuel Lewin of Hackney. Some attacks having been made upon Unitarianism by the Rev. Thomas Best, M.A., Vicar of St. James, Sheffield, Piper was singled out for the repulse of these onslaughts, and his efforts so commended themselves to his fellows that he was presented by them with a hundred pounds and a silver inkstand. At Norton, in the house now known as the Grange, Piper founded a school which promised well at times, but shrunk at others, and ultimately was closed. In Asline Ward's diary there are allusions to this venture. At first it was a school for girls, " not too successful " ; in 1814 it was made into a boys' school, but Asline Ward's opinion was that Piper " has not the art, or heart, to puff. He is too modest to state what I think is the fact, that his fifty guineas school is as good as most at double the price, and as cheap as most at half, because of their extras." In 1820 it was flourishing, and Piper spent two hundred pounds in enlarging the premises, and he built also some cottages on Dore Moor ; but in 1831 it had become very small, and in 1833, when it was down to eight pupils, Piper decided to close it, and to give the time to study and to writing. When the Rev. J. E. Manning wrote his valuable *History of Upper Chapel, Sheffield*, he received a most interesting letter from one of Piper's old pupils, Mr. Holbrook Gaskell, of Woolton Wood, near Liverpool, who was in Norton in 1825–7. Mr. Gaskell wrote that "Mr. Piper was universally respected by his pupils, and beloved by most of them. I felt much attached to him and to his family. The school house faced Norton Park, and the chapel was in the Park, directly opposite the school house. Mr. Piper was tall, and of good figure. He wore knee-breeches, as was general in those days, but did not sport a pigtail; though I can remember at least one old gentleman who did, and wore powdered hair. Mr. Piper's preaching was didactic, dwelling chiefly on the moral virtues and formation of character—probably intended mainly to influence his pupils, who formed a large part of the congregation. There were thirty or forty boarders at the school. Among them I recall the names of Rodgers, son of the celebrated Sheffield cutler; and a young Bagshaw, whose family, I think, were of some consequence in the neighbourhood. There was also Frank Hollins, from Mansfield, who subsequently settled in Liverpool as a cotton broker— now dead. Four or five boys came from Liverpool, viz. two Lewins, one Harvey, my brother, William Broadbent, and myself. Of these I think I am the only survivor. . . . The school was detached from the dwelling house. There was some land attached to the school, partly used as a playground, and partly cultivated by Mr. Piper. I remember when I was confined to my bed by rheumatic fever, Mr. Piper bringing me under a napkin, with much form and ceremony, a singular specimen of mangold-wurzel, a product of his farm, grown in the form of a human being, with arms and legs. When this freak of nature was exposed to view I felt bitter disappointment that it was not something good to gratify my appetite! Mr. Piper had a considerable fund of humour. The family consisted of an elder son, who was educated at York; a younger son, Lewin, and several daughters—Alicia, Emily, and Fanny—who were great favourites with the schoolboys."

Pupils came to this school here at Norton from distant

places. There were some connections of Dugald Stewart from Edinburgh, and two sons of Professor Milne from Glasgow. There seems to have been a home life of more than usual happiness at Piper's house. The genial father amongst his children and pupils, the gentle mother spending herself for their comfort, young life abounding everywhere, girls and boys glad in their surroundings ; but the impartial hours could not be stayed there, the hands of the clock were ever moving forward, and the cold shadows began to fall across the warm hearth. That time came in this family too that causes parents to become pensive upon a past when their girls and boys knew no other world than the home and the garden ; those days arrived here at last when mothers long to fold their children in their arms again, when they would give all they have if they might hang once more over their girls and boys sleeping innocently in cot or cradle ; but here at Norton as elsewhere such wishes were in vain. Significant entries begin to appear in Asline Ward's diary. " Mr. and Mrs. Piper have been to London, where they went to see their son Henry embark for India, he having relinquished his studies for the ministry. He is gone with Capt. Brodie in the *Charles Kerr* as a midshipman, and his parents are reconciled to the change, though it has been a source of affliction to them." This was in 1829, and six years later we read that Henry Piper is home again, " where he behaves well, but is resolved not to go to sea again, and seems very slow in looking out for other employment." During the same period we are told that " Mr. Piper's second son, Lewin, has a fancy to see if he shall like Canada. His father and mother are gone to Liverpool to see him embark. Their eldest is on a voyage to Calcutta." This was the son born in 1816, whom Ward describes as " an uncommonly strapping cub." Piper's daughter Fanny died in 1854. In 1836 she had married George Elliott, and when the end came was visiting at Lewes to welcome back from Australia her brother Frederick, his wife and two children.

Unitarianism does not seem to have satisfied one of Piper's daughters, for Asline Ward wrote in 1849 that " Eliza Piper is a considerable bit of a Puseyite, illuminates books, copies *Holy Thoughts* from old masters, paints ancient robes of priests, and I know not where she will *rest*."

Piper was fond of active manual work and had his garden and his workshop. " He once bought a small tract of land on the moors of Derbyshire, and on this he often went and laboured with all the peasant's energy." This property at Dore still bears Piper's name. At one time he " is so bitten with a fishing enthusiasm that he rises at four o'clock to sally forth with rod and line." He was also particularly fond of music, and himself a musician. In Asline Ward's diary we are enabled to see some old friends at one of his musical parties. In 1811 " I drank tea and supped at Mr. Piper's with Miss Shore, Miss Read, Sir William and Lady Bagshawe, Mr. J. Rodgers, Dr. Jonn. Stokes, Capt. Thompson, etc., it being a musical party. Mr. Ellis and Mr. Piper were the principal performers. It was nearly two o'clock before we left Mr. Piper's, an hour which I should suppose the annals of Norton, or at least those of the Dissenting minister there, can furnish no parallel for lateness."

Piper had at Norton too a good library, especially of Greek and Latin classics, and so he bore his part in the maintenance of that air of scholarship that has prevailed from time to time in old Norton. The friendship between Asline Ward and Piper was close and lasting. Ward writes in his diary in 1811 " Piper I have long respected ; if there be a domestic, honest, intelligent, friendly frank, agreeable, social being in the world, he is one." When Asline Ward was married to Mrs. Piper's sister, Piper sent the pair thirty-two bottles of red currant wine, towards their housekeeping. Piper and Montgomery were very congenial too, and Montgomery came often to Norton to see his friend. When Montgomery's *Wanderer in Switzerland* was published Piper wrote a review of the poem in the *Monthly Theological Repository*, and when Piper's eldest child was born Montgomery wrote the poem of seven stanzas entitled *The Roses. Addressed to a Friend on the Birth of his First Child.* It opens with the lines

> Two Roses on one slender spray
> In sweet communion grew,
> Together hail'd the morning ray,
> And drank the evening dew ;
> While, sweetly wreathed in mossy green,
> There sprang a little bud between.

With Chantrey too Piper was on the best of terms. He is said to have helped Chantrey in the early days of struggle, and whether this is so or not, the two were warmly attached to each other to the end, and Chantrey painted Piper's portrait. Interested in Sheffield affairs, Piper was a shareholder in the *Independent* in its early days, helped to found the Literary and Philosophical Society, and his name is on the roll of its presidents.

Asline Ward once preached for Piper at Norton, " where I was accidentally one forenoon, after he had been much alarmed during the night by his boy being attacked with the croup, who, however, soon recovered from the danger. But the fatigue Mr. Piper had undergone, the want of sleep, the anxiety of a parent, etc., had so unnerved him, that, when he began the prayer, he could not proceed, and after several ineffectual attempts, he desisted, when Mr. Shore requested me to read a service, which I did." On another occasion in 1812 Ward officiated for Piper on two Sundays, and he tells us in his diary he has heard of Mr. Pearson, the Vicar of Norton, complaining of this on the ground that the novelty might attract some, and asserting that such conduct exposed the lay preacher to a penalty. " It was, he declared, in his power, if the regular minister were three weeks absent, to alienate some lands from the chapel." At this time Nonconformists were still under a number of disabilities, since removed,

and there can be no doubt that all this dissent at Norton,
and that too not in the cottages but in the halls, amongst
a class that has since found its way back to the Church,
must have been a source of chagrin to the vicars of
Norton.   Not only have we this complaint from the
Rev. H. Pearson, but some one asking the Rev. Peter
Robinson why his congregation was so small he replied,
" Well, you see, I am crucified between two thieves, one
an Independent and the other Unitarian," an allusion
to two of the dissenting bodies of the parish.   Again,
in a petition for more assistance for church work in
Norton, it is set forth that Cavendish Nevile, " to secure
his congregation from separating to a Dissenting Meeting
House adjoining to his church, doth preach twice every
Sunday throughout the year."

There is a reference in Asline Ward's diary to the
presence at Norton of a once shining light, for he wrote
in 1818 " I have had only a short view of Read since
his return.   It was at the Norton Chapel, where he had
gone to hear Mr. Belsham preach."   The Wesleyan
Chapel at Backmoor was built in 1854.

Piper left Norton in 1843, and writing six years later
Asline Ward says " I was very much grieved last week
to see the Norton grounds so much out of order, and
cattle pasturing in the flower gardens become a wilderness."

Chiefly in Asline Ward's diary we are permitted one or
two more glimpses of Piper after he had gone hence.   In
1853 he tells us that " Mr. Piper is leaving Banbury.
He attempted to introduce a Liturgy, which has been very
unpalatable to some of his congregation.   He will go to
Lewes, where some relations reside, and retires from the
ministry."   Then he is hurt in a railway accident and
walks with crutches.   Next we hear of him " at Taunton
but not settled there.   His son-in-law Edward Cole
does not find schools suitable to his eight children, and
wishes to remove ; so the Pipers will bear him company.
Frederick Piper is with his father, having retired from
Australia with three children, whose mother died above

a year ago. He is. a partner with Levicks, and will remain in England if he can so arrange it." It is evident, however, that he could not so arrange it, for a newspaper notice of 1860 runs : "PIPER—At the North Shore, Sydney, on the 22 Sept. last, Frederick Piper, Esq., of the firm of Levicks and Piper, son of the Rev. H. H. Piper, formerly of Norton near Sheffield."

Piper himself died on Jan. 13, 1864, at No. 2, Church Row, Hampstead, survived by his wife, and he lies buried at Highgate, far from these scenes amongst which the most fruitful years of his life were spent and away from his old friends Ward, Montgomery and Chantrey.

Piper has a claim to be remembered in these parts as a pioneer amongst its scholars, for he compiled a glossary of local words as early as 1825, a few years before Hunter's glossary appeared. Piper embodied his work in a paper read before the Sheffield Literary and Philosophical Society, and it has been pointed out that an entry in Asline Ward's diary may indicate in what manner Piper had his attention drawn to this interesting subject, for Ward wrote that Maria Lewin, Mrs. Piper's sister, "is so wicked as to have composed what she calls a Derbyshire Dictionary, a small quarto volume containing words peculiar to the neighbourhood of Norton and Sheffield, so that she evidently intends, on her return home, to expose us to the criticisms of the circle at Hackney." Ward records also that " Mr. Piper's lecture on the peculiarities of our dialect was very amusing, and has attracted much notice. It will be printed in the *Provincial Magazine*, a new work now published at Leeds." It was printed in full in the *Independent*, and reprinted in a pamphlet now prized for its rarity by collectors of local books and papers, though both Piper's and Hunter's glossaries were superseded by the one published in 1888 by Mr. Addy.

In connection with these allusions to Norton Nonconformists it would be unpardonable to omit mention of the visits to this place of a preacher recognised as great alike by churchman and dissenter. On Tuesday, June 5, 1753, John Wesley was in Sheffield. Upon the previous day he had ridden from Manchester to Chelmorton in the Peak, where he had preached in a little meadow, and had then ridden forward to Sheffield. He rode over to Jonathan Booth's at Woodseats, "whose daughter had been ill in a very uncommon manner." The account her parents gave of it is given by Wesley in his journal, where we read that "About the middle of December, 1752, Elizabeth Booth, junior, near ten years old, began to complain of a pain in her breast, which continued three days : on the fourth day, in a moment, without any provocation, she began to be in a vehement rage, reviling her mother, and throwing at the maid what came next to hand. This fit continued near an hour ; then in an instant she was quite calm. The next morning she fell into a fit of another kind,—being stretched out, and stiff, as a dead carcase : thus she lay about an hour. In the afternoon she was suddenly seized with violent involuntary laughter ; and she had some or other of these fits several times a day, for about a month. In the intervals of them she was in great heaviness of soul, and continually crying for mercy ; till, one Saturday, as she lay stretched out on the bed, she broke out, 'I know that my Redeemer liveth.' Her faith and love increased from that time ; but so did the violence of her fits also. And often while she was rejoicing and praising God, she would cry out, 'O Lord ;' and losing her senses at once, lie, as dead, or laugh violently, or rave or blaspheme.

" In the middle of February she grew more outrageous than ever. She frequently strove to throw herself into the fire, or out of the window. Often she attempted to tear the Bible, cursing it in the bitterest manner ; and many times she uttered oaths and blasphemies, too horrid to be repeated. Next to the Bible, her greatest rage was against the Methodists,—Mr. W. in particular. She frequently told us where he was, and what he was then doing ; adding, 'He will be here soon ;' and at another time, 'Now he is galloping down the lane, and two men with him.' In the intervals of her fits she was unusually stupid and moped, as if void of common understanding ; and yet sometimes broke out into vehement prayer, to the amazement of all that heard.

"Sometimes she would strip herself stark naked, and run up and down the house, screaming and crying, 'Save me ! save me ! He will tear me to pieces !' At other times she cried out, 'He is tearing off my breasts ; he is pouring melted lead down my throat. Now I suffer what the Martyrs suffered ; but I have not the Martyrs' faith.'

"She frequently spoke as if she was another person, saying to her father, 'This girl is not thine, but mine. I have got possession of her, and I will keep her ;' with many expressions of the same kind.

"She often seemed to be in a trance, and said she saw many visions ; sometimes of heaven, or hell, or judgment ; sometimes of things which she said would shortly come to pass.

"In the beginning of March, Mrs. G. came over to Rotherham, who herself made me the following account : 'Soon after I came in, she fell into a raging fit, blaspheming and cursing her father and me. She added, "It was I that made Green's horse so bad the other day :" (which had been taken ill in a most unaccountable manner, as soon as he was put into the stable) : "I did it that thou mightest have the preaching no more ; and I had almost persuaded thee to it. It was I that made thee bad last night." I was then taken in an unusual way. All the time she spoke she was violently convulsed, and appeared to be in strong agony. After about a quarter of an hour she brake out into prayer, and then came to herself ; only still dull and heavy.'

"John Thorp, of Rotherham, had often a desire to pray for her in the congregation ; but he was as often hindered, by a strong and sudden impression on his mind that she was dead. When he came to Woodseats, and began to mention what a desire he had had, the girl, being then in

a raging fit, cried out, ' I have made a fool of Thorp ! '
and burst out into a loud laughter.

" In the beginning of May all these symptoms ceased ;
and she continues in health both of soul and body."

Wesley came to Woodseats on several occasions.
His journal shows that on Thursday, July 28, 1757,
" About noon I preached at Woodseats ; in the evening
at Sheffield. I do indeed live by preaching ! " An
entry for August 29, 1761, shows this tireless man
preaching at Matlock Bath at five o'clock in the morning,
at Woodseats at two o'clock in the afternoon and at
Sheffield in the evening.

In his account of Methodism in Sheffield, James Everett
alludes to Norton, and tells us that " it was some time
in the course of this year, [1761] that Elizabeth Booth
[apparently the mother of the other Elizabeth Booth]
became acquainted with experimental religion, and led
the way to another favourite Methodist station, namely,
Woodseats, about three miles south of Sheffield,—a place
frequently visited by Mr. Wesley, and whose chief importance consisted in being a kind of retreat from the
violence of persecutors in more populous places, and a
constant home for the preachers. She was born in the
year 1725 ; her maiden name was Wood, and she was
the daughter of Stephen and Isabella Wood, of Summer-
ley, near Dronfield, Derbyshire. She was the subject
of serious impressions from her childhood, and regularly
attended the service of the Established Church at Norton.
Her impressions were deepened under the ministry of
David Taylor ; but it was not till the year of her
marriage to Mr. Jonathan Booth, of Norton Woodseats,
Derbyshire, who had a small farm there, that she possessed the consolations of religion, which was about the
eighteenth of her age. The opposition which she first
met with from her husband, who, through the persuasion
of his relatives, threatened to turn her out of doors,
was considerable. Though she brought him a fortune,
he would not, on the testimony of a daughter, suffer

her to have a halfpenny in her possession to his knowledge, and she frequently contributed to her class by
the saving of a farthing at a time. She generally attended preaching at Sheffield at five o'clock in the morning, carrying the child in her arms that she was then
nursing. Through her perseverance and exemplary
conduct she at length so won upon him, as to suffer
preaching to be established in the house ; and through
some severe affliction in the family, he was brought to
serious reflection, and lived in the fear and love of God
several years. She led a class in the neighbourhood,
attended the different prayer-meetings which were established in the villages and hamlets around, and often gave
a word of exhortation. In many of her religious excursions she went as far as Totley, Highlane, Penistone,
and Staincross, the last of which places is about eighteen
miles from Woodseats, and there prayed with the people,
and there spake to them as she was able. Her house
was the grand resort of all the first preachers, as the
Messrs. Wesley, Whitefield, Grimshaw, Nelson, and
others; and among pious females, Mrs. Green, of Rotherham, Mrs. Crosby and Miss Hosmer, of Leeds. Whenever Mr. Wesley visited Woodseats during the summer
season, he almost invariably went to the brook, now
called London river, near Heeley, and bathed himself,—
a recreation conducive to health, and to which he was
very partial.

" Norton, near Woodseats, was one of those places
in which several early attempts were made to form a
society. Two of the first members were Hannah Bramley
and Dorothy Bingham, both of whom died in peace at
a good old age—one of them betwixt 90 and a 100.
There seems to be a striking coincidence, in many cases,
between the introduction and reception of Christianity
and Methodism in various places ;—females distinguishing
themselves among its first embracers, and, by the influence of their conversation and example, among the
first of its propagators."

A writer in the *Sheffield Independent* for July 15, 1875, says that "Jonathan Booth's house at Woodseats is down a lane opposite Mr. Cammell's school, and is now divided into two dwellings."

Years after the great preacher's death there lived at Norton Woodseats a man whose lot would have had an intense interest for John Wesley ; for the career of this wretched creature of Woodseats was all of a piece with the weird narratives which accompanied the history of early Methodism, and its tragedy strikes even a deeper note than the strange case of Elizabeth Booth.

In and about the year 1828 there was published in Sheffield, during the theatrical season, *The Sheffield Postscript*, a periodical devoted chiefly to theatrical criticism. Copies are very rare now, but as they do exist it goes without saying that Mr. W. T. Freemantle, of Barbot Hall, has specimens, and he has the issue for November 17, 1828, containing the remarkable article

PETER RAENEY

The Maniac of Woodseats, Norton, Derbyshire.

"Truth is more wonderful than fiction."—BYRON.

An abridged version of the article appeared in the *Sheffield Courant* for November 28, 1828.

So vivid is this arresting contribution to local history that it is reproduced as it stands in the *Postscript* ; but most readers will agree that the writer, though he did his work uncommonly well in other respects, was somewhat bumptious and theatrical, and in his quest for "copy" had small regard for other people's feelings and sanctities, for apparently this article was published when all the chief people concerned were alive.

"I had been acquainted by rather extraordinary means, that the little village of Woodseats, three miles from Sheffield, contained a living object of the most

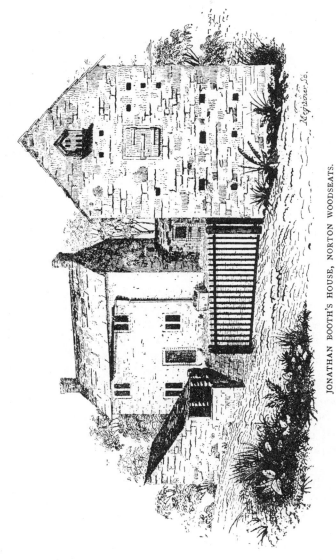

JONATHAN BOOTH'S HOUSE, NORTON WOODSEATS.

From the plate in Everett's *Historical Sketches of Wesleyan Methodism in Sheffield and its Vicinity*, 1823.

painful interest ; and moreover that notwithstanding it had existed upwards of fourteen years, that few of the old villagers had seen it, or been at the pains to satisfy themselves—this object was not the victim of cruelty or avarice. Possessing sufficient information to lead me to the precise spot, where it was said the wretched human being was imprisoned ; in company with a friend, I set out on Thursday morning, determined either by stratagem or force to satisfy the demands of my humanity or curiosity. On arriving at the public house called Freemason's Arms, I mentioned privately to the owner the object of our errand. The man appeared surprised at our questions, but shortly admitted that the object we sought, might, he believed, be found in a certain spot, to which he pointed through the casement ; but added he with the animal ease of the genuine Derbyshire boor, ' I know naught about him, only he used to scare our folks years ago, at night time 'ith Pinfold.' ' Then . . . you have SEEN him.' ' Nay (said he) none on us have seed him, we only heard his shrieks.' With our curiosity if possible more inflamed we left his house and followed the directions we had received.

" We proceeded towards Chesterfield about two hundred yards, where, on the right hand the road opens, and bears the appearance of the beginning of a cross bridle way. Two or three hundred yards up this way, brought us to a few tenements, beyond, but almost opposite which we recognised by the description previously given, in a little croft, the miserable abode of the creature of whose wrongs or miseries we sought to enquire. It was one of those cabins, which are so frequently found in those parts of the country which offer stone merely for labour ; originally a square enclosure, made in the primitive manner, of stones, put one on the other, to protect the Lord's cattle from thieves or storms. Afterwards abandoned and seized by the peasant, who year after year adds turf, a little lime to the inside, a cross piece of wood, and at harvest time some straw, until he has converted it into a little homestead. Such was the house, in which we had been told Peter Raeney had been confined fourteen years. After traversing the extent of the enclosure which we had to do before we could reach the doorway, we stopped to listen if the inmates were stirring. No sound however reached us, and I tapped seriously against the broad low door. Upon a second application of my knuckles, we heard the latch gently raised, and the door giving way a few inches, I pressed against it rather strongly, and without ceremony, the interior of the hovel was at once presented to us. The first object we observed was sufficient to reprove the manner of our entry. It was an old woman apparently about eighty, who seemed to regain with great difficulty, the chair from which she had just risen. Our errand however appeared understood, and before a word was uttered we were seated face to face on such chairs as the place afforded. ' You have a son (said I) I have been told, a poor boy who is——' The old woman stopped my enquiries, and her eyes running over with tears, (but whether they should rather be put to the account of the aged body than the afflicted mind, I know not) said—'Is it that you want ? God's will be done—Yes, I have, but I will let no one see him.' This was said, in a tone which impressed us at once, with the conviction, that under the colours of demand, the old woman would surrender nothing either to our vision or information. Talking with her was now our business—three fine young children were playing on the black stone floor,—' Whose are these ?' said I. ' My daughter's (she replied) pointing to a young woman, washing in one corner, whom the gloom of the place though scarcely five yards square, had hidden from our sight. ' You are a grandmother then ' ;—We had touched the sympathetic chord, the old dame's countenance brightened, and the stream of talk was let loose ; my little notebook and pencil were out in a moment, my friend filled up the few pauses which her failing memory or many infirmities made necessary, and aided by a few simple interrogatories, we obtained the 'heart of her mystery.' The following broken sentences (how they were produced and as it were eked out by my friend in the manner I have described, can be left to the dullest imagination) kept me in breathless attention for a quarter of an hour—' Aye, my daughter's there—I have a son that's got fourteen and all bonny, and one of the fourteen has gotten six—I am mother, and grandmother, and great-grandmother to eighty on 'em—God's will be done—Job had trust and so have I—But I have not been in bed since my husband died—he died ten years ago—God's will be done,—I am a poorly woman—You see I am dropsical—Yes, they heed me little—Miss Eliza—of—[Shore, of Meersbrook, probably] she has called and given us something, but she has never seen *him*—Peter—Peter my boy—Yes, if they do come —they come,—But my boy shall not be taken from me while I live.—It is now fourteen years, they say it is fifteen, but I know it's only fourteen—God's will be done—He took to his bed through the lass—He did not speak for a month, and when he did speak, he said

> ' No greater grief, no meikle pain
> Than for to love, and not be lov'd again.'

I shall never forget it—but ! God help you gentlemen —he once fell downstairs in the night, but now he's stricken, he knows me, and calls me mother—no, my trust is in God.' At this moment something seemed to move above us, and as we turned our eyes to the blackened board which made the imperfect ceiling, a moan which we knew to be human was heard, and losing all patience, I started from my seat, put my book in my pocket, and said, ' I must see him.' My friend shewed more wisdom, commiserating with the old woman, he offered her a few shillings, and said that we were strangers in these parts, but being on our way to Derby he hoped we should not be denied a sight of her poor son. She accepted the money, and without saying a word, the daughter pointed to a few crazy steps which led from the corner of the miserable dwelling to the loft above the ceiling we had just observed. In six strides, a tall man might have encompassed the entire edifice, but to ascend these few steps was a work of some difficulty and danger, for the greater portion of the light we enjoyed came through a few 'wintry flaws' which the poverty or carelessness of the inmates had neglected. The fragile board, bending beneath our weight, and the slender railing giving way at our touch, our physical senses gave us the first intimation that we were near the object of our search. 'There,' said the daughter—'Where—I can distinguish nothing but a foul discoloured sheet, wrapped about what seems to be a log of wood'—'Look nearer.' I stooped lower, (I was already stooping, being within four feet only of the ancient drooping roof) and shuddering while I put my hand upon a mass of human hair, the face of one of my fellow-creatures suddenly presented itself! After the first shock which so strange a sight must have caused the least superstitious or at least pitiful, I set about examining the lost being before me with the same feeling, which the anatomist owns, when he plunges his scientific knife in the dead mass which lies upon his table. The face of course attracted my first notice. I brought my own almost close to his, but I could discover none of the usual physiognomical marks of mere physical insanity. The forehead and nose were rather finely marked, and the eyes which appeared to me (in the imperfect light) a deep black, were large, and though they betrayed the restless motion of insanity, were totally without what may be termed the gazeless look of mere idiotcy. The lower part of his face was buried in hair, and even the orifice of the mouth appeared shut up in the growth of years. The next thing which attracted my attention, was the lower part of his body ; the space which he occupied was sufficient only for the trunk of an ordinary man, and my curiosity was painfully excited to discover how he had disposed of his thighs and legs. While he was eyeing

me with the greatest intensity I drew aside part of the
coarse sheet which was upon him, and I saw the points of
his shoulders, and the caps of his knees drawn closely
together, allowing only a little room for his arms which
were between them, leaving his hands upwards. The
whole body was in the attitude of an ape sitting, but then
the body was turned on one side, without that attitude
being destroyed. Upon closer examination it appeared
that the particular position I found him in, must have
been assumed at an early period of his mental disease, for
I discovered that he was perfectly sinew bound, and
could not in the smallest degree relax or alter the position
of a single joint. Consequently the only change of
attitude of which he was capable, was rolling from side
to side, or balancing himself on the centre. His state of
health, I am not a competent judge of, but I can assert
that he exhibited most of the popular signs of con-
valescence, a clear full eye, and a sound skin, though the
last had evidently taken a hue foreign to its nature. I
looked round the miserable loft, which for so many years
had been his resting place, and it literally contained
nothing but the naked body of the poor maniac, and the
dirty sheet I have spoken of, myself, my friend, and the
woman who conducted us. In spite of my appetite for
information I grew physically as well as mentally sick,
when to my surprise, and almost horror, the poor wretch
who had kept his wild looks continually upon us, turned
his face to the floor, and said in a tone which smote the
heart, 'I am bound to sleep.' We hurried down the
dangerous stairs, and in a moment we were breathing
the fresh air ;—after we had recovered the surprise, which
the sound of the maniac's voice had produced, (for imagination had nothing to do with our emotion, he, whom
we looked upon as lower than the brute, spoke our
language with a tone and pathos deeper than those of the
most gifted actors) we thought we could converse with
the madman's sister, who might supply us with that
portion of the poor man's tale which had escaped the old

woman's garrulity. Their story is the following :—' Fourteen years ago, my brother was about twenty years old,
and as fine a young man, about six feet high, as you
would see anywhere. He courted one Mary Jones whose
father owned a bit of land just yonder opposite us. It
was at last settled that one day they should be married at
Dronfield Church—my brother was ready at the time
appointed, but Mary Jones without giving any notice, on
the same day, at a Church in a different part of the
country, married one W——, of Sheffield. It was too
much for Peter, who doated upon her. He returned
home, and going into the loft which you have seen (it
then had a bed, a chair and a table in it,) he merely said
he would never leave it, and he went to bed. We took
him food, but he would not speak, we left the door open
at night time and after a while he would creep down
when it was dark, and nearly bury himself in the earth of
the garden, or roll in any pool he could find. Many a
time has his father wheeled his barrow over his naked
body, when he was lying in his gait early in the morning,
and he could not see him. At last he refused to go out
any more, and pulled his bed all to pieces ; everything
which has since been given him, for bedding or clothing
he destroys, and the hole which you saw in the loft,
through which the light and air is let in, he tore with his
hands. He afterwards put himself in the position you
saw him in, and years many, have gone by, since he has
moved a foot from the spot in which you saw him.' We
enquired if he had ever before his intended marriage
shewn symptoms of insanity, or during any lucid interval
he had spoken of his fatal disappointment. She said that
he had never spoken anything about the matter, excepting the words which her mother had told us of :

> No greater grief, no meikle pain
> Than for to love, and not be lov'd again.

And that before he fell in love, he was the smartest young

man of the place. She added that he was inoffensive in his manner, excepting that he sometimes cried out dreadfully in the night time, but that on such occasions, he always exclaimed, ' Mother ! Mother ! ' and was instantly pacified as soon as she had hobbled up to the loft, and he saw her.

" During our return, as may be supposed, we were ruminating on the frightful sight, to which we had been witnesses. The first idea was that of surprise, that the maniac's parents and family should have so kept the secret of his miserable existence, that scarcely one of the neighbouring cottagers knew anything more than that there was something strange to see in Raeney's house, but what, they knew not. In Sheffield, and as we may charitably suppose at Norton, (especially to the parish officers of fourteen successive years) the existence, and as it may be termed, the horrid imprisonment of the pauper lunatic has not been known ; or doubtless the magistracy would have committed his care, and possible cure to the great public asylums, which the public maintains out of its own purse. The possibility that the poor son of humanity may yet be returned to the world of which he is insensible he forms a part, I think merits attention. His physical powers can never be restored, but it is impossible to suppose that the poor wretch, who could with a manner and tone not to be mistaken, distinctly say ' I am bound to sleep,' is irretrievably fallen to the state of the lowest animal,—yet is his treatment and his lodging inferior to that of the ox or the ass. The cause of his malady is deeply interesting— mentally *he has died for love*. In our boyhood we thought this possible, nay likely—in youth, we doubted if it could happen, in our manhood we laughed at the mere idea, and said with Shakespeare :—' Men have died and worms have eaten them ere now—but not for love.' Alas ! we must go back to our juvenile faith, for it cannot be doubted, that the falsehood of Mary Jones, broke the heart of Peter Raeney.

" Since the preceding hasty sketch was written, we have been assailed by the incredulous and the pitiful. The latter, and least impertinent of our annoyers, require further information respecting poor Peter ; the former attempt the excuse of society, by denying the existence of the maniac, or palliate its carelessness and neglect, by declaring that if the horrible object do exist, the romance by which we have surrounded him—the nakedness, the sinew-bound limbs, the dark loft, &c. are but ingenious fictions. To those we reply, ' there he is ; ' —the sun and moon have appeared in their orbits ten times, and the world-forgotten madman is still to be found lying on the boards of his prison. We have likewise received communications from a respectable individual of Norton, who seeks to apologise for the ignorance or neglect of the officers of his parish. He informs us that the mother of Peter receives relief for him from the overseers. If this be the case we decidedly say that those Derbyshire guardians of the poor, have shown themselves to be very ignorant or very cruel. We have reason however to believe that the relief alluded to (which is 3s. 6d. per week, and has been allowed only during the last year), is given on account of the alleged pauperism of the mother. Our feelings are also appealed to, and we are asked, if we would separate the old woman from her son, upon whom even in his forlorn state she doats ? Without any compromise of our humanity, before we answer this question we may ask another—How was it, the first years of Raeney's malady, and his consequent confinement were unvisited, untalked of, by the neighbourhood, or its proper officers ? A studied secrecy must have been observed on one side, or a gross inattention to a great violation of decency and humanity existed upon the other. Therefore we say, all that can be done to remedy the great abuse which neglected or unknown has existed for fourteen years should be done, and Peter

Raeney ought to be instantly removed, where he might
have at least the animal comforts, which a proper asylum
would afford, together with the chance of those benefits,
which proper physical and scientific treatment, might
afford.   We before mentioned the circumstance of his
speaking to us very clearly, we have since been informed
that he frequently, though seldom articulately, indulges
in speech.   He likewise distinguishes his mother and
his sister, and appears sensible of any attention they
may bestow upon him.   It may be remarked too, that
his mental disease arose from a great excitement, which
it must be admitted, youth only is capable of self-creating.
That period has now passed, he is between thirty and
forty years of age, and we hazard the conjecture, that with
the physical calmness which age induces, a mental placidity
and consciousness, might be attendant.   We had been
led to suppose that Raeney was totally unknown in
Sheffield, this however is not the case.   He was known
to many persons in the town as an industrious scythe
maker, but soon after he became insane, his acquaintance
missed him, and it was the general belief that he was dead.
Amongst these persons, is Flather, the active and ex-
perienced officer, who visited him on Thursday last, and
as he informs us to his great grief found the dreadful
creature we have described to be Peter Raeney, who
fourteen years ago, was a fine youth standing upwards of
six feet high, at that time endeavouring under his tuition
to qualify himself as a fugleman.   His existence was likewise known to Mr. Holland, though it would seem that
gentleman never saw him.   The following pleasing lines
in the first part of his poem entitled 'The Hopes of
Matrimony,' published in 1822 with a few alterations,
would tell the sad story of Peter Raeney, with as much
feeling as fidelity."

In this poem of Holland's, though the victim is named
Walter, it is clear that the author, who mentions the case
in *Sheffield Illustrated*, had Peter Raeney in his mind when
he wrote :

Beside yon hill, whose steep and wooded brow
Casts a broad shadow o'er the vale below,
In the same cottage where his life begun,
There dwelt a youth, his mother's only son ;
Whose heart was fix'd, in buoyant seventeen,
On the gay charmer of the village-green :
He loved and hoped, till love and hope became
That wild desire which reason cannot tame.
Intense and ardent while his passion grew,
Through every vein the strong infection flew :
His cherish'd visions of prospective bliss
Brighten'd in fancy, and the unripe kiss
Of green virginity seem'd mellowing fast,
And half the term of anxious courtship past.
Alas ! while Walter thus confess'd her charms,
The faithless maiden bless'd a rival's arms !

. . . . .

Thus Walter felt ; and at an ardent age,
While lash'd and fever'd by his passion's rage,
He vow'd, in utter hopelessness of prayer,
The felon vengeance of his own despair.

. . . .

He left mankind, and dwelt through years forgot,
In the lone attic of his mother's cot ;
Where sickness spared, and death delay'd to strike,
Till shrunk and shrivell'd from aught human-like,
The monster manikin at length resign'd
The upright figure and the reasoning mind ;
Crouch'd on his calves, with beard and nails unshorn,
Uncheer'd alike by midnight, noon or morn—
Racking his maudlin brain, the idiot gropes,
A wretched suicide of marriage hopes.

The cottage in which Peter Raeney dragged out his miserable life still stands, but it has been altered ; so the sketch in this book is from a drawing of 1850 by Hugh Thompson, in the High Hazels Museum at Darnall. The artist is not to be confounded, however, with the charming illustrator of our own time, Hugh Thomson. I have been told by an old inhabitant of Norton who remembers the Raeneys that the end of a brother of the recluse was not very different from that of Peter himself. He remained indoors, allowed his hair to grow long and never suffered any washing operations in house, clothes or person.

The strange cases of Jonathan Booth's daughter, and of Peter Raeney, were long the talk of Woodseats, and in *Sheffield and its Neighbourhood Illustrated* (1865) Holland wrote that " driven by a shower into one of the cottages

REANEY'S COTTAGE
from a drawing in High Hazels Museum

for shelter, we were reminded by the woman of the attention attracted to the spot some years since by the discovery there of a deplorable victim to the effects of
disappointed love ! and of a still more remarkable case
of mental aberration, which is recorded in Wesley's
' Journal.' " He goes on to say that he remembered
Jonathan Booth's daughter " a sensible, pious, single
woman, upwards of sixty years of age, when she shewed
us several letters addressed to her by the founder of
Methodism."

Religion has failed in Norton, as in most other places

and in most other ages, to displace completely the old
superstitions.   There are still people here who believe
that he who hears Gabriel's whelps will die in the year.
The mysterious sounds which are supposed to be caused
by the hounds of Gabriel as he hunts across the sky in
the night are now attributed by naturalists to the nocturnal
migrations of birds, to wild geese, that yelp like dogs,
and to such wanderers ; but notwithstanding this explanation the superstition maintains its hold upon the
credulous.

These midnight journeyings across the sky, and the
environment of mystery in which they are accomplished,
have attracted the attention of poets and other writers,
and so we have Sir Samuel Ferguson's

> But when the wintry frosts begin,
>   And in their long-drawn, lofty flight,
> The wild geese with their airy din
>   Distend the ear of night.

Tennyson too had noted this weird phenomenon and
wrote of
> . . . wild birds that change
> Their season in the night and wail their way
> From cloud to cloud.

Some have regarded these strange cries as the gabblings
of witches as they sweep through the air in the dark
astride of their broomsticks.

A curious story has been perpetuated by James Linacre.
John Bingham lived with his parents at Sheephill, and
one day, without telling them, he set off to Bolsover with
Cornelius Crich, apparently with the notion of running
away from home.   Growing anxious, Mrs. Bingham
mentioned her son's continued absence to Thomas
Greaves, her neighbour.   " Look at noon next day
towards the Woodbent," he said.   This was a narrow
wood three hundred yards away, and looking there at
the time appointed Mrs. Bingham saw her son approaching.

A number of questions revealed the circumstance that young Bingham " was so troubled I could not stay away any longer." This strange incident seems to have been set down to witchcraft.

The superstition of telling the bees of a death in the family, which seems to have prevailed in most parts of the world, survives in and around Norton. I have heard of cases near Holmesfield, quite recently, and Mr. Addy has noted a form of the custom at Norton, where if a man or woman who keeps bees dies cake and wine must be given to them upon the day that he or she is buried, or they will die too. It was said that some bees at Hazelbarrow did die because this custom was not observed, and such coincidences give another lease of life to these ancient notions.

One of the superstitions of Norton is that if a calf is born prematurely a fire is made, and upon it the dead body is burned, while the cow, and probably other cows, are driven round the fire, a process held to prevent similar mishaps in the future. At Norton, too, Mr. Addy found the superstition that if a pig's hock be hung in the farm-house, and whitewashed whenever the house is whitewashed, the cattle upon the farm will be protected from disease. No farther away than Dronfield an old man used to sit in the church porch on the eve of Saint Mark at midnight to watch the spirits of those who would die that year pass into the church, and on the eve of another saint an old woman of Troway told Mr. Addy that it was the custom of girls who wanted to see their future husbands to hang a wet smock or chemise before the fire, and to put a loaf of bread and a knife upon the table. If the apparition of the man who appears turns the smock towards the girl he will marry her. If he cuts a piece from the loaf of bread and eats it he will be a good husband; if he cuts the smock in two a bad one. On one occasion she said there came during such a vigil a large black dog "as big as an elephant."

A boggard is said to have haunted Bunting Nook at one time, and there are traditions of ghosts at Norton House, and of the Lupton ghost at Greenhill Hall, in addition to the ghost of Edmund Offley that we saw at Norton Hall.

Amongst James Linacre's notes are a few brief, hurried entries indicating a Norton tragedy. Thomas Knowles was hanged for forgery about 1800; but it was said that old Thomas Marsden, of Bole Hill, was the actual offender, and sent Knowles to get the forged notes cashed, and that Knowles did not know a letter of the alphabet. After the execution Marsden never dared to stir out of his house after dark. An older tragedy is indicated in an entry on the Patent Roll of Richard the Second concerning a pardon in 1397 to Robert Vykerman *alias* Bikerman, of Norton, for the death of John Fundelyng of Staveley, killed at Bremyngton on Thursday after the Purification in the seventh year.

In the matter of village customs it may be said that at Norton, as in some other villages in this district, the old Christmas pastimes, like mumming, are dead or dying. In 1907 Mr. Addy wrote with regard to " The Old Tup" that "at Norton a sufficient number of boys could not be got together at Christmas 1901, when I made enquiry. Both the 'old tup' and 'the old horse' were performed at Norton and Dronfield when I was a boy about 1855. I have remembered the tunes since boyhood, having frequently heard them sung." At Cold Aston people used to go round begging corn on St. Thomas's Day to make frummety at Christmas. My father remembers this practice at Whiston. The children went round in little companies, each child with a small bag. They called at all the farms, obtaining a little wheat at most of them. At Cold Aston it used to be the practice when a lover was forsaken by his mistress to make an oval-shaped garland of leaves, flowers and ribbons, and to hang this at night in a tree near his house, so that this sign was likely to be the first thing he would see in the morning. Then, like so many other villages, Norton had its town song. There is an idea that these town songs are not only very old, but that in Roman times they had some relation to the taking of the census. The Norton town song was sorry doggerel, and not complimentary enough to families still alive to bear reproduction. A similar song at Cold Aston relates of a man who was said to be frightened at the moon,

> And old George B——
> Took boggart at t' moon,

a curious use of the word "boggart" for "fright." The town song of another part of this district imparted the valuable information that

> Old Billy M—— at Fulud [Fulwood] Booth
> Stands all weathers, rough and smooth.

At Whiston a town song was composed in my father's youth by Billy Street, the blacksmith, but no doubt he followed an old tradition. His song was not forgotten when I began to go to Whiston in the early seventies of last century. The boys used to go to the first house in the village and sing the couplet which had been composed for the benefit of the family there, and so on through the village, unless, as often happened, their vocal ardour was quenched under a bucket of cold water, or ended untimely by the application of an ash plant. A few of the lines I can remember. In cases where members of the family are alive still fictitious names have been substituted.

> At bottom o't tahn the row begins,
> Owd Ann Pilley taks lodgers in.
>
> . . . .
>
> And her son Tom's a rovin spark,
> For he neer cooms hooam while reight pitch dark.
> Owd Mary Yeardley shoo sells flour,
> An' as it gets lower owd Tommy looks sour.
> Owd Timmy Elliott, he sells meight,
> An' if yo' don't watch him he'll gie yo' short weight.

In old wills a frequent provision was that the heir should not turn out the widow from her late husband's house. For instance, at Martinside, near Chapel-en-le-Frith, was a house belonging to the Kirkes in which part of one of the wings was set aside as "the Widow's Corner." The apartments in this portion of the house belonged by right to any mistress of the house who became a widow, and the arrangement was made so that no heir could turn her out. The right was exercised in 1789. Upon this point Mr. Addy has given us a de Hooch-like picture in his Glossary, where we have it—page xlviii—that "Upon the death of a farmer or yeoman it was, until recent years, the custom in this district for the widow to occupy a distinctly separated portion of her late husband's house. In one case in Norton the widow, an old woman, spent her time in spinning. The room which she occupied, and in which she slept, was on the ground floor, in a corner of which was her bed, hung with homespun linen in blue and white 'checks' or squares. When she was tired of spinning she sat near the fire and smoked her pipe. The spun thread was woven in the adjacent village of Dronfield. In old Derbyshire wills I have several times noticed directions as to the room or rooms in the testator's house which the widow was to occupy." A widow was entitled to the *flet*, or inner portion of the house, from a very early time.

It is wonderful how old customs survive in some places. So recently as 1902 I saw a man, near Dronfield, use sand instead of blotting-paper, a practice I thought was obsolete in England, though still usual in cafés in Venice, and so probably in other places in Italy. In France the practice still survives.

A grotesque figure, out of German mythology, one Nicobore, has managed to obtain a firm footing at Norton, and some legends make him a jester, or at any rate a servant, in the Bagshawe family at the Oakes. One day a visitor was expected who had a large red nose, and

Nicobore was warned that he was not to mention nor to seem to notice this extraordinary feature. However, coming into the room where host and guest sat, Nicobore fancied his master looked at him angrily, whereupon he excused himself hurriedly in an injured tone by the exclamation " Well, I've said nowt about his nooas yit ! " Some of the Nicobore tales have become attached to Mosbro' Hall, and another version of the nose legend found there is that when the guest arrived Nicobore exclaimed in his presence " Oh, what a nooas ! " and then added hurriedly " But there's no sayin' nowt." When Nicobore swept the stairs at Mosbro' he began at the bottom, and when he sawed the branch off a tree over a stream he sat upon the wrong end of the branch and came plump into the water. Another Norton tale is that Nicobore, having received a sixpence, buried it in the garden that it might grow bigger. A fellow-servant, who had watched him, took the sixpence and put a shilling in its place, and Nicobore's appetite for gain having been roused he reburied the shilling. This process went on until by stages a five-shilling piece had been attained, and then the coin began to diminish until a threepenny piece reposed under the gooseberry bush. " I will put thee in my pocket," said Nicobore, " or thou wilt grow away altogether." There is a version of this tale that Nicobore hid his sixpence and pocketed it when it had reached its maximum of five shillings. On another occasion Nicobore is said to have drowned a litter of pigs because they had " prick ears," Nicobore's standard of what ears should be having been arrived at by his observation of hounds, which he noticed had drooping ears. Hunter says there was a story about an errand of Nicobore's to Mr. Jollie's academy at Attercliffe, but he adds, tantalisingly, that he has forgotten the particulars.

In Stannington, people have been known to throw contempt upon a story or excuse by retorting " Tell that to Nickybore ; don't tell me." Mr. Addy, who gives

Nicobore a place in his *Household Tales*, says the name evidently contains the Old English *nicor*, or Old Norse *nykr*, a water goblin.   The *bore* is doubtful.

One more curious old Norton folk-tale is of a hen-pecked husband, who, fleeing from his wife, heard a farmyard cock crow " Women are masters here ! " and a few miles farther another that crew " Aye, and everywheer ! " and so resolved to go back to his wife and bear the inevitable as best he could.   Of these old folk-tales, reminiscent of the stories of the wise men of Gotham, and similar to those which to-day we attach vaguely to an Irishman, a handloom weaver, a Sheffield grinder or a Lincolnshire man, it is not easy to discover who told them originally, but we may imagine family groups sitting round the wood fires across the North Sea, in the timbered homelands of the fatherland of the English race, spending the long winter evenings in the narration of these old tales that have been handed down orally for many generations since the song of Beowulf was sung in the hall of Hrothgar the Dane, until Jacob Grimm and other scholars gave them the permanence of print.   In these later times we find the descendants of the race that once lived in the Baltic region still dwelling in " tuns " and " hams," but on this side of the German Ocean, and still laughing heartily over the escapades of Nicobore and of the henpecked husband.

CHAPTER XVI

INDUSTRIES

DIVISION of labour makes its way apace even into domestic work ; but though in the south of England it has become the rule to take your bread from a cart at the door, here it is possible still to taste the sweeter home-made loaf. In Norton it is yet one of the delights of life to enter the cottage upon a frosty afternoon, to find it full of hospitable warmth and penetrated with the grateful aroma that comes from the baking bread in the oven, from the slowly rising tea-cakes that warm themselves in front of the fire, welcome accompaniments of a cosy home life in which we are not held at arm's length in the drawing-room, but have access to the well-ordered kitchen, the very heart of the house, and to the roaring north-country fire, where the bright kettle sings, where the comfortable cat blinks and purrs, where the grandfather's clock shines with beeswax and turpentine as he ticks solemnly and leisurely, where the fender gleams above the white hearth and where haply the sprightly cricket chirps.

As baking is now, so brewing once was amongst the household duties in this neighbourhood. This close connection of brewing and baking is shown in an old play by Robert Green, who has the line " Even as you have baked so brew." The older housewives still make wine from the flowers of the colt's foot, from gooseberries, rhubarb and other available material ; and in the dog days they fill great stone bottles with herb beer, but the national beverage is not now brewed at home, the people buying the more sophisticated concoctions that issue from the laboratories of the brewers. Traditions of the older practice remain in Norton, and James Linacre has recorded a brewing match " betwixt grandmother Ravel Linacre and John Gillatt, butler to John Read," and he adds triumphantly " Grandmother won ! " Bravo, Grandmother ! Thou hast been dead these many years, but thy victory over the butler shall not be forgotten. Another tale of his which seems to have some connection with baking or with brewing is one concerning Joshua Fox, who lived at Gleadless, and trained the singers, but had more than a sneaking regard for hunting, and loved the horn in the fields as well as the psalms in the church. His wife was carrying a " doachen of leaven " on her head when the bottom came out and covered her with barm. " Whativver mun I do ? " she exclaimed, looking helplessly at her husband. " Goo an' cleean theesen," he replied with true north-country directness.

Words are not wasted in this northern region. " My boy, can I see your uncle ? " asked a gentleman of a lad digging in a Norton garden. " Me ooncle's as droonk as moock," said the boy laconically, and went on with his digging.

The word " doachen " is not heard often now, if at all. Mr. Addy gives it as " doshun " in his Glossary and says it means a tub in which bread is kept. In Lancashire it is found in the form of " dashin " or " deashon," and signifies a tub in which oatmeal dough is kneaded. Pancheons are still in use about Norton, a picturesque kind of earthenware, beloved of artists, that we hope will long survive, though they are beset by the ugly blue and white enamelled ware to which no self-respecting artist would pay any regard.

James Linacre's tale will remind some readers of one which the late Councillor Nadin of Sheffield used to tell from his great store of local anecdotes, rivalled only by those accumulated by the Rev. T. W. Holmes, or those in Mr. Robert Eadon Leader's *Sheffield in the Eighteenth Century*, a book racy of the soil and smoke. One hot Sunday morning, when the doors of the Scotland Street chapel were left wide open to obtain some of the delightful air that blows in that salubrious region, a youth strolled along on his way to minister to the pigs with a wooden bucket of swill upon his head. The boy " gawmned " in at the open door, the preacher prayed with his eyes open and then the bottom of the bucket shot upwards and the boy was drenched with hogswash. The minister had to explain as best he could why he had interrupted the flow of his supplications with a wild shriek of laughter.

Even when brewing was done at home there was, for other reasons than mere drinking, the demand for the village alehouses, and in the year 1577, during the reign of Queen Elizabeth, Sir Francis Leek supplied to the Privy Council " the nowmber and namys of all such as kepe any alehowsis, Innys and Taverns within this Countie of Derbie whereof many are very poore." At Norton there were ten such places, kept by Christopher Chapmon, Thomas Arom, Edwarde Kirke, John Felde, Thomas Bullock, Charles Benyt, Mrs. Blyth, Edward Malam, Mrs. Gostilan and William Feyth.

In Dr. Cox's *Three Centuries of Derbyshire Annals* (Vol. II. p. 257) there is an account of an affair in a Norton public house in 1746 which recalls an "interior" by Jan Steen or by some other Dutch painter of card-playing topers. Some men who had been in a public house at Heeley came to Four Lane Ends, at Norton, and visited two public houses there, in the second of which they were joined by other men from Dronfield and Unston, who had come " with the intent to spend a shilling." They were all drinking together, their imbibings including a tankard of punch, when Sarah Marsh, the wife of the innkeeper, brought in a pack of cards. The men played putt and then brag, and from playing they sank to cheating and to a grabbing of the stakes. One swore before Richard Bagshawe, the magistrate, that he was cheated of £18, and that then all fell upon him " and struck and abused him after a barbarous manner."

Older than police organisation as we know it to-day is the " Norton Association for the Prosecution of Felons and other Depredators," which claims a history of nearly a hundred and twenty years. There used to be an old copy-book with particulars of the formation of the society, but this has been lost. The rules were drawn by Thomas Fox, Chantrey's schoolmaster, and the first meeting was held in 1784 at the Bowling Green, Magathay, now a private residence. The Ravel Linacre of that day was amongst the founders of the association. The subscription, based upon rateable value, was really a voluntary police rate, and the members received aid for the capture and prosecution of horse stealers, sheep stealers, fowl robbers, garden robbers, burglars and other reprobates. The Shores, the Bagshawes and other local gentlemen, gave liberal support to the association, and the Rev. H. Pearson, the Rev. H. H. Piper, John Read, Mr. Booker and Mr. Webster appear as members. Much of the money went in eating and drinking, and the prosecutions cost more than the stolen goods. For instance it cost £14 15s. to convict James Hines of stealing fowls, so that the lawyers must have had even better pickings than the thieves, to say nothing of the expenses of the numerous committee meetings, at which members were fortified with brandy, held to discuss the position, though " when Mr. Booker's fowls was stolen " the committee spent no more than 4s. 4d. in investigations.

In 1840 the committee agreed that "several highway robberies having been committed, in the neighbourhood of Greenhill, and in consequence of the gentlemen of the parish entering into a subscription for a night police, we, the members of the association consider that the sum of £5 be paid from their funds for that purpose, if necessary, towards the expenses of the apprehension and conviction of the above." This resolution is not very skilfully drawn, and hypercritical persons might ask whether the police or the gentlemen of the parish were to be apprehended and convicted, or haply the members of the association themselves.

It goes almost without saying there was an annual dinner, and this was a moveable feast, dominated by the January full moon, to improve perhaps the chance of the members finding their way home after their convivialities. It may be also that the members thought the January frosts would " sharpen their nip." That usually most stupid thing the after-dinner speech was not introduced, but the evening was spent in informal conversation and in music. It was the period not of machine-made music, phonographs and their kind, but of glees, and it is said that on one occasion a long journey was made after midnight to fetch from his bed a particular vocalist to take part in a popular glee.

For thirty-two years Mr. G. H. Osborne of Holmesfield was secretary of this organisation ; he attended its meetings for sixty years, and his father was a member before him. Mr. E. Hunstone is the secretary now, for it has not been found desirable to dissolve the association.

The people of Norton did not combine only for the suppression of thieves. They had also a Sick Club, whose meetings were held at the Masons' Arms, then at Little Norton, and about the time of the battle of Waterloo a momentous struggle was being waged here at Norton too. Every club night twopence was to be spent with the landlord for each member, whether the member was present or not ; and as the drink was ordered at the beginning of the evening those who were early came in for more than their share, at the expense of those whose work had detained them. It was agreed, therefore, that the twopences of absent members should go to the funds of the club ; but in this the members agreed without their host, for the landlord, James Firth, or Frith, insisted that all these twopences should be spent. The club flung down its ultimatum : if the landlord would not agree, then must the club remove to the inn at

Hemsworth. The landlord remained inexorable, and, moreover, being now thoroughly roused, he refused to yield the club's box and temporalities, whereupon John Linacre and Constable Reaney, armed with an authority they had obtained through Thomas Fox, who was both schoolmaster and clerk for the magistrate, Sir William Bagshawe, entered the Masons' Arms and at last went triumphantly to Hemsworth with the property of the club.

If all stories be true, this parish officer did not act always in harmony with the magistrate. A sheep had been stolen at Gleadless, and the thief was taken before the resident justice. The constable, "old John Reaney," got the mutton as his perquisite, but claimed also a reward which he said had been offered. The magistrate refused to grant this, and there seems to have been a dispute about it outside, for the story goes that they fought and that the constable threw the justice into a garden (Wilkinson's) and then called out to him, perhaps as much in sorrow as in anger, "Damn you, an' I 'ave been like a father to you!"

In addition to the self-supporting Sick Club there have been charities in Norton for many years. The Rev. Francis Gisborne (1817) left money to buy flannel and woollen ; Robert Newton (1784), money for the old and poor ; Richard Rose (1774), assistance for six poor widows ; William Scriven (1724), clothing ; John Storie (1674), help for needful, aged and impotent poor ; John Wingfield (1731), clothing and money for poor old people ; Isaac Shepherd (1811), bread for the people of Greenhill and Bradway ; Samuel Butcher (1892), clothing for children. We have seen that the Gills were benefactors, and we shall see that Sir Francis Chantrey did not forget his native village in his will. These bequests, however, have not met every case of poverty, and sometimes an appeal has been needed to the Guardians of the Poor. Relief of this kind was at one time bestowed by the Justices at Quarter Sessions, and at the Easter Sessions of 1683 one

shilling weekly was ordered to be given " unto Thomas
Marradin " of Cold Aston. Formerly each parish had
its own workhouse; but in 1834 an Act was passed by
which parishes were joined in union to provide a union
workhouse, colloquially known now amongst some people
as "t'Union"; but as early as 1800 Norton, which we
have seen already with a voluntary police rate, belonged
to a voluntary and permissive union sending its paupers
to Ashover, where a building which had failed as a bathing
establishment designed to rival Buxton and Matlock was
used as a workhouse. In this pioneer amongst poor law
unions in 1809 were 61 parishes and 38 inmates. Later,
in 1828-9, there were 43 parishes with 61 paupers, and
with an increased cost of maintenance from £10 10s. to
£11 4s. per head.

There have been attempts too to reduce poverty in
Norton, as in other places, by the artificial coddling of
industries. In the reign of Henry the Eighth the growing
of flax and hemp was made compulsory, though Bishop
Latimer suggested that the area of land allotted in the
Act of Parliament to hemp "were all too little were it so
much more." He argued benevolently that the hemp
produced would not be half sufficient with which "to
hang the thieves that be in England." However the flax
and hemp industries flagged in spite of legislation, but
again it was sought to revive them by keeping out foreign
linen in the reign of George the Third, when the English
production was encouraged by bounties to the producers.
Between 1783 and 1797 much flax was grown in this
part of Derbyshire "in the moist meadows amid the
moor-lands of Scarsdale."

Traces of the former cultivation of hemp and flax may
still be found in many places. People interested in the
names of fields will find often near a town or village a
Flax Piece, Hemp Lands or some other name that indicates that here flax or hemp was grown; and we know
that in Norton and Unston, as well as in Dronfield, flax
was cultivated, and the Hemper, Hempard, or Hemp-

yard Lane from Greenhill to Bradway may have some connection with the industry. Again, we may recall that James Montgomery, the poet, walking near Sheffield with Robert Montgomery, of Woolwich, on a September day of 1808, came suddenly upon a field of flax in full flower, an expanse of beautiful blue. " Brother, what sort of corn is that ? " exclaimed Robert. " Such corn as your shirt is made of," answered James. Another poet once had similar natural history difficulties with a Cockney, for Harriet Westbrook, during a coach journey between Edinburgh and York, besought Shelley to teach her how to discriminate between turnips and barley.

In Cold Aston there are the Henpepper fields, a name which Mr. Addy suggests has been derived from *henep*, hemp, and *æcer*, a field ; there is a Hemp Lane, mentioned in the court rolls of the manor of Holmesfield, of 1674, leading down to Horsleygate Lane. Flax lands are mentioned in 1807 at Ecclesall, and Linker Lane at Woodseats may be Old Icelandic *lin—akr*, flax field. Linley Bank near Gleadless may have a similar derivation, and the personal name Linley the same origin. When it is remembered that " line " is another word that means flax, that linseed is flaxseed, then Line Croft, a field in Heeley, Line Croft in Ecclesfield and the Norton family name Linacre become for us names that are full of signification. In Iceland there is *Linakra dala*. The Anglo-Saxon *heordan* is associated with flax also, and to-day the Norton housewife does her rough work in what she calls a harden apron, that is an apron of coarse linen. In some districts the word is pronounced " harding."

Having some recollection of hearing an allusion to flax growing near that village, during a visit when I was a boy to my grandmother at Whiston, I wrote to my father for confirmation. His reply was that the inquiry " brings to my mind that I was born just in time to see what I believe was the very last field of flax that was ever grown in Whiston. It belonged to Timothy Elliott, who kept the Chequers Inn, and was growing in the croft facing the inn. It caught my boyish imagination, and is still a most vivid and beautiful memory : when it was in flower it looked like a bit of blue sky come down to earth. Whether that particular flax was dealt with at Whiston I could not say, but I should be disposed to think not. There was, however, a flax-pit at the bottom of the Bank in that marshy bit of land where you will probably remember the yellow iris grew so abundantly and where the sewage-farm now is. It was a shallow

pool, oblong in shape, about 24 ft. by 12 ft., and my grandmother told me it was used to lay the flax stems in to rot away the softer parts so that the fibres could be more easily separated. I believe those who separated them did so with a coarse kind of comb and were called flax-dressers. It would probably then be sent away to be dealt with—there was a considerable linen industry at that time at Barnsley in which my grandfather's brother John was engaged, whether as a manufacturer or not I could not say, but certainly as a merchant. It just comes to my mind that the father of old Dicky Cutts (the sexton when I was young), whom I do not remember, was a weaver and lived at the bottom of the Green, and that he and his loom were both objects of lively interest to the lads and lasses of the time of Napoleon Buonaparte. There may have been more hand-looms in Whiston, but I am not certain." People who know Rotherham may remember Smith's flax mill, near the river, to the north of the church, and an old lane called Mill Gate leading to it.

Much folklore has gathered round the hempseed, and in Derbyshire many a maiden has sown the seed on St. Valentine's Eve, believing that he who mowed the crop would be her lover.

Norton's natural, unprotected, bounty-free industry has not been connected with hemp, nor with flax, but with iron and steel. Scythes and sickles and such manly implements have been her contribution to industrial evolution, and not shirts, aprons, nor hangmen's ropes. Her annals are full of references to this work, her Registers crowded with the names of those who have been engaged in it. Many of her sons have wrought, not in factories, but in picturesque workshops in the country lanes, and sometimes their anvil has been set up in a shop attached to their home and with the pleasing surroundings of apple-blossoms, vegetables and flowers, with ready access to the dinner and tea table and other homely advantages. I remember being invited to take shelter in such a cottage once at Meadow Head, when I had been caught in a storm as I was making a sketch of the place. The anvil and other implements were in a workshop that formed part of the same building as the worker's home, and the scent of the hay came in at the workshop door.

Pilkington, who wrote at the end of the eighteenth century, noticed that " in this parish the manufacture of scythes is carried on to a very great extent. The number of persons employed by it is one hundred and thirty-six makers, and twenty-five grinders. Besides these some of the principal scythe-smiths furnish work for both makers and grinders in other neighbouring parishes." Already have we read that the iron gates at the Oakes are of Norton iron and Norton craftsmanship.

In much more recent times reference has been made to Norton in association with iron work by Mr. Robert Eadon Leader, B.A., whose removal from Sheffield to London caused no loss of attachment on his part to the history of the district in which he and his forefathers were born. On May 20th, 1908, Mr. Leader, a past President of the British Archæological Association, read a paper on *Alien Refugee Cutlery Traditions*. His purpose was to examine a persistent tradition that, of the artisans who, in the reign of Queen Elizabeth, fled from the Netherlands before the cruel Duke of Alva, certain workers in metals were settled in the neighbourhood of Sheffield, bringing with them some cutlery crafts not previously practised, and introducing improvements in other branches already followed by the Hallamshire work-men. According to this, sickle makers were established at Eckington, scythe makers at Norton, the makers of scissors at Attercliffe and button makers in Sheffield. In disproof of the allegation that local scythe-making was thus begun, Mr. Leader shows that fourteen years before Alva arrived in the Netherlands " a family named Urton, *alias* Stevyn, scythesmiths with every appearance of English origin, were firmly seated at Norton— possessing freeholds, marrying into other yeoman households, and on terms of friendly equality with their substantial neighbours. Six years after Alva's descent upon the Netherlands, that is in 1574, John Vrton *alias* Steven was taking an apprentice, one John Clayton, to learn the craft of making scythes, as an existing indenture shows. Mr. Leader then turns to the Norton Registers and points out that the first three entries disprove this tradition of an alien origin for the local industries.

Old Cottage at
Meadow Head

347

" They record, in 1559 (1st and 2nd Elizabeth), the
baptisms of children born to two scythe-smiths, John
Grene and William Camme, and to a scythe-striker,
Thomas Rose. Then in the succeeding years, from 1561
to the end of the century, we find employed in the
same trade, men bearing the names of Padley, Brownell,
Biggen, Allen, Pearson, Perkyn, Fielde, Wainwright,
Meller, Cowleye, Barten, Bullocke, Barnes, Tayler, Bates,
Clayton, Parks, Bore, Gryme, Clarke, Turner, Walker,
Hallam, Roper, Staniforth, Levicke. And in the period
that follows, the industry remains in the hands of these
twenty-nine families, the occurrence of a name other than
those in this list being exceedingly rare. I do not lay
stress on the fact that, interposed among these scythe-
makers is a certain sprinkling of cutlers, sickle-makers,
and sheathers, because it is enough to find before the
Netherland persecutions began, say 1568, nine families
actively engaged in the production of scythes, as well as
of children, in Norton parish. Further, these, as well as
the twenty others who appear in succeeding years, mostly
bear English names. In view of all this we may
well ask where are the traces of a refugee settlement?
And how can individual immigrants have brought in an
industry shown to be in existence at least ten years
earlier ? "

Mr. Leader proceeded to show that the case against
this tradition with regard to sicklesmiths and shear-
smiths was equally strong, and that in the matter of
knives, fact and chronology are entirely against the
notion that native craft was capable only of making the
ruder shapes, and owed the finer forms to the superior
taste and skill of alien artisans. Dr. Smiles in *The
Huguenots* cites the Gillots as a family that found refuge
in England when the Huguenots were persecuted in 1685,
but Mr. Leader's triumphant rejoinder is that there have
been Gillots in Yorkshire from 1297 and in Norton from
1575, and that before 1685 " Gillots, mostly scythe-
makers, were as plentiful as blackberries in Norton

parish." If Gillot is a French name at all, and if the founder of this family in Norton was driven here by religious persecution, it may have been during the time of the St. Bartholomew's massacres of 1572, but clearly it could not have been, as Dr. Smiles suggested, during the persecutions attendant on the Revocation of the Edict of Nantes in 1685, a hundred years later. Mr. Leader urged that "the names in the Norton deeds, of the Urtons and their neighbours, and of those recorded in the Registers as resident in Norton parish, are almost wholly such as are found in common use in England during several previous centuries." The scythesmiths of Norton from 1559 bore, with but few exceptions, essentially English names. In consideration of these facts and of others we have not repeated, Mr. Leader concludes " that the numbers of the incomers have been exaggerated ; that their introduction of new industries is a fiction ; and that their contributions to raising the standard of manufacture have been inordinately appraised to the unfair disparagement of workers of earlier, or English origin. This applies with equal cogency to any immigrants and to any period."

Since he wrote this paper Mr. Leader has found evidences of much earlier scythe-making in Norton and the neighbourhood. Ancestors of the Parkers of Woodthorpe included yeoman followers of this craft. In 1459 John Parker of Little Norton, scythesmith, held a building on the Beauchief Abbey estate ; and his son, Thomas Parker of Whitley, had in 1486 carried the industry to Ecclesfield. There are, too, in *Derbyshire Charters*, a particularly valuable work compiled by Mr. I. H. Jeayes, allusions to a scythesmith at Holbrook, near Staveley, in 1489 ; and to another at Derby in 1511. It is thus clear that although a few names, such for instance as Gillott or Richard Levicke, otherwise Leathwicke, mentioned in the Norton Register as a scythe-striker in 1599, indicate a certain infusion of alien craftsmen, instead of introducing a new manufacture, they only joined a long practised craft.

In the days before it was lawful for workmen to combine to increase the price of labour some Norton scythesmiths were sent to gaol for their devotion to trades-unionism, and the event was celebrated by a local poet.

THE NORTON SCYTHESMITHS' SONG.

At the Bowling Green the Meeting was held,
We Journeymen Scythesmiths there did attend;
We drew up a statement as all had agreed
And sent to our Masters, but did not succeed.

We were summoned the Magistrate's court to attend;
Justice Jebb and Sir William nine of us did send
(Because we'd no money nor friend to give bail)
For a fortnight free lodgings in Derby jail.

And when we got there some drinking, some smoking,
While others looked sad,
We thought it was Bedlam and all going mad.

Hard boards and Long Straw we had for our Beds,
We pulled off our Breeches to put under our Heads,
We pulled off our Coats for both Blanket and Sheet,
We pulled off our Waistcoats to wrap our cold feet.

Thomas Asline Ward was opposed to the idea of sending men to prison because they joined trades unions, and entered in his diary on May 23, 1814, "I cannot help pitying the poor men who are to be punished for combination, one of whom is George Richardson, of Norton, a man who works like a slave for the decent maintenance of his family. It is a shameful thing they have no other means of raising their wages, and that the only one is punishable. Surely the masters should agree to give a proper proportion of gains."

Not only could they make scythes in this district, but they could use them too, and remembering some allusion of my father's to the annual visits of "Grennel Mowers" to his native village of Whiston, near Rotherham, I wrote for some particulars, whereupon he replied that "in the days before mowing machines were invented, and after the sickle had been superseded by the scythe, Greenhill was noted for the skill and rapidity of its mowers. I remember when I was a little lad a gang of them being engaged year after year at Whiston Hall farm, which then contained, I should think, almost three times the acreage it does now, and was farmed by a 'gentleman' farmer named Francis Moss, who used to ride round his extensive lands on a little grey cob. He was a terror to the village lads, and had the knack of getting value for his money both out of man, beast and land. Nobody else after he died could make a living out of it ; at any rate, nobody ever kept it long, and ultimately it was divided into smaller holdings, and the glory of the Old Hall departed. This band of 'Gren'ill mowers,' as they were called, were looked upon as prodigies by the villagers ; and their feats with the scythe were the talk of the country side. They lived 'in ' and slept 'out.' That is, they were fed in the Hall kitchen and slept among the hay in the hay-mow. Uncle William once suggested to some old lead miners at Eyam that their scythes were attached to a belt round their waist by a swivel which enabled them to use their scythes both left and right ! He had a taste for romancing."

Traditions of prowess with the scythe in Norton parish are not yet dead, for the Vicar, Mr. Hall, mentioning to an old inhabitant that Chantrey was able to mow an acre in a day, found that this was not considered by any means a feat, for the old man declared that he had himself mowed two acres, and "done a day's work after that."

Greenhill is an interesting place, with other old houses beside the Hall that was mentioned in Chapter XI. There was once a second hall here, Suarte Hall, but all traces of this seem to have been lost. The village

was one of the possessions of Beauchief Abbey, and
Mr. Addy commenting upon its name has written : " I
cannot believe that the village of *Green-Hill* was so
named arbitrarily, for the grassy slopes which lead up
to the village from the north are a sufficient explanation.
There must have been, at this place, an expanse of bright
green turf, free from gorse or underwood, and probably
the site of an old British settlement, which would strike
the eye of the Anglo-Saxon settler, and hence give rise
to the name."

From several points of view you obtain the idea
of a village upon a green hill, but the poetry of the
impression is utterly spoiled upon the Bradway side by
a vulgar, flaring, red and yellow sign of immense size
put there in the interests of some bottler of ale and
beer.   A replica of this sign appears in another part
of Norton, for there seems to be no power in inhabitants,
sometimes, unhappily, no desire, to preserve the amenities
of their village, so that tobacco manufacturers, brewers,
distillers, compounders of pills and other people of
that kind, giving so little or no value for money in
" goods," find themselves able to spend a great deal too
much of that " fool's money " which is said to go a long
way in obtruding their low taste for ostentatious adver-
tisement into places whose beauty they completely ruin.

Greenhill Moor was a marshy waste between Norton
and Greenhill.   A deed of 1384 gives William of the
Moor, that is, of Greenhill Moor.   Stage-coach travellers
have spoken of it as the coldest place on the road between
London and York.   I have heard a similar description
applied to the hill at Highfield, near the Highfield
Library and Trinity Wesleyan Church, between Heeley
and Sheffield, a locality formerly known as Goose Green,
though the name seems now to have been lost to the
people.   It survives in Georgian Highway Acts and in
other documents.

At one time races were held on Greenhill Moor.   A
public house kept by Benjamin Cavill served as grand

stand, the spectators occupying what was known as the dancing chamber, for here the village balls took place, and there is a fondly cherished memory of an heroic age when old Josh Reaney, the fiddler, was dragged out of his bed in his shirt to provide the music.

Within the radius of a few miles of Norton church there used to be many nailmakers' shops, but the jealous, greedy cities have clawed the craftsmen who worked there away from their village homes and gardens into crowded streets and factories, making these erstwhile somewhat free-and-easy workers

> Slaves to an hour, and vassals to a bell.

A few file-cutters have been able to retain their position as outworkers, so that the tap-tap-tap of the " nicker peckers " may yet be heard in some places as an accompaniment to the droning of the bee ; but even they are not beyond the reach of authority, and in Ebenezer Downing's *Smook thru a Shevvield Chimla* we have a file-cutter, in a lament to Liberty, complaining querulously amongst other things that

> . . . for ivvry bloomin stidda
> There's sooa many cubic feet,
> We'st ha' room to play at 'idda—
> Uz 'at isn't aht i't street.

CHAPTER XVII

PLACE NAMES

HEEDLESS of stern philologists, John Holland has told us of Norton that "there is in the village a well-known public-house, called ' Mag-o'-th'-hay,' *i.e.* [*pace* Mr. Addy] the Magpie-on-the-hayrick : the pleasant style in which parties from Sheffield are accommodated with tea, and the nice bowling-green, with its weekly parties, are sources of grateful reminiscence with holiday visitors, old and young."   When Holland and Montgomery were at Norton in May 1850 to see Chantrey's grave they came to Magathay, and Montgomery remarked that he had never been able to make out the meaning of this odd name Mag-o'-th'-hay, whereupon Holland replied " I never doubted that it signified *the magpie on the haycock*."   Montgomery was a polite man and not given to contention, so all he said was " You *may* be right ; but it is spelled Maugherhay in the early parish records."   What puzzled Montgomery, and drew such complacent response from John Holland, has been a long-standing problem to scholars with much greater experience in place names than Montgomery or Holland could hope to attain in those days.   There have been more than twenty ways of spelling the name during the last three hundred years ; but the termination " hay " or " hey " has persisted through all these mutations, and most philologists agree that this part of the name indicates an enclosure.   Innumerable examples of its use in this way might be compiled from Chaucer,

354

old deeds, Domesday Book and other sources, and *Haie* is still the French word for a hedge. In Belgium too we have La Haye Sainte. In Fairbank's survey of Norton he mentions fields near Magathay with such names as Rough Hay, Roe Hay, Maga Allotment, Mag Green and Maga Green allotment. Haw is a variation of Hay and occurs with great frequency, often meaning a park. In another part of Derbyshire is Parsley Hay, and there is Birley Hay, near Eckington. At Slaithwaite near Huddersfield is Calf Hey.

Many are the suggestions that have been made for the meaning of the term Magathay ; but as these conjectures are untenable in the presence of recent discoveries in philology it would be idle to repeat them. Mr. Addy, who has given much consideration to the question at different times for many years, thinks the name has been derived from *mægeth*, a maid, and *hay*, an enclosure, and that it indicates the place to which the milkmaids drove the cows to be milked—maiden croft or milking fold. There is a Maggath Lees at Holmesfield, and I have seen the map of a farm at Dore of 1767 in which one of the fields was called "Milking Place."

The meaning of the name would give little concern to a past generation of Sheffield people who used to obtain here that solace from business cares which they now seek at Scarborough or on the Alps. Those who read the annals of Sheffield will find themselves intruding often upon little parties of townsmen gathered here at Magathay to play bowls or to sit and gossip. Already we have seen that James Montgomery and John Holland came here, and many are the allusions too in Asline Ward's diary. In the summer of 1805 "My mother and I drank tea at the Bowling green, Norton, with the Wilsons, Leaders, Wreakes, Pearsons, Newboulds, Watsons, Harrisons, Mackenzies, J. Roberts, my brother S.B.W., etc.—above 30 in all." He was there also on one occasion with Montgomery and Piper, and during another visit he was shown an old book of visitors

1792–1800, and he gives names. He reveals too that not only were teas provided here but dinners also. In his *Sheffield and its Neighbourhood Illustrated* John Holland wrote that "there is but one public house, the Mag-o'-th'-Hay, and many a merry party have enjoyed their tea in the little parlour, and their sports on its pretty bowling-green ! the latter, indeed, was not always free to social interlopers, for more than one set of 'Old Sheffielders' had their fixed afternoons once a week for making a game at bowls. But of these it is melancholy to reflect how many, whom we well knew, does the green sod or the cold gravestone now cover ! "

A charming article recalling in style and matter the writing of Gilbert White was contributed to *Notes and Queries* for January 15, 1887, by Mr. Addy, with this old green for subject.

"I find from the Norton church registers," he wrote, "that there has been a bowling-green at this place since the year 1681, when it is first mentioned as such. It might have been so used long before the year 1681, for previous to that time the names of houses are rarely given in the register. The date, however, is sufficiently remote to show the long-continued usage of a favourite English game.

"The green itself, laid down at least two centuries ago, is composed of the finest peat turf, on which grows mountain grass, mingled with patches of moss which look like green velvet. The subsoil is a yellow marl. In shape the green is nearly square, and till recently was surrounded by ditches and banks, upon which grew foxgloves, sweetbriar, lad's love (southern wood), pinks, bachelors' buttons, and many other flowers more common in old than in modern gardens. On the western side are a number of quaintly contorted sycamore-maples (*Acer pseudo-platanus*), whose main stems have been cut away, and whose lateral branches have been trained over the green, so that their leaves might afford a pleasant shade in summer to bowlers and holiday-makers. These

trees, doubtless, were planted for the shade which they
afford ; though Evelyn, in his *Sylva*, says the sycamore
is ' much more in reputation than it deserves, for the
honey-dew-leaves, which fall early, turn to mucilage and
noxious insects.' The north side is bounded by a tall
hedge of holly and thorn, in which are planted at
intervals hollies of great age, trained into somewhat
fantastic shapes.

" For many years the green at Norton has been
haunted by a species of small bees (*Andena vicina*), which
have perforated and undermined the whole of its surface.
On taking up a piece of the turf, it was observed that
these industrious insects had bored down into the marl to
the distance of five to twelve inches. At the approach
of summer the green, whose fine grass and moss, living
on a substratum of marl, had been trodden and pounded
by the feet of two centuries of bowlers and village
revellers, was perforated all over with little round perpendicular holes or shafts, into which you might push
a tobacco pipe for several inches. For a time bowling
was prevented or made difficult, for the green was covered
with little hillocks of earth. Attempts were from time
to time made to destroy these industrious miners, in the
belief that they would destroy the grass, and in ignorance
of the useful part they played in the economy of nature ;
for it cannot be doubted that without the aid of the
bees the grass would have perished altogether. In the
hot summer of 1868 the green was almost burnt up ;
and, after heavy rains, pools of water which could find no
exit might have been seen standing upon it. The insects,
by boring into the marl which lay immediately beneath
the turf, enabled water to get away. They were the
means of admitting air to the soil below. They
performed, in short, many of those useful services
which Mr. Darwin, in his delightful book on ' The
Formation of Vegetable Mould through the Action of

Worms,' has shown to be the peculiar work of the common earthworm.

"The green had probably attained its peculiar velvet-like appearance from the careful weeding out, during a long period, of everything except the finest grasses and one or two kinds of moss ; and at the approach of every summer these little insects seemed to duly play their part in the long process of making a perfect bowling-green. They deigned not to make their nests elsewhere. . . ."

The house named Norton Green adjoins this old bowling green. It was rebuilt and enlarged by Mr. James Addy, the father of Mr. Sidney O. Addy, in 1866, and was purchased afterwards by Sir Nathaniel Creswick, K.C.B., who resides there now. A part of the old house remains embodied in the new, and the school to which Chantrey went as a boy stands now in the grounds of Norton Green, and has been adapted to the uses of a private theatre. An early portrait by Chantrey formerly belonged " to Mrs. Bunting, at the Bowling-green House, who was the intimate friend of old Mrs. Chantrey."

The derivation of Magathay is not the only bone of contention amongst Norton place names. In the seventies of the nineteenth century there was much discussion of local antiquities carried on with great vigour in the *Sheffield Independent,* and at one time these wit combats raged furiously round the derivation of Cold Aston. Even in those days it was recognised that Henry Bradley, one of the combatants who wrote as " Leofric," was " a man o' parts," but few if any in Sheffield would foresee his present eminence as Dr. Bradley, co-editor with Sir James A. H. Murray, LL.D., D.C.L., D.Lit., of the great *New English Dictionary.* He was not born amongst us, but at Manchester, yet was he educated no farther away than Chesterfield Grammar School, and he worked in Sheffield as a foreign correspondent before he wrote the books and attained the position in learned societies which led to the post he holds to-day in Oxford.

It has been found that the name Aston is common to

many villages, and I have counted sixty-seven.   There is
a Cold Aston in Gloucestershire and another in Wiltshire,
and indeed Cold affixed to a place name occurs often.
There is Cold Eaton in this county, a Cold Norton in
Essex and another in Staffordshire, and Cold Ashton in
Sussex.   To-day Cold Aston has become Coal Aston, but
this seems to be a corruption from the earlier form,
though the fact that coal is got here has confirmed and
has seemed to justify the corruption.   Glover says un-
blushingly in set terms that " from the coal strata with
which this lordship abounds this village derives its
first name [Coal Aston], and from its elevated and
bleak situation its second [Cold Aston]."   Many have
been the suggested derivations of this name.   One of the
earlier essays in solving the riddle was that the name
came from Anglo-Saxon *æsc*, an ash tree, a tree sacred
among the Saxons, or Anglo-Saxon *ást*, a kiln, and Anglo-
Saxon *col*, meaning coal—the coal-kiln town or the
ash-tree town.   Then another philologist gave Anglo-
Saxon *ceald*, meaning bleak, cold.   Aston may be East-
town, as Norton is North-town, and some have held
that the place has its name from standing upon what
farmers call cold land, but others rejoined that the land
is not cold at all.   A few years ago Mr. Addy made
the following suggestion.   He pointed out (*Notes and
Queries*, 6 S., XI. 122) that Shakespeare uses collied
for blackened, just as we might say coaled.   In
Domesday Book the place is called Estune, and Cold is
not used before the fourteenth century.   It is Haston
in a deed of 1541.   The word Cold appeared about the
middle of the fourteenth century in a rent roll of the
Abbey, though it was probably current before that.   It
persisted during the sixteenth and seventeenth centuries,
became Cole in the eighteenth and Coal in the nineteenth.
Mr. Addy gives no countenance to a derivation based on
cold soil, because he says the soil is rich and fertile.
Then, having drawn attention to the spellings Could and
Coled, he gives this significant extract from Mower's

Memorandum Book, a local manuscript of the sixteenth century : " Mem : That the Rose Hedge was *coaled* the yeer of our Lord God 1563, and had XI dozen of coal in it." Another entry shows that the charcoal which resulted was sold for £50 6s. 8d., about £600 of our money. Here is one of many indications of the great importance of charcoal before the coal we know had been adopted generally, and even now there are some processes of steel manufacture which demand the use of charcoal. Mr. Addy mentions that there were many lead mills in Abbeydale that would use charcoal, and that the Norton Register shows that charcoal burners, wood colliers, *carbonarii lignarii*, were the most numerous of the Norton workmen in the sixteenth century. He adds that at Cold Aston the ploughshare still turns up pieces of charcoal. Now when a piece of land had been cleared of its wood and the wood had been made into charcoal the land was said to have been coaled. Thus does Mr. Addy think we have *coaled* Aston, and the rest is easy. Another idea has been based upon the same foundation. The local pronunciation of ashes is *ass* ; ass-nook is the place under the kitchen fire into which the ashes fall. From the process of coaling we should get ashes or ass, and so Ass Town, meaning ash town. An open space in the middle of Cold Aston, where three roads meet, is known as Kiln Hill.

Charcoal burning, an ancient and often hereditary occupation that still lingers in some English forests, used to be pursued in neighbouring woods. There is a stone in Ecclesall Wood in memory of George Yardley, " wood collier," burnt to death in his cabin there on October 11, 1786, and a deed of 1613 at Norton Vicarage complains that " Mr. North's ill husbandry in cutting down the Wards woods and buylding of lead mills which he is bound to mainteyne with woods . . . in a short tyme will make destruction of all ye Ward's woods."

It is a co-incidence that ordinary coal too has been obtained at Aston in early days. Mr. Addy has written

that " we learn from the Chartulary [Beauchief Abbey]
that coal was worked at Cold-Aston and Alfreton as
early as the beginning of the fourteenth century ; for
Sir Thomas [Chaworth] gives the canons permission to
dig for it ' in the land belonging to the chantry of the
Blessed Virgin in Alfreton, in the land of their own
tenants, and in their land and wastes in the manors of
Alfreton and Norton.' Now, as Cold-Aston is part of
the Manor of Norton, there can be no doubt that coal
was got there . . . in places where it would not lie
deep." There is an Elizabethan deed giving free ingress
to get the coal and ironstone "growing" at Bradwaie
More, Graynill More and Weltsick Lane, and a
specific association of Aston with early coal mining
is found in a document which declares that " Thomas
Gladwine hath unlawfully entered uppo a piece of
wast grownd called Holmbey lyinge and beinge in Aston
al' Cold Aston within the manor of Norton . . . and
there digged a pit for gettinge of coales."

Aston, quiet as it seems to-day, has had its internal
commotions, and in *Three Centuries of Derbyshire Annals*,
by Dr. Cox, we see in progress a number of disputes
about who had and who had not served his term of
a year as Thirdborrow, a kind of under constable.

During the reign of Elizabeth, Henry Babington of
Dethick, whose wife was Mary, the sister of John,
Lord d'Arcey, settled land at Cold Aston on his
children. According to James Linacre's notes, Joseph
Biggin, antiquary, of Cold Aston, died in 1871. He
was a collector of books, and was related to Mr. Addy's
mother.

Norton, like so many other neighbouring places,
Crookes, Barlow, Treeton, Troway, Wirksworth, Totley,
Padley and others, has her Bole Hill. About the
meaning of this name there is no dispute. The name
signifies that here lead was smelted, and this industry
sought the tops of hills for the same reason that windmills occupied such sites, for here the breeze that sent

the mill sails round fanned the furnace and caused the
lead to melt and run.   Sheffield has a Furnace Hill.
Mr. Addy in his Glossary has shown that in West's
Symboleographie, 1647, sect. 133, is a form of bond
whereby the obligor is bound to deliver " ten foothers
of good, pure, and merchandizable *boole* lead of the
weight commonly called the *boole* weight, most commonly
used within the county of Derby, that is, after the rate
and weight of thirty foot to the foother, every foot to
containe six stone, and every stone to containe fourteen
pounds, at his *Boole Hill* at Hardwicke, in the county of
Derbyshire where commonly he used to burn his lead."
In connection with this industry Mr. Addy reminds his
readers that the Gills of Norton and the Rotherhams
of Dronfield were great lead merchants here in the
seventeenth century, and we have met John Storie
already in this capacity.   Mr. Addy mentions the shot
tower of the Gills at Greenhill, and he adds that lead was
carried by pack horses to places many miles distant from
the mines, and wood and charcoal were taken back in
return.   From old deeds Mr. Addy discovered that the
Rotherhams had a large lead mill near Beauchief, supplied
with charcoal from the neighbouring woods.   The name
occurs too in the court rolls of the manor of Holmesfield
for 1669, where we are told of " a paine set that noe
person or persons shall digg, hack, or break upp any old
bole works upon the commons or lord's wast within this
said manor upon payne for every such offence six shillings
eight pence."   Again, a definition of 1670 tells that Boles
or Bolestids are places where in ancient times (before
smelting mills were invented) " the miners did fine their
lead."

There is another old place name that survives hereabouts which merits at least a passing mention.   I
remember that the long narrow wood to the west of
Fawcett's farm near Lees Hall was known amongst the
boys of the district as Fawcett's Lumb, and I was per-
plexed often concerning the meaning of the word.   Why

should all the other woods be called woods and this
a lumb? A lumb is a deep cleft, or a pool in the bed
of a river, and if we leave that arm of the wood which
goes towards Fawcett's farm, Coneygreave Wood, and
go straight forward to Harvey Clough we find there the
explanation in a cleft down which the stream flows.

Fawcett's Lumb is not the only lumb in this district,
for there is Hemsworth Lumb running from Mawfa
Lane to Rollinson's Wood. In a Norton deed of 1584
is Oldfield Lume, North. Then we have Dowel or
Dowie Lumb, below Hazelbarrow; Black Car Lumb,
near Holmesfield; Sherwood Lum, near Horsley Gate,
in the same locality; and lumbs at Wardsend, Dore and
Bradfield. In the neighbourhood of Worral it is usual
to hear "Awm gooin' round by t' lumb." Farther
afield we have Depth of Lumb near Belper, Lumsdale
near Matlock, and Lumb, a stream near Todmorden,
and an old Rotherham rhyme begins

Down in yon lum we have a mill.

The study of field names and of place names generally
is a fascinating pursuit, but needs scholarship both wide
and deep. It would be possible to compile for Norton a
book upon this phase of the place alone, and it is to be
hoped that some attempt will be made to collect and
arrange all the field names and place names around
Sheffield. Isaac Taylor tells his readers that "what
has been affirmed by the botanist as to the floras
of limited districts, may be said, with little abate-
ment, concerning local names—that they survive the
catastrophes which overthrow empires, and that they
outlive devastations which are fatal to almost everything
besides."

Sick, of frequent occurrence in Derbyshire place names,
with sic or syke means a ditch, trench, small valley,
furrow, gutter, stream or other water course. Thus Sick
Mead is a meadow with a brook in it. At Norton is
Syke, or Sick, and James Linacre mentions a reference of

1712 to Sick House, then divided into two dwellings, and fields called Limepit meadow, the Wheat field, the Broom close and the Infield near Hemsworth. He has another note that Jarvis had a malthouse at Sick, which was quite a little town once. John Morewood had a butcher's shop there. Jarvis was of Sheffield, or perhaps of Heeley, and gave a tea to twenty old women of Norton at the Bagshawe Arms for several years, about 1880, during the Christmas holidays.

Far away as Norton is from the metropolis, the place has been long known by the tax collector, and by those who had to recruit for the army. In the reign of Edward the Third a subsidy of one-twentieth of all movable goods was granted by his first parliament for the defence of the King against the Scots. The principal people who paid at Norton upon this occasion were Thomas de Chaworth, Thomas de Bircheved, Gilb. de Grenhell, Robt. de Sellioke, Rad. Payn, John del Grene, Isabella de Norton, Gilb. del Leyes, Robt. Heron, Will Picard, Thomas de Gotham, Roger fil. Bate.

When Elizabeth came to the throne in 1558 one of her first acts was to test the military strength of some of the counties, and to see that the laws regulating the local forces were being regarded. Returns were prepared, and that for Norton shows

NORTON.—Itm̃ Able men in the same towne without
          harness iiij.
          Archer j—byllmen iiij.
          Harnes for j archer.

For the better understanding of this and subsequent records it may be explained that a byllman is a bill man, a man who carries a bill ; a bill, sometimes indicated by b., was a kind of sword or battle-axe. Calliu' indicates a caliver, a sort of firearm known also as a harquebuss. There is a specimen in the Tower of London that came from Penshurst. Ar' is an archer ; cor., co. or corslet means a breastplate, sometimes the whole armour of a pikeman. Pikeman is shortened to p.; m. or musk. is musket. A petronel is a large horse pistol.

In 1585, still in the reign of Queen Elizabeth, there were compiled "the names of all suche men as are appointed for to be in redines in Skarsdale . . . at a muster taken at Chesterfeelde, . . . and a particular note w^{th}all of all suche armo^r and weapons as euery Towneship hath in redines for the ffurnishinge and settinge forthe of the same." This return shows

Nortton—Christopher Rose, John Bartyn, Reynold Cowley, [name crossed out,] Thomas Savage, Hughe Sherte, ffrancis Bate ij calliu', j ar', j corslet, j bill.

In 1587 there was the alarm of the Spanish Armada and a threatened invasion, and so another muster being called, Norton was ready with "Phillope Bate ; Ric. Cleyton, calliu' ; Robert Hunter, ar' ; George Atkinson, cor. p. ; and Peter More, cor. b." Robt. Allen is entered but crossed out. In 1599 John Parker and John his son of Norton Lees contributed 20s. towards the Queen's service in Ireland.

The warriors of Norton and their accoutrements in 1624, during the reign of James the First, were

Philip Gill	co. p. musk.
John Stevens *alias* Urton, Wm. Blith and John Parker of Little Norton	co. p. & m.
James Bullock, gen.	m.
Leonard Gill	m.
Godfrey Barton, Edw. Outram and Ellis Poynton	m.
Rolland Morewood	m.

"The Board of Green Cloth was, in the Elizabethan and Stuart times," writes Dr. Cox, "the worst remainder of the ancient right of purveyance for the King's use.

Under the authority of this board, victuals for the use of the royal household were exacted at prices far below the real value, and in quantities far beyond any possible requirement." In 1596 an account of arrears was compiled for this district, when it appeared that Norton for the year owed 26s. 8d. of this exaction. Again, during the time of Elizabeth, loans were levied upon the gentry, who were thus compelled to lend money to the Queen. At Norton there was collected in this way

John Gyll, £xxv ;
John Parker, £xxv ;
James Bullock, £xx, and
William and George Gill, £xx.

Another subsidy was collected from the Norton landowners in 1599, full particulars of which appear in the *Proceedings of the Derbyshire Archæological and Natural History Society*, XXIV. p. 10.

During this period, when the long bow was of such importance, laws were enacted which forbade the export of English yew, and which provided also for the importation of foreign yew. Each parish must have so many bows, and often these were kept in the church. The inhabitants of Norton were compelled to maintain two butts at which to shoot, and penalties were inflicted if they allowed them to fall out of repair. They were obliged also to provide their sons and their menservants with bows and arrows.

Although soldiers and maintenance for soldiers have been found at Norton, there is no record of any stirring national incident having disturbed the quiet of this place ; but the noise of battle, or of coming battle, has sounded more than once upon its borders, and Norton's neighbours have heard " the drums and tramplings of war." Far back in history we have our country as a place of many small kingdoms, with sometimes one and sometimes another gaining a kind of supremacy over the others. In

the year 825 Egbert of the West Saxons was winning
such a domination. Kent, Sussex, Essex and East Anglia
were already subdued, and soon the Mercians fell before
his prowess. It needed now only that he should conquer the
Northumbrians to make himself King of the whole of
England, and he marched north to give them battle. No
battle, however, was needed. The Northumbrians were
in a state of degeneracy and unreadiness, and already the
pirates were harrying their coasts. The northern nobles
marched to meet Egbert, but they carried no longer their
defiance but their surrender ; and so it has come about
that we read in the Saxon Chronicle that Egbert led an
army to Dore in the year 827 and received the homage
of the Northumbrians :

> ꝺ se Ecgbryht lædde fierd to Dore wiþ Norþan hymbre,
> ꝺ hie him þær eaþmedo budon ꝺ geþuærnesse, ꝺ hie
> on þam tohwurfon :

> . . . and this Egbert led an army to Dore against the
> Northumbrians, and they offered him their humble
> and friendly submission, and thereupon dispersed.

Thus do our neighbours at Dore, under Hankirk Hill,
that lift of dark moorland, that mass of lofty and frowning
millstone grit, with its crown of heather, live where
history has been made, where England became at last
more like the country that we know to-day, with " one
flag, one fleet, one throne."

Norton too was disturbed when Sheffield Castle was
besieged and reduced, and before that, in the early years
of Henry the Third, was in the region of strife when the
nobles rebelled, and when Prince Henry, a nephew of the
King, marched into Derbyshire and sought to intercept
Baron D'Ayville or D'Egville, who was hastening from
Yorkshire to support Ferrers, Earl of Derby, one of the
King's enemies, who had reached Dronfield. D'Egville
succeeded in joining Ferrers at Chesterfield, but the King's
forces gained the victory, and Ferrers, hiding amongst

some wool that had been stored in the church, was betrayed.

Norton people from time to time have been called upon to fill the post of Sheriff of the county, or High Sheriff as he has come to be called, and thus we have a list which includes Wilhelmus de Chaworth, 1383 ; Thomas Chaworth, 1403 ; Thomas Chaworth, 1417 ; Sir Thomas Chaworth, 1423 ; William Chaworth, 1457 ; George Chaworth, 1512 ; Sir John Chaworth, 1556 ; Sir Peter Frecheville, 1571 ; Sir Peter Frecheville, 1605 ; Cornelius Clarke, 1670 ; Samuel Hallowes, 1674 ; Stephen Offley, 1716 ; George Mower, Woodseats, 1734 ; Robert Newton, 1746 ; Samuel Shore, 1761 ; Joseph Greaves, Cold Aston, 1765 ; William Chambers Bagshaw, 1805 ; Samuel Shore, jun., 1832 ; and Francis Westby Bagshawe, 1868.   Surely a large contribution for a place so small as Norton, but in this too is made manifest the truth that Norton is a village unusually interesting, a place of exceptional distinction and fame.

CHAPTER XVIII

CHANTREY

THERE have been mentioned in this story of Norton many villagers who have won repute in their parish, in their county or even beyond the shire ; but the fame of all these has been eclipsed by the renown of Norton's favourite son, Sir Francis Chantrey. His romantic career makes a powerful appeal to our love of the marvellous : the child of the small farmer and joiner whose mother was housekeeper for Robert Newton, who yet became the chosen sculptor of monarchs and statesmen ; the grocer's boy who lived to mould the sleeping children of Lichfield Cathedral with such feeling that their beauty cannot be denied the tribute of our tears ; the picture cleaner's drudge who has given to London, to Liverpool, to Dublin, to Edinburgh, to Glasgow, to Calcutta, Madras, Bombay, and, across the Atlantic, to Boston, the monuments that have become amongst the landmarks for which people look in their daily goings to and fro, like the Wellington monument in front of the Royal Exchange in London, the statue of Pitt in Hanover Square.

It is less than half a mile from the church at Norton to the unpretentious home at Jordanthorpe in which Chantrey was born. Even now the farm-house, covered with a kind of stucco that was formerly used in this district, makes no pretence to be an imposing building ; but before Chantrey enlarged it for his mother's comfort it was humble indeed, as may be seen from the sketch which Miss Shore made of the place before it had been altered. Chantrey's father and grandfather, who worked as joiners also, rented this little house and forty-five acres of land from the Offleys, and then from their successors, the Shores. The place has most charming surroundings of green croft, willows, oaks and sycamores, and one ancient oak, standing in the line of the garden wall, has been saved by some lover of trees, for the wall runs to the tree, stops, and continues on the other side. There are old fruit trees in the garden, no lack of homely flowers, and so we may recall that, coming here in 1850, John Holland noticed the snowdrops in the garden and thought of those in the hand of one of Chantrey's sleeping children in Lichfield Cathedral. A wide expanse of country may be seen from the farm, for the view includes Cold Aston and Holmesfield, where Chantrey's grandmother lived, topping the rising ground beyond Greenhill. Chantrey loved his old home and its surroundings, and when the Rev. Henry Pearson preached his funeral sermon he remarked that the great sculptor " was much attached to the place of his birth. Prevented by numerous demands on his time, and pressing avocations from making frequent visits to it, he delighted not only to talk of it, but he had it in his heart."

The Chantreys had lived in other houses in Norton, including a small house in Sheephill Yard, long before Sheephill Hall was taken down, for that was not until the early seventies. The family is not to be ranked with those whose traditions are of persistent poverty, for the Chantreys had possessed land, some members of the family received a university education and one held a rectory, all circumstances which indicate prosperity ; but that prosperity seems to have waned before the sculptor was born, and his uncle George, sheepshear-maker, has the discredit, rightly or wrongly, of having contributed to this diminution of the family possessions. A piece of Norton property which remained with the Chantreys was a half of a freehold estate known as Dych Lane, between

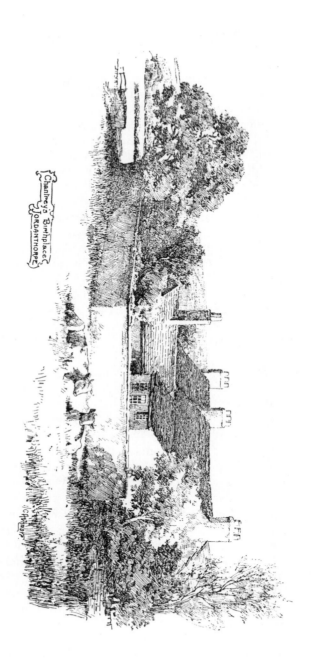

Chauncey's Birthplace,
JORDANTHORPE.

Norton and Cold Aston, and a spring wood known as
Norwood. This estate, whose name has various spellings,
Ditch Lane, Dykes Lane, Dyks Lane, is mentioned
often in the Registers, and James Linacre remarks that
" Old Ruth Gascoigne lived there and brewed a strike
of malt every Saturday." He adds that George Cooper,
by will dated September 19, 1763, gave money to Dronfield out of his estate at Ditch Lane, and refers to a house,
smithy and fields. Dych Lane may be the property from
which came the tenant of Chantrey's father, to whom
allusion is made in the *Gentleman's Magazine* of 1842,
who " used to tell of the goose pie which old Dame
Chantrey was wont to bring out of the meal-ark on the
rent day."

An old account book of the Chantrey family, now
in the possession of Mr. Addy, presents a hodge-podge
of entertaining matter, a delightful salmagundi of all
sorts of quaintness. Some day, perhaps, all these
entries will be printed carefully in the *Proceedings of
the Derbyshire Archæological and Natural History Society*,
or in the *Reliquary*, because they afford information
of prices and customs and of other matters. Meanwhile here are a few skimmings. There is a list
of " prises of Woolshers [wool shears] maad **By**
George Chantrey and Thomas Buck," references to
" plough bites " and " spock shaves," to dealings with
Nicholas Jackson and Mr. Newton, and entries concerning a door sneck, a graterboard that was made for
ninepence, a coffin, ointment, and the charge for " re-
pareing chist." In the year 1778 there was the " anging
barne doore," and an entry " Began with the Sheffield
paper " on February 5, 1790. The book too mentions
farming operations " for horses five days leading muck,"
and " stooping railins at Gleadlis." In 1787 there is
an entry against " Mr. Armitag for 800 of Lats," and
a payment to " Fox for scoolwage," together with " Expenses on journey and toulbars." Sickness, death, a
wake and a funeral appear apparently in 1789, and we

have " 1 Qr of Brandy, two pints of Hollands Gin, 2 Bottle of Wine, Advise and Medisans, Assistance to Wake etc., cofing a guinea, shroud, Wine 4 Wite 4 Red, Biskets 16 lb at 1s. 3d. £1, Diner £1, Grave fees 2s. 9d." Expenses for Uncle funaral etc., paid to Women for attendance 5s., William Crooke 2s., Jon Raworth Junr. 2s., Grave fees 3s., Ale 8s., Bisket 4s.,

A Chantrey Pocket-book in the possession of S. O. Addy Esq.

Grave Close etc 17s. 11d., Wine 10s., Cofin 18s., Raisins and Curran, hears 5s., Meat 7s. 6d., A Gown for the Girl 7s. In 1789 a "coffing for a Child" of Joseph Reaney cost 3s. 9d. Then there is work for Mr. Shore, "Mowing in Little Hallfield," and "One day Work in Mr. Bagshow Wood." An estimate for desking Norton School by F. Chantrey is fourteen guineas. At another time he is "making wascot" (wainscot), and

CHANTREY'S BIRTHPLACE.
From Miss Shore's sketch.

then there is an expenditure for "½ yard of rushey duck" for a smock frock. In the same book are some of the quaint remedies of the period, including "An Exalant Drink for a Hors" suffering from rheumatic : "4 oz. Casteel sope shaved thin, quart of warm ale," which would make probably an effective emetic whether it eased rheumatic or not, and may indeed have given rise to the saying "as sick as a horse." Then there are directions for treatment "for a beast that has over-eat themselves in Clover &c.," mixtures for "when the Coff is troublesome," "for a Consumtion," and "Huney Tracle" has a prominent part. "A handfull of Dale Shavings" preserves an old pronunciation of deal, and recalls that Brindley used to write and talk of a "loog of daal" for a log of deal. In addition to this account book amongst the archives of the Chantreys is an old diary and pocket-book in which appear such frank entries as "got drunk."

In Miss Shore's unassuming but valuable and apparently veracious sketch of the little farm-house at Jordan-thorpe, as it appeared before Chantrey had it enlarged for his mother's comfort, one bedroom window is shown ;

and this represents the window of the room in which
Chantrey was born at about seven o'clock in the morning
of April 7, 1781. He learned his letters at home, and
when he was six years of age, having imbibed such
education as it was in the power of Dame Rose to
bestow, he was sent to the village school, whose desks
his father had made, kept at that time by Thomas
Fox. He attended very irregularly, for no doubt there
was much for him to do on the farm or in the workshop.

"When we called there the other morning," writes
John Holland in his *Sheffield Illustrated*, published in
1865, "we found the son and successor of 'Old Fox,'
Chantrey's schoolmaster, seated at the desk, under the
roof where he had found himself almost every week-day
for sixty years. He well remembered Chantrey, as a
'bright' schoolfellow—heard of his reputation as an artist
—saw him on his visits to Norton—helped to carry him
to his grave—but never went to London either to see the
great sculptor's gallery, where he would have been 'so
welcome'—nor to the 'Great Exhibition,' of 1851, whither
'every one else went!'"

The school is now enclosed in the grounds of Sir

The Old School
NORTON

Nathaniel Creswick, and is used as a private theatre,
but many will remember it as a feature of the lane
skirting the western side of the Oakes park. Frequenters
of the village hear not now, however, the murmurs that
they used to hear as they strolled past on a summer
afternoon, when, with the doors and windows of the
school open, the lads and lasses droned their lessons,
longing for the time when they might burst out with
wild shouts in a way that was reminiscent of Hood's lines
in which

> . . . four-and-twenty happy boys
> Came bounding out of school ;
> There were some that ran, and some that leapt,
> Like troutlets in a pool.

In winter the race was for the lake there in the Oakes
park, and though at such times the park gates were
generously thrown open, the boys found a shorter way
by scaling the wall, for it is not in boyhood that we look
for the line of least resistance.

The children of Norton are at the new school now,
and though probably the change had become necessary,
yet would most people be touched to see the old room,
once so full of vivid life, looking so desolate "without
fire, without light, without songs," its door fast closed
and all its windows broken. I came here after it had
been abandoned to look again at the place, but by that
time the patient plantain, all these years no doubt biding
its hour, as the grass bides its hour on London Bridge,
had thrust its leaves and seed stalk from the crevices in
the pavement, where so many light and restless feet had
bounded to and fro ; and grass and chickweed, Spenser's
"weedes and wastefull gras," had invaded even the
doorstep. My ears asked in vain for the accustomed
murmurs and the cheerful commotion, and there was
more than a hint of sadness in the silence that prevailed.
A current of life that had its beginnings here a long time
back had been broken abruptly. As Dr. Johnson has
written, we never do anything consciously for the last

time without sadness of heart, and when not a single child remained it is easy to imagine there would be a feeling of melancholy as the key was turned upon the empty, silent schoolroom, at the end of the last afternoon upon which the school was used. Many in this parish would feel that a silver cord had indeed been loosed.

Around Chantrey's boyhood many entertaining stories have gathered. Each Saturday, before his mother washed the flags upon the kitchen floor for Sunday, Chantrey was allowed to cover them with drawings. Then there is the story that Widow Chantrey's landlord, or some other local magnate, calling for luncheon, chided her gently for going to the cost of an elaborate pork pie which appeared to have come from some expensive establishment. She explained that the modelling in pastry upon the summit of the pie of a sow and her young pigs that had attracted the guest's attention had been done in her own kitchen by young Frank. In his memorials of Chantrey, John Holland treats this as one of the apocryphal tales of the great man's boyhood, and indeed with regard to this particular story goes so far as to say it is " pure invention " ; but since John Holland's death there have been published the Memoirs of Anna Maria Wilhelmina Pickering, and she tells the story as she heard it from Chantrey himself, who said the circumstance was the cause that he received assistance from this Norton gentleman in his early struggles.

It is further stated that Chantrey moulded butter and candle ends into shapes before he worked in more lasting marble ; but the most interesting of these stories are those which refer to the days when, with his donkey Jock, he went with the milk, eggs and butter of the farm to the neighbouring town of Sheffield. One of these stories, which so far as I know has never yet been published, illustrates that kindness of which more will be written soon. On one of the occasions when the late Dr. Sorby, the geologist and biologist, was at Norton, he

asked the present vicar, the Rev. G. W. Hall, to show
him the hollow on a wall into which Chantrey used to
pour milk for a cat. At that time Mr. Hall had not
heard of the incident, but Dr. Sorby said he had received
the story from a friend who had got it from the vicar's
coachman. The coachman accordingly was sent for, and
related that when Chantrey was on his rounds he used to
pour milk for a cat into a hollow which he had scooped
out in the top stone of a wall, and that each morning
pussy used to sit beside the hollow waiting for her friend
to come along with her breakfast. The wall unhappily
was taken down during the erection of the schoolroom
at the bottom of Derbyshire Lane.

One hot day when Chantrey was returning home from
Sheffield with Jock, who carried the week's groceries, he
allowed the ass to stand in a pond. Not content with
this indulgence, Jock calmly proceeded to roll upon his
back in the water, and a companion used to give a vivid

description of the future modeller of
monarchs raking in the pond with a
hay rake endeavouring to recover
his mother's tea and sugar by a
similar method, and with about as
much chance of success, as the
process used by the wise men of
Gotham in the neighbouring county
when they tried to scrape the reflection of the moon
from the waters of the
Trent.

There is too a fondly
cherished Norton tra-
dition that one day as
Chantrey sauntered
along by the side of
his donkey he was
noticed to be whittling
the nob of a stick ;

A PRESENT-DAY NORTON MILK BOY.

and when he was asked what he was doing he replied that he was carving a likeness of " Old Fox," the schoolmaster. The story goes that the gentleman who thus accosted Chantrey thought the head so well carved that he gave the boy sixpence, the first money he gained for his skill in sculpture. This incident is one of those which H. P. Parker, the artist, has embodied in a picture, and still with reference to Chantrey he painted another entitled *Milk Boys*, reproductions of which in line or colour used to be in many Sheffield houses. A few are still to be found there, and the original picture is not far away, for it is in the possession of Mr. W. T. Freemantle, at Barbot Hall near Rotherham. A wood engraving of the subject by E. Dalziel was used as an illustration in *The Land we Live In.*

Many years after his Norton days, Chantrey, taking leave in London of a gentleman going into Yorkshire, said " You are going in the coach ; you will reach Sheffield in the evening, for all the coaches arrive there about that time. A few miles on this side the town, you will pass a number of asses carrying milk in barrels, with boys sitting on their croups behind the saddles, and merrily jogging along the road ; think then of your friend. I was a milk lad, and travelled in the same manner, and along the same road from my native village, morning and evening to Sheffield with milk."

Chantrey's father died when Francis was twelve years old, and Mrs. Chantrey had for farm servant one Job Hall, who, though he could not spell his own name, seems to have understood agriculture, and upon him she relied much in the conduct of the farm. From being her chief adviser he became her second husband, and as it happened that he was related to Ebenezer Birks, a grocer of Fargate, Sheffield, the suggestion arose that Chantrey should be apprenticed to the Fargate tradesman, and he went there on trial, or as the local expression has it " a liking," so resembling another Sheffield celebrity, James Montgomery the poet, who was once a grocer's assistant. A few weeks' experience in the doling out of tea and sugar convinced Chantrey that he had missed his vocation. Moreover, he was given during his spare time to peering into the shop window of Robert Ramsay of High Street, wood-carver, and dealer in prints and plaster models. For most boys such a shop has a fascination, but for a boy with artistic instincts it is a veritable cave of Aladdin, and the windows of Messrs. Hibbert Brothers have served the same purpose as Ramsay's for some later generations of potential Hallamshire artists. Amongst the treasures at Ramsay's were James Taylor's wax figures of Faith and Charity, afterwards reproduced as the statues which to-day stand sentinel at the main portal of the Sheffield Infirmary, statues which seem to have been executed by Chantrey himself. One of the results of this window gazing was that when his mother called to see her boy he walked out with her into the town, explained the misery of his present position, and then taking her to the shop window of Mr. Ramsay, besought of her to get him placed there rather than in the grocer's shop. So Chantrey came from behind the counter, and he does not seem to have seen Mr. Birks again until the year 1806, when the Sheffield tradesman went with others to see Chantrey at work upon the model of Mr. Wilkinson's bust, and received a cordial welcome from the sculptor.

For the majority of apprentices sufficient for the day is the work thereof; but Chantrey had more ambition and energy than to be satisfied with the work he did for his master, and renting a room of his own spent his evenings and holidays there drawing and modelling and generally fitting himself for his distinguished career. When Chantrey came to these parts for the last time in 1840, the year before his death, he called upon John Rodgers, the famous cutler, and together they walked about the Sheffield streets. When they reached High Street Chantrey took his friend up Hutton's Yard, a narrow place that was opposite the end of George Street, and pointed out the little room he had rented nearly fifty years before when he was an unknown apprentice. John Holland says that many of Chantrey's sketches remained upon the walls of this room for years after Chantrey had relinquished his tenancy.

Even at this busy period, however, not the whole of Chantrey's time was spent between Ramsay's shop and Hutton's Yard. He was welcome always in Shemeld Croft, where lived Nicholas Jackson, the file manufacturer, who came of a Norton family, and, like Billy Batty, wrote songs that were sung at those more homely Cutlers' Feasts of the past, when the guests were free to drink themselves under the table and nothing said. In the family at Shemeld Croft the principal attraction seems to have been the handsome and loveable Susannah Jackson, with her golden hair and blue eyes, whose portrait Chantrey painted. There was no end of romping at the Jacksons', and one night Chantrey's bolster bolted from under his head as he lay in bed, drawn by a string with no doubt a Jackson girl at the other end, haply the handsome Susannah herself.

In 1802 Chantrey, who had been to Ireland, was in Shrewsbury, whence he wrote this letter to his mother :

SHREWSBURY *Septer 21st Monday* 1802.

DEAR MOTHER,

I now take the opertunity of writing you a few lines in the first place I shall inform you that I have had a bad cold but I thank god I am now recovering very fast it effected my bones and made them very soor but that in a day or two I hope will be better Mr. Tayler is with me and is very well I hope you have had a good harvest the Crops seems to be very good pray make my best Love to my Father and if he will give me leave I will come and stay a few days at Norton with you it perhaps may be a fortnight three weeks or more before I can be with you that depends on business you need make no preparations there will be nobody but myself I would

write more but I have no more Ink so you must excuse
me believe me a your ever Dutiful Son

F. CHANTREY.

John Holland mentions an early drawing by the artist,
of a tuft of snowdrops, but says that " the earliest existing
specimen of Chantrey's attempts at drawing with which I
am acquainted, is of a periwinkle flower, framed and
glazed, in the house of Mr. Biggins, adjacent to the
cottage at Jordanthorpe : it is inscribed—F. Chantrey,
fecit, 1798. It is pleasing to find early mementoes of the
artist prized at his birth-place." At first Chantrey divided
his time between painting and modelling, and when it
came to a matter of earning his living he painted portraits. Although he lived to work for monarchs, one of
whom, William the Fourth, knighted him, his early work
here was amongst humbler people. He painted his
schoolmaster, Thomas Fox, and a son Robert Fox ;
one of the sons of Peter Robinson, Vicar of Norton ;
and as Holland wrote an " old man and woman, formerly
of Norton. Heads, life-size, in crayons ; in the possession of Miss Shore of Meersbrook. These are highly
characteristic likenesses, painted at the expense of the
late Samuel Shore, Esq., of Norton Hall." One was
a portrait of Samuel Daken, who completed ninety-four
years in the latter end of November 1800. He was formerly a gardener, and when young, lived three years and
a half at Norton Hall, in the service of Mr. Stephen
Offley. The portrait of the woman represented old Dame
Lee, of Norton Green.

Chantrey painted the portrait of the Vicar of Sheffield,
the Rev. James Wilkinson ; the Rev. Thomas Sutton,
another Vicar of Sheffield ; his friend Mr. Jenkin of
Hazelbarrow ; local manufacturers, professional men,
shopkeepers and other friends who came to his studio.

In addition to portraits there are amongst Chantrey's
earlier works Murillo-like subjects. *A Sleeping Boy* is
said to have been inspired when Chantrey, walking in his

mother's fields on a hot day, found a farm lad asleep under a hedge, his dog keeping watch and ward at his feet. This was a favourite picture with Mrs. Chantrey, and became the property of John Read of Norton House. *Two Beggar Boys* by Chantrey found its way to the same appreciative owner.

Not much of Chantrey's work as a sculptor is to be seen in his own district. Norton church has nothing that he chiselled, but there are examples of his skill at the Oakes. Some of his Sheffield work used to be at Sheaf House, built by Daniel Bramall,—hence Bramall Lane — a friend of Chantrey even before he had shown signs of genius and when he was a fatherless boy at Norton. Mrs. Bramall was a near relation of the Rev. Peter Robinson, then Vicar of Norton. Bramall died in Paris in 1830, and Sheaf House was afterwards habited by George Younge, another friend and patron of the rising sculptor. Chantrey, who appreciated Bramall's kindness, painted his portrait, and also the portrait of Mrs. Bramall and of other members of the family, including Mary Bramall, with whom as with Susannah Jackson, under similar circumstances, Chantrey fell in love ; but, as Holland has written, " In reference to the case before us, it must suffice to add, that while the lady went down to the grave in her maiden name, the recollection of her piety in life and death, exists as a more precious memorial to her friends, than the fact that she was painted by the hand, and flattered with the admiration of one so pre-eminently distinguished in art."

Chantrey's career in London is so full of interest that the temptation to leave Norton to record all his achievements there is great, but such a chronicle would need a book all its own. He worked in London as a journeyman wood-carver, and had a struggle to make ends meet. The struggle did not last long, however, for Chantrey had energy, courage and skill to overcome every difficulty. He did not lose touch with Sheffield,

and obtained a commission for a monument to Vicar
Wilkinson and for other work in the parish church, and
in St. Paul's in addition to a number of other local
commissions, including one for a bust of Samuel Shore
of Meersbrook. In 1809 Chantrey married, not Susannah
Jackson with the blue eyes and the golden hair, nor
Mary Bramall the poetess with the raven tresses, but his
cousin Mary Ann Wale, of Twickenham, and she brought
Chantrey a fortune.

The statue of the Duke of Wellington on his horse
in that most thronged and animated part of London
environed by the Bank, the Royal Exchange and the
Mansion House, is one of Chantrey's most telling
works, and to the native of Hallamshire it may serve,
in this restless centre with the crowd of busiest London
surging at its base, to conjure the thoughts away to the
sequestered farm at Jordanthorpe, to Norton church yard,

Far from the madding crowd's ignoble strife

The statue stands aloof, silent, stately and austere
amidst all this fussiness. It is in the crowd but not of
it, and indeed is in the most striking contrast to the
general effect caused by the running to and fro of
bumptious stock-jobbers' clerks, the noisiness of shrill
whistling errand-boys, the " whiffling activity " of pursy
City men, the clamour and gesticulations of febrile 'bus
conductors straining for passengers, the gibes and
derision of cab drivers, the dictatorial hoots of motor
horns and the raucous crying of costers and of *camelots*.

Some have thought the bust of Rennie was Chantrey's
masterpiece, and he was particularly proud of this achieve-
ment, and others have favoured his statue of Watt or
that of Bishop Ryder in Lichfield Cathedral, designed for
a higher pedestal. The Pike Watts memorial in Ilam
Church, near Dovedale, has many admirers, but the most
popular of all the works by Chantrey is the monument
in Lichfield Cathedral known as *The Sleeping Children*. It
was erected in memory of the daughters of the Rev.

William Robinson, and the granddaughters of Dean
Woodhouse. Both their mother and their aunt had been
belles of the county, so that handsome faces were in the

BISHOP RYDER.

family, and Chantrey has given a fitting grace and loveliness to these children, who lie asleep in each other's arms,
and so reveal the surpassing beauty which is characteristic
of children when they slumber, an added angelic grace;

25

loveliness lifted to a higher plane even than the witchery
of children in their waking moments, and touching deeper
feelings in those who so behold them. Such beauty too
is more within the compass of the artist who works in
marble than are the colour, the movement and the joy of
life, and in the presence of this touching memorial of the
two sisters we feel the lack of no element to complete
the appeal to our sense of what is perfect, the absence of
no quality that could sustain this siege of our emotions.

In her right hand the younger sister still holds a posy
of snowdrops, meet symbol surely of that youth and
stainlessness that were cut down in the springtime of
her life ; but there is no hint here of ruthlessness in
her end, and we think rather of her of whom Hood
wrote :

> Our very hopes belied our fears,
> Our fears our hopes belied—
> We thought her dying when she slept,
> And sleeping when she died.

Before the monument was erected in Lichfield it was
exhibited in London, and each day crowds flocked to see
it to the neglect of all other works. Mothers pushed
their way to the front and sobbed as they gazed upon
the artless beauty of the sleeping sisters. Reluctantly
they tore themselves away, but returned again and again,
and lingered there, but, blinded by their tears, how could
they hope to see the monument?

Loving architecture, and knowing something of the
principles of this fascinating and virile art, it is not
surprising that Chantrey indulged sometimes in the
designing of buildings. If his bent had been that way
he would probably have become as great in architecture
as in sculpture. At Norton he designed the terrace at
the Oakes, and presented two vases, one for each end
of it. Even when he abandoned painting for sculpture,
Chantrey did not cease to sketch. He made a series of
drawings in the beautiful valley of the Rivelin, one of the
Sheffield streams beloved by Ebenezer Elliott.

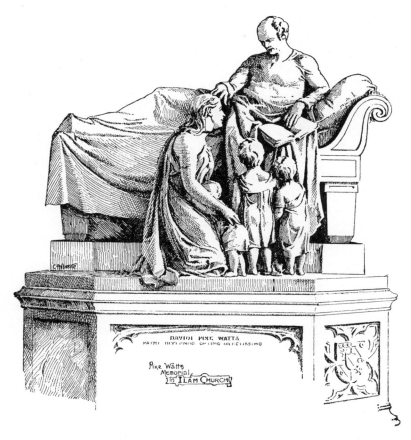

DAVIDI PIKE WATTS
PATRI DEFLENDO OPTIMO DILECTISSIMO

Pike Watts
Memorial
in Ilam Church

One of Chantrey's many good traits was his kindness, and speaking to John Holland, and holding out one of his hands, a man who had been at intervals a fellow milk boy with Chantrey said " When I lost these two fingers, he sent me ten guineas, besides many smaller sums afterwards," and when Ebenezer Rhodes fell upon evil days in his old age Chantrey sent secretly each quarter the interest upon £2,000. Chantrey's kindness to his mother is shown in many ways, and it is a pleasing circumstance that she lived to see him at the height of his glory. She died at Jordanthorpe when she was 81 years of age. She visited his great house in Eccleston Street, and wept for joy at home when Ebenezer Rhodes, at the request of Chantrey, came one memorable day to tell her that her son had been appointed to execute the statue of George the Third for the council chamber at the Guildhall. His kindness to his mother ran through his life. He reconstructed her house, and ministered to all her needs. "I beg of you," he writes to Ebenezer Rhodes during a "terrible bout" of illness, "not to make any talk of this lest it should reach my mother's ears; she supposes I have had a trifling cold." In Ward's diary we read that "After church Chantrey walked through the romantic grounds of Mr. Shore, and drank tea at his mother's—a decent, motherly villager of Jordanthorpe." Again, "Chantrey has paid a short visit here lately. He came to see his mother who was in a weak state. He had just arrived at home from France, and among 30 or 40 letters saw 2 or 3 from his aunt expressing a wish to see him at Jordanthorpe. He opened only these, and left the others to await his return."

Letters to his mother are full of kindness, and accompanied by generous presents and things for her comfort.

"DEAR MOTHER—I have only time to say that I enclose you half of £100 note; will send the other half to-morrow. When you receive them both, write a line to Mrs. Wale. We are all well, and I am going to Winchester to-day. You will see us this autumn.

"The stuff which Mrs. Wale made for you is at one of the coach offices in Sheffield, directed to Mrs. Chantrey, Jordanthorpe, Norton near Sheffield. You must enquire for it; it is a small brown paper parcel."

"DEAR MOTHER—The red French scarf is a present from Mrs. C. to Miss Jenkins, and the light blue French handkerchief and sash is a present from Mrs. Wale, also to Miss Jenkins. All the rest is for yourself. Mrs. Wale sends you a red ribbon, and I send you a blue ribbon and blue kerchief to match, and some peppermint drops and a little of preserved ginger, to warm your stomach in cold weather. You must take a lump or two of ginger before you go out, and remember it will not keep good long, therefore you must eat it and not keep it. All the other odds and ends are from Mrs. C."

In another letter he says : " I have ordered for you

6 lb. of black tea, in lead.
3 gallons of brandy.
4 dozen of Lisbon, and one dozen of port.
$\frac{1}{2}$ lb. of ginger, and
$\frac{1}{4}$ lb. of rhubarb.

I have ordered these things to be packed immediately, and you shall be informed by what waggon they will be sent, and when they will arrive in Sheffield. I trust that when you get the wine you will enjoy at least two glasses every day with your dinner. You must know that you are not very young, and that you require a good deal more comfort than you used to do, and you do know very well that you can have *plenty*."

A further letter tells his mother that " there will be three hampers at Hunts' waggon office, in Sheffield, on Monday next, so that on the day following, which will be next Tuesday, you must send down a one-horse cart and money to pay the carriage. The hampers contain,—

Port wine 2 dozen.
Madeira 1   ,,
Lisbon 4   ,,
Brandy 3 gallons or 13 bottles and a half.
Tea 6 pounds.
Ginger $\frac{1}{2}$ pound.
Rhubarb $\frac{1}{4}$ pound.

Now, I beg and desire that you will take at least a couple of glasses of Lisbon every day with your dinner ; and don't give the Madeira away, because it is very fine and a good cordial for yourself ; and when any portion of this parcel is done let me know and you shall have plenty more.   Let all the bottles be laid flat, and put

your port wine on the cold floor in your pantry, with the side of the bottle washed with chalk uppermost.   The brandy may stand upright."

Portraits of Chantrey and all we read of him give the impression of a man overflowing with vitality ; but for such too, as for the frailest, comes the inevitable end. "What shadows we are ; what shadows we pursue." Two years before his death Chantrey began to decline. His mind was active, but his hilarity forsook him, his cheeks fell, his eyes lost their sparkle, his gait its spring and elasticity, his mouth its expression "and often fell uncontrolled during fits of somnolency." His friends urged him to retire and rest, but he clung to his work and replied "My retirement must be my death," and so it happened. In August 1841 when for grouse shooting he paid his last visit to John Read, who was now at Derwent Hall, he could not keep up with his dog in the heather without the aid of a pony. It was in that year too that he saw Norton for the last time, and on November 25 he died suddenly in his chair.

His body lay in a gallery surrounded by the models of his works and by the work of others he had admired, the Laocoon, Venus, Apollo, Ilissus, Theseus and such immortal statues. Wax lights burned and people came in silently to see the great sculptor lying there, his eyes closed, his face calm, like some of his own figures in the cathedrals. " They said it was a most affecting sight," wrote Lady Pickering in her memoirs.

The day after Chantrey's death his old and close friend Turner the artist called. Jones was there, but Turner could not speak to him. He wrung his hand vehemently and rushed out of the house without uttering a word.

To those who are dead it matters nothing where their bodies lie ; but the living are not able to divest themselves of sentimental feelings, and for us it seems more congruous that Chantrey should lie in this cool corner of Norton church yard, under the southern face of the old tower, under these beautiful trees near Norton Hall and near his birthplace, rather than in St. Paul's Cathedral or Westminster Abbey. It was natural that Chantrey should desire to come to Norton, but in his case circumstances had strengthened this yearning for the quiet of this church yard. Many years before his death he was in the burying ground of St. Martin-in-the-Fields in London, upon the occasion of the funeral of Scott who had been shot by Christie in a duel. There were heaps of human bones in the church yard, and the sexton with all the nonchalance of the grave-digger in *Hamlet* kept tossing others upon the piles. " And what becomes of these bones ? " asked Chantrey. The sexton told him that when they began to be in the way they were carted in

loads down to the Thames and so shot into the river.
The colour left Chantrey's face and he broke into a cold
perspiration. " I will take care they do not cart my
bones to the Thames. They shall lie undisturbed under
my native sod."

It is a coincidence that another local celebrity, Ebenezer
Elliott, received a similar shock upon seeing a dog gnaw-
ing a human bone in a church yard. In Windmill Street,
Finsbury, there was a windmill built on the top of a large
mound composed of bones and earth which had been
carted from the church yard of old St. Paul's.

So some years before his death Chantrey came to
Norton church yard to find his last resting-place. " I am
looking out a place for my grave," he said to the old
sexton, " but I do not mean you to dig it." " I hope I
shall," replied the grave-digger naively, not quite seeing
where he was going ; but as matters turned out the old
sexton had the honour for which he longed. There still
survives a Norton man who saw Chantrey on this occasion, our old friend Mr. Rhodes of the Post Office, who
was attending a Dame's School at the time.

When Chantrey's body had lain in state in his gallery
the journey to the north began. The undertaker left
London with it on December 1, Wednesday, and upon
the following Sunday had reached Chesterfield, where he
remained for that day. On Monday came the last stage
to Norton, and during the morning the watchers in the
village saw the hearse and a mourning coach, each drawn
by four horses, and preceded by four men on horse-
back, coming along the road from Chesterfield. The
travellers went to the Oakes, where Mr. W. J. Bagshawe
had provided breakfast and had hospitably made the
house the headquarters of the local arrangements. Soon
after twelve o'clock the bells which when Chantrey had
last visited his native place not long before had rung
joyously in honour of his visit now rang a muffled peal,
and the funeral procession issued slowly from the gates
of the Oakes. Names that have now become familiar

THE BURIAL OF CHANTREY.

P. 392]

to us appear amongst those who came after the hearse : Mr. Bagshawe, Mr. Shore, John Read, the Rev. Henry Pearson, vicar, and his brother the Rev. William Pearson, curate, the Rev. E. Bagshawe, the Rev. Henry Hunt Piper, John Parker, M.P. for Sheffield. Sheffield was well represented. The Master and members of the Cutlers' Company, the Town Trustees, members of the Literary and Philosophical Society, and a host of other people and children from Chantrey's old school crowded together in the rain or in the shelter of the yew trees to see the end of a romantic local story, the burial amidst this pomp and circumstance of the Norton milk boy who had risen to such eminence. " I noticed," says John Holland, " a branch of laurel on the coffin as it lay in the vault, though how, when or by whom placed there did not appear." At Holland's suggestion the whole scene was painted by Henry Perlee Parker in a picture now in the High Hazels Museum at Darnall and reproduced in this book.

As far as had been possible the bearers were men who had known Chantrey as a boy here at Norton : John Linacre, James Linacre, Charles James Fox, the schoolmaster, who had succeeded his father, Chantrey's teacher, and his brother Robert, in that office, Peter Linley, George Cocker, Samuel Slack, who was the steward at the Oakes, Joseph Booth and George Bailey. The Rev. Henry Pearson, who afterwards preached the funeral sermon, now committed the body to its tomb.

During the time that this account of Chantrey's country was being written Norton supplied an interesting memory of Chantrey's funeral. Those who know the people of this district intimately will scarcely need to be told that the drawing over leaf is the portrait of a native ; and they will at once see that he is a file-cutter. Him Charles Ashmore found in the Bagshawe Arms, and he remembered Chantrey's funeral. He went to it, losing a day's work to be there.

" And were you working so long ago as that ? "

"Ah, I'd been graftin' nearly two year' then. Tha kno's aw wor ten year owd at Chantrey's funeril, an' awd started to work when aw wor seven an' a haafe.

10 years old
at Chantrey's
Funeral

Ah! he wor a fine chap wor Chantrey. Tha kno's it wor t' Bagshawes 'at shoved him on at first—just at first, tha kno's, an' then he shoved his sen on."

Chantrey's tomb has been formed in accordance with his own directions. His dislike for ornament is seen here in a severe plainness. In avoiding everything that is finicking he has gone almost to the other extreme of clumsiness. Cut deeply in a huge slab of granite overlying some ponderous grit-stone is this inscription, in which V is used instead of D :

M.
FRANCIS CHANTREY,
DIED MVCCLXVI. AGED LVI.

FRANCIS CHANTREY,
DIED MVCCXCIII. AGED XXXXV.

SARAH, HIS WIFE,
DIED MVCCCXXVI. AGED LXXXI.

SIR FRANCIS CHANTREY,
SCULPTOR,
R.A. — F.R.S.
BORN IN THIS PARISH
VII. APRIL,
MVCCLXXXI.
DIED IN LONDON
NOV. XXV
MVCCCXXXXI.

The question of perishing inscriptions also had engaged
Chantrey's attention, and once "when selecting a place
for Mr. Watt's statue in Westminster Abbey, he was

Chantrey's
Grave

accompanied by the late Lord Liverpool and Mr. C.
Hampden Turner, and the subject of durability of monu-
mental memorials was discussed. The sculptor took

Lord L. to the spot where William Pitt and Charles James Fox lay, nearly side by side, and it was observed that the stones over the graves were cracked, and the engraved letters almost obliterated; this occasioned regret to all the party, and the Earl, with a tear standing in his eye, asked Chantrey what could be done to prevent

SIR FRANCIS CHANTREY, R A

SCULPTOR

H DCL _ FRS _ MA

BORN APRIL VII MDCCLXXXI DIED NOV. XXV. MDCCCXLI

such effacement, when the sculptor replied 'If your Lordship will obtain permission for me, I will place stones that are not liable to suffer, or the writing to be defaced.' The consent was obtained, and after a short time Chantrey showed to his friend Mr. Hampden Turner two blocks of stone of almost imperishable thickness, and the inscription so deeply cut, that erasure must be the destruction of the granite."

Thus do we see why Chantrey took such pains that his grave should not be violated, and why he made his tomb so massive, the inscription so deep, that it may survive the frost, the rain and the heat for ages.

Lady Chantrey is not buried here at Norton, and so finds no mention upon the inscription. She is interred at Twickenham. The Sarah Chantrey of the inscription is Chantrey's mother, who died at Jordanthorpe. For several years there had lived with her her elder maiden sister, Miss Leggitt, who died in 1818. This aunt, who claimed to have initiated Chantrey into the mysteries of modelling in paste, was for a time the housekeeper for the notorious Marchioness of Hertford. The other Francis Chantreys whose names are inscribed upon the tomb are the sculptor's father and grandfather. Job Hall, Chantrey's step-father, died at Jordanthorpe in 1804, leaving £20 to his niece Sarah Nadin, wife of Robert Nadin, labourer, of Bulwell, Nottinghamshire, and the rest to his wife for life, and then to his step-son Francis Chantrey. His grave stone is close to Chantrey's tomb.

The tomb is not the only memorial. In the chancel of the church there is a tablet with a medallion portrait by Heffernan, who was with Chantrey as an assistant for thirty years. This medallion is inscribed

SIR FRANCIS CHANTREY, R A

SCULPTOR

H D C L — F R S — M A

BORN APRIL VII MDCCLXXXI   DIED NOV. XXV. MDCCCXLI

During later years there has been put in the church a full-length plaster cast of Chantrey that was executed by John Bell, the sculptor who designed the Montgomery monument in the Sheffield cemetery. It was presented to Norton church by Mr. Charles Stoatt of Kensington, who purchased the contents of Bell's studio.

In 1854 the Chantrey obelisk was erected on the little patch that remains of Norton Green. It is of Cheeswring granite, brought from Cornwall to Hull by sea, nearly twenty-two feet high in one piece, fixed upon steps three feet high, the whole designed by an old friend of Chantrey, Mr. Philip Hardwick, of the Royal Academy. It bears no other inscription than the word " Chantrey " cut deeply.

Chantrey's will showed that he left the greater part of his fortune, after the death of Lady Chantrey, who died in 1875, to trustees chosen from the Royal Academy for the purchase of works of art. The bequest was singularly free from conditions. The painting and the sculpture were to be the finest, and the works were to be executed on British soil. The purchases under the Chantrey bequest may be seen at the Tate Gallery. They were all executed on British soil.

For Norton Chantrey left £50 annually for the school-master for the education of ten poor boys of the parish ; £10 annually to each of five poor men and five poor women, and £50 a year for the vicar. He made these bequests depend upon the endurance of his tomb, in an anxiety about his last resting-place which has been explained.

Chantrey's funeral has brought us back to Norton church yard, to our starting-place ; but it is no longer summer. The earth has prepared for her long sleep. The great brown fields that are at rest now around Chantrey Land lie between us and the leafless elms, behind which the sun has set. Greyness steals over all these large spaces of earth and sky, and the world seems without sounds. A lonely labourer, who, standing in the great dim field, has looked like a part of inanimate nature, like a part of the earth itself, detaches himself now, and moves towards the house among the trees, making a Millet-like picture as he goes. In his home is a yellow light, and we think of the great fire on the hearth where he will soon slumber in his chair all through

the long evening ; but for the present we lose him and
we are alone again in Chantrey Land, for to us this will
be always Chantrey's country.   Generation after generation, this table-land waited for its hero, and now he has
been, and has gone ; yet his name will never be forgotten
in the region of the church, the halls and the cottages
that stand in the midst of Norton's quiet fields.

SOURCES OF "CHANTREY LAND"

PERSONAL observations, conversations with Norton people, books and manuscripts have gone to the making of this volume. The Vicar, the Rev. G. W. Hall, M.A., has helped me at many points, and the residents have been very kind in answering inquiries. Not only have I had the great advantage of access to the published writings of Mr. Sidney O. Addy, M.A., but he suggested generously and hospitably that I should stay at his house and rummage amongst his papers. During my visits to his home, and at other times, I have learned much about Norton from one peculiarly well informed concerning this district. In 1880 Mr. Addy published, in the *Proceedings of the Derbyshire Archæological and Natural History Society, A Contribution towards a History of Norton.* Mr. Charles Ashmore, who has illustrated the book, has not rambled about Norton without gleaning much interesting matter, and that too has been placed at my disposal. In talks with Mr. Charles Dixon, the naturalist, I have added much to my store of information concerning the Meersbrook side of the parish, and here too Mr. Alfred Dyson has drawn my attention to features that else would have been overlooked. It is scarcely necessary to add that in writing this book the author came into touch with Mr. W. T. Freemantle of Barbot Hall. He is inevitable. Too many years has he been studying the history of Hallamshire and its surroundings, that he might gather every scrap of printed matter that has any sort of relation to the district, for any local historian to be able to disregard his accumulations, and let us hope that what he has collected so well may never again be dispersed. *A Bibliography of Sheffield and Vicinity*, upon which he is at work now, will be a most useful contribution to the sum of Hallamshire books.

I have drawn a little upon the manuscripts at the British Museum and at Norton Vicarage, but without exhausting those stores.

Most of the books I have consulted have been indicated in the text, and so there is no need to repeat their titles here. The many volumes of the *Proceedings of the Derbyshire Archæological Society* and of the *Reliquary* have been particularly interesting and valuable, and the local *Notes and Queries* that appeared in the *Sheffield Independent* contain many references to Norton. *Thief Catching in Olden Times*, which appeared in the *Sheffield Telegraph*, March 4, 1898, is an account of the Norton Association for the Prosecution of Felons. Hunter's *Hallamshire* has frequent references to Norton people, and a compact account of the place is given in the volume on *Derbyshire* by Daniel and Samuel Lysons. A few Norton folk find mention in the *Dictionary of National Biography*, and there are Norton items in John Pym Yeatman's *Feudal History of the County of Derby*. A recent work of great value is a *Descriptive Catalogue of Derbyshire Charters* by Isaac Herbert Jeayes. The reader will notice many allusions to the industry and learning of Dr. Cox, a veteran in antiquarian work. His *Three Centuries of Derbyshire Annals* and *Calendar of the Records of Derbyshire* contain a number of interesting references to Norton. Asline Ward's diary has furnished many a welcome item. John Holland and John Daniel Leader drew upon it, but since their day it has been made available as *Peeps into the Past. Being Passages from the Diary of Thomas Asline Ward*. Edited by Alexander B. Bell. With an Introduction and Annotations by Robert Eadon Leader, B.A. I am indebted also to Mr. Robert Eadon Leader for more even than appears in his published works, useful as they have been, and Mr. H. C. Fanshawe has supplied me with information about the Fanshawes and about the Bullocks. A number of allusions to Norton appeared also in the short-lived *Sheffield Miscellany*.

Amongst others to whom I have applied for information and have not been sent empty away are Mr. E. Howarth, Curator of Weston Park Museum, Sheffield, Mr. Samuel Smith, Chief Librarian of the Sheffield Free Library, and Mr. Alfred Doxey. Like most other writers I am indebted for much to current issues and past volumes of *Notes and Queries*, and without the British Museum I could not have written the book at all.

At the last moment before this book went to press, I received an interesting communication from my friend Dr. Frederick Arnold Lees, of Meanwood, Leeds, who tells me that Meersbrook is classic to botanic geographers in that in 1865 it was the home of a famous flower, "The Happy Medium" (*Epimedium alpinum*), which has never had but three or four surviving localities of growth in all England. It is common in Switzerland, possibly was once so in Hallamshire, and, in 1865, Dr. J. Deakin Heaton gathered it in a spot by the Meersbrook. Dr. Lees acquired the Heaton Herbarium in 1899, or thereabouts, and wrote an article upon it entitled "An Old Leeds Herbary." Dr. Heaton was Dean of the Leeds Medical School from 1855 to 1880, and the late Sir (T.) Wemyss Reid wrote his life, published in 1883. Dr. Lees, who is well known as an authority upon Yorkshire botany, was Dr. Heaton's clinical clerk, and he assures me that Dr. Heaton was unable to find the flower anywhere else in this country but by the Meersbrook.

INDEX

INTRODUCTION

It is almost forty years since I had the good fortune to go to London, and visit Mr. and Mrs. Armitage for the first time; I had read most of his books, including Chantrey Land, (which is my favourite). I made my way to their home in Hampstead, and when I arrived I was cordially given a very warm welcome, to say we were strangers it was really wonderful. We talked all afternoon about books, early days in Sheffield, and reminiscences of Norton, etc. I was soon made to feel at home, and the time passed very quickly.

The most interesting part of the conversation was how the book Chantrey Land came to be written. Harold Armitage was born in Heeley, and as time went on he made friends with Charles Ashmore, the artist, who also lived in Heeley, and was a silver engraver by trade. At this time, Mr. Armitage was a reporter on the Sheffield Independent, and these two gentlemen used to go for walks every Saturday and Sunday, around Old Norton and the surrounding district. Every so often, they would rest a while, either sit down on a wall or a style, then Ashmore would take out his sketch book and make a drawing of some nearby object. This went on for quite a long time, when one day Ashmore said to Armitage "Eh, Harold, I've got a lot of these sketches at home, what do you say if you write a bit of a story to go with the sketches, and make a book of it?" Mr. Armitage agreed, and that is how the book Chantrey Land came to be written, but it finished up in being much larger than was intended.

Mr. Armitage also told me that on Saturday afternoons they would often call in at the Old Norton Post Office for a cup of tea and a chat with Mr. and Mrs. Rhodes, who conducted the business in their old-world cottage, and when one entered through the door, your presence was made welcome by a homely atmosphere.

After a most exciting day, and enjoyable afternoon, I bid my hosts farewell and returned home; I must add that Mr. and Mrs. Armitage were a grand old couple, who belonged to an earlier generation.

The book was published in 1910 by Sampson Low Marston & Company, from London. At the time it didn't prove to be a good seller, however, a few years later, Cadman's one of the leading booksellers in Sheffield, bought all the remainders and sold them, as low as 6/d per copy, but today first edition copies are fetching a high price.

The year 1981 was the bicentenary of Liz Francis Chantrey's birth, and to mark the occasion a second edition of Chantrey Land was published by the Sheffield City Library issuing on one thousand copies, needless to say they were all dispersed in a very short time.

It goes without saying, that after all these years the book is still very popular.

Edward Jessop
1988

The following supplementary chapters have never been published in either of the two previous editions. Although certain details are covered in the book, the publisher felt that the inclusion of these scripts, which have only recently come to light, to be important in this latest edition.

BEAUCHIEF ABBEY

DERBYSHIRE

A drawing of Beauchief Abbey by Sir Francis Chantrey.
Executed for Rhodes' book on Peak Scenery published in 1818.

CHAPTER XIX

The bright yellow charlock is a thing of beauty, and yet it is not a joy forever. The poet who has no more to do with the wheat-fields than to look over the fence has been inspired to sing the praises of this golden weed, but the farmer views its blooms with irritation and dismay. Not merely does the charlock choke his cornfields and impoverish his soil, but men behold afar off its bright gold and fall to talking of the shortcomings of his husbandry. The charlock taunts him to his face with failure, it insults him in his own house.

Grant Allen, pushing impertinent enquiries into the antecedents of the corn-cockle thanked heaven for slovenly fields; but the farmer knows that very few regard his acres with the eyes of the naturalist, and that very many judge his farming by bread alone. That this has been the more usual attitude during the last five hundred years at least is evident from a document of the fourteenth century which contains the particulars of a grant of land, by Sir Thomas Chaworth, to Beauchief Abbey. 'I give and grant' says the charter 'to the abbot and convent, libery and power to cleanse their lands and the lands of their tenants, as well freemen as bondmen, from "golda" according to the customs of the manors of Norton and Alfreton, and if they find any neglect in this respect, they may punish their tenants and receive fines from them, just as they have heretofore been punished by me and my ancestors; so that neither I, nor my heirs, will interfere in the said cleansing. Nor shall the abbot and convent, if any neglect be found in the cleansing of their own cornfields from the said "golda", be punished or blamed, but shall forever hereafter remain in peace'. Scholars of an older generation were baffled by the world "golda" in the original Latin charter. The most that their dictionaries could do for the student was to suggest dams in watercourses, mill-dams; but this assumption did not agree with the context in the Beauchief deed; yet Du Cange and succeeding writers learned as they were on most points had nothing better to offer. They were like the Sunday School teacher who told his pupils when they came to a hard word to say 'London' and pass on. In this old deed the most you could do when you came to "golda" was to say dam and proceed with the context, and this very anomalous state of affairs continued until Mr. Addy's brilliant solution - the word was an attempt to Latinise goldies, the popular word for a golden flower, the charlock, the wild mustard, the sinapis aroensia of the botanist, an ill weed which grows apace around Beauchief to this day.

In these times most students agree that the word "golda" means a weed but they do not all accept Mr. Addy's suggestion of the charlock, some urging that children call the corn-marigolds (chrysanthemum segelum) goldies, and certainly a number of writers have known these flowers as golds. However, if it were the charlock, or catlock as it is called at Norton, that was meant it has managed to survive the old document here at Beauchief and contrives somehow to hold its own in spite of all the methods that have been devised for its eradication as we may see for ourselves if, when we have torn ourselves from Greenhill Hall, we go at the right time of year along the delightful path that leads from Greenhill through the fields and through the steep wood to the back of Beauchief Abbey. This wooded hill shelters the abbey upon its southern side, which is the "bello capite" or "beau chef", the beautiful headland from which the abbey has derived its name, and here the monastery lifts what is left of its old western tower in a dale that runs almost parallel with the valley of the Sheaf, a peaceful pastoral region 'where one might expect to meet Pan, Apollo, or the Muses', that has succeeded so far in retaining much of its quiet, remaining today a realm of ancient peace remote from the city life, away from the 'dust of the struggling outer world'. Whether it will much longer remain so is a question to give us pause, for it is threatened by the same doom that is so rapidly substituting ugliness for beauty in the valley of the Sheaf, and not far away there may be witnessed those disconcerting tendencies towards the outbreaks of the architectural scarletina, modified by the cool tints of the blue slate, to which the country hereabouts is so liable, notwithstanding that stone is so plentiful. Since the first words of this book were written hitherto, rural Woodseats has more than commenced to emulate Attercliffe and no one knows how far this kind of blight may spread; for just as Leeds is catching up to her Kirkstall so may Sheffield surround her Beauchief Abbey, and Abbey Lane its wild rose blooms notwithstanding may yet become as is Carlisle Street east.

Whatever may happen in the future, however, no spoiler can take from us the pleasures we have enjoyed here in the past, not forgetting even the boyish slides upon the abbey fish-ponds in winter nor the delight of seeing this sequestered place under deep and unpolluted snow. Pleasant has it been too in summer to sketch the great oak in Beauchief park or to sit under is wide-spread boughs reading "Ivanhoe", or watching the sheep and cows browsing quietly or languorously chewing their cud; to drink at the cold spring that runs into its mossy trough under the trees not far from Beauchief Hall which itself, upon a summer afternoon, seems like a poem by Tennyson; to loiter in the cool woods where patches of oak fern used to grow, to watch the mad gambols of the water shrews in the little river Shene, that runs through the abbey grounds to join the Sheaf. In any case these joys could never return with the same zest for are they not associated with the

Dreams that the soul of youth engage
Ere Fancy has been quelled?

With regard to the name of Beauchief there is precisely the same word in Beachy Head. In the State Papers of Henry the Eighth Beachy Head is given as Cechiff, Bechiefe, Beauchif and Beauchief, beautiful headland so that it was pure ignorance which added the word 'Head' when it was there already.

A beautiful headland this one at Beauchief truly is though, its beauty is of a different kind compared with the famous Sussex cape, and here many a local artist has been tempted to take out his sketchbook at sight of the ruin and its lovely surroundings. Tom Creswick, R.A., the Sheffield artist who became famous for his beautiful paintings of English landscape and for his exquisite book illustrations made a drawing of Beauchief Abbey, and picturesque old Christopher Thompson who lived for some years in Sheffield, sketched many of her beautiful scenes and wrote that the most interesting "Autobiography" of an Artisan, painted

Beauchief Abbey too, a work now in the possession of Mr. W. T. Freemantle of Barbot Hall. Not only innumerable local artists, but others of national fame who were not, like Creswick, born here have yet found their way to Beauchief for here came Dayes who we have met already at Smithy Wood Bottom and he tells us that 'four miles from Sheffield, at the sign of the Hammer and Pincers, I turned into an indifferent cross road, which, at the end of two miles of pleasant country conducted me to Beauchief Abbey which is situated in a delightful vale, near the northern boundary of Derbyshire. The remains of the Abbey, though inconsiderable, are nevertheless sufficiently attractive, by the aid of the rich surrounding scenery; the background being formed by bold hills, richly decorated with wood... Beauchief being highly enriched with wood, will afford some excellent studies, in which the building will happily unite'.

Others have left evidence of their admiration of Beauchief beside Dayes. On April 24 1822 James Montgomery and some of his friends drove along here in a gig. James Everatt describing this Spring jaunt says 'We were presently in Abbeydale, that charming scene in all seasons! – the monastic ruin and rising woods of Beauchief on our left – the young leaves of the latter just tinting and softening the dark masses'. 'How beautiful the trees are' exclaimed Montgomery... this is a lovely valley'. Again on July 24 1838 Montgomery called upon John Holland to walk with him to Beauchief. 'He had, he said, a particular reason for a ramble thither at this time; and his companion naturally concluded that their visit to the Abbey had some poetic or at least some picturesque bearing. It turned out, however, that the main object of the poet was to enjoy the appearance of the roses which generally at that season festooned the hedges along the

Beauchief Abbey and cottages.
June 1941

entire length of the lane, from Norton Woodseats
to Beauchief Abbey with the most luxuriant profusion. We were indeed late for the heyday of their
bloom, but still the scene was beautiful; and the
two friends enjoyed, for its own sake, the summer
afternoon walk, partly amidst suburban scenery
such as perhaps is not to be found about iron forges
and grinding mills except in the immediate neighbourhood of Sheffield'.

Ebenezer Rhodes too has written in praise of the
place remarking that the hills in the vicinity of
Beauchief are singularly graceful in form, and the
long line of luxuriant wood with which they are
adorned gives them an air of grandeur.

None of these artists, none of these writers, however, saw Beauchief Abbey except as a fragment of a ruin.

This solitary truncated tower and the fragments
which cling to it give no idea of the extent of the
monastery. If the foundations are ever exposed by
excavations an abbey not amongst the greatest but
one of considerable proportions will be revealed.
Meanwhile Mr. Addy thinks that the less demolished abbey at Dryburgh furnishes an idea of what
Beauchief was like. The west doorway is of thirteenth century architecture, the tower itself of
fourteenth century. The doorways which now flank
the tower are not in their original positions but
were placed there when they were discovered
amongst the ruins. They do not appear, for
instance, in Grimm's drawing of 1785 nor in Bucks
of 1727. That doorway upon the north side of the
tower is of Norman architecture, that upon the
south is Early English.

Little as remains of Beauchief Abbey we are better off here in this respect than at Premontre, for
there the building which occupies the site of the
abbey was built no longer ago than the eighteenth
century, and it is used as an asylum for lunatics.

Not far from the abbey of Premontre is the town and abbey of St. Quentin, or St. Quintin, and it may be that a well near to Beauchief Abbey was named St. Quintin's well by the canons. The name survives to this day as Twenty Well, or Twenty Well Sick, sick being a denomination for a stream and appearing in this district in Sickleholme near Troway, and in other place names. The lane from Bradway to Dore and Totley Railway station is known as Twenty Well Lane. The stream itself that adds the 'sick' to the Twenty Well is the one that belongs to the deep valley in which today we find the Bradway tunnel of the Midland Railway between Dore and Totley station and Dronfield. There is a reference to Quintine well during the time of Edward the First, but Mr. Addy has shown in his "Glossary" that an alternative derivation may be from Centing, the son of Centa or Quenta. In 692 there was in England a man of this name, and there is Centing's tree. Moreover there are examples of names composed of welle and a person's name.

The abbey at Beauchief was founded about 1175 by Robert Fitz Ranulph, whom we have already seen as lord of the manor of Alfreton and Norton, and it was dedicated to the Virgin Mary and to St. Thomas the Martyr that is to Thomas a Becket who had been canonized a little before the foundation of the monastery. Fitz Ranulph bestowed upon the abbey seven hundred acres of land and the churches of Norton and Alfreton in Derbyshire, Wymeswold in Leicestershire and Edwalton in Nottinghamshire. Earlier writers upon the abbey, Dugdale and Tanner, for instance – say that Fitz Ranulph founded it in expiation of his crime in being concerned in the murder of Thomas a Becket in Canterbury Cathedral; by Dr. Samuel Pegge set himself the task of proving there was no truth in this tradition, though Glover denies that he succeeded. A middle course was taken in 1878 by Mr. Addy who, thinking probably that Pegge had denied too much, argued that though Fitz Ranulph was certainly not one of the principals in the crime yet it might be as indeed Dean Stanley wrote that he was there in the background, not striking a blow but, like Saul of Tarsus at the martyrdom of St. Stephen, consenting to his death and ready if need should arise to aid and abet the murderers in more active ways. The altarpiece of alabaster that stood in the abbey and is now in the possession of the Foljambe family represented the murder of Thomas a Becket and the seal of the abbey bore a similar design. Subsequent writers, however, have stoutly resisted the expiation theory and the "Victoria County History" gives no countenance to the idea.

The canons at Beauchief were under the rules framed by St. August with a few added austerities and upon their intellectual side it was ordained that they should be able to read well, to understand grammar and that they should have a knowledge of Latin.

In 1490 the abbey agreed with Christopher Haslam, who bore a name very frequent to this day in these parts, to teach such boys as should be elected from time to time in singing and grammar for 26s.8d annually with food and a decent chamber in the abbey. Haslam was a chaplain and this agreement, though it gave him security of tenure, was not to be binding if he received promotion to a benefice. Their days were apportioned by rule and well-defined periods allotted to sleeping, eating, reading, ceremonies, fasting, prayers and work. Those who toiled far from the abbey at harvest time sang their vespers in the fields before they returned home.

The abbey grew wealthy with its thousands of acres. Like Jeshurun it 'waxed fat and kicked' and in time the rules were relaxed and concessions made to human frailty. From vegetarianism the canons passed to flesh, and some of them to gluttony and drunkenness, fasting giving way to feasting. Instead of going abroad in groups and couples according to the wise ordinances of their house, they sneaked off alone and from time to time involved the abbey in squalid scandals.

These scattered abbeys were subjected to visitations from Premontre and the abbot of each went from time to time to attend general gatherings of the order at headquarters. For instance, in 1284 the Abbot of Beauchief went to Premontre, without the aid of the railway which now runs less than a mile away from us for we read that he crossed the sea from Dover with four horses. In the reign of Edward the first the Abbot was summoned to attend Parliament.

Not always, however, did the days pass at Beauchief in a monotonous peace. On more than one occasion there was flat rebellion. During the time that Downman was Abbot his conduct was called in question and the Abbot of Shap was asked to visit Beauchief to hold an inquiry. He found Downman guilty of 'solemn perjuries', wasting of the convent's goods, incontinence, insubordination, and many other notorious crimes. 'Nay, when he was proved guilty, he rebelliously shunned the discipline of our order, and, led by the evil spirit, rose in insurrection with armed men and defensive arms, with swords and with staves, and departed the monastery, despising altogether the legal process of our order, and associated with him seven canons joined in his apostasy'. Downman was asked to appear in the chapter house to defend himself and show cause why he should not be deposed, but he had left the abbey. He was then deposed and excommunicated, and John Swift, already at Beauchief, and more amenable than

Downman to the wishes of those in authority was appointed in his place, 'and so, signing "Te Deum laudamus" they brought him to the church, and we gave him corporal possession of the same by delivering the bells into his hands, and according to our customs, installed him'.

Downman appealed and asked for reinstatement, and for more than one year afterwards, for the laws delays as well as the laws verbiage seem to have been inherited from ecclesiastics, a court of appeal was constituted at Nottingham. It decided against Downman, and the other recalcitrant canons, now that their leader was finally defeated, deserted him and made their peace with the abbey. Swift remained at Beauchief till 1478, when the abbey at Newhouse, having fallen into disrepute under a frail old abbot, he was sent there with a view no doubt to reducing canons at Newhouse to order for Swift had a reputation for organising ability, and was 'famed for the purity of his life and morals'. When he left Beauchief the Prior, and five others rebelled against his successor who was a stranger amongst them.

The abbey was inspected from time to time by representatives of the Abbot of Premontre or of Welbeck and the reports of these visitations show the visitors instructing the canons where they should sing Alleluia, for evidently they had been singing it in the wrong place in their service. They were commanded to sing the psalms with care at the end of each verse, not lengthening the note, nor lowering their voices, but rather lifting them up. Some of the lay brothers seem to have thought it would be nice for them to have tonsures and had affected this style of hairdressing, but the visitors forbade this as being contrary to the rules of the order. Then the tonsures of the canons themselves were not of the regulation kind and had to be decreased. At another visitation 'we ordered that the tonsures of the brothers be reformed, so that there may be, at the least, three fingers breadth of hair above the ears, according to the institutes of our order'.

Amongst the complaints of another visitation is one 'that in the evening, after complines, the brethren go outside the cloister, stay out so long, and get so much to drink, that at midnight, when matins should be said, they cannot keep awake'. Sometimes the visitors warn a brother, others are put on bread and water for a day, and in one case the visitors 'inflicted a penalty of ten days upon a sub-prior, because he strove contentiously with his prior, in the presence of the secular brethren'. It is laid down in another place that the canons were not to be allowed to go beyond the boundaries of the monastery to see common shows without a special licence of the Abbot.

The land of the abbey was at Norton, Bradway, where there was a water-mill, Norton Lees, Dronfield, Cold Aston, Greenhill, Woodseats, Alfreton, Sheffield, Fullwood, Wymeswold (Leicestershire), Edwalton (Nottinghamshire), Holmesfield, Unston, Dore, Totley, Stubley, Povey, Cowley, Barlow, Birchet, Harwood, Beeley, Walton, Chesterfield, Tivershall, Wadsley, Bizley, Beighton, Glapwell, Ashover, Bakewell, Eckington, Handsworth, and other places. Some of the grants are interesting from their mention of places or persons; for instance, Sir Thomas Chaworth gave a bovate of land which Adam, son of John, of the Cliff some time held of him in Norton, and five acres of essarted land and a piece in Norton Wood, which the said Adam held of him. Essarted here means cleared of wood and made ready for cultivation. Not only land was given but the people upon it, as though they had been stocks and stones, Adam, son of John, of the Cliff, with his whole family, and their chattels; Thomas son of Hugh de Bosco, with all his family and their chattels and Wynora, (what a pretty name to become obsolete) with all her family and their chattels. The canons did not cultivate the whole of the land themselves, but let it to tenants with buildings, mills and other property like other landlords.

In addition to the land they possessed the canons were allowed to drive their cattle freely upon other territory to graze. For special purposes they made special appeals to the wealthy and they were able also to obtain funds by the sale of indulgences. The canons too had 'licence and full liberty of getting coals, drawing of them and carrying them away, both for their own use and the use of their tenants, whether bond or free, whenever they want, and that both in the lands of the tenants and the said abbat and convent, and in their own lands, and in the waster lands lying amongst their lands, within the Sokes of Alfreton and Norton'. Wool from the abbey flocks was conveyed to the merchants of Chesterfield, who disposed of it abroad, for in those days, England, who now imports wool, had not begun her career of manufacturing activity. Also it may be that the canons shared in the lead mining of the country for as Mr. Addy has remarked there was a mine called Beauchief mine.

We have seen that in the days of the manors vassals were compelled to grind their corn at the lord's mill; and as the land of Beauchief Abbey constituted a manor it was natural that the abbey too should have its mills and indeed it has been found that it had at least four mills besides a fulling mill, and rents issuing out of other corn mills. The first of these mills of which there is any record is that of Hastona, or Cold Aston, which was given to the abbey by William, Baron of Alfreton, apparently about the year 1200. This mill was on the stream at

Haslehurst, near to Cold Aston, and just outside the boundary of Norton parish. Thomas Jones Junior, writing in the Sheffield "Independent" for March 8, 1877 upon this subject says the mill at Haslehurst was on the brook just at the junction of the three parishes of Eckington, Norton and Dronfield, in the wood lying between Haslehurst, Povey and Carter Hall farms. He mentions also that the faint outline of the mill dam and the foundation of the mill may still be traced and adds that a number of ancient bridle roads radiate from this place, and that the fields on each side bear the names of Mill Meadow, Mill Field and Mill Holt. Still upon the same point there is a note by Mr. James Linacre that the mill 'is said to have been near Povey on the stream running through Parsons wood. An old bridle road leads to the site of the mill from Hazlehurst farm'.

This mill at Haslehurst seems to have been moved from the east side of the steam, when it was Eckington to the west side when it was in Norton for we read that Sir Thomas Chaworth gave the canons 'half a rood of land lying near their mill of Aston, Or Hesilhyrst, on the west side of the water-course of the mill, for the purpose of transferring the mill from the east side to the west, for the greater advantage of the mill, to be erected on that spot which Roger Pykard held of him. The canons gave him in exchange a rood of land in Aston-Field'. In the time of Queen Elizabeth there was considerable litigation concerning the mill and the boundaries hereabouts. 'Heardinge land', 'Roileswood', 'a ryver called Harebeck "alias" Mearbeck', Whelefeld... good and fertile land' are mentioned in the documents and it is stated that two (mills) are under one roof – one called Parke Mill and the other called Eamylles Sett' Heardinge Lane is the disused bridle path from Norton to

Ridgeway running up the side of Roileswood, now Royals Wood and it has been suggested that Eanilles Sett is a corruption of Ea myln seta, the water mill place or Eah myln seta, the island mill place.

About the time of Edward the First Sir Thomas Chaworth, a grandson of Sir Thomas the great bene factor of the abbey, erected a windmill at Cold Aston within the manor of Norton. The canons objected to this, saying it was to the prejudice and detriment of their mill at Norton and thereupon he gave the windmill to them on condition that he and his heirs and his free family should grind their corn toll free so long as they resided at Norton.

The abbey had also in addition to the mill at Bradway, another mill called the New Mill, which is described as being the parish of Norton but which, though in the parish was really at Heeley for the parish of Norton extends to Heeley. At least Mr. Addy takes this to be the case because, besides the stream at Hazlehurst, which itself is only very small, there is no stream in Norton strong enough to turn a mill, and because mention is made of a certain Hugh Hanslen, of Little Sheffield, who 'gave the canons leave to make a dam for their mill, called the New Mill, in his "cultura" de Holleford, so that they might conduct the river Sheaf at pleasure and as convenient through his alder-plot'. As one of these mills was three and the other four miles from the abbey, however, the canons would probably make use of the mill at Ecclesall, which was afterwards given them by Robert de Ecclesall. With regard to the fulling mill of the canons Ralph de Ecclesall gave 'a spot of ground near the river of Schefeld, for the erection of a fulling mill, with leave to turn the river if necessary; he to have one-third of the profits, and to bear one-third of the expense'. It has been said that this fulling mill upon the river Sheaf, was opposite

Jowitt House, on the east side of the stream, not far from the Tunnel, and writing to the Sheffield "Independent" in 1871 Mr. Addy stated that 'there may now be seen on the Sheaf a mill (formerly a paper mill) in which are two heavy oaken mallets of very ancient appearance. I believe paper making and cloth making both require the process of fulling, and this, may, therefore be the very mill which Robert Ecclesall gave to the canons'.

The Sheaf without bridges seems to have been at times a formidable barrier for Ralf, son and heir of Robert de Ecclesall when he left the mill at Ecclesall to the canons at Beauchief in return for celebrations at Ecclesall, excuses their attendance at Ecclesall 'in case of great floods or snow' when they might celebrate at Beauchief. This shows there were times when Beauchief was cut off from Ecclesall, and we know today that after a heavy rain upon the moors or a sudden thawing of the deep snow there the Sheaf swells rapidly and becomes a torrent, in a way to surprise those who know only the streams of the more deliberate level lands.

Beauchief Abbey was founded on December 21, 1183 upon the feast of St. Thomas the Apostle and in honour of St. Thomas the Martyr. There are two documents, each professing to be the deed of foundation and both are addressed to Richard Pecke who was Bishop of Coventry from 1162 to 1183. These documents, given in full by Mr. Addy, are of great local interest from their references to familiar places. In the first we read 'To Richard, by the grace of God, Bishop of Coventry, and to all the children of Holy Mother Church as well present as future, Robert Fitz-Ranulph sends greeting. Know ye that I have given to God, Saint Mary, and St. Thomas the Martyr, and to the professed bretheren of the Order of Premontre, in free and perpetual alms, for the building of an abbey, the place which is called

Beuchef in Doresheles, and whatsoever is within
the boundaries of Doresheles that is to say, from
Grenhilheg along the field of Clebinus (Clebini?) to
the fields of Gervase, Gamel, Haco, and Gerard,
along the hedge to the brow of the hill which is
called Dorehegset, and then as you descend over
the brow of the same hill to the field of Roger, and
so along the hedge of the same Roger beyond the
water, across the footpath, to the field of Robert the
Forester, and so by the way which leads to the aforesaid Grenhilheg aforesaid, and whatsoever is contained within the limits of these boundaries; and the
church of Norton with all its appurtenances...'

The second deed is richer in place names and
therefore more interesting for our purpose. Fitz-
Ranulph grants 'for the building of an abbey, the
place which is called Beauchief, and which is situate in Doreheseles, that is to say, from Grenhilheg,
through Aldefelds, as far as Quintinewelle and so
as you descend by the brook of the said
Quintinewelle to the stream which is called Shava
(Sheaf) and along the same stream as you descend
to the Broc, and by the Broc as you ascend to the
ford of the Broc, which is near the path which
descends from the house of Alan, and so by his
field to the fields of Robert and Peter, and so as
you ascend to Grenhilheg aforesaid, and whatsoever is contained within the limits of these boundaries, and the church of Norton with all its appurtenances and the church of Alfreton... and the mill
of Norton, with all its multure, its appurtenances
and gearing, so that neither I nor my heirs shall
build any other mill in the liberty of the said village, nor permit this to be done by any man save
the canons; but it shall be lawful for the canons
themselves to erect other mills in the liberty of the
same village, whenever they wish, and wherever
they shall consider it advantageous to themselves.

And also the field of Hugh near Mersbroc, with one toft in Leis (Norton Lees) and one toft near the house of Alan...' There is a third description of the canon's land at Beauchief entered in the Obituary, a curious and irregular place for it. The entry is very short and it takes us 'from Quintinwell along the brooklet which descends into the river Scheth to Le Broke, and so as you ascend along the Le Broke as far as Tachellforth, and so from Tachellforth, as far as Hulstorth across and from Hulstorth across the hill to Grenhyll hege, and from Grenhyll to Quintinwell. These are the boundaries of the site of the abbey of Bewchiff'.

The "Obituarium" or "Necrologium" in which someone had entered the bounds of the estate was amongst the more important books of an abbey. In its proper use it was a kind of diary, a list of appointments, for it showed the canons each day for whose souls they should pray. Each morning, in the chapter house, after Prime, the entries for the day were read aloud. Entered in this book were the names of canons now lying in their graves, of people who had given land or goods to the abbey, or of others who had by one way or another commended themselves to the canons. Not many of these books have been preserved, but two books from Beauchief Abbey have been saved and the more important found by Mr. Addy was published for the first time in his "Memorials of Beauchief Abbey".

Without reproducing the whole of this necrology we may select a few of the entries that refer to Norton or that have other local interest. On Feb 10 each year was commemorated Galfird de Arnesby, a canon of the abbey, and vicar of Norton church, and two days later John Croke, formerly vicar of Norton, who died A.D. 1510. Upon March 11 was the commemoration of John Moor of Grenhill, 'who gave us two silver spoons'.

With regard to the commemoration of 'Jordan our brother', Mr. Addy has remarked that 'Jordanus is the name of one of the earliest abbots of Beauchief, and also of one of the vicars of Norton. The place name Jordanthorpe, Norton, near the abbey doubtless comes from this word'.

Other commemorations mention Sir William de Chaworth; Lady Alice wife of Sir William Chaworth, our advocate, for whom a full service shall be said in the convent with great commendation; Lady Alice wife of Sir Thomas Chaworth; John de Norton, our assistant brother; and the Lady Matilda Lovetot, wife of Sir Gerard Furnival, lord of Hallamshire who gave us one mark of yearly rent for a pittance, from her mill in Sheffield, to be received on the day of St. Denis and his companions to sustain a solemn service for the souls of Sir Gerard, her husband, and herself which appears by a charter which she gave us. The canons were to commemorate also Isabella de Norton and Adam her son; Gerard de Furnivall, son of Thomas 'who gave us thirty acres of land in Fulwode; Henry the mason of Eccleshale: Hundehowe, and Isabella his wife, an entry upon which Mr. Addy remarks that there is a place called Hundow near Dronfield; Ranulph, vicar of Norton; John Rovecester, lord of Dore, who had given to the abbey a very liberal grant of land in Dore; Robert Fitzranulph, canon, and founder of this place, who gave us four churches, that is to say, Nortone, Alfretone, Wymondewolde and Eadwalton, for his a solemn service ("Solempne Servicium") shall be said in the convent. William de Eylborn, formerly vicar of Norton; Sir Thomas de Chaworth, our advocate, for whom a full service shall be said in the convent with great commendation, and for whom a mass shall be celebrated for ever at the altar of St. Katherine the Virgin A.D. 1314 he gave us

Grenhyll and Wodcetes with divers parcels of rent and land in Alfretone.

Sir Gerard Furnival the first, who gave us sufficient pasture in his forest of Fulwode for thirty cows, with their young under three years and one acre of land to build our cottages upon and who also gave us 20s. rent from his mill of Sheffield, to sustain the lamp of our church, for whom a service shall be said in the convent with great commendation. This service was to be accompanied by music. Mr. Addy thinks the cottages would be houses for the neat herds or shelters for the cattle in winter, and he has added that Gerard de Furnival died at Jerusalem in the third year of the reign of Henry III.

Further commemorations include Symon Bolar, of Holinesfeld (Holmsfield) a name that has survived at Heeley; William, priest, and vicar of Norton; William Parker, of Eston (Cold Aston) and Abe his wife; Adam, called 'the Cook' of Schefeld, our assistant brother; Sir Thomas de Furnivall, for whom a full service shall be said in the convent with great commendation. He gave us land to enlarge our grange in Fulwode (Fullwood) and confirmed all the donations of his ancestors of Halumshyre.

During the reign of Henry the Eighth a survey of the monasteries was made and the returns, known as the "Valor Ecclesiasticus", are in the Record Office. They have also been printed with an introduction by Joseph Hunter. The return shows that the annual income of Beauchief in 1535 was £126.3s.3d. and when it was decided that the smaller monasteries, those with an income of less than £200 must go, the fate of Beauchief was sealed. Abbot Greenwood, or Sheffield as he is called sometimes from the place of his birth, surrendered the monastery on Feb 4 1536 'without giving any trouble or opposition' and it is believed that in the same year he died.

This is no place in which to fight all over again the battle of whether or not the monasteries should have been surpressed; but here as in the suppression of the chantries there can be no defence of the manner in which the suppression was executed. Apart even from the question of whether the land should have been passed so completely into private hands or not, the demolition of the buildings which might have served for schools, colleges, libraries or other appropriate and useful purpose was an act of the most wanton waste and savagery. In the destruction of these noble buildings it was not an unknown proceeding for the carved woodwork to be made into a bonfire to melt the lead from the roofs. Local farmers dug up the stone coffins for swine troughs, scattering to the winds their contents of bones and wrappings. Fences, farmhouses outbuildings were erected with the abbey ruins as the quarry, drains were made with its carved stones, and even the roads were mended and ditches were bridged with material from the same source, so that it was quite a common thing for the wayfarers of that day to see pieces of carved and inscribed stone lying in the deep ruts of the hitherto neglected lanes. During the year 1909 an examination of some masonry forming a grotto in a garden at Radford a suburb of Nottingham disclosed a block about 18 inches square which had been hollowed out and used as a feeding trough. In spite of the defacement there was still sufficient indication in the shape and the carved ornamentation to show that it was at one time one of the Norman capitals in the Cluniac Priory of Holy Trinity at Lenton, Nottinghamshire, founded by William Peverel at the beginning of the twelfth century. So instances might be multiplied of the degradation of buildings, the beauty of which has never been surpassed before nor since.

An inventory of all the goods in the abbey has survived, and is printed in Mr. Addy's work. He utters his protest against the burning of the books and here again the illiteracy and brutality of the despoilers of monasteries appears.

The estates given by the Chaworths and others were sold amongst local and other magnates. Land at Eckington, Dronfield and Newbould went to the Fanshawes; Woodseats, Greenhill, Little Norton and other land hereabouts went to Sir William West and other partakers in the spoiling of the abbey estates were Strelley, Leake, Talbot Earl of Shrewsbury, Cavendish, Foljambe, and the Duke of Portland. At the time of the dissolution the founders of the abbey were represented by two daughters and co-heiresses of John Ormond, who were mentioned in the account of the descent of the manor of Norton. Thus all through its existence the lords of the manor of Norton had been the patrons of the abbey.

The Strelleys were prominent people during the reign of Elizabeth. A member of the family who was lord of the manor of Ecclesall was buried at Sheffield in 1602, though he seems to have lived at Beauchief. Their descendants were attached to this district and records of their baptisms and burials are contained in the registers of Norton, Dronfield and Sheffield. The William Strelley who died in 1635 married Gertrude daughter of Adam Eyre of Bradway a younger son of Rowland Eyre of Hassop. It was their daughter Gertrude who married Edward Pegge at Norton in 1648 and so transferred the Strelley estates to the Pegges. A third Gertrude, their daughter, was the maternal grandmother of Dr. Samuel Pegge, the antiquary and the historian of Beauchief. Edward was high sheriff of the country in 1644 and he it was who built Beauchief Hall in 1671 finding the ruins of

Beauchief Abbey a convenient quarry of wrought stone. It is said he lived first in the abbey grange and then built the Hall upon the site of the grange. He built also the little chapel behind the tower and caused those services to be held there which are still continued; and when he died in 1679 he was buried in the abbey where other Pegges and Strelleys were interred. Quoting from Bishop Kennett's Register, Samuel Pegge has told us with regard to the services at the abbey, which are still continued that Nathaniel Baxter from Lancashire came into Yorkshire after 1662 and being in these parts he fell into company of (Edward) Pegge, Esquire, of "Beauchief Abbey", in Derbyshire, a very sober gentleman, who invited him to give them a sermon at an old abbey church called Beauchief Abbey, and he complied with the notion. After this gentleman told him, that if he would let him have the benefit of his labours at Beauchief Abbey, his steward should pay him sixteen pounds "per annum", for that there was nothing belonging to the place but what he thought fit to allow. Mr. Baxter being then a single man, accepted the offer; and afterwards marrying lived within a mile or thereabouts of the abbey; and, in a little time, with his wife's fortune, he purchased a small estate, about the same distance from it, and continued there several years'.

This little estate leased from Cornelius Clarke in 1674 was at Woodseats, where was born Baxter's daughter Mary whose baptism appears in the Norton register March 8 1677. Before he went to Woodseats Baxter had been living at Brincliffe Edge.

The Pegges and Strelleys are not the only people buried at Beauchief Abbey for here lies too a game-keeper of the eighteenth century whose epitaph shall speak for him.

A gamekeeper I was at Beauchief Hall;
At Dore my fatal gun caused me to fall,
Which made a speedy passage through my head,
And sent me to the mansions of the dead.
Repent in time; consider, mortal man,
Thy race's end no longer than a span;
Man's like a flower that's in the morning blown,
Before the night is withered and cut down.

A tradition has survived that the great bell whose deep tolling used to break the stillness of this quiet dale was stolen at midnight and that in order to baffle pursuers the horses had their shoes reversed. The bell was taken to Lincoln, runs the tradition, and is indeed none other than Tom of Lincoln whose ringing even at the distance sours all the milk for several miles round Beauchief Abbey. Writing in 1878 Mr. Addy, while ridiculing the absurdities of the story, remarked that it may have been built upon a foundation of truth. He pointed out that the obituary mentions a great bell. This distinction suggestions that there were other bells. Buck's drawing of 1727 shows that the present tower once carried a belfry, and a large steeple and five bells are mentioned in a law suit between William Bullock and Edward Pegge. As the five bells would probably monopolise the belfry it may be that the great bell had a belfry of its own. There is no reason why this bell should not go to Lincoln for did not Tom of Oxford come from Oseney Abbey? Moreover many horses would be needed to draw a great bell from Beauchief to Lincoln so that altogether it may be that the unbelievable elements in the story are no more than mediaeval embellishments of a straightforward tale.

Beauchief too has its variant of the absurd stock tradition of Oliver Cromwell setting his canon upon Bole Hill to blow away the top of the tower;

but Buck's drawing of 1727 shows that the tower was still at its full height sixty nine years after the death of the Protector, and he of course had more pressing use for his powder, shot and men than to use them needlessly upon abbey ruins held only by the bats and owls.

There has been in later years a revival of the order of St. Norbert in this country, and at Crowle is a small Norbertine Priory. The revival took place in 1872 when a canon came from Tongerloo Abbey, not far from Antwerp, to re-establish the order in England and houses have since been founded at Spalding, Manchester, Storrington, Bedworth, and Wigton. The building at Crowle was designed by Mr. A. M. Hadfield of Sheffield, whose architecture in that city was amongst the author's earliest loves in seemly building. So far the revival of the order in England has not led to the rebuilding of Beauchief Abbey, and may never so lead; but sauntering in this quiet, beautiful place we may still endeavour to see in our mind's eye the stately abbey, to put ourselves in the position of those who in 1491 'beheld the said monastery adorned with such fair decorations, buildings, and repairs, that well may it be said with the prophet 'O Lord, I have loved the beauty of thine house'

CHAPTER XX

NORTON IN BOOKS AND PICTURES

When we come to consider those who have helped us to a history of our own countryside we think first of Joseph Hunter. He doth bestride our world of Hallamshire like a Colossus; and we petty men walk under his huge legs and peep about; for whoever endeavours to puzzle out the story of Sheffield or its outlying places will be sent sooner or later to those 'Switzer-like tomes' those generous folios of his, "Hallamshire" and "South Yorkshire" that answer 'the place of our kindly engendure' amongst the great works on topography standing sentry near the door at the British Museum. Dr. Gatty has told us that in personal appearance Mr. Hunter was the "beau ideal" of an antiquary, in manners most courteous, and quite of the old school. Tenacious he was too, and on one occasion arguing a point with Sir Henry Ellis as they crossed the Strand, Hunter to emphasize his point seized his friend so tightly by the arm and so rooted himself to the spot to settle the matter there and then that the two ran the greatest peril of annihilation by an omnibus.

Joseph Hunter, born in 1783, had many qualifications for the role of a local historian. He was born in Sheffield, an important point; for many things come to a native that are denied to a stranger, and an understanding too of the spirit and temper of a place. Locally too he learned his first steps in Latin for when his father Michael Hunter, cutlery manufacturer died, his guardian Joseph Evans, minister at Upper Chapel, Sheffield, sent him to receive a classical education at a school in Attercliffe kept by a Mr. Sorby. At York he found a friend in Samuel Shore who was studying there and another in James Yates, who we have met already at Norton Hall.

Dr. Gatty has related that upon the last occasion upon which Hunter visited the Ecclesfield vicarage he walked off to the vestry, as he did always, to renew his acquaintance with the register. Upon this occasion the old man turned faint 'but he went into the churchyard and selected the place of his own interment under the waving shadows of some ancient willows; and there, within a few months' Dr. Gatty read the funeral service over this remains. Gales uprooted the ancient willows, but others were planted in their place as Hunter would have wished for they seem to have decided his choice of a grave.

Associated more closely with Norton is a scholar of a later generation Mr. Sidney Oldall Addy, M.A., who was born in 1848, in the parish, at Hemsworth, has never lived far away and spent the most impressionable years of his life within the sound of Norton church bells. Today his library window in Sheffield commands a view of that line of trees that has already been noticed as forming the northern boundary of the park at Norton. On his mother's side he is connected with the famous old Derbyshire family of Balguy. George Addy, cutlery manufacturer, of Gell Street, Sheffield at that time a rural retreat, married Rose, the daughter of John Radcliffe of Sheffield, the eldest of three beautiful sisters. Rose Addy is the subject of an obituary notice in the "New Methodist Magazine" for March 1833, and Mr. Addy has her portrait in oils.

Their youngest child was James Addy, colliery and landowner born in Gell Street in 1816, and he married Sarah Oldall, hence Sidney Oldall Addy. James Addy died in 1900. In view of what has been written of Hazlebarrow Hall in Chapter X, it is interesting to know that Sarah Oldall was the daughter of Mary Jenkin, who, in her turn, was the daughter of James Jenkin of Hazlebarrow. Mary Jenkin married Sidney Oldall of Cold Aston. Mr. Addy received his education first at the Sheffield Collegiate School, afterwards at Lincoln College, Oxford, and became a solicitor, but spent the whole of his leisure in historical philosophical and antiquarian studies, and many carefully considered papers and books show how wide and deep his researches have been.

Mr. Addy's predecessor as the historian of Beauchief Abbey was the Rev. Samuel Pegge, a man of erudition when there were fewer workers in the field of English antiquities. He was born in 1704 and belonged to an old Derbyshire family. A Katherine Pegge of the time of Charles the Second bore that faithless monarch a son who became Earl of Plymouth, distinguished himself in the navy and lies buried in Westminster Abbey. Samuel was born no further away than Chesterfield and was educated there too and afterwards at Cambridge, his goal the church. He had livings elsewhere, but to us is known as Rector at Whittington, a post he held for forty-five years. At Whittington too he died in 1796 in his ninety-second year and in the chancel of the church there we may see his monument today. His writings were manifold and scholarly and Oxford conferred upon him the degree of Doctor of Laws. Like other authors who have loved the county, Blore Jewitt and the rest, he contemplated that impossible task for one man a history of Derbyshire, and his laborious accumulations, carefully and affectionately arranged by Joseph Hunter, are now in the Herald's College in London. Pegge was agreeable and vivacious in conversation, in manners gentlemanly and dignified. We know him best by his book of Beauchief Abbey, a work it was particularly appropriate he should write for he was connected with the Beauchief Pegges and had access to family papers as well as to national records. So he tells us that 'although I am derived directly from, and indeed am the representative of, the elder branch of the little family of Pegge of Osmaston juxta Ashbourn, co. Derby; yet am I also descended from the second line of that house seated at Beauchief, by the intermarriage of my father with the granddaughter of Edward Pegge, of Beauchief, Esq.'

Beauchief Abbey has a place too in Notes on the Church of Derbyshire by Dr. Cox who devotes also a section to Norton church in that work of sustained interest and endless research published in 1876 – it is not the fault of Dr. Cox that with regard to Norton the 'restorers' of the building have made his notes no longer a description of what may be found at Norton; but perhaps they are all the more valuable in another way as recording what has been there but now is there no more. Since he wrote about Norton church to the present day the zeal and industry of Dr. Cox have been exceptional; book has followed book with bewildering rapidity and many a budding antiquary has had cause to bless his name for his admirable little volume entitled "How to write the History of a Parish", to say nothing of innumerable articles, papers and reviews. Dr. Cox is the grand-son of Major John Cox of Derby and the son of the Rev. Edward Cox, Rector of Luccombe. He was born in 1843 educated at Bath and at Queen's College, Oxford and like his father entered the church. Though other counties have benefited by his labours, Derbyshire has been his favourite. Dr. Cox lived at Sydenham but recent books and reviews show that he has not forgotten Derbyshire.

Many interesting features have gone from Norton church since Dr. Cox was there, but the registers repose intact in the vestry and recently a useful work has been accomplished by Mr. Lloyd Simpson of Littleover, who has transcribed them for the printer translating the parts in Latin into English. His interest in Norton springs from the circumstance that his maternal ancestors were the Blythes of Norton and Dronfield and in an endeavour to learn all he could about them he naturally came into touch with the registers and eventually arranged with Mr. Hall, the vicar who has borne the cost, to have the registers printed. Mr. Lloyd Simpson is not new to such work for he has prepared parts of the registers of a number of Derbyshire parishes for Mr. Phillimore's series. These volumes of the Norton registers constitute a most valuable contribution to the history of this parish.

There are many things about Norton that we owe to John Holland. Sheffield may have nurtured more profound scholars, and more distinguished writers both of poetry and of prose, but no one could have had a more sincere love for the place of his birth than this kindly man nor a more genuine desire to preserve local traditions. There are those who speak slightingly of John Holland, and his life of Montgomery long and occasionally diffuse has been described as the worst biography ever written; but for all that there will be people in each succeeding generation glad to turn to John Holland's books and to his scattered writings to learn something gratefully from his recollections of the features of this countryside that are disappearing now with such disconcerting rapidity. If when we have died, our spirits haunt the places we have

loved on this earth, we may depend upon it that
the ghost of John Holland often seeks for the traces
of the bygone narrow High Street of Sheffield, but
still more often flits past the old yew and moulder-
ing cross of Norton churchyard. He was born in
1794 in a delightful old cottage in Sheffield Park
near the ruins of the Manor House of the Earl of
Shrewsbury in which Cardinal Wolsey was once
received with hospitality and in which Mary Queen
of Scots passed some of her captivity. His father
made optical instruments, not in a factory, but in
the home garret; his mother was a model housewife, who added spinning to her other household
activities. John took to books early and to the writing of verses and prose, with strong leanings to
antiquities and topography. His religious instincts
too were strong and much of his time went in
Sunday School work. Ebenezer Elliott admired
Holland, Montgomery became his close and lifelong friend. He succeeded Montgomery as editor
of the "Iris" in Sheffield, later was co-editor of the
"Mercury" and afterwards contributed to the
Sheffield "Times" and the Sheffield "Telegraph".
Amongst his literary work away from Sheffield
were his contributions to Dr. Lardner's "Cabinet
Cyclopedia". For forty years he was curator for the
Literary and Philosophical Association in Sheffield
and if old age had caused him to give up that office,
an annuity of £100 had been provided by ten gentlemen of the town. However, he died in harness in
1873, 78 years of age and was buried with his parents and other ancestors at Handsworth. A biography by William Hudson was published in 1874.
Holland lived a blameless, contented and useful
life on small means, and on his death-bed was able
to say 'I think no man has had a brighter life than
mine'. A number of the poems he left, including
his "Diurnal Sonnets" have reference to Norton,

but none touch the place so intimately as one of 1848 "A Meditation on May-Day Morning, in Norton Churchyard" and from the twenty-one stanzas a few may be selected – the sixth, ninth and sixteenth. The poet mentions the 'sombre yews' and proceeds,

> On that damp stone round which the nettles grow,
> I read the name which from my sire I drew;
> And many, many a nameless grave I know,
> Holds kindred dust; for near this village grew
> My ancestral race; while many a bough,
> Its faithful shadow o'er the farm-stead threw:
> For simple yeoman - men of daily toil,
> Were they who flourished in this Norton soil.

Holland finds his ancestors in the days of James the Second and traces them in the registers

> Methinks I see them now, on Sabbeth morn,
> Advancing Churchwards with their neighbour friends;
> From Jordanthorpe, where Chantrey since was born -
> From yonder cottage home at Four-lands-Ends
> From breezy Bolehill, whence, abrupt descends
> To Woodseats, the deep lane all water-worn:
> From where yon avenue of lofty trees,
> O'er tops the ancient mansion at the Lees.

> That quaint, gray, ivy-mantled mansion seems
> While wizard shadows round its windows fails –
> As if it beckoned from the land of dreams,
> An apparition of "old" Norton Hall;
> What time discoursing stern polemic themes,
> "There" Newton, and "here" Offley we recall:
> Names which Tradition's legendary page,
> And grave historian's pen did erst engage.

Chantrey

A pencil sketch *by Weekes made in 1839*

Norton has frequent mention too in the writings of both the late John Daniel Leader, F.S.A. and of his brother Robert Eadon Leader, B.A., and as we read their books we may regret that so many days of their lives were spent in work now embedded deeply in the accumulating strata of the Sheffield "Independent" files and, relatively, so few days in the production of volumes like "Mary Queen of Scots in Captivity" and "Sheffield in the Eighteenth Century". Many could have done the jounalistic work if not as well or as soundly as the Leaders did it at least well enough for its ephemeral purpose for while a locality produces many who can do its newspaper work it nurtures but few who can write its history. As a young man John Daniel Leader loitered about Norton church making notes, for though the accident of birth made him the son of a newspaper proprietor, the son of a journalist of much more than the ordinary capacity and energy, a fighter who scented the battle afar off, yet at heart the younger man conscientiously and well as he did his work for the "Independent" cared more perhaps for old churches, old records and old books than for the passing show or for the chronicling of the small beer of the daily round, and when the chance presented itself was apt to steal away from the contentions of partisans or it may be from the fever of a Pot Square meeting which was as the breath of life to 'Bobby Leader', his father, to the quiet of the library or to the silence of the long-deserted Roman camp. Mr. J. D. Leader made notes here at Norton and copied the inscriptions both inside the church and outside; but these notes were not printed, and he has too a number of references to Norton and to Norton people in his "old Sheffield Jottings", a pamphlet printed for private circulation in 1891. When the restoration operations began in 1881 he went to Norton church with

Mr. Addy to see the last of the old arrangements and probably the article on the church which appeared soon afterwards in the "Independent" was one of the fruits of this little jaunt.

Though not as far as his writings are concerned in such intimate association with Norton as his brother, yet Mr. Robert Eadon Leader has many references to Norton folks in his books and papers so that a number of intimations of indebtedness to Mr. Leader are found scattered through these pages. Mr. John Daniel Leader, born in 1835, died in 1899 but his brother is still with us, although he no longer lives in Sheffield, but does not leave Hallamshire out of his literary activities.

Although it is not in the Peak of Derbyshire, Norton finds more than a passing mention in "Peak Scenery" because its author, Ebenezer Rhodes, was fond of the place and had friends here in the Shores and in Chantrey. Rhodes was a native of the Holmes near Masborough where he was born in 1762. Ten years before there was born, not far away, the Corn Law Rhymer, Ebenezer Elliott. Both Rhodes' and Elliott's fathers worked at Masborough for the Walkers the iron masters who built from Rennie's design the Southwark Bridge. Rhodes was apprenticed to a scissor manufacturer in Sheffield but was given to walking in the country admiring the scenery and to poring over books. For a short time he was an actor but returned to his scissors though he retained his fondness for the drama, wrote a play and acted in the principal part himself in the Sheffield theatre. Wandering one day in 1792 towards Eckington he lighted upon James Montgomery on a field path near Ridgeway and the two became attached for life. This friendship with the poet and with Chantrey strengthened Rhodes' bent towards art and literature and much of the time he could spare from his cares as a manufacturer of scissors and razors went in writing his books or in miscellaneous articles, some of which were sent to the "Northern Star". It was at the suggestion of Rhodes that Montgomery wrote "The Wanderer in Switzerland". Rhodes was master Cutler in 1809 and three years later went to London upon a deputation to protest against those Orders in Council which a few weeks later were revoked. Reader of Charlotte Bronte's "Shirley" will remember her vivid pictures of the stagnation in trade and other dire results of these orders and in Sheffield as well as in Briarfield there were scenes of violence and there was widespread starvation. Rhodes was sociable, much given to clubs and societies and of handsome presence.

From prosperity Rhodes declined until in 1827 he became bankrupt and died 77 years of age in 1839, living the last years of his life upon the bounty of his friends the Duke of Devonshire, Chantrey, Montgomery and less known men. Montgomery, the kindly poet, as usual was most generous and quietly spent more than a thousand pounds in his manifold endeavours to put Rhodes' unfortunate family beyond the dismal atmosphere of need when their father lay in his grave in the old parish churchyard of Sheffield.

Another important contribution to the story of Norton is that embodied in Mr. Henry Kirke's book on "The First Conquest of Canada".

Just as we have derived information of the Kirkes from a Kirke, so also do we hear of the Fanshawes from a Fanshawe. Mr. Herbert Charles Fanshawe, the historian of his family, was born in 1852 a son of the Rev. Faithfull Fanshawe, he was educated in Derbyshire at the ancient school of Repton. Entering the Indian Civil Service he was in succession settlement officer at Rohtak, chief secretary Punjab government, a commissioner for the same region, a member of the legislative council of the Punjab and in 1900 a member of the Legislative Council of the Governor General of India. Upon his retirement and return to his native country he spent some of his leisure here in our colder greyer climate away from the glories and colour of Delhi 'hearkening after the memory of his ancestors', with the result that the libraries of those who have a love for this upland region have been enriched by "The Memoirs of Ann, Lady Fanshawe" with valuable and exhaustive editorial notes, many of them of great local interest.

A very concise account of Norton appears in the Derbyshire volume of Lyson's Magna Britannia projected by Daniel Lysons (1762-1834) assisted by his brother Samuel (1763-1819) a clever draughtsman. The Lysons belong to Gloucestershire and Daniel, educated at Bath Grammar School and Oxford, entered the church and devoted his leisure to topography with the result that many large and important volumes stand to his credit. His portrait was painted by Sir Thomas Lawrence and by Dance.

In her "Vignettes of Derbyshire", Mrs. Sterndale gives a 'vignette' of Norton and dedicates the whole book to Chantrey, upon whose monument of vicar Wilkinson she wrote some poetry. At the top of Angel Street in Sheffield, a little below Watsons Walk upon a site absorbed since by the premises of Messrs. Cockayne and was, as Mr. R. E. Leader has told us, a druggist's shop kept by Robert Handley from Hall-Carr and continued when he died, by his widow. Handley's father had intellectual tastes and supplied Hunter with information for his "Hallamshire". Mary Handley the daughter of the druggist married John Sterndale, the surgeon, and she wrote a number of books. John Holland has mentioned her persistence in the stately and ceremonious manners of the 'old school' when a more casual kind of deportment had been adopted and he has added that 'Mrs. Sterndale was pointed out to me as the friend of Anna Seward; and I recollect congratulating myself, when I first spoke to the Sheffield authoress, on having talked with the lady who had talked with the lady who had talked with Dr. Johnson, and, if we may "not" believe Boswell, had the best of the conversation too!'

Chantrey contemplated painting a portrait of Mrs. Sterndale but it is a pity that nothing came of the plan. Mrs. Sterndale was one of those who used to pop in at Everett's bookshop in Sheffield where Joseph Hunter, Montgomery Holland, Ebenezer Elliott, and other lovers of letters used to gather; and this recalls that the history of Norton owes something to Everett himself from whom particulars are to be obtained concerning John Wesley at Norton, Chantrey, and the artist Hofland. James Everett was born at Alnwick in 1784 and after an uproarious youth, part of it passed as a poacher and the friend of poachers, he became a Methodist. In his childhood he had heard of John Wesley preach, and he himself became and effective preacher at Shields, Belpher, Manchester and other places. Throat trouble drove him from the pulpit for a time, and it was then he became a bookseller in Sheffield and afterwards in Manchester; but in 1834 he was able to return to the ministry and was stationed at Newcastle and later at York. Again his health failed for a time, but once more he was able to go back to his work. Then in 1849, he was expelled from the church for his criticisms and attacks upon the Methodist constitution, and especially for his strictures contained in some anonymous 'flysheets'. He and others who were expelled at the same time, and many followers, now formed the United Methodist Free Church and Everett was made first president in 1857. He died in Sunderland in 1872. Everett wrote much, made notes of famous people he had met, including Southey and Montgomery; and he had a very large accumulation of books and manuscripts relating to Methodism. Those went to the Rev. Luke Tyreman that he might draw upon them for his life of John Wesley. Everett was the historian of Sheffield Methodism and he combined with John Holland in a life of Montgomery. In Parker's Wesleyan Centenary picture, suggested by Everett, of John Wesley saved from the burning of his father's house at Epworth the artist introduced Everett running with outstretched hands to receive the child and Everett supplied many of the historical details for the work. Everett's portrait appears also in the very interesting life written by the Rev. Richard Chew, a Sheffield minister, and published in 1875.

Although there is nothing to show that George Jones R.A. ever came to Norton yet his book Recollections of Chantry brings him within the scope of this chapter. He painted landscapes, battle scenes and other pictures and served as a soldier on the Continent during the Napoleonic wars. In this way he was with the army in the occupation of Paris. Jones was librarian for the Royal Academy, afterwards keeper, and enjoyed the friendship of Chantrey Turner and other artists. Turner made him one of his executors. Jones born in 1786 lived on until the year 1869.

Thus do we see that many authors have written about Norton and of Norton people and artists too have been drawn to the little place. It will be shown that "Milk Boys", with Sheffield in the background, by Henry Perlee Parker is not without reference to Norton, and the same artist painted Chantrey's funeral, a picture that has been

reproduced to face page 392 of this book. It is
strange that Parker should ever have come into
such close association with Norton for he was born
at Devonport in 1795. He became a portrait painter
at Three Towns, but with small success, and wandered to the north of England. In 1816 he was in
Newcastle and managed to attract attention there
by his picture of some Newcastle eccentrics, and
he helped to establish the Northumberland
Institution for the Promotion of the Fine Arts. He
went on painting historical and marine subjects but
with such a great likings for smugglers that he
became known as 'Smuggler Parker'. Ceremonial
pictures, coronations and such things too he painted and also the Grace Darling incident. His very
popular picture of the rescue of John Wesley from
the flames of Epworth rectory was presented in
1840 to the Wesleyan Conference and engravings
used to be seen, and may still be seen, in many a
Methodist home. Thus in one way or another he
became widely known and came into touch with
our own countryside by his appointment as drawing
master at Wesley College, Sheffield. Hence his
interest in Chantrey and Norton and his pictures of
"Milk Boys" and "Chantrey's Funeral" of which
more hereafter. In 1844 Parker settled in London
and died in 1873.

From time to time topographical artists have
been attracted to Norton, from distant parts of the
country. Of these, Samuel Hieronymous Grimm
who made a drawing of Norton church and the old
hall, and another of Beauchief Abbey both adopted
by Pegge for his book on Beauchief, was born at
Burgdof, Berne, the son of a miniature painter. He
was brought to London about 1778 and was in
request for the illustration of many topographical
works amongst them books on Derbyshire and
Nottinghamshire, two countries in which he made

many drawings for Sir Richard Kaye. The Society of Antiquaries too employed him to make sketches of ancient buildings. He died in 1794, sixty years of age, in London and in the following year five hundred of his drawings were sold by auction. A reproductions of his drawing can be found in this volume facing page 96. The Norton church plate was given in the "Gentlemans Magazine" Jan – June 1818, Vol. 88, page 497.

The artist of the more recent, but still old drawing of the church and hall at Norton, Thomas Malton, was the son of an architect's draughtsman of the same name and Malton the younger was born probably in London in 1748. His early life was spent in Dublin. Girtin and Turner were amongst his pupils at an evening drawing class in London. 'My real master was Tom Malton' said Turner and he used also to remark that 'If Tom Girton had lived I should have starved'. Malton drew seats of the nobility for the publishers, painted scenes for theatres, and worked in aquatint. He died in 1804.

The best representation of a Norton scene known to the author is the drawing of the old house at Norton Lees, by Edward Blore, contributed to "Peak Scenery", and reproduced in this book in reduced form to face page 44. It is one of the ornaments of Rhodes' account of the Peak and reveals careful loving work and deep feeling. Edward Blore was the son of the topographer Thomas Blore, both Derbyshire men of whom the county is proud, and Thomas born in 1787 early revealed his instincts for the delightful arts of sketching and architecture and made drawings for his father's books. He drew many of the illustrations too for the great topographical works of his day including Hunter's book on Hallamshire for which he sketched Chantrey's Wilkinson monument in the Sheffield Parish church, and Carbrook Hall.

A friend of Sir Walter Scott, he was the designer of Abbotsford, and illustrated some of Scott's antiquarian writings. As an architect he took part in the gothic revival, achieved fame, and won the confidence of King William the Fourth and of Queen Victoria. He was a most industrious man, and when he died in 1879 left nearly five thousand sketches as the fruit of merely one of his many absorbing activities. His career and work are full of attraction and it is pleasing to feel that he has been in touch with Norton.

Already mention has been made of the view that Thomas Christopher Hofland drew of Sheffield from Meersbrook. He was born no further away than Worksop in 1777. An only child he grew up in an environment of indulgence and prosperity with no more to do than to win an easy excellence in athletics and field sports and to mix in a society that welcomed him for his handsome face, winning ways and wealth. Then his father, a manufacturer of cotton machinery, failed and Hofland turned for a living now to art, which hitherto had been one of his amusements. He did well as a teacher amongst the wealthy folk about Kew. When Napoleon threatened to invade England, Hofland volunteered, won favour from George III who gave him some art work to do and would have given him more if he would have left his mother to go abroad as artist for a foreign expedition.

Leaving Kew he lived afterwards at Derby and Doncaster painting and teaching, and he was fond too of sketching in the Lake District. In 1812 he won a hundred guinea prize for "A Storm off the Coast of Scarborough". He married a famous Sheffield lady, Barbara Wreaks, born in 1770. She had previously married T. Bradshaw Hoole, who died two years later, and she lost also a daughter. For her own maintenance and that of her son, four months old, she then established, with money obtained from a volume of her poems, a boarding school at Harrogate, and it was here that she became acquainted with Hofland. The two struggled on, he with his pencil, she with her pen, and story after story, not many of them read now, were the results of her labours. She lost her husband in 1842 and two years later she followed him to the grave. Her son, a London clergyman, had died some years before. On one occasion, however, fate favoured Mrs. Hofland. After a money reverse, she had her foot upon a coach to go upon some business when she remembered she could save sixpence by going another way, and she went the other way. The coach she had left was overturned on its journey and the woman who had taken Mrs. Hofland's place was killed. Hofland was acquainted with Montgomery, who was of service to him, and James Everett too was his friend. He dedicated his book on angling to Chantrey, and to Chantrey Mrs. Hofland wrote some lines of verse. Not far from the point from which Hofland made his drawing of Sheffield David Martin must have stood to draw his picture of Little London Dam, one of six sketches of local places he engraved, scarce now and sought after eagerly by Sheffield collectors. Mr. Addy has a set, and there is a set at the Weston Park Museum. Martin, an engraver of Norfolk Street, Sheffield, was at one time in partnership with Joseph Gales as proprietor of the "Sheffield Register" and afterwards emigrated to America where things went from bad to worse and ended in Martin's suicide. He engraved the copperplate title page for the Sheffield Director of 1787 and for the same book a view of the facade of the old meat market of 1786. When he quitted Sheffield he was at work upon "Flora Britannica" and had issued about twenty numbers.

Little London Dam engaged the attention of another artist, Bonnington, a ne'er do weel Nottingham man. Bonnington had succeeded his father as governor of Nottingham gaol, but lost the post and took to painting. He exhibited a landscape at the Royal Academy in 1797 and a portrait in 1808 and he published a few coloured prints. He spent much of his life in Calais. His son, Richard Parkes Bonnington, became famous for beautiful landscapes and his works are still held in great esteem and that deservedly.

As he was born in Sheffield it was natural that Thomas Creswick should sketch Beauchief Abbey. His belongs to the year 1811, and he left Sheffield for Birmingham and proceeded thence to London where his landscapes won him a place in the Royal Academy. He died in London 1869, and in the International Exhibition of 1873 in London more than a hundred of his pleasing works were exhibited. It is always a solace to see a painting by Creswick, who gives homely English scenery with simplicity and charm; graceful elms, quiet pastures woods and streams, those peaceful rural outlooks that never lose their allurements. Many books too received his illustrations delicately engraved on wood and he contributed to the work of the Etching Club.

Another representation of Beauchief Abbey is one of 1727 in a publication known by its short title of Buck's Views issued in three volumes in 1774 the work of the brothers Samuel and Nathaniel Buck, and containing their portraits. Samuel was born in 1696 and died in 1779, eighty three years of age. Nathaniel had died some years before. Their numerous engravings of ruins and other buildings are very interesting to the topographer. The brothers used to go about sketching in summer and they engraved at home in winter. Samuel became very poor in his old age, but was relieved by the subscriptions of friends and admirers. Buck's view of Beauchief was reproduced in the "Reliquary" for April 1867.

The full length plaster cast of Chantrey in Norton church introduces us to John Bell, sculptor, born in Norfolk in 1811. As long ago as 1832 he exhibited at the Royal Academy and his "Eagle Slayer" exhibited in 1837 is now at South Kensington. Bell designed the gates of Kensington Gardens and the group America for the Albert Memorial. In Sheffield there is an example of his skill in the Montgomery monument at the General Cemetery. Books and articles as well as sculpture are amongst his works. The Chantrey cast was presented to Norton church by Mr. Charles Stoatt of Kensington who purchased the contents of Bell's studio.